COLLECT
BRITISH
FIRST DAY COVERS

by

N. C. PORTER

Designed & Edited by

A. G. BRADBURY

PUBLISHED BY A.G. BRADBURY

3 Link Road, Stoneygate, Leicester LE2 3RA

© N. C. PORTER, 1993

ISBN 0 9517463 2 4

Typeset by Plyglen Ltd., Leicester.
Printed by A. T. Shelley (Printers) Ltd., Leicester.

Royal Mail Covers of Quality Awards

1992
**CHARITY
CATEGORY**
WINNER : *A. G. Bradbury*

1993
**PROMOTIONAL
CATEGORY**
WINNER : *A. G. Bradbury*

1993
**COMMEMORATIVE
CATEGORY**
WINNER : *A. G. Bradbury*

for Award Winning Covers contact :

A. G. BRADBURY
3 LINK ROAD, STONEYGATE, LEICESTER LE2 3RA
Telephone : (0533) 705367 office hours

PREFACE

At the time of writing, there was still some uncertainty as to whether the long awaited economic recovery was set on a sustainable course. Despite the severe recession, it has been noticeable that, in the past year or so, a significant number of new collectors have begun collecting official, slogan and cds covers. The catalogue may, in some small way, have contributed to this trend with a large increase in sales, resulting in a reprint having to be organised. Four times as many copies were sold of the twelfth edition when compared with the previous edition.

We are pleased to note from our correspondence that the amended format was received positively by collectors; many of the new collectors commented that they had not previously realised, until they read the catalogue, the breadth of interest that the hobby was able to offer.

The price of the catalogue makes it, in our view, the best value for money of any catalogue of British first day covers and we are pleased to be able to hold the price at its present level for a further year.

As we have said in many of the previous twelve editions, we view the compilation of the catalogue as being one of a constant process of improvement, and so if you have any suggestions which you believe could improve the format or content of the catalogue, please write to the publisher.

Finally, we have noted that in some recent first day cover auctions, particularly high prices have been achieved for the exceptionally rare cover and that recession or not, there will always be a strong demand for the better item – the lesson is clear – be discerning in your purchases of covers whether new issue or otherwise.

ACKNOWLEDGEMENTS

As always, we thank all those who have contributed with the compilation of this work. In particular: Alan Finch and Colin Peachey of the British Postmark Society; Ghazi Choudhury (Sajal), Brian Reeve, Peter Middleton, Mark Grimsley and Steven Scott for help with prices; Mr. Wellman, Geoff Todd, Colin Young and all those collectors who take the time and trouble to write in with their new discoveries; Peter Withers for all his help with the slogan listings; and John G. Rice, John Swanborough and other dealers who supply their postmark listings for each issue. All of this assistance is greatly appreciated.

A final note to all collectors: Please mention this book when replying to advertisements – thank you.

N. C. PORTER

A partner in Greenberg & Porter – a cover producing partnership formed in 1981 – he is responsible for the text and compilation of the prices in the catalogue.

A. G. BRADBURY

Specialist in covers, trading under his own name since 1974 and producing 'official' covers since 1980. Besides being the editor and publisher, he is also responsible for design and layout – and searching out all those postmark illustrations!

GENERAL NOTES

The General Notes set out below should answer most questions concerning the hobby – 'Collecting British First Day Covers'. After studying these notes and the body of the catalogue, it will become apparent that this fascinating subject can prove to be a very worthwhile and absorbing hobby with the added bonus of being educational.

It is beyond the means of most people to be able to afford a collection comprising every available cover. However the number and range of covers produced should be viewed as an advantage since this provides the collector with a wide variety to choose from – a decision that once made should make for an interesting collection.

(A) WHAT IS A FIRST DAY COVER?

First day covers are essentially newly issued postage stamps affixed to an envelope and franked with a postmark on the first day that those stamps are placed on sale by the Royal Mail. Early first day covers, in the main, are usually available only on plain envelopes – specially designed envelopes only began appearing regularly in the 1950s. Further details of the variety of covers and postmarks available are provided in these notes.

An example of a first day cover issued for the 1993 Swans stamp issue.
The stamps were franked with a special postmark on 19th January 1993,
the first day of sale of these stamps. All first day of sale dates are listed
alongside each stamp issue in the catalogue.

A first day cover should not be confused with souvenir or commemorative covers which are usually produced to celebrate or commemorate a particular event or anniversary. Souvenir covers are normally issued on the actual day of the anniversary or event being commemorated and their value is more related to the collector's own connection with the event. First day covers, on the other hand, are issued on the day of a particular stamp issue and command a more universal appeal.

(B) SCOPE OF THE CATALOGUE

This catalogue lists all standard first day covers for both British commemorative, definitive and greetings stamp issues. The number of different combinations and variations available for each cover is so large that it precludes the economic production of a catalogue to cater for such detailed variations; and it is doubtful whether there are enough collectors who would be willing to purchase an expensive volume (which would be nearer the size of the Encyclopaedia Britannica!). This catalogue makes no judgement as to the suitability of various types of covers for their 'collectability' – this is a decision solely in the hands of collectors. It should be remembered that, like many things in life, a cover may come into fashion and increase in value. Likewise, covers which are fashionable now may not be sought after in 10 years time.

(C) FORMAT

The layout of this catalogue has been established to reflect the changing nature of British first day covers over the years. On compiling the catalogue it was found that commemorative issues could be divided into three distinct periods, viz:

(1)   1924 Wembley – 1961 Parliament issues
Prices for this period have been set out in two columns – the first is for illustrated covers and the second for plain covers (i.e. non-illustrated covers).

(2)   1962 National Productivity Year – 1967 Wild Flowers
For this period commemorative stamps were issued both with and without phosphor bands. The two column price structure reflects prices for both of these types of first day covers. All prices from this date are for illustrated covers. Plain covers are often available for this period but not generally collected. They are usually only worth a small fraction of their illustrated equivalent.

(3)   1967 British Paintings – present day
With effect from this issue all commemorative stamps were phosphor coated. It was also around the late 1960s that more 'official' or sponsored covers were being produced. Consequently the two columns now reflect prices for 'ordinary' covers and 'official' covers (see para (F) 'Types of Covers')

Definitives, regionals, booklet panes etc. on first day covers are all listed together in an easy to follow section at the end of the catalogue.

(D) PRICES & CONDITION

This catalogue has been compiled as a work of reference and is not the publisher's or author's own price list. **The prices quoted are intended as a GUIDE ONLY and are based on clean, undamaged covers and unless otherwise stated, serviced with a full set of stamps.** Many factors may affect the price of first day covers, for example:

(1)   Condition The general condition of covers, including the quality of postmarks, proper siting of stamps and the neatness of the address are important in determining the price of a cover. It should be remembered that invariably the older covers will be of inferior quality when compared to their modern counterparts. However shortages of available older covers should be taken into account by the collector when buying such covers. As a general guide the prices quoted in the catalogue are for clean covers with a small address label, or a printed, typed or rubber stamped address. Earlier covers, primarily before 1964, are acceptable with neat hand-written addesses, whilst later covers from, say 1970, usually command a premium if unaddressed.

The very scarce covers may well retail at full catalogue value even if they do not conform to the above guidelines. Condition is everything – a scruffy cover will only be worth a fraction of its pristine counterpart.

Study for a moment the cover illustrated below – it has almost everything wrong with it, viz (i) hand written address; (ii) a postmark which bears no relevance to the stamp issue; and (iii) the stamps are not aligned.

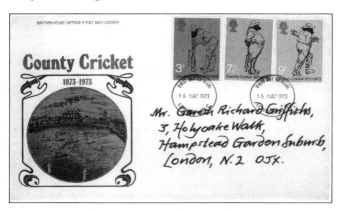

Now compare this to the cover illustrated on page 4 — a much better proposition.

(2) Supply and Demand The market in first day covers is no different from the market in any commodity and is subject to the same economic forces. For example, if 600 collectors wish to purchase a cover of which only 500 were produced, then that cover will inevitably rise in price. Conversely, if only 100 of a particular cover exists but a mere 50 collectors wish to buy that cover, then the price will remain static or even fall until demand exceeds supply. The early 1980s is a good example of a period when several covers were over-produced and are now only beginning to recover their new issue prices.

In addition there may be significant variations in the stock position of individual dealers at any particular time. A dealer holding a stock of say 50 covers may well be prepared to sell that cover for less than a dealer holding a stock of only one or two covers.

(3) Locality In the same way that house prices vary according to the locality, to a lesser degree this can also affect first day cover prices.

In the final analysis, the value of a cover is determined at a price at which both the dealer and collector feel is acceptable to them. The prices quoted in the catalogue are based on the **AVERAGE** of several dealers' lists, and, for the scarcer covers on auction realisations.

Prices quoted with **(s)** appended indicates that covers are only known to exist with a single stamp or incomplete set. The initials **'n.k.'** in the price columns indicate that as far as the author and publisher are aware the covers do not exist. Prices include VAT @ 17½%.

(E) TYPES OF POSTMARKS

Each commemorative stamp issue has been classified according to the type of postmarks found. They can be divided into four distinct categories: special handstamps, ordinary first day of issue postmarks, counter date stamp (C.D.S.) postmarks and slogan postmarks.

(1) SPECIAL HANDSTAMPS

These are specially designed postmarks which until recently were mostly applied by hand. Today first day covers are usually franked with the more advanced 'pad canceller' machines which give much better impressions, and allow for more detailed designs.

Any member of the public is permitted to sponsor a special handstamp – at a current cost of £195 (plus VAT) – providing that they adhere to certain Royal Mail rules governing their use. The special handstamp remains the property of the Royal Mail and is applied to philatelic items by trained Royal Mail staff. Controversial subjects are not permitted on handstamps, including political propaganda and offensive subjects. All special handstamps to be used are advertised in advance in the "Postmark Bulletin" – a fortnightly newsletter issued by the Royal Mail (currently £10 per annum available from Philatelic Bureau in Edinburgh). Any member of the public can subscribe to the Bulletin and thereby know which handstamps have been sponsored before the stamp issue date. They can then send their first day covers to the Head Post Offices or Special Handstamp Centres for franking with the special handstamps. This is known as the "re-posting facility".

In a move to improve the quality of service offered to collectors Royal Mail Stamps set up seven Special Handstamp Centres with effect from 23rd January 1990, the RSPCA issue. These centres are intended to provide a quicker and more efficient service for customers, employing staff working full-time on philatelic items. All special handstamps are now applied at these centres, each of which covers a specific area, viz:

Royal Mail City & International – for London, north of the Thames
Royal Mail London SW – for London, south of the Thames
Royal Mail Windsor – for the rest of SE England and most of East Anglia
Royal Mail Cardiff – for Wales and SW England
Royal Mail Birmingham – for the Midlands and east to the Wash
Royal Mail Newcastle – for N England
Royal Mail Glasgow – for Scotland and Northern Ireland

All special handstamps in use on the first day of an issue of a set of commmemorative stamps are included in the catalogue whether they are relevant to the stamp issue or not. Some covers serviced with handstamps which are not relevant are priced higher than others with more relevant postmarks. This is because they are often more difficult to obtain – especially with a full set of stamps.

There are special handstamps which are available on every first day of issue but, except where relevant to an issue, these have been omitted. These postmarks are illustrated and listed in Section (G).

(2) ORDINARY FIRST DAY OF ISSUE (F.D.I.) HANDSTAMPS

These are circular postmarks specially made and paid for by the Royal Mail and used in many towns and cities throughout the United Kingdom. They are in use for all commemorative stamp issues and many of the definitive stamp issues. F.D.I. handstamps – like special handstamps – are applied by Royal Mail staff usually by hand. These are also made available to collectors under the "re-posting facility".

It was not until the 1960s that the then G.P.O. recognised a need for proper philatelic handstamping. The F.D.I. handstamps are listed from their introduction (1964 Shakespeare issue) up to the Christmas issue of 1970. The start of the decimal period saw a much wider use of special handstamps. However there are numerous examples where no special handstamps were available at places with an obvious connection with the stamp issues. In such cases, where a F.D.I. postmark was available, these have been listed.

King's Lynn F.D.I. postmark (the local F.D.I. office for Sandringham) used on the 1978 Coronation issue.

(3)   COUNTER DATE STAMP (C.D.S.) POSTMARKS

Sometimes known as circular date stamps, these are ordinary everyday cancellations available at all Post Office counters. To obtain such operational cancellations, it is usually the case that the philatelic item has to be registered except where the post office concerned still handstamps its own ordinary mail. It is sometimes difficult to obtain these cancellations on first day covers because the Royal Mail insist that covers for registration are physically handed over at the Post Office counter concerned. No re-posting facility is permitted.

During the early years, first day covers were generally only available with circular date stamp (C.D.S.) postmarks. Whether such postmarks had any connection with an issue was, in most cases, fortuitous. Relevant C.D.S. postmarks were clearly the exception rather than the rule.

During the 1960s and up to the present day the collecting of relevant C.D.S. postmarks has become a specialist interest. The criterion used for the inclusion of these C.D.S. postmarks is that they should have a direct bearing on the theme of the stamps. Items which are 'one-off' or have a dubious connection with the issue concerned are not included. The items included were available in commercial quantities – i.e. twenty or more covers. The C.D.S. postmarks are included even if there is a special handstamp or ordinary F.D.I. postmark available for the same area because often they are more valid. A good example of this is the 1992 Civil War issue where the special Naseby handstamp was applied at the Midlands Special Handstamp Centre therefore the only authentic Naseby cancellations are the C.D.S.

The proliferation of C.D.S. postmarks (from the 1979 Christmas issue) has necessitated the classification of C.D.S. postmarks into main and ancillary listings. Those postmarks which, in the opinion of the Author, have a close or direct connection with an issue, are given a full listing with a descriptive note where necessary. Other C.D.S. postmarks are recorded in italics below the main listing.

Broadly speaking, the criteria used for determining whether a particular postmark is included in the main listing are as follows:

(a) Name association
Where the name of a Post Office has a strong link with the issue concerned. For example with the 1976 and 1991 Roses stamp issues, first day covers were postmarked at the village of 'Rose' in Cornwall.

(b) Place association
Where a Post Office is located in, or is the nearest to, an area which is being commemorated by the stamp issue, or otherwise has geographical connections with the subject matter of the issue. For example, with the 1991 stamps featuring Maps, first day covers were franked at 'Maybush', Southampton — the headquarters of the Ordnance Survey.

(c) House of Commons & House of Lords
These C.D.S. postmarks are not ordinarily available to members of the general public, the cancellation of mail being primarily on correspondence sent by members of either House of Parliament. These postmarks are only listed where they are relevant, viz:
(i)   Where an issue commemorates the passing of legislation (e.g. the 1974 issue commemorating the 200th anniversary of the first fire service legislation); or reform (e.g. the 1976 issue commemorating Social Pioneers and Reformers); or
(ii)   Where an event commemorated is connected with Parliament (e.g. the 1973 issue commemorating the 19th Commonwealth Parliamentary Conference); or
(iii) Where a featured individual has a connection with Parliament (e.g. the 1974 issue commemorating the centenary of the birth of Sir Winston Churchill); or
(iv)   Royalty issues.

(d) Balmoral Castle, Buckingham Palace, Sandringham House and Windsor Castle
Postal facilities in Balmoral Castle, Buckingham Palace, Sandringham House and Windsor Castle are only available to members of the Royal Family or staff of the Royal Household. Whilst these types of covers are extremely scarce and therefore valuable, they are only relevant where an issue of stamps involves a 'Royal' theme. Prices in the catalogue reflect their rarity. Postmarks at Sandringham House and Balmoral Castle are more rare than those at Buckingham Palace and Windsor Castle.

(e) Other associations
This final criterion embraces any of those associations which do not readily fit into the four categories mentioned above, but nevertheless merit inclusion. For example, 'Paquebots' used on the 1973 European Communities issue or the 1970 Direct Elections issue; Travelling Post Office (T.P.O.) cancellations on railway related issues; etc.

House of Lords C.D.S. postmark used on the 1992 Alfred, Lord Tennyson issue.

(4) SLOGAN POSTMARKS

These are machine cancellations applied to the vast majority of British mail. A slogan postmark consists of two parts viz: a circular element which incorporates the sorting location, time and date; and more often than not, an advertising 'slogan'. These postmarks can be sponsored for a specified period of time at a cost of £300 or more depending on the number of 'dies' (postmark cancellation) and length of time these are in operation. Again, they are advertised in advance in the "Postmark Bulletin" and are available to collectors under the "re-posting facility".

Three types of slogan postmarks are available to the collector, viz:

(a) First Day of Issue Slogans

These were first introduced with the 1963 Paris Postal Conference issue. They were used on covers posted in special posting boxes at selected Post Offices. From 1964 slogans were mostly replaced by ordinary F.D.I. handstamps (see para (2) above). However slogans continued in use mainly for bulk mailings. Where F.D.I. slogans are used at a place connected with an issue they have been listed. For the 1963 Compac issue the Philatelic Bureau used this type of slogan postmark.

(b) 'Wavy line' machine cancels

These have only been listed if the location at which they were used was connected with the stamp issue.

(c) Commemorative or Campaign slogans

The criterion used to determine whether a particular slogan should be included depends on its relevance to the stamp issue concerned. Unlike C.D.S. postmarks, the location of a Post Office at which a slogan is used is not as important as the wording or illustration of the slogan, which should have a good connection with the stamp issue. The proliferation of slogan postmarks (from 1979 Christmas issue) has necessitated their classification into main and ancillary listings. Those which, in the opinion of the Author, have a close or direct connection with an issue, are given a full listing. Other, less relevant slogans are recorded in italics.

'Smugglers Adventure' slogan postmark used on 1992 Gilbert & Sullivan. Notice the way the stamps have been carefully positioned so that the slogan is clearly legible.

Earlier covers are usually only available with a slogan which obliterates the stamps – often making the slogan difficult to read. However, with effect from 1974 most covers are available with the stamps positioned in such a way as to make the slogan clearly legible. To achieve this the stamps have to be sited in such a way that the slogan will only cancel one stamp, the remaining stamps being franked with a C.D.S. or ordinary F.D.I. postmark.

(F) TYPES OF COVER

Nowadays first day cover envelopes fall into two categories: ordinary (or commercial) covers and 'official' (or sponsored).

(1) ORDINARY (OR COMMERCIAL) COVERS

These are produced primarily for the general philatelic market and are usually sold as 'blanks' (i.e. with no stamps affixed). They are available from most good stamp shops before the day of issue of the postage stamps. Collectors purchase the 'blanks' and then affix the stamps to the covers themselves. They then have to make their own arrangements concerning franking. The covers produced by the Royal Mail are additionally available from most Post Office counters.

The different makes of covers are listed below. The Publisher is indebted to S.C.R. Nowell without whose help this list would not be possible.

 Abbey: These covers were produced from 1969 until 1982. They were not sold as blanks but fully serviced – usually with appropriate special handstamps. They were all numbered limited editions and recognisable by their 'Abbey' logo.

 Artcraft: This company was based in America – their first cover was for the 1948 Games issue with several more up to and including the Battle of Hastings issue of 1966.

Benham 'silks': These are only available fully serviced – usually sets of single stamp covers. They have been produced from the 1980 Birds issue to date. See also entries in 'official' covers section.

Benham 'woodcut': The only Benham covers which were available as blanks were first produced for the 1968 Bridges issue. The series ended with the 1978 Historic Buildings issue.

 Cameo: The Cameo Stamp Centre produced a few covers in 1970 and 1971 and these bear a 'Cameo' logo.

Colorano 'silk': These were first produced for the 1974 Horse Chestnut issue and appeared for most issues up to the early 1980s.

 Connoisseur: These were produced for all issues from the 1963 Freedom from Hunger issue until 1970. Recognisable by an Old English 'C' logo they were produced by R.F. Grover of Fareham, Hants.

Cotswold: Cotswold die-stamped covers were first introduced with the 1970 Christmas issue and have appeared ever since. They are easily recognisable by their large 'C' border which is common to all their designs.

 Mercury: These were first introduced in 1972 and have appeared for all stamp issues to date. Produced by Harry Allen of Rickmansworth they all have a 'Mercury' logo. These are also die-stamped.

 Philart: First produced in 1964 for the Geographical issue, they ceased production in 1990. Philart 'Luxury' die-stamped covers were sold from the 1969 Ships issue until the early 1980s.

PPS: Presentation Philatelic Services (PPS) produced their first blank for the 1981 Butterflies issue. Christmas 1981 saw their first 'silk' – these continued until Christmas 1983. With effect from the 1984 Heraldry issue the SOTHEBY'S 'silk' range was introduced. The Cigarette Card 'silk' series commences with the 1988 Linnean issue.

PTS/BPA: The Philatelic Traders Society and the British Philatelic Association produced a number of covers jointly. These commenced with the 1948 Olympic Games issue and continued through to the early 1960s.

Peter Scot: Peter Scot covers were introduced with the 1978 Energy issue and ceased in 1988.

Royal Mail: The first Post Office first day covers appeared for the 1964 Shakespeare issue. They have been produced for all subsequent issues with the following exceptions: 1965 Salvation Army, Joseph Lister, Commonwealth Arts, U.N., I.T.U., and 1966 England Winners.

Save the Children Fund: These were produced for the earlier decimal issues, commencing with the 1973 Royal Wedding.

Stuart: The first Stuart cover was for the 1965 Churchill issue. They are still available for all the current issues. The covers are die-stamped and have a 'thistle' logo.

Thames: These were first issued for the 1968 Bridges issue and continued until the 1974 Christmas issue. The covers have a similar appearance to die-stamping. The earlier covers had a 'Thames estuary' logo printed on their flaps.

Trident: These were produced for some of the 1969/70 issues and bear a 'Trident' logo.

Wessex: These have a 'Wyvern' logo and were first produced for the 1967 EFTA issue and regularly until 1973. A few have been produced since, most notably for the 1977 Queen's Silver Jubilee. The covers are still produced by Rembrandt Philatelics but are now souvenir covers – no first day covers are produced.

(2) 'OFFICIAL' (OR SPONSORED) COVERS

In the context of this catalogue, 'official' covers are defined as covers produced by private organisations or their philatelic agents, who at the same time sponsor a special handstamp to accompany their cover. Such covers, bearing the full set of stamps, are invariably rarer than the 'ordinary' covers, and their prices reflect this. Some are particularly so, e.g. the 'Jeol' cover on the 1989 Microscopes issue where probably fewer than 60 official covers exist with full sets of stamps. Sometimes an organisation will not affix the full set of stamps, preferring to market their covers with just a single value. Often the only way to get a cover cancelled with the full set of stamps is to obtain blank covers from the sponsors and service the cover yourself. However this is often not possible because of a reluctance to sell blank covers.

The Royal Mail has recently relaxed its rules governing the sponsorship of special handstamps. As a result the concept of an 'official' cover has changed over the last few years. It is now possible for anyone to sponsor postmarks mentioning such places as Clarence House, Glamis Castle, Windsor Castle etc. which were used on the 1990 Queen Mother issue. The covers produced to accompany these handstamps are only official in the sense that the sponsor of the handstamp has also provided his/her own envelope. No special sanction is necessarily conferred upon a cover by a particular place or organisation. This will help explain why there were four Westminster Abbey, and two Dummer handstamps for the 1986 Royal Wedding stamp issue.

The numerous official covers have been categorised below together with the abbreviations used in the text of this catalogue.

(a) Covers marketed by First Day Cover Producers

  (i) those forming a F.D.C. series (numbered or otherwise)

*BL**	– British Library (1976-1982)
BLS	– Benham large 'silk' (1982-1984)
BLCS	– Benham large cover series (1985 to date)
Benham L	– Benham limited edition (1981 to date)
B'ham 500	– Benham 500 (1985 to date)
BOCS	– Benham official covers (1978-1984)
Benham SG	– Benham Special Gold (1986 to date)
Fine Art	– Fine Art covers of Brentwood (1985-1986)
LFDC	– Leicester first day covers (1980 to date)
Brad. V.P.	– Bradbury's Victorian Prints (1991 to date)
RFDC	– Forces first day covers (1981-1992)
RAF FDC	– Forces Charities (1992 to date)
Havering	– Havering covers of Romford (1980-1984)
Hawkwood	– Hawkwood covers of Chingford (1980-1986)
S. Petty	– Stewart Petty covers of Weybridge (1981-1984)
B. Reeve	– Brian Reeve/B. Alan (1992 Only)
(f)	– denotes forerunner to the series

Official covers forming a numbered series are listed with the appropriate number after the abbreviation, e.g. *BOCS (2) 3* indicates the third cover in the second series of the Benham official cover series. Sometimes the sequence of numbers will be broken, because no handstamp was sponsored.

*BL covers – values quoted are for British Library covers with British Library handstamps. Many B.L. covers exist with other handstamps.

  (ii) those not forming a F.D.C. series

Cotswold }	– These should not be confused with the 'ordinary'
Philart }	covers which were available for the same issues.
Cotswold (g)	– Where Cotswold sponsored a handstamp and utilised their ordinary cover, not producing a separate cover.
A.C.C.	– Action for the Crippled Child (Philart)
Arlington	– J. & M. Arlington of London
Benham	– Benham of Hythe (other than series above)
Bradbury	– A.G. Bradbury (other than LFDC or VP series)
Cameo	– Cameo stamps of London
Cam. S.C.	– Cambridge Stamp Centre
CoverCraft	– Cover Craft (R. de Swarte), Beckenham
Dawn	– Dawn covers of Stockport
D.F.	– David Fletcher of Coventry
Des. Enc.	– Design Encounter (R. de Swarte), Beckenham
F.A.A.	– Fleet Air Arm Museum
G. & P.	– Greenberg & Porter of Horsham
H.R.	– Historic Relics
K. & D.	– K. & D. Covers of London
Markton	– Markton Stamps of Norwich
S. Muscroft	– Stan Muscroft of Guisborough
Pilgrim	– Pilgrim Philatelics of Canterbury

P.P.S.	– Presentation Philatelic Services, Leicester
R. Skinner	– R. Skinner of Epsom
S.P.	– Stamp Publicity of Worthing
Sumner	– The Sumner Collection
D.G.T.	– D.G. Taylor of Harrow
B. Travers	– Travers Publications of Cleveland
W & W	– Warwick & Warwick
P. Withers	– P. Withers of Stoke-on-Trent
*BFPS	– British Forces Postal Services
*Royal Eng.	– Royal Engineers
*B Legion	– British Legion
*RH/RHDR	– Railway History/Romney Hythe & Dymchurch Rly.

*These belong to a series of covers but the majority are souvenir or commemorative covers.

Other abbreviations used in the official covers column:

n.o.c.	– indicates that no official cover exists, or is known but NOT with the commemorative stamps of the issue concerned.
Post Office } *Royal Mail*	– indicates a special handstamp sponsored by the Post Office, no special cover being produced.

(b) Covers produced by Private Organisations

Many organisations have produced their own special covers to raise funds or to foster public relations – usually where their work/activity is related to the theme of the stamp issue. Abbreviations used in the official covers column should be easily interpreted by referring to the wording of the handstamp.

(c) Other categories

There are many so-called 'official' covers produced which use special handstamps sponsored by other organisations or by the Royal Mail, e.g. 1971 Christmas issue with Canterbury Post Office handstamp used on a special Canterbury Stained Glass Window cover; 1975 Jane Austen issue with Steventon Post Office handstamp used on a special cover produced by Jane Austen Bicentenary Committee.

Neither Canterbury Cathedral nor the Jane Austen Bicentenary Committee sponsored these handstamps, but made use of the handstamp provided free of charge by the Royal Mail. It would be almost impossible to list all such privately sponsored covers which have been produced, so we have made no attempt to do so.

(d) C.D.S. and slogan postmarks used on offical covers

It has been the practice in recent years for official cover producers, amongst others, to offer their covers with alternative postmarks – C.D.S., slogans, etc. It would be impossible to list all these variations. Such covers usually command a premium over, say the same C.D.S. on an ordinary cover. This is especially so where there is a direct link between the cover and postmark.

(G) PERMANENT PICTORIAL HANDSTAMPS

As mentioned earlier (see section E (1)), there are now numerous philatelic handstamps available to the collector which are in use on each first day of issue of new stamps. These have been omitted from the text except where relevant to particular stamp issues, e.g. the Shakespeare handstamp is listed under the 1982 British Theatre issue; London SW (Buckingham Palace) and Windsor Philatelic Counter are listed under the royalty issues, and so on. These handstamps are available under the "re-posting facility" and are shown below:

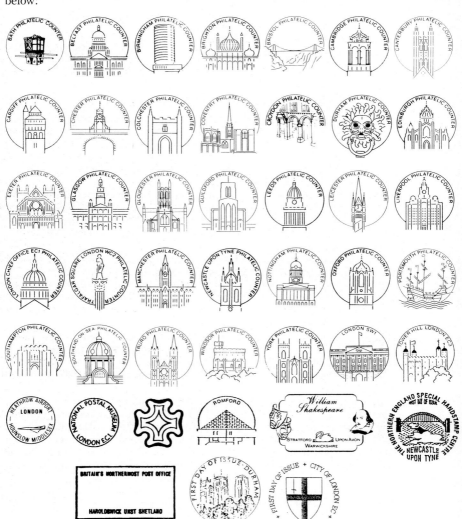

Beautiful covers - yours to treasure

(1) Queen's Accession -Windsor Official   £15

(2) Queen Mother - 90th Birthday   £15

(3) Crufts with 1979 and 1991 Dog stamps   £15

(4) Spirit of Britain (1974 Churchill+1990 Gallantry) £10

(5) Jodrell Bank signed by Patrick Moore   £15

(6) Roses on stamps - 1976 and 1991 stamps   £15

(7) Civil War - National Army Museum   £10

(8) Royal Wedding - Three Generations   £15

(9) Marine Clock and 1969 Ships   £15

(10) 'O, My Luve's Like A Red Red Rose'   £15

To order: List your requirements and send with a cheque/PO made payable to A. G. BRADBURY.
Sorry no credit cards. Overseas please remit in £ Sterling and add £1
A. G. BRADBURY, 3 LINK ROAD, STONEYGATE, LEICESTER LE2 3RA

Cover Classics...

(11) 1991 Greetings - Luckington official £8

(12) 1991 Greetings - Stan Laurel 'Smiles' £10

(13) Bismarck with 1982 Maritime stamps £10

(14) Mountbatten signed by Winston Churchill MP £15

(15) Star Trek 25th Anniversary £9

(16) Sir George Everest 200th Anniversary £10

(17) 1987 Flowers signed by Percy Thrower £20

(18) Ten Years At No. 10 £12

(19) 1992 Greetings - Portobello Road official £9

(20) 1993 Greetings - Alice official £8

To order: List your requirements and send with a cheque/PO made payable to A. G. BRADBURY.
Sorry no credit cards.   Overseas please remit in £ Sterling and add £1

A. G. BRADBURY, 3 LINK ROAD, STONEYGATE, LEICESTER LE2 3RA

... for the Discerning Collector

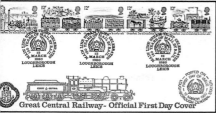

Great Central Railway- Official First Day Cover

) Great Central Railway official £7

INTERNATIONAL SPACE YEAR 1992

(22) International Space Year £10

) Single Market - Europe Workers slogan £12

A QUESTION OF SPORT

(24) Question of Sport signed by Bill Beaumont £7

) PDSA signed by James Herriot £12

Skegness is so Bracing

Premier Seaside Award for clean water and beaches.

(26) Skegness is so Bracing slogan postmark £12

) Alfred Lord Tennyson Heroes and Heroines £20

The Worshipful Company of Dyers

(28) Swans - The Worshipful Company of Dyers £8

The Aintree Legend

The Aintree Legend £5

The Sealed Knot

(30) Civil War - The Sealed Knot official £10

Beautiful covers - yours to treasure

(31) Rail Riders 'Mallard' 50th Anniversary £3

(32) Friends of the Earth official £

(33) NSPCC Signed Judi Dench £10

(34) The Flying Scotsman visits Australia £1

(35) Kensington Palace - 300th Anniversary £5

(36) Australia Double pmk in UK & Australia £1

(37) Ministry of Agriculture official £15

(38) Cunard 150 Years - double postmark £

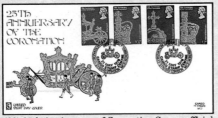

(39) 25th Anniversary of Coronation Cameo official £5

(40) Apollo 11 Moon Landing 20th Anniversary £

To order: List your requirements and send with a cheque/PO made payable to A. G. BRADBURY
Sorry no credit cards. Overseas please remit in £ Sterling and add £1

A. G. BRADBURY, 3 LINK ROAD, STONEYGATE, LEICESTER LE2 3RA

LONDON ROAD STAMPS

54a LONDON ROAD, LEICESTER LE2 0QD
Tel : Leicester (0533) 551544

Publishers of the **COVER NEWS** magazine (formerly published by Benham)—a must for all Collectors of first day covers. Write for your free copy now.

We also publish two series of first day covers:

PRESENTATION PHILATELIC SERVICES
54a LONDON ROAD, LEICESTER LE2 0QD

SOTHEBY'S COLLECTION

This beautiful collection commenced in 1984 and has become extremely popular, some of the early covers now being very elusive. The Collection is planned to continue for many years and is building into a fascinating miniature art gallery. Each cover has a reproduction on 'silk' of a painting, or other collectable, auctioned by Sotheby's which reflects the theme of the stamps. Serviced covers with a full set of stamps and pictorial handstamp cost £4.20 plus 50p P.&P. (for a standard 4 stamp issue). Blank covers are available at £1.10 each from ourselves (5 or more post free) or from good stamp shops. Definitive, Regional and Railway Event 'silk' covers also available. Send for our list of past 'silk' issues.

THE FIRST ADHESIVE POSTAGE STAMP

PRESENTATION PHILATELIC SERVICES
54a LONDON ROAD, LEICESTER LE2 0QD

CIGARETTE CARD SERIES

This fine series commenced with the Linnean Society issue of 1988 and has developed into a beautiful compliment to our Sotheby's Collection. Pre-war Cigarette Cards reflecting the theme of the stamps are superbly reproduced on 'silk' and each issue is limited to 1000 numbered covers.

A few of the previous Year Sets are still available. 1993 covers cost £5.25 each. Fifty covers are serviced with a relevant C.D.S. and are available, subject unsold, at £7.25 each.

For free lists and details contact us now and reserve your limited edition cover. ALL PRICES PLUS 50p P.&P.

Greenberg & Porter

...fine first day covers

Greenberg & Porter · Farnham House · 2 Beedingwood Drive · Forest Road · Colgate
Horsham · West Sussex RH12 4TE   (Telephone 0293 851174)

Listed below are the **OFFICIAL COVERS** we have produced:

1982	Motor Cars	Dagenham Motors – THE OFFICIAL cover	£25
1983	Engineering	Thames Flood Barrier	£6
		Thames Flood Barrier signed by the	
		Senior Partner of the Barrier Designers	£7
1983	Army	Royal Military Academy, Sandhurst	£12
1984	Heraldry	City of London, Square Mile – set of four covers:	
		Lloyds, Stock Exchange, Bank of England	
		and the City of London Corporation	£45
1984	Urb. Renewal	Abbey National Building Society	£6
		Abbey National Building Society	
		signed by Clive Thornton	£7
		Commercial St., Perth	£7
		Commercial St., Perth	
		signed by Provost (Perth District Council)	£9
		Commercial St., Perth,	
		signed by James Parr (Architects)	£9
1984	Br. Council	British Council, ...BUY	£7
1985	Railways	Golden Arrow/V.S.O.E. ....BUY	£8
1985	Film Year	Goldcrest, B.F. ....BUY	£6
1986	Industry Year	Osram, Wembley..BUY	£50
1986	Queen's 60th B	Lombard North Central, Birthplace	£6
1986	Wedding	Dummer	£7
1987	Flowers	Stephen Thomas Flora Exhibition	£6
1987	Victoria	Marconi's First Broadcast to France.................BUY	£5
1988	Transport	Laser Transport, Hythe	£6
1990	Kew Gardens	Ash cds	£8
		Elm cds	£8
		Kew Gardens cds	£12
		"Pass on your postcode" slogan, in black	£8
1990	Hardy	Dorchester cds	£7
		Puddletown, Dorchester cds	£7
		Fordington, Dorchester cds	£7
		Sturminster Newton cds	£8
		"Pass on your postcode" slogan, in black	£8
		"Pass on your postcode", Dorchester slogan	£7
1990	Queen Mother	Bowes cds	£10
		Mey cds	£10
		Queen Elizabeth Ave., cds	£6
		"Forres Europe in Bloom" slogan	£7
1990	Gallantry	High Cross cds	£10
		"RAF Finingley Air Show" slogan	£7
		"Royal Engineers Museum" slogan	£7
1990	Xmas	"Please control your dog/postman calls" slogan	£15
		"Stampway to the World" slogan	£8
1991	Dogs	Isle of Dogs cds	£10
		N.E.C. Birmingham cds	£10
		Dog Kennel Lane cds	£12
	Greetings	"The Magic of British Music" slogan	£25

O ver the past ten years or so we have offered numerous 'double-postmarked' covers, i.e. covers postmarked in Britain on the first day of issue of a set of commemorative stamps and sent overseas to a connected place of interest and (usually) a foreign stamp affixed and cancelled in that place. The following covers are available currently from stock (except three):

1979	*E.E.C.*	*Entente Cordiale, Stowmarket – VERY RARE*	*£65*
		Strasbourg cds/Leicester S/H	*£10*
1982	*Xmas*	*Bethlehem cds (fdi)/Bethlehem, Israel (Xmas Eve)*	*£12*
		Nasareth cds (fdi)/Bethlehem, Israel (Xmas Eve)	*£12*
1983	*Xmas*	*St. Mary-le-Strand (fdi)/Bethlehem, Israel (Xmas Eve)*	*£10*
		Winchester Cath. (fdi)/Bethlehem, Israel (Xmas Eve)	*£10*
		Minster Gatehouse (fdi)/Bethlehem, Israel (Xmas Eve)	*£10*
		St. Augustines cds (fdi)/Bethlehem, Israel (Xmas Eve)	*£10*
1984	*E.E.C.*	*Euro Elections, Strasbourg*	*£10*
1984	*Greenwich*	*Greenwich Meridian (fdi)/Washington, USA*	*£20*
1984	*Br. Council*	*Br. Council, official (fdi)/Ausipex – SAME DATE SUPERB*	*£30*
		Br. Council, official (fdi)/Lagos	
		Br. Council, official (fdi)/Athens SET OF	*£60*
		Br. Council, official (fdi)/Colombo FOUR	
		Br. Council, official (fdi)/Muscat	
1984	*Xmas*	*Norwich Cath. (fdi)/Bethlehem, Israel (Xmas Eve)*	*£10*
		Weybridge (fdi)/Concorde to Lapland (Xmas Day)	*£12*
1985	*Railways*	*Orient Express, Victoria (fdi)/Venice*	*BUY £15*
1985	*Music*	*Delius, Bradford (fdi)/Finland (Sibelius)*	*£10*
		Elgar (fdi)/Vienna (Fux-fdi)	*£10*
		Handel, Royal Opera House (fdi)/Warsaw (Chopin)	*£10*
		Holst, Cheltenham (fdi)/Bucharest (Enescu)	*£10*
		Elgar (fdi)/Prague (Dvorak)	*£12*
		Holst, Cheltenham (fdi)/Tivoli Gardens, Copenhagen	*£10*
		Delius, Bradford (fdi)/Grez-sur-Loing	*£15*
		Handel, R.O.H. (fdi)/Leningrad on Tchaikovsky stamp	*£15*
1985	*Film Year*	*Goldcrest, London (fdi)/Hollywood, USA*	*£20*
		Goldcrest, London (fdi)/Cannes, France	*£20*
		Goldcrest, London (fdi)/Italia '85 Rome	*£20*
1985	*Xmas*	*Drury Lane, (fdi)/Christmas Island (Xmas Day)*	*£20*
		Drury Lane (fdi)/Concorde to Lapland (Xmas Day)	*£10*
1986	*Halley*	*Giotto, Bristol (fdi)/Kouro, Fr. Guiana (13.3.86)*	*£20*
		Giotto, Bristol (fdi)/Padua, Italy (13.3.86)	*£10*
		Giotto, Bristol (fdi)/Bayeux, France (13.3.86)	*£10*
		Giotto, Bristol (fdi)/Austria (Astro-Phil. Society)	*£10*
		Giotto, Bristol (fdi)/St. Helena (13.3.86)	*£15*
		Giotto, Bristol (fdi)/Kennedy Space Centre (13.3.86)	*£20*
1986	*Domesday*	*Battle, Hastings (fdi)/Bayeux, France (fdi)*	*£15*
		Battle, Hastings (fdi)/Caen, France (fdi)	*£15*
1987	*Architects*	*London W1 (fdi)/Paris*	*£15*
		London SW1 (fdi)/Luxembourg	*£20*
1987	*Victoria*	*Chelmsford (fdi) Boulougne official cover*	*BUY £10*
1987	*Xmas*	*Hamley's S/H (fdi)/North Pole, Colorado (Xmas Eve)*	*£20*
1988	*Sports*	*Question of Sport S/H (fdi)/Innsbruck cds*	*£10*
1988	*Aus. Bic.*	*Botany Bay cds (fdi)/Kurnell S/H (Australia) (fdi)*	*£25*
		Stratford cds (fdi)/Sydney S/H (Australia) (fdi)	*£25*
		Lords S/H (fdi)/Perth S/H (Australia) (fdi)	*£25*
		Wimbledon S/H (fdi)/Melbourne S/H (Australia) (fdi)	*£25*
1988	*Armada*	*Gravelines, Dover (fdi)/Gravelines, France (fdi)*	*£20*
		Plymouth, Devon (fdi)/Cadiz, Spain	*BUY £12*
1989	*Microscope*	*Oxford S/H (fdi)/Delft (Holland)*	*£15*
1990	*Gallantry*	*George Cross S/H (fdi)/Valetta, Malta*	*£15*

We advertise all our covers mainly through our FREE Newsletter (published for each commemorative stamp issue) and if you would like to be added to our mailing list WRITE NOW.
We stock 'official' covers cds and slogan postmarks and welcome Wants Lists – send today for a quote.
BUYING: We are always interested in buying good quality covers.

PLEASE MENTION THIS CATALOGUE WHEN REPLYING TO ADVERTISEMENTS

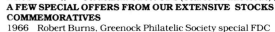

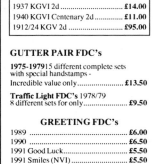

HOW TO USE THIS CATALOGUE

This section (commemoratives) follows the format below:

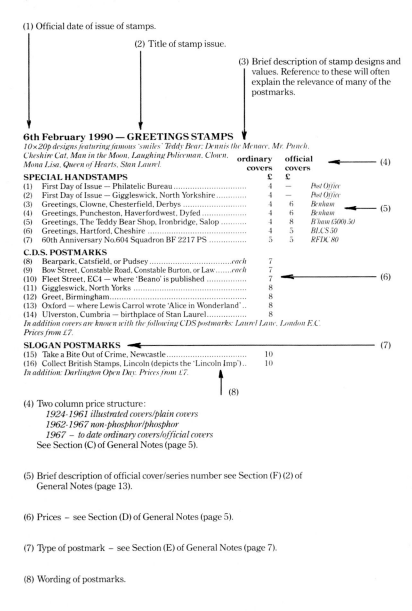

(1) Official date of issue of stamps.

(2) Title of stamp issue.

(3) Brief description of stamp designs and values. Reference to these will often explain the relevance of many of the postmarks.

6th February 1990 — GREETINGS STAMPS
10×20p designs featuring famous 'smiles' Teddy Bear; Dennis the Menace, Mr. Punch, Cheshire Cat, Man in the Moon, Laughing Policeman, Clown, Mona Lisa, Queen of Hearts, Stan Laurel.

	ordinary covers £	official covers £	
SPECIAL HANDSTAMPS			
(1) First Day of Issue — Philatelic Bureau	4	—	*Post Office*
(2) First Day of Issue — Giggleswick, North Yorkshire	4	—	*Post Office*
(3) Greetings, Clowne, Chesterfield, Derbys	4	6	*Benham*
(4) Greetings, Puncheston, Haverfordwest, Dyfed	4	6	*Benham*
(5) Greetings, The Teddy Bear Shop, Ironbridge, Salop	4	8	*B'ham (500) 50*
(6) Greetings, Hartford, Cheshire	4	5	*BLCS 50*
(7) 60th Anniversary No.604 Squadron BF 2217 PS	5	5	*RFDC 80*
C.D.S. POSTMARKS			
(8) Bearpark, Catsfield, or Pudsey ....*each*	7		
(9) Bow Street, Constable Road, Constable Burton, or Law.......*each*	7		
(10) Fleet Street, EC4 — where 'Beano' is published	7		
(11) Giggleswick, North Yorks	8		
(12) Greet, Birmingham	8		
(13) Oxford — where Lewis Carrol wrote 'Alice in Wonderland'	8		
(14) Ulverston, Cumbria — birthplace of Stan Laurel	8		

In addition covers are known with the following CDS postmarks: Laurel Lane, London E.C. Prices from £7.

SLOGAN POSTMARKS		
(15) Take a Bite Out of Crime, Newcastle	10	
(16) Collect British Stamps, Lincoln (depicts the 'Lincoln Imp')	10	

In addition: Darlington Open Day. Prices from £7.

(8)

(4) Two column price structure:
   1924-1961 illustrated covers/plain covers
   1962-1967 non-phosphor/phosphor
   1967 – to date ordinary covers/official covers
   See Section (C) of General Notes (page 5).

(5) Brief description of official cover/series number see Section (F) (2) of General Notes (page 13).

(6) Prices – see Section (D) of General Notes (page 5).

(7) Type of postmark – see Section (E) of General Notes (page 7).

(8) Wording of postmarks.

COMMEMORATIVE ISSUES

·23rd April 1924 — BRITISH EMPIRE EXHIBITION, WEMBLEY
1d, 1½d

	illustrated covers £	plain covers £
SPECIAL HANDSTAMPS		
(1) Empire Exhibition Wembley Park 1924 (double ring)...........	n.k.	225
(2) Empire Exhibition Wembley, Palace of Engineering	n.k.	475
SLOGAN POSTMARKS		
(3) Wembley Park (Lion) 1924 Empire Exhibition 1924	275*	200
H. R. Harmer Ltd. 'semi-display' cover.		
POSTAL STATIONERY		
(4) 1d Postcard – Wembley special h/s or slogan........................	—	75
(5) 1½d Postcard (foreign) – Wembley special h/s or slogan	—	100
(6) 1½d Printed envelope – Wembley special h/s or slogan	—	125

9th May 1925 — BRITISH EMPIRE EXHIBITION, WEMBLEY
1d, 1½d

SPECIAL HANDSTAMPS		
(1) British Empire Exhibition Wembley 1925 (double ring)........	n.k.	900
(2) Empire Exhibition Wembley, Palace of Industry	n.k.	1,000
C.D.S. POSTMARKS		
(3) British Empire Exhibition Wembley	n.k.	950
SLOGAN POSTMARKS		
(4) Wembley Park (Lion) 1925 Empire Exhibition 1925	n.k.	900
POSTAL STATIONERY		
(5) 1d Postcard – Wembley special h/s or slogan........................	—	150
(6) 1½d Postcard (foreign) – Wembley special h/s or slogan	—	175
(7) 1½d Printed envelope – Wembley special h/s or slogan	—	200

WEMBLEY PARK 1924

WEMBLEY PARK 1925

10th May 1929 — 9th UNIVERSAL POSTAL UNION CONGRESS
½d, 1d, 1½d, 2½d King George V; £1 St. George and the Dragon

C.D.S. POSTMARKS		
(1) Postal Union Congress, London (double ring) — £1 value......	n.k.	5,500
(2) Postal Union Congress, London (double ring) — 4 low values	n.k.	700
(3) -do- on P.U.C. stationery or P.U.C. envelope (crest on flap)......	—	700
(4) – do- on P.U.C. stationery – all 5 values	—	3,500
(5) Registered P.U.C., London (oval) — 4 low values	n.k.	750
(6) Any other postmark — £1 value.......................................	n.k.	4,500
(7) Any other postmark — 4 low values	n.k.	350
(8) Any other postmark — all five values	n.k.	5,000
SLOGAN POSTMARKS		
(9) Any postmark — 4 low values...	n.k.	200

7th May 1935 — KING GEORGE V SILVER JUBILEE
½d, 1d, 1½d, 2½d King George V

C.D.S. POSTMARKS		
(1) Windsor, Berks..	600	200
(2) London SW1	525	150
(2a) -do- on Westminster Stamp Co. cover	550	—
(3) Any other postmark	500	75
SLOGAN POSTMARKS		
(4) London SW1 or Windsor — wavy line cancellations	12(s)	6(s)
(5) Any other postmark	375	75

13th May 1937 — CORONATION OF KING GEORGE VI
1½d King George VI and Queen Elizabeth

C.D.S. POSTMARKS		
(1) Windsor, Berks..	150	25
(2) Hampton Court Camp, Kingston-on-Thames	150	n.k.
(3) Pirbright Camp — used to accommodate troops for Coronation.....	100	n.k.
(4) Any London SW postmark	25	8
(5) Any other postmark	20	4
SLOGAN POSTMARKS		
(6) London SW1 or Windsor, Berks. – wavy line	125	30
(7) Any other postmark	15	3

6th May 1940 — CENTENARY OF FIRST ADHESIVE POSTAGE STAMPS

½d, 1d, 1½d, 2d, 2½d, 3d Queen Victoria and King George VI

	illustrated covers £	plain covers £
SPECIAL HANDSTAMPS		
(1) 27th Philatelic Congress of Gt. Britain, Bournemouth	65	20
(2) Adhesive Stamp Centenary Exhibition, Bournemouth	35	7
(3) Stamp Centenary (Red Cross) Exhibition, London (struck in red)	35	7
(3a) -do- on Perkins Bacon cover	50	—
(4) Pavilion Bournemouth	35(s)	20(s)
C.D.S. POSTMARKS		
(5) Dundee (James Chalmers — maker of first adhesive postage stamps)	150	—
(6) Any other postmark	30	5
SLOGAN POSTMARKS		
(7) Post Early in the Day	—	50
(8) Any other postmark	25	4

11th June 1946 — VICTORY COMMEMORATION

2½d, 3d Symbols of Peace and Reconstruction

C.D.S. POSTMARKS		
(1) Any central London postmark	50	5
(2) Jersey or Guernsey — only German occupied part of U.K.	50	10
(3) Any other postmark	40	4
SLOGAN POSTMARKS		
(4) Don't Waste Bread — Others Need It	60	20
(5) Any other postmark	35	3

DON'T ═══
WASTE BREAD
OTHERS NEED IT

26th April 1948 — SILVER WEDDING OF KING GEORGE VI & QUEEN ELIZABETH

2½d, £1

C.D.S. POSTMARKS		
(1) Georgetown, Jersey	400	175
(2) London EC	325	100
(3) Any central London postmark	300	75
(4) Any other postmark	275	70
SLOGAN POSTMARKS		
(5) Any postmark	250	60

10th May 1948 — 3rd ANNIVERSARY OF THE LIBERATION OF THE CHANNEL ISLANDS

1d, 2½d Gathering Vraic

C.D.S. POSTMARKS		
(1) Guernsey or Jersey	20	4
(2) Sark or Alderney	45	10
(3) British Industries Fair, Birmingham (registered)	45	25
(4) Any other postmark	20	3
SLOGAN POSTMARKS		
(5) Guernsey or Jersey — wavy line cancellations	20	4
(6) A Distinguished Career — Nursing	60	20
(7) British Industries Fair, Birmingham	n.k.	35
(8) Any other postmark	15	4

A DISTINGUISHED
CAREER ────┐ (6)
NURSING
BRITISH INDUSTRIES FAIR
MAY 3RD-14TH 1948
(7) LONDON & BIRMINGHAM

29th July 1948 — OLYMPIC GAMES, WEMBLEY

2½d, 3d, 6d, 1s Olympic Symbols

C.D.S. POSTMARKS		
(1) Wembley, Middx. (single ring or double ring)	40	12
(1a) ditto — used at Games (bearing nos. 11 to 16 in pmk.)	45	30
(2) Any other postmark	25	4
SLOGAN POSTMARKS		
(3) Olympic Games Wembley, Gt. Brit.	40	20
(4) Any other postmark	20	3

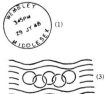

PRICES & CONDITION – PLEASE READ GENERAL NOTES

10th October 1949 — 75th ANNIVERSARY OF UNIVERSAL POSTAL UNION
2½d Two Hemispheres; 3d UPU Monument, Berne; 6d Goddess Concordia; 1s Posthorn and Globe

	illustrated covers £	plain covers £
C.D.S. POSTMARKS		
(1) London Chief Office — postal headquarters	75	30
(2) Any other postmark	45	8
SLOGAN POSTMARKS		
(3) Any postmark	45	13

3rd May 1951 — FESTIVAL OF BRITAIN
2½d Commerce and Prosperity; 4d Festival Symbol

C.D.S. POSTMARKS		
(1) British Industries Fair B'ham (double ring)	n.k.	10(s)
(2) British Industries Fair B'ham (single ring)	n.k.	10(s)
(3) Registered B.I.F. Birmingham (oval)	n.k.	10(s)
(4) Battersea SW11 (Festival Gardens were in Battersea Park) ..	40	12
(5) Buckingham Palace, SW1	125	50
(6) London SE1 (Festival site was on the South Bank, London SE1) ...	40	15
(7) Any other postmark	25	3
SLOGAN POSTMARKS		
(8) Battersea, SW11 — wavy line	50	15
(9) Festival of Britain May 3-Sept 30 (used at Cardiff)	300	175
(10) Any other postmark	25	3

3rd June 1953 — CORONATION OF QUEEN ELIZABETH II
2½d, 4d, 1s 3d, 1s 6d

C.D.S. POSTMARKS		
(1) Arundel (Earl Marshal responsible for Coronation arrangements)	100	—
(2) Buckingham Palace SW1	675	—
(3) Windsor Castle, Windsor, Berks. or Sandringham	675	—
(4) Windsor, Berks.	200	50
(5) Queen's Head, Queensborough, Queen Camel, Queensferry or Queensbury	10(s)	n.k.
(6) Any central London postmark	40	15
(7) Any other postmark	30	10
SLOGAN POSTMARKS		
(8) Long Live the Queen, Windsor	200	40
(9) Long Live the Queen, London SW1	60	20
(10) Long Live the Queen, any other location	50	15
(11) Any other postmark	25	7

1st August 1957 — WORLD SCOUT JUBILEE JAMBOREE
2½d, 4d, 1s 3d Scouting Symbols

C.D.S. POSTMARKS		
(1) Sutton Coldfield	60	20
(2) Any other postmark	15	4
SLOGAN POSTMARKS		
(3) World Scout Jubilee Jamboree, Sutton Coldfield	20	5
(4) Wavy line cancellation — Sutton Coldfield	20	5
(5) Any other postmark	15	3

12th September 1957 — 46th PARLIAMENTARY CONFERENCE
4d

SPECIAL HANDSTAMPS		
(1) 46th Parliamentary Conference, London SW1	80	20

The special handstamp is known both with and without a time recorded in its design (found above the date). The version without the time recorded was used on registered mail and is more scarce, thus commanding a premium.
Collectors are advised that a London W1 handstamp is known used on illustrated covers, but was not officially applied by the Post Office.

C.D.S. POSTMARKS		
(2) Northern Parliament, Belfast	200	80
(3) Any London SW postmark	70	20
(4) Any other postmark	60	15
SLOGAN POSTMARKS		
(5) Any postmark	60	7

18th July 1958 — 6th BRITISH EMPIRE & COMMONWEALTH GAMES, CARDIFF

3d, 6d, 1s 3d Welsh Dragon and Games Emblem

	illustrated covers	plain covers
	£	£
C.D.S. POSTMARKS		
(1) Empire Games Village, Barry (double ring pmk)	200	75
(2) Empire Games Village, Barry (single ring pmk)	250	90
(3) Empire Games Village, Barry (registered — 'hooded' pmk)	300	75
(3a) -do- on R.A.F.A. Philatelic Society cover	325	—
(4) Any other postmark	35	7
(5) Empire Games Village, Barry Parcel Post	n.k.	25(s)
SLOGAN POSTMARKS		
(6) VIth British Empire & Commonwealth Games — Barry	65	25
(7) VIth British Empire & Commonwealth Games — Llanberis..	80	35
(8) VIth British Empire & Commonwealth Games — Cardiff	80	35
(9) Any other postmark	30	5

7th July 1960 — TERCENTENARY OF THE ESTABLISHMENT OF THE GENERAL LETTER OFFICE

3d, 1s 3d Post boy and Post horn of 1660

C.D.S. POSTMARKS		
(1) Lombard Street, EC3 (General Letter Office)	60	20
(2) London Chief Office, EC (Site of postal headquarters)	60	20
(3) Any other postmark	35	5
SLOGAN POSTMARKS		
(4) International Postal Conference 1960 Eastbourne	150	50
(5) Any other postmark	30	5

19th Sept. 1960 — 1st ANNIV. EUROPEAN POSTAL & TELECOMMUNICATIONS CONFERENCE (CEPT) — 'EUROPA'

6d, 1s 6d Conference Emblem

C.D.S. POSTMARKS		
(1) Lombard Street, EC3 (General Letter Office)	45	n.k.
(2) London Chief Office, EC (Site of postal headquarters)	45	20
(3) Norwich (first use of postal coding in 1960)	40	17
(4) London F.S. (Foreign Section)	50	25
(5) Any other postmark	30	7
SLOGAN POSTMARKS		
(6) Any postmark	30	5

28th August 1961 — CENTENARY OF THE POST OFFICE SAVINGS BANK

2½d, 3d, 1s 6d Thrift Plant and Growth of Savings

C.D.S. POSTMARKS		
(1) Blythe Road, West Kensington, W14 (HQ of the P.O.S.B.)	200	75
(2) London Chief Office, EC (Site of postal headquarters)	60	25
(3) Any London postmark	50	20
(4) Any other postmark	45	7
SLOGAN POSTMARKS		
(5) Express Good Wishes by Greetings Telegrams	75	15
(6) Any other postmark	40	6

18th Sept. 1961 — EUROPEAN POSTAL & TELECOMMUNICATIONS CONFERENCE (CEPT)

2d, 4d, 10d Doves and CEPT Emblem

C.D.S. POSTMARKS		
(1) London Chief Office, EC (Site of postal headquarters)	30	n.k.
(2) Any other postmark	3	1
SLOGAN POSTMARKS		
(3) CEPT European Conference, Torquay, Devon	6	2
(4) Post Office Savings Bank 1861-1961	175	25(s)
(5) Any other postmark	3	1

25th September 1961 — 7th COMMONWEALTH PARLIAMENTARY CONFERENCE

6d Hammer Beam Roof, Westminster Hall;
1s 3d Palace of Westminster

	illustrated covers £	plain covers £
C.D.S. POSTMARKS		
(1) House of Commons, SW1	175	45
(2) House of Lords, SW1	200	60
(3) London SW1	40	20
(4) Any other postmark	25	5
SLOGAN POSTMARKS		
(5) Commonwealth Parliamentary Conf.25-30 Sept. 1961, SW ..	35	8
(6) Post Office Savings Bank, Windsor	50	n.k.
(7) Any other postmark	25	4

With effect from the National Productivity Year issue, all commemorative stamps were produced with and without phosphor bands. All prices listed from this issue are for illustrated covers only. Plain covers are generally available for subsequent issues but are worth considerably less than illustrated covers.

14th November 1962 — NATIONAL PRODUCTIVITY YEAR

2½d, 3d, 1s 3d Productivity Emblems

	non-phos. covers £	phosphor covers £
C.D.S. POSTMARKS		
(1) Any postmark	40	80
SLOGAN POSTMARKS		
(2) National Productivity Year November 1962-63	70	120
(3) Export & Prosper, NW1 (on plain covers)	40(s)	40(s)
(4) Southampton T — wavy line cancellation	n.k.	110
(5) Any other postmark	35	80

21st March 1963 — FREEDOM FROM HUNGER CAMPAIGN

2½d, 1s 3d Campaign Emblems

SPECIAL HANDSTAMPS		
(1) Tenth Anniversary Stampex 1963, London SW1	60	60
C.D.S. POSTMARKS		
(2) Any postmark	25	30
SLOGAN POSTMARKS		
(3) Freedom From Hunger Week 17-24 March 1963	35	40
(4) Southampton T - wavy line cancellation	n.k.	35
(5) Any other postmark	20	30

With effect from the next issue 'Any other postmark' in the SLOGAN POSTMARKS section is not listed. Special 'First Day of Issue' (envelope design) slogan postmarks were introduced and are listed for the remaining issues of 1963 (and some later issues where relevant).

7th May 1963 — CENTENARY OF THE PARIS POSTAL CONFERENCE

6d

SPECIAL HANDSTAMPS		
(1) Post Office Tercentenary Dover Packet Service 1633-1963 ...	20	400
(1a) -ditto- Dover Philatelic Soc. official cover	25	n.k.
C.D.S. POSTMARKS		
(2) Any postmark	10	20
SLOGAN POSTMARKS		
(3) First Day of Issue — any office	10	20
(4) Southampton T - wavy line cancellation	n.k.	20

16th May 1963 — NATIONAL NATURE WEEK

3d Posy of Flowers; 4½d Woodland Life

SPECIAL HANDSTAMPS		
(1) Brownsea Island Opening Week, Poole, Dorset	80	80
C.D.S. POSTMARKS		
(2) Botanic Gardens, Belfast	—	100
(3) Selborne, Hants. (Gilbert White's 'Natural History of Selborne')...	75	75
(4) Forest Row, Sussex	100	100
(5) Any other postmark	20	25
SLOGAN POSTMARKS		
(6) First Day of Issue — any office	20	25
(7) Southampton T — wavy line cancellation	n.k.	25

31st May 1963 — 9th INTERNATIONAL LIFEBOAT CONFERENCE

2½d Rescue at Sea; 4d Lifeboat; 1s 6d Lifeboatmen

	non-phos. covers £	phosphor covers £
C.D.S. POSTMARKS		
(1) Edinburgh	50	n.k.
(2) Sites of Lifeboat Stations, e.g. Cromer	60	60
(3) Any postmark	25	30
SLOGAN POSTMARKS		
(4) International Life-Boat Conf. Edinburgh 1963 — Edinburgh	50	65
(5) International Life-Boat Conf. Edinburgh 1963 — any other office	40	55
(6) Southampton T — wavy line cancellation	n.k.	45
(7) First Day of Issue — Edinburgh	40	55
(8) First Day of Issue — any other office	25	40

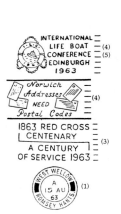

15th August 1963 — RED CROSS CENTENARY CONGRESS

3d, 1s 3d, 1s 6d

C.D.S. POSTMARKS		
(1) West Wellow, Romsey Hants. (home of Florence Nightingale)	90	100
(2) Any other postmark	30	45
SLOGAN POSTMARKS		
(3) 1863-1963 Red Cross Centenary A Century of Service	65	100
(4) Norwich Addresses need Postal Codes	65	n.k.
(5) Southampton T — wavy line cancellation	n.k.	70
(6) First Day of Issue — any office	35	50

3rd December 1963 — COMMONWEALTH PACIFIC CABLE (COMPAC)

1s 6d

C.D.S. POSTMARKS		
(1) Any postmark	20	25
SLOGAN POSTMARKS		
(2) First Day of Issue — Philatelic Bureau GPO London EC1	25	35
(3) Southampton T — wavy line cancellation	n.k.	30
(4) First Day of Issue — any other office	20	25

The 'Ordinary F.D.I. postmarks' were introduced with effect from the 1964 Shakespeare issue. In general, these were collected in preference to the F.D.I. slogan (envelope design). The latter are now only listed if used at an office relevant to the issue. The Post Office also issued their own first day covers commencing with this issue.

23rd April 1964 — SHAKESPEARE 400th ANNIVERSARY FESTIVAL

3d, 6d, 1s 3d, 1s 6d + 2s 6d (non-phos. only) scenes from plays

SPECIAL STAMPS		
(1) Shakespeare 400th Anniversary Stratford-upon-Avon	30	22

There were available six different covers each bearing the legend 'Official First Day Cover' or 'Official Cover'. Each cover depicts places of interest connected with the life of Shakespeare.

ORDINARY F.D.I. POSTMARKS		
(2) Stratford-upon-Avon, Wks.	15	15
(3) Any other office	7	10
C.D.S. POSTMARKS		
(4) Any postmark	5	7
SLOGAN POSTMARKS		
(5) Shakespeare Anniversary Year, Stratford-upon-Avon	475	600
(6) First Day of Issue, Stratford	15(s)	15(s)

1st July 1964 — 20th INTERNATIONAL GEOGRAPHICAL CONGRESS

2½d, 4d, 8d, 1s 6d

SPECIAL HANDSTAMPS		
(1) The Lawn Tennis Championships AELTC, Wimbledon	200	n.k.
ORDINARY F.D.I. POSTMARKS		
(2) GPO Philatelic Bureau, London EC1	25	35
(3) London	25	35
(4) Any other office	20	30
C.D.S. POSTMARKS		
(5) South Kensington, SW7 (Home of Royal Geographical Society)	100	100
(6) Any other postmark	15	20
SLOGAN POSTMARKS		
(7) First Day of Issue — Greenwich SE10 (Geographical expeditions)	275	275
(8) First Day of Issue with triangle — SE10 (also used at Greenwich)	275	275
(9) Ralph Allen of Bath, Postal Pioneer, Bath	275	n.k.
(10) The Country Code — Leave no litter	200	n.k.

5th August 1964 — 10th INTERNATIONAL BOTANICAL CONGRESS
3d Spring Gentian; 6d Dog Rose; 9d Honeysuckle; 1s 3d Water Lily

	non-phos. covers £	phosphor covers £
SPECIAL HANDSTAMPS		
(1) Tenth International Botanical Congress, Edinburgh	180	200
ORDINARY F.D.I. POSTMARKS		
(2) GPO Philatelic Bureau, London EC1	25	30
(3) Edinburgh..	30	50
(4) Any other office	20	30
C.D.S. POSTMARKS		
(5) Kew Gardens, Richmond, Surrey	200	200
(6) Primrose Valley, Filey, N. Yorks.......................................	100	125
(7) Forest Row, Sussex	100	100
(8) Any other postmark	18	28
SLOGAN POSTMARKS		
(9) First Day of Issue — Richmond & Twickenham (local slogan for Kew)	150	175

4th September 1964 — OPENING OF THE FORTH ROAD BRIDGE
3d, 6d

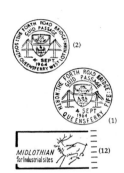

	non-phos.	phosphor
SPECIAL HANDSTAMPS		
(1) The Forth Road Bridge Guid Passage North Queensferry, Fife	20	90
(2) The Forth Road Bridge Guid Passage South Queensferry, Lothian	15	70
(3) Apostolatus Maris — 14th Int. Congress, Liverpool	n.k.	150
ORDINARY F.D.I. POSTMARKS		
(4) GPO Philatelic Bureau London EC1	10	15
(5) Edinburgh (local F.D.I. for Forth Road Bridge).....................	10	15
(6) Any other office	7	10
C.D.S. POSTMARKS		
(7) Balmoral Castle (The Queen proceeded to Balmoral after opening the Forth Road Bridge)	225	225
(8) South Queensferry, West Lothian	90	90
(9) North Queensferry, Fife...	125	125
(10) Any other postmark	6	9
SLOGAN POSTMARKS		
(11) First Day of Issue — Edinburgh (local slogan for Forth Road Bridge)......	40	50
(12) Midlothian for Industrial Sites	50	n.k.

8th July 1965 — SIR WINSTON CHURCHILL
4d, 1s 3d

ORDINARY F.D.I. POSTMARKS		
(1) Bladon, Oxford (Churchill buried at Bladon)	15	20
(2) London SW1	10	15
(3) GPO Philatelic Bureau, London EC1	9	12
(4) Any other office	5	7
C.D.S. POSTMARKS		
(5) Churchill, Bristol or Oxford..	75	75
(6) House of Commons, SW1	65	65
(7) House of Lords, SW1	125	125
(8) Marlborough (the Churchill ancestral home)	200	n.k.
(9) Woodford Green (Churchill was MP for Woodford)..............	125	n.k.
(10) Any other postmark	4	6
SLOGAN POSTMARKS		
(11) First Day of Issue — Westminster, London SW1	95	95

19th July 1965 — 700th ANNIVERSARY OF SIMON DE MONTFORT'S PARLIAMENT
6d De Montfort's Seal; 2s 6d (non-phos. only) Parliament

ORDINARY F.D.I. POSTMARKS		
(1) Dover or Lincoln	40	40
(first boroughs to be represented at the Parliament by commoners)		
(2) Evesham, Worcs. (Simon De Montfort killed at Battle of Evesham)	30	30
(3) London SW	20	20
(4) Leicester (Simon De Montfort was Earl of Leicester)...........	25	25
(5) Oxford (Parliament sometimes met at Oxford)....................	25	25
(6) GPO Philatelic Bureau, London EC1	10	15
(7) Any other office	9	12

Simon De Montfort's Parliament (contd.)

	non-phos. covers £	phosphor covers £
C.D.S. POSTMARKS		
(8) Buckingham Palace, SW1	100	100
(9) Dover or Lincoln (see note in F.D.I. section)	60	60
(10) Evesham, Worcs. (Simon De Montfort killed at Battle of Evesham)	90	90
(11) House of Commons, SW1	90	80
(12) House of Lords, SW1	125	100
(13) North Warnborough (De Montfort's home was Odiham Castle, North Warnborough)	200	200
(14) Parliament Street, SW1	100	n.k.
(15) Any other postmark	8	10

9th August 1965 — CENTENARY OF THE SALVATION ARMY
3d, 1s 6d

SPECIAL HANDSTAMPS		
(1) Portsmouth & District Philatelic Society	90	100
(1a) -ditto- on Philatelic Society official cover	90	100
ORDINARY F.D.I. POSTMARKS		
(2) London EC (International HQ of Salvation Army)	35	40
(3) Nottingham (Birthplace of William Booth)	45	45
(4) Any other office	20	25
C.D.S. POSTMARKS		
(5) Any postmark	18	23

(1)

1st September 1965 — CENTENARY OF THE DISCOVERY OF ANTISEPTIC SURGERY BY JOSEPH LISTER
4d Carbolic Spray; 1s Lister

SPECIAL HANDSTAMPS		
(1) Eyam Plague Tercentenary Commemoration, Eyam, Sheffield	125	n.k.
ORDINARY F.D.I. POSTMARKS		
(2) Edinburgh (Lister was Professor of Clinical Surgery here)	40	40
(2a) -ditto- on Royal Infirmary Edinburgh special cover	60	60
(3) Glasgow (Lister was Professor of Surgery here)	40	40
(4) Any other office	10	12
C.D.S. POSTMARKS		
(5) Paddington W2 (Lister was House Surgeon at Kings College)	125	150
(6) Royal Infirmary Edinburgh on R.I. cover (Professor of Surgery)	225	225
(7) Glasgow (Lister was Professor of Surgery here)	100	125
(8) Any other postmark	9	11
SLOGAN POSTMARKS		
(9) First Day of Issue — Paddington	110	n.k.
(10) First Day of Issue — Edinburgh	110	110

(1)

1st September 1965 — COMMONWEALTH ARTS FESTIVAL
6d Trinidad Carnival Dancers; 1s 6d Canadian Folk Dancers

SPECIAL HANDSTAMPS		
(1) Eyam Plague Tercentenary Commemoration, Eyam, Sheffield	125	n.k.
ORDINARY F.D.I. POSTMARKS		
(2) Cardiff, Glasgow, Liverpool or London (major events held here)	30	30
(3) Any other office	15	20
C.D.S. POSTMARKS		
(4) Balmoral Castle (The Duke of Edinburgh travelled from Balmoral Castle to open the Festival)	150	150
(5) Stratford-upon-Avon (on Arts Centre cover)	80	n.k.
(6) Any other postmark	14	18
SLOGAN POSTMARKS		
(7) Commonwealth Arts Festival, Glasgow 18 Sept-2 Oct 1965	500	550
(8) Commonwealth Arts Festival, Liverpool 17 Sept-2 Oct	450	500
(9) Commonwealth Arts Festival 16 Sept-2 Oct — any other office	375	425
(10) 4th Bach Festival Bath 23-30 October 1965, Bath	500	n.k.

(10)

(7) COMMONWEALTH ARTS FESTIVAL GLASGOW 18 SEPT – 2 OCT.

COMMONWEALTH ARTS FESTIVAL LIVERPOOL SEPT 17- OCT 2 (8)

(9) COMMONWEALTH ARTS FESTIVAL 16 SEPTEMBER - 2 OCTOBER 1965

PRICES & CONDITION – PLEASE READ GENERAL NOTES

13th September 1965 — 25th ANNIVERSARY OF THE BATTLE OF BRITAIN

6 × 4d, 9d, 1s 3d Battle Scenes

	non-phos. covers £	phosphor covers £
ORDINARY F.D.I. POSTMARKS		
(1) Biggin Hill, Westerham, Kent	60	70
(2) GPO Philatelic Bureau, London EC1	12	15
(3) Any other office	18	20
C.D.S. POSTMARKS		
(4) Biggin Hill, Westerham, Kent	70	80
(5) Churchill, Bristol	75	n.k.
(6) Dover, Kent	30	30
(7) Any RAF Post Office postmark	70	80
(8) Any other postmark	16	18

8th October 1965 — OPENING OF THE POST OFFICE TOWER

Tower and 3d Georgian Buildings; 1s 3d 'Nash' Terrace

SPECIAL HANDSTAMPS		
(1) Leicester Philatelic Society Diamond Jubilee, Leicester	30	25
(1a) ditto — on Leicester Philatelic Society official cover	40	40
ORDINARY F.D.I. POSTMARKS		
(2) London W1 (Site of P.O. Tower)	20	20
(3) GPO Philatelic Bureau, London EC1	4	5
(4) Any other office	6	8
C.D.S. POSTMARKS		
(5) Gt. Portland St. (nearest P.O. to the Tower)	n.k.	75
(6) Any other postmark	5	7
SLOGAN POSTMARKS		
(7) London W1 (wavy line) — site of P.O. Tower	20	n.k.

25th October 1965 — 20th ANNIVERSARY OF THE U.N. & INTERNATIONAL CO-OPERATION YEAR (ICY)

3d U.N. Emblem; 1s 6d I.C.Y. Emblem

SPECIAL HANDSTAMPS		
(1) Leicester Philatelic Society Diamond Jubilee, Leicester	50	50
(1a) ditto — on Leicester Philatelic Society official cover	75	75
ORDINARY F.D.I. POSTMARKS		
(2) First Day of Issue — London SW (U.N. London offices are here)	10	12
(3) Any other office	12	15
C.D.S. POSTMARKS		
(4) Any postmark	10	12
SLOGAN POSTMARKS		
(5) Int. Co-operation Year 1965 Reading, Great Britain — Reading	425	425

15th November 1965 — CENTENARY OF THE INTERNATIONAL TELECOMMUNICATIONS UNION (ITU)

9d Telecommunications; 1s 6d Radio Waves

ORDINARY F.D.I. POSTMARKS		
(1) Any office	12	17
C.D.S. POSTMARKS		
(2) Helston, Cornwall (Goonhilly Downs Ground Station)	200	200
(3) Any other postmark	12	17
SLOGAN POSTMARKS		
(4) Have You Taken Out Your Licence for Radio-TV?	250	n.k.

25th January 1966 — ROBERT BURNS

4d, 1s 3d Portraits of Burns

SPECIAL HANDSTAMPS		
(1) The friend of man — to vice alone a foe — Dumfries	7	7
(2) That man to man the warld o'er shall brothers be — Alloway	5	5
(3) That man to man the warld o'er shall brothers be — Ayr	9	9
(4) That man to man the warld o'er shall brothers be — Edinburgh	7	7
(5) That man to man the warld o'er shall brothers be — Glasgow	7	7
(6) That man to man the warld o'er shall brothers be — Greenock	35	40
(7) That man to man the warld o'er shall brothers be — Kilmarnock	9	9
(8) That man to man the warld o'er shall brothers be — Mauchline	35	40

These special handstamps were sponsored by the Post Office. Although various organisations produced their own covers using these handstamps, they are not 'official' as described in the General Notes. Such covers though, do command a premium.

Robert Burns (contd.)

	non-phos. covers £	phosphor covers £
ORDINARY F.D.I. POSTMARKS		
(9) Any Scottish postmark	7	7
(10) Any other office	4	4
C.D.S. POSTMARKS		
(11) Burns Statue, Ayr	200	200
(12) Any other postmark	3	3

28th February 1966 — 900th ANNIVERSARY OF WESTMINSTER ABBEY
3d Abbey; 2s 6d (non-phos. only) Henry VII Chapel

ORDINARY F.D.I. POSTMARKS		
(1) London SW	15	15
(2) GPO Philatelic Bureau, London EC1	6	9
(3) Any other office	7	10
C.D.S. POSTMARKS		
(4) Buckingham Palace SW1	120	120
(5) House of Commons SW1 (Early Parliaments were often	100	100
(6) House of Lords SW1 held at Westminster Abbey)	100	100
(7) Any other postmark	6	9
SLOGAN POSTMARKS		
(8) Westminster Abbey 900th Anniversary Year, London SW7	140	120
(9) First Day of Issue — Westminster, London SW1	120	100

2nd May 1966 — BRITISH LANDSCAPES
4d Sussex; 6d Antrim; 1s 3d Harlech; 1s 6d The Cairngorms

ORDINARY F.D.I. POSTMARKS		
(1) Lewes, Sussex (appropriate to view on 4d value)	40	60
(2) Harlech, Merioneth (appropriate to view on 1s 3d value)	60	70
(3) Coleraine, Co. Londonderry (appropriate to view on 6d value)	60	80
(4) Grantown-on-Spey, Morayshire (appropriate to 1s 6d)	100	125
(5) GPO Philatelic Bureau, London EC1	10	10
(6) Any other office	8	8
C.D.S. POSTMARKS		
(7) Antrim (appropriate for 6d value)	100	100
(8) Coleraine, Co. Londonderry (appropriate for 6d value)	100	100
(9) Grantown-on-Spey, Morayshire (appropriate for 1s 6d value)	100	125
(10) Harlech, Merioneth (appropriate for 1s 3d value)	100	100
(11) Any other postmark	7	7
SET of four single stamp covers with appropriate postmarks – usually (1), (2), (3) and (4)	30	40

1st June 1966 — WORLD CUP FOOTBALL COMPETITION
4d, 6d, 1s 3d

ORDINARY F.D.I. POSTMARKS		
(1) Wembley, Middx.	20	20
(2) GPO Philatelic Bureau, London EC1	9	9
(3) Birmingham, Liverpool, Manchester, Middlesbrough, Sheffield or Sunderland (sites of World Cup Games) *each*	15	15
(4) Any other office	9	9
C.D.S. POSTMARKS		
(5) Any postmark	9	9
SLOGAN POSTMARKS		
(6) First Day of Issue — Harrow & Wembley	60	60
(7) World Cup City, Sheffield, City of Steel	425	n.k.
(8) The Dairy Festival Time for Sport	275	n.k.

8th August 1966 — BRITISH BIRDS
4 × 4d Black-headed Gull; Blue Tit; Robin; Blackbird

ORDINARY F.D.I. POSTMARKS		
(1) GPO Philatelic Bureau, London EC1	8	8
(2) Any other office	7	7
C.D.S. POSTMARKS		
(3) Any postmark	7	7

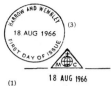

18th August 1966 — WORLD CUP FOOTBALL COMPETITION — 'ENGLAND WINNERS'

4d (non-phos. only)

	non-phos. covers £	phosphor covers £
SPECIAL HANDSTAMPS		
(1) World Methodist Conference, SW1 (on plain covers)	50	—
(2) Opening of the Tay Road Bridge, Dundee	50	—
ORDINARY F.D.I. POSTMARKS		
(3) Harrow & Wembley	6	—
(4) Birmingham, Liverpool, Manchester, Middlesbrough, Sheffield or Sunderland (sites of World Cup Games) ......*each*	10	—
(5) Any other office	4	—
C.D.S. POSTMARKS		
(6) Harrow & Wembley, Middx.	25	—
(7) Any other postmark	4	—

1st June & 18th August 1966 — WORLD CUP & 'ENGLAND WINNERS' DOUBLE DATED COVERS

As no 'England Winners' phosphor stamps were issued, these double dated covers may exist with phosphor and ordinary stamps.

(1) Harrow & Wembley F.D.I. — both dates on one cover............	175
(2) Birmingham, Liverpool, Manchester, Middlesbrough, Sheffield or Sunderland — both dates on one cover...............	100
(3) Any other postmark — both dates on one cover	50

19th September 1966 — BRITISH TECHNOLOGY

4d Jodrell Bank; 6d Motor Cars; 1s 3d Hovercraft; 1s 6d Nuclear Power

ORDINARY F.D.I. POSTMARKS		
(1) GPO Philatelic Bureau, Edinburgh 1	6	6
(2) Birmingham, Coventry or Oxford (car industry)...................	9	10
(3) Carlisle, Cumberland (Windscale Reactor)	9	15
(4) Manchester (Jodrell Bank)...	9	10
(5) Newport, Isle of Wight (Hovercraft)	9	15
(6) Portsmouth (Hovercraft)	9	15
(7) Luton, Beds. (car industry)	9	15
(8) Any other office..	4	4
C.D.S. POSTMARKS		
(9) Macclesfield, Cheshire (with Jodrell Bank cachet)	150	200
(10) Cowes, I.O.W. (on British Hovercraft Corp. cover)	175	150
(11) Calderbridge, Seascale (Windscale reactor).......................	10(s)	—
(12) Lower Withington (Jodrell Bank)	10(s)	—
(13) Any other postmark	4	4
SLOGAN POSTMARKS		
(14) Build Your New Factory at Grimsby................................	60	—
SET of four single stamp covers with appropriate postmarks — usually (2), (3), (4) and (5)...	25	40

14th October 1966 — 900th ANNIVERSARY OF THE BATTLE OF HASTINGS

6 × 4d, 6d, 1s 3d Battle Scenes

SPECIAL HANDSTAMPS		
(1) Battle of Hastings 900th Anniv. Battlefield, Battle, Sussex...	7	8
ORDINARY F.D.I. POSTMARKS		
(2) Battle, Sussex	6	7
(3) Hastings, Sussex	5	6
(4) GPO Philatelic Bureau, Edinburgh 1	3	5
(5) Any other office..	2	3
C.D.S. POSTMARKS		
(6) Battle, Sussex	30	n.k.
(7) Any other postmark..	2	3
SLOGAN POSTMARKS		
(8) Channel Islands Les Iles Normandes 1066-1966 Guernsey (on 2 covers) .	175	175
(9) Channel Islands Les Iles Normandes 1066-1966 Jersey (on 2 covers)	175	175
(10) Hastings Popular with Visitors since 1066.........................	20(s)	20(s)

PRICES & CONDITION – PLEASE READ GENERAL NOTES

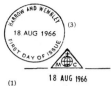
(1) 18 AUG 1966 WORLD METHODIST CONFERENCE, LONDON, S.W.1

(3) HARROW AND WEMBLEY 18 AUG 1966 FIRST DAY OF ISSUE

(2) DUNDEE 18th AUG. 1966 OPENING OF THE TAY ROAD BRIDGE

(2) OXFORD 19 SEP 1966 FIRST DAY OF ISSUE

(14) BUILD YOUR NEW FACTORY AT GRIMSBY Details of sites from the Town Clerk

(1) BATTLE OF HASTINGS 900TH ANNIVERSARY POSTED FROM 14 OCT 66 THE BATTLEFIELD BATTLE, SUSSEX

(8) (9) CHANNEL ISLANDS 1066 1966 LES ILES NORMANDES

HASTINGS POPULAR WITH VISITORS SINCE 1066 (10)

1st December 1966 — CHRISTMAS
3d, 1s 6d Children's Paintings

	non-phos. covers £	phosphor covers £
SPECIAL HANDSTAMPS		
(1) British Stamp Exhibition BF 1000 PS	30	30
(1a) ditto — on BFPS official cover	25	25
ORDINARY F.D.I. POSTMARKS		
(2) Bethlehem, Llandeilo, Carms	2	2
(3) GPO Philatelic Bureau, Edinburgh 1	1	1
(4) Any other office	1	1
C.D.S. POSTMARKS		
(5) Bethlehem, Llandeilo, Carms	250	250
(6) Nasareth, Caernarfon, Gwynedd *(Registration label shows 'Nazareth')*	250	250
(7) Isle of Whithorn (first seat of Christianity)	150	n.k.
(8) St. Nicholas, Guildford	100	n.k.
(9) Any other postmark	2	2
SLOGAN POSTMARKS		
(10) Reedham School Caring for Children	60	
(11) Britain Leads the World in Helping Spastics	25	n.k.

20th February 1967 — EUROPEAN FREE TRADE AREA (EFTA)
9d Sea Freight; 1s 6d Air Freight

SPECIAL HANDSTAMPS		
(1) Radiation Biology Conf. Portmeirion NATO Portmadoc	30	30
ORDINARY F.D.I. POSTMARKS		
(2) GPO Philatelic Bureau, Edinburgh 1	4	4
(3) London SW	6	6
(4) Hull, Grimsby or Newcastle (UK/EFTA Trading Ports)	10	10
(5) Any other office	2	2
C.D.S. POSTMARKS		
(6) House of Commons, SW1	25	30
(7) House of Lords, SW1	40	45
(8) Any other postmark	2	2
SLOGAN POSTMARKS		
(9) Ship Early Through the Port of London	175	175
(10) Southend — Modern Centre for Business and Industry	50	50

24th April 1967 — BRITISH WILD FLOWERS
4d Hawthorn, Rosaceae, Bramble; 4d Larger Bindweed, Echium;
4d Ox-eye Daisy, Coltsfoot, Buttercup; 4d Bluebell, Red Campion, Wood Anemone;
9d Dog Violet; 1s 9d Primroses

SPECIAL HANDSTAMPS		
(1) RSH Health Congress, Eastbourne	175	175
ORDINARY F.D.I. POSTMARKS		
(2) GPO Philatelic Bureau, Edinburgh 1	5	5
(3) Kingston-upon-Thames, Surrey (local F.D.I. for Kew)	10	10
(4) Any other office	3	3
C.D.S. POSTMARKS		
(5) Bluebell Hill, Nottingham	175	175
(6) Flore, Northamptonshire	150	n.k.
(7) Hawthorn, Wilts.	175	n.k.
(8) Kew Gardens, Richmond, Surrey	150	125
(9) Primrose St., Alloa	175	n.k.
(10) Any other postmark	3	3

**With effect from the 1967 Paintings issue all stamps were phosphor coated.
It was also around this time that more 'official' covers were being produced (see
General Notes). C.D.S. postmarks are now only catalogued if relevant to an issue.**

10th July 1967 — BRITISH PAINTINGS
4d 'Master Lambton' (Lawrence); 9d 'Mares and Foals in a Landscape' (Stubbs);
1'6d. 'Children Coming Out of School' (Lowry)

	ordinary covers £	official covers £	
SPECIAL HANDSTAMPS			
(1) Art on Stamps Exhibition, Strand Stamp Centre, London WC2	15	40	*P.R. O'Connell*
ORDINARY F.D.I. POSTMARKS			
(2) GPO Philatelic Bureau, Edinburgh 1	5		
(3) Bishop Auckland ("Master Lambton" painting is at Wilton Castle)	25		
(4) Any other office	3		

24th July 1967 — WORLD VOYAGE OF SIR FRANCIS CHICHESTER
1s 9d Gipsy Moth IV

		ordinary covers £	official covers £	
SPECIAL HANDSTAMPS				
(1)	Sir Francis Chichester, GPO Philatelic Bureau, Edinburgh	2	—	*Post Office*
(2)	Sir Francis Chichester, Greenwich, London SE10	3	—	*Post Office*
(3)	Sir Francis Chichester, Plymouth, Devon	3	—	*Post Office*
(4)	International Camp, E. Mersea, Colchester	100	—	*n.o.c.*
ORDINARY F.D.I. POSTMARKS				
(5)	Barnstaple (Birthplace of Sir Francis Chichester)	8		
(6)	Chichester, Sussex	4		
(7)	Gosport, Hants.	8		
(8)	Any other office	1		
C.D.S. POSTMARKS				
(9)	House of Commons, SW1 (on Outward Bound Trust cover)	10		

19th September 1967 — BRITISH DISCOVERY
4d Radar; 1s Penicillin; 1s 6d Jet Engine; 1s 9d Television

SPECIAL HANDSTAMPS				
(1)	Penicillin Discovered 1928 Sir Alexander Fleming St. Mary's, W2	12	—	*n.o.c.*
(2)	Grant Exhibition of F.D.C.s aboard HMS Discovery, London WC	12	—	*n.o.c.*
(3)	BF 1000 PS (used at RAF Bruggen Stamp Exhibition)	70	50	*Forces*
ORDINARY F.D.I. POSTMARKS				
(4)	GPO Philatelic Bureau, Edinburgh 1	3		
(5)	Coventry (birthplace of Frank Whittle)	9		
(6)	Hounslow, Middlesex (associated with jet aircraft)	10		
(7)	London SW — on British Drug Houses cover	3(s)		
(8)	Paddington W2 (discovery of penicillin)	10		
(9)	Plymouth, Devon — with Westward TV logo	15		
(10)	Any other office	2		
C.D.S. POSTMARKS				
(11)	Benenden Chest Hospital, Cranbrook, Kent	275		
(12)	Brechin (birthplace of Sir Robert Watson-Watt)	5(s)		
(13)	Darvel (birthplace of Sir Alexander Fleming)	5(s)		
(14)	Helensburgh (birthplace of John Logie Baird)	150		
SLOGAN POSTMARKS				
(15)	First Day of Issue — Paddington W2	100		

SET of four single stamp covers with appropriate postmarks
— usually (5), (11), (12) and (13)....... 40

18th October 1967 — CHRISTMAS
4d 'Madonna and Child'

ORDINARY F.D.I. POSTMARKS			
(1)	Bethlehem, Llandeilo, Carms	2	
(2)	GPO Philatelic Bureau, Edinburgh 1	2	
(3)	Any other office	1	
SLOGAN POSTMARKS			
(4)	First Day of Issue — Bethlehem, Llandeilo, Carms	10	
(5)	Visit Roman Bath	100	

27th November 1967 — CHRISTMAS
3d, 1s 6d 'Adoration of the Shepherds'

SPECIAL HANDSTAMPS			
(1)	Dulwich Millennium AD967-1967 SE21	100	100
ORDINARY F.D.I. POSTMARKS			
(2)	GPO Philatelic Bureau, Edinburgh 1	2	
(3)	Bethlehem, Llandeilo, Carms	2	
(4)	Any other office	1	
SLOGAN POSTMARKS			
(5)	First Day of Issue — Bethlehem, Llandeilo, Carms	75	
(6)	See the Christmas Illuminations December 1st-27th, Cheltenham	325	
(7)	First Ever Christmas Present God Gave His Son, Londonderry	325	
(8)	The National Postal Museum	50	
(9)	Visit Roman Bath (plain cover)	25	

18th Oct. & 27th Nov. 1967 — CHRISTMAS
(DOUBLE DATED COVERS)

(1)	Bethlehem, Llandeilo, Carms — both dates on one cover	25
(2)	GPO Philatelic Bureau, Edinburgh 1 — both dates on one cover	12
(3)	Any other office — both dates on one cover	10

29th April 1968 — BRITISH BRIDGES

4d Tarr Steps, Dulverton; 9d Aberfeldy Bridge;
1s 6d Menai Bridge; 1s 9d M4 Viaduct, Chiswick

	ordinary covers	official covers	
	£	£	
SPECIAL HANDSTAMPS			
(1) First Day of Issue GPO Philatelic Bureau, Edinburgh 1	4	—	*Post Office*
(2) First Day of Issue, Bridge, Canterbury, Kent	4	—	*Post Office*
(2a) RSH Health Congress, Eastbourne	130	—	*Post Office*
ORDINARY F.D.I. POSTMARKS			
(3) Perth (local office for Aberfeldy).....................................	4		
(4) Any other office	2		
C.D.S. POSTMARKS			
(5) Aberfeldy (featured on 9d value)	100		
(6) Chiswick (featured on 1s 9d value)...................................	150		
(7) Dulverton (featured on 4d value).....................................	150		
(8) Menai (featured on 1s 6d value)	100		
SLOGAN POSTMARKS			
(9) First Day of Issue — Bridge, Canterbury, Kent....................	50		
(10) First Day of Issue/Diwrnod Ymddangosiad Cyntaf — Menai Bridge	50		
(11) First Day of Issue — Aberfeldy, Perthshire	50		
(12) Chiswick — wavy line cancellation..................................	100		
SET of four single stamp covers with appropriate postmarks — usually (7), (10), (11) and (12)......................	25		

29th May 1968 — BRITISH ANNIVERSARIES

4d TUC; 9d Votes for Women; 1s RAF; 1s 9d James Cook

SPECIAL HANDSTAMPS				
(1) TUC 100 First Day of Issue, Manchester	60	—	*Post Office*	
(2) First Day of Issue Women's Suffrage, Aldeburgh, Suffolk.....	60	—	*Post Office*	
(3) First Day of Issue Hendon, London NW4	60	—	*Post Office*	
(4) First Day of Issue, Whitby, Yorkshire................................	60	—	*Post Office*	
(5) 50th Anniversary RAF Leuchars, Fife	175	10(s)	*Forces*	
(6) 50th Anniv. RAF Medmenham RAF Post Office, Marlow, Bucks. .	175	—	*n.o.c.*	
(7) RAF 50th Anniv. Fylingdales RAF Post Office, Pickering, Yorks. .	175	10(s)	*Forces*	
(8) RAF 50th Anniv. RAF College Cranwell, Sleaford, Lincs.	175	10(s)	*Forces*	
(9) RAF Escaping Society 1945 1968 BF 1067 PS	175	10(s)	*Forces*	
(10) BF 1000 PS (used at RAF Laarbrucke)	175	—	*n.o.c.*	
(11) Post Office Engineering Union 100000, Ealing W5..............	175	—	*n.o.c.*	
(12) RNIB Centenary Exhibition, London SW1	175	—	*n.o.c.*	
ORDINARY F.D.I. POSTMARKS				
(13) GPO Philatelic Bureau, Edinburgh 1	5			
(14) Any other office	4			
C.D.S. POSTMARKS				
(15) House of Commons SW1	35			
(16) House of Lords SW1	45			
(17) Digby Aerodrome, Lincoln (usually found on RAF Digby cover)....	10(s)			
(18) Marton-in-Cleveland (birthplace of Captain James Cook)......	10(s)			
(19) Any R.A.F. Post Office e.g. Hawkinge, Syerston	100			
(20) Tolpuddle, Dorset (Tolpuddle Martyrs)	15(s)			
SLOGAN POSTMARKS				
(21) Bi-centenary Captain Cook 1768-1968, Whitby....................	25(s)			
SET of four single stamp covers with appropriate postmarks — usually (1), (2), (3) and (4)......................	8			

12th August 1968 — BRITISH PAINTINGS

4d Elizabeth I (artist unknown); 1s Pinkie (Lawrence);
1s 6d Ruins of St. Mary le Port (Piper); 1s 9d Hay Wain (Constable)

SPECIAL HANDSTAMPS				
(1) Philatex 68 Woburn Bletchley, Bucks..............................	10	20	*Woburn*	
(2) Portsmouth & District Philatelic Society, Portsmouth..........	25	30	*Phil. Soc.*	
(3) Parish Church Restoration Kettering, Northants	25	30	*Parish Ch.*	
(4) SAGA, Beeley Matlock	—	20(s)	*Scout & Guides*	
ORDINARY F.D.I. POSTMARKS				
(5) GPO Philatelic Bureau, Edinburgh 1	5			
(6) Bristol (Lawrence born at Bristol)...................................	6			
(7) Ipswich (local F.D.I. for 'Constable Country')	8			
(8) Any other office	4			

1968 Paintings (contd.)

		ordinary covers £	official covers £
C.D.S. POSTMARKS			
(9)	Blackheath SE3 (Queen Elizabeth's portrait probably commissioned by a member of the Admiralty)	150	
(10)	East Bergholt, Colchester, (Constable's birthplace)	350	
(11)	Greenwich, SE10 (Birthplace of Elizabeth I)	175	
(12)	Richmond, N. Yorks ("Pinkie" associated with Richmond)	175	
SLOGAN POSTMARKS			
(13)	First Day of Issue — Hatfield (QEI associated with Hatfield House)	30	
(14)	First Day of Issue — London SE1 (Birthplace of Elizabeth I)	30	
(15)	First Day of Issue — London W1 (London art galleries)	30	
SET of four single stamp covers with appropriate postmarks ....from		8	

25th November 1968 — CHRISTMAS
4d. 9d. 1s 6d Childrens Toys

SPECIAL HANDSTAMPS			
(1)	Selfridges Christmas Toy Fair, London W1	8	—	n.o.c.
(2)	HMS Hermes BF 1074 PS	100	100	Forces
ORDINARY F.D.I. POSTMARKS			
(3)	GPO Philatelic Bureau, Edinburgh 1	3	
(4)	Bethlehem, Llandeilo, Carms	4	
(5)	Any other office	1	
SLOGAN POSTMARKS			
(6)	First Day of Issue — Bethlehem, Llandeilo, Carms	40	
(7)	See the Christmas Illuminations during December in Cheltenham	30(s)	

15th January 1969 — BRITISH SHIPS
5d 'Queen Elizabeth 2'; 9d 'Cutty Sark'; 9d Elizabethan Galleon;
9d East Indiaman; 1s 'SS Great Britain'; 1s RMS 'Mauretania'

SPECIAL HANDSTAMPS			
(1)	Lloyd's of London New Coffee House Opened 1769, London EC3	80	—	n.o.c.
(2)	Cutty Sark Stamp Day, Greenwich SE10	25	—	n.o.c.
ORDINARY F.D.I. POSTMARKS			
(3)	GPO Philatelic Bureau, Edinburgh 1	5	
(4)	Belfast, Glasgow or Newcastle (Shipbuilding traditions)	9	
(5)	Bristol, Liverpool, Plymouth or Portsmouth (Maritime traditions)	8	
(6)	London EC or SE1	7	
(7)	Southampton (Home port of the QE2)	8	
(8)	Any other office	4	
C.D.S. POSTMARKS			
(9)	Clydebank, Dunbartonshire (Cutty Sark built here)	175	
(10)	Maritime Mail, London I.S.	250	
(11)	Southampton (Home port of the QE2) or Plymouth	60	
(12)	Seaview, Isle of Wight	35	
SLOGAN POSTMARKS			
(13)	First Day of Issue — Greenwich SE10	80	
(14)	First Day of Issue — Great Britain W2 (SS Great Britain on 1/- stamp)	50	

3rd March 1969 — FIRST FLIGHT OF CONCORDE
4d, 9d, 1s 6d

ORDINARY F.D.I. POSTMARKS			
(1)	Filton, Bristol	4	
(1a)	ditto — with 'Conseil de L'Europe' postmark	15	
(2)	GPO Philatelic Bureau, Edinburgh 1	4	
(3)	Hounslow, Middx. (Heathrow)	10	
(4)	Any other office	2	
SLOGAN POSTMARKS			
(5)	The National Postal Museum	30	

2nd April 1969 — NOTABLE ANNIVERSARIES

5d Alcock & Brown; 9d Europa; 1s International Labour Organisation;
1s 6d NATO; 1s 9d 1st England/Australia flight

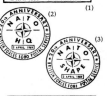

	ordinary covers £	official covers £	
SPECIAL HANDSTAMPS			
(1) 50th Anniv. 1st Atlantic Flight, Alcock & Brown, Manchester	25	12(s)	*Man. Int. Airp.*
(2) 20th Anniversary NATO HQ BF 1080 PS	175	120	*N.A.T.O.*
(3) 20th Anniversary NATO SHAPE BF 1081 PS	175	10(s)	*N.A.T.O.*
(4) Hoverlloyd Inaugural Flight, Pegwell Bay, Ramsgate, Kent ..	225	8(s)	*Hoverlloyd*
(5) BF 1000 PS (used at Mill Hill)	175	150	*Forces*
(6) The Grammar School Centenary, Doncaster, Yorks	150	100	*Grammar Sch.*
ORDINARY F.D.I. POSTMARKS			
(7) Hounslow (Eng./Aust. flight took off from Heathrow)	15		
(8) London SW (Int. Labour Organisation)	10		
(9) Manchester (Alcock & Brown)	10		
(10) GPO Philatelic Bureau, Edinburgh 1	6		
(11) Any other office	3		
C.D.S. POSTMARKS			
(12) Farnborough, Hants.	100		
SLOGAN POSTMARKS			
(13) Manchester Airport Salutes Alcock & Brown 1919-1969	40(s)		
SET of five single stamp covers with appropriate postmarks	from 8		

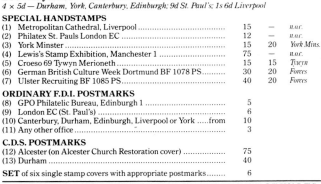

28th May 1969 — BRITISH CATHEDRALS

4 × 5d — Durham, York, Canterbury, Edinburgh; 9d St. Paul's; 1s 6d Liverpool

SPECIAL HANDSTAMPS			
(1) Metropolitan Cathedral, Liverpool	15	—	*n.o.c.*
(2) Philatex St. Pauls London EC	12	—	*n.o.c.*
(3) York Minster	15	20	*York Mins.*
(4) Lewis's Stamp Exhibition, Manchester 1	75	—	*n.o.c.*
(5) Croeso 69 Tywyn Merioneth	15	15	*Tywyn*
(6) German British Culture Week Dortmund BF 1078 PS	30	20	*Forces*
(7) Ulster Recruiting BF 1085 PS	40	20	*Forces*
ORDINARY F.D.I. POSTMARKS			
(8) GPO Philatelic Bureau, Edinburgh 1	5		
(9) London EC (St. Paul's)	6		
(10) Canterbury, Durham, Edinburgh, Liverpool or York	from 10		
(11) Any other office	3		
C.D.S. POSTMARKS			
(12) Alcester (on Alcester Church Restoration cover)	75		
(13) Durham	40		
SET of six single stamp covers with appropriate postmarks	6		

1st July 1969 — THE INVESTITURE OF THE PRINCE OF WALES

3 × 5d Caernarvon Castle; 9d Celtic Cross; 1s Prince Charles

SPECIAL HANDSTAMPS			
(1) Diwrnod yr Arwisgiad Croes Geltaidd, Margam Abbey, Port Talbot	80	—	*n.o.c.*
(2) Croeso 69 Diwrnod yr Arwisgiad, Investiture Day, Cardiff	80	—	*n.o.c.*
(3) Greetings from Talyllyn Railway (in Welsh) Tywyn, Merioneth	35	40	*Tywyn*
(4) Nettleham, Lincoln	80	80	*Nettleham*
(5) BF 1000 PS (used at camp of troops involved in Investiture) ..	100	75	*Forces*
ORDINARY F.D.I. POSTMARKS			
(6) GPO Philatelic Bureau, Edinburgh 1	5		
(7) London SW	3		
(8) Windsor, Berks.	3		
(9) Dydd yr Arwisgo Day of Investiture, Caernarvon	3		
(10) Any other Welsh postmark	2		
(11) Any other office	1		
C.D.S. POSTMARKS			
(12) Buckingham Palace, SW1	200		
(13) House of Commons, SW1	60		
(14) House of Lords, SW1	70		
(15) Windsor Castle, Berks.	200		
SLOGAN POSTMARKS			
(16) Dydd yr Arwisgo, Investiture Day, Caernarvon	225		
(17) Wales Tomorrow Exhibition, Cardiff	50(s)		
(18) The National Postal Museum	50		

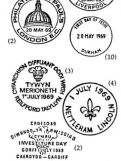

13th August 1969 — GANDHI CENTENARY YEAR 1969
1s 6d Mahatma Gandhi

	ordinary covers £	official covers £	
SPECIAL HANDSTAMPS			
(1) Gandhi Centenary Year HCRC Exhibition, London E8	5	20	*Hackney CRC*
(2) Trade Fair & Exhibition Llanelli, Carms	100	—	*n.o.c.*
(3) 21st International Youth Camp Colchester	100	—	*n.o.c.*
ORDINARY F.D.I. POSTMARKS			
(4) GPO Philatelic Bureau, Edinburgh 1	2		
(5) Any other office	1		

1st October 1969 — POST OFFICE TECHNOLOGY
5d Giro; 9d & 1s Telecommunications; 1s 6d Automatic Sorting

SPECIAL HANDSTAMPS			
(1) Posted in the Post Office Tower, London W1	5	—	*n.o.c.*
(2) Post Office Technology Exh. University College, WC1	5	—	*n.o.c.*
(3) Philatelic Stand Ideal Homes Exhibition, Birmingham	150	—	*n.o.c.*
(4) 1st Southampton Boat Show, Mayflower Park, Southampton	150	20(s)	*Boat Show*
(5) National Postal Museum, London EC1	60	—	*Post Office*
ORDINARY F.D.I. POSTMARKS			
(6) GPO Philatelic Bureau, Edinburgh 1	2		
(7) Norwich (first use of postal coding)..................................	4		
(8) Any other office	1		
C.D.S. POSTMARKS			
(9) Bootle (National Giro HQ — featured on 5d value)................	15(s)		
SLOGAN POSTMARKS			
(10) Remember to use the Postcode..	400		
SET of four single stamp covers with appropriate postmarks			
— usually (1), (2), (7) and (9)...	20		

26th November 1969 — CHRISTMAS
4d, 5d, 1s 6d The Nativity

SPECIAL HANDSTAMPS			
(1) Jerusalem, Skellingthorpe, Lincs.	40	40	*Temple of Jerusalem*
ORDINARY F.D.I. POSTMARKS			
(2) GPO Philatelic Bureau, Edinburgh 1	2		
(3) Bethlehem, Llandeilo, Carms...	2		
(4) Any other office	1		
C.D.S. POSTMARKS			
(5) Bethlehem, Llandeilo, Carms...	150		
(6) Nasareth, Gwynedd	150		
SLOGAN POSTMARKS			
(7) First Day of Issue – Bethlehem, Llandeilo, Carms...............	60		
(8) See the Christmas Illuminations during December in Cheltenham	40(s)		
(9) National Childrens Home	50		

11th February 1970 — BRITISH RURAL ARCHITECTURE
5d Fife harling; 9d Cotswold limestone; 1s Welsh stucco; 1s 6d Ulster thatch

ORDINARY F.D.I. POSTMARKS		
(1) British Philatelic Bureau, Edinburgh 1	2	
(2) Aberaeron, Diwrnod Ymddangosiad Cyntaf (1/- Welsh stucco).......	5	
(3) Belfast (1s 6d Ulster thatch) or Dunfermline (5d Fife harling)	5	
(4) Edinburgh (5d Fife harling) or Gloucester (9d Cotswold limestone)	5	
(5) Any other office	1	
C.D.S. POSTMARKS		
(6) Auchtermuchty, Fife (5d Fife harling)	10(s)	
(7) Bibury, Cirencester, Glos. (9d Cotswold limestone)..............	90	
(8) Chipping Campden (9p Almshouses)	90	
(9) Cirencester, Glos.; or Stroud, Glos. (9d Cotswold limestone)..	60	
(10) Culross, Dunfermline, Fife (5d Fife harling)........................	70	
(11) Holywood, Co. Down (1s 6d Ulster thatch)..........................	20(s)	
SLOGAN POSTMARKS		
(12) Keep Britain Green — European Conservation Year.............	100	
(13) Visit the 1970 Furniture Show — on plain cover	20	
SET of four single stamp covers with appropriate postmarks	6	

1st April 1970 — GENERAL ANNIVERSARIES
5d Declaration of Arbroath; 9d Florence Nightingale;
1s International Co-operative Alliance; 1s 6d Mayflower;
1s 9d Royal Astronomical Society

		ordinary covers £	official covers £	
SPECIAL HANDSTAMPS				
(1)	British Anniversary Stamps, Canterbury, Kent	17	—	*n.o.c.*
(2)	Florence Nightingale Hospital, London NW1	50	—	*n.o.c.*
(3)	Nat. Florence Nightingale Mem. Ctte. B'day Exh. 1820-1910, SE1	30	40	*F.N. Cttee*
(4)	The Crimean War BF 1206 PS	275	12(s)	*Forces*
(5)	150th Anniv. Florence Nightingale BF 1121 PS	175	12(s)	*Forces*
(6)	150th Anniv. Florence Nightingale BF 1205 PS	200	12(s)	*Forces*
(7)	London Co-op Golden Year 1920-1970 London E15	225	12(s)	*Co-op*
(8)	World HQ International Co-operative Alliance ICA London W1	175	—	*n.o.c.*
(9)	Mayflower '70 Scrooby Doncaster, Yorks.	175	12(s)	*Scrooby*
(10)	Sir William Herschel 1st Pres. Royal Astronomical Soc., Slough.	65	—	*n.o.c.*
(11)	Air-sea Warfare Dev. Unit Disbandment RAF Ballykelly	225	—	*n.o.c.*
(12)	Air Mountains Expedition Base Post Gibraltar BF 1112 PS.	225	12(s)	*Forces*
ORDINARY F.D.I. POSTMARKS				
(13)	British Philatelic Bureau, Edinburgh 1	2		
(14)	Arbroath, Angus (5d value Declaration of Arbroath)	25		
(15)	Billericay, Essex (associated with 'Mayflower')	12		
(16)	Boston, Lincs. (associated with 'Mayflower')	10		
(17)	London W1 (World HQ of ICA)	8		
(18)	Plymouth (1s 6d Pilgrim Fathers)	8		
(19)	Rochdale, Lancs. (first Co-op founded here)	10		
(20)	Southampton (The Pilgrim Fathers set sail from here)	8		
(21)	Any other office	3		
C.D.S. POSTMARKS				
(22)	Immingham or Scrooby (associated with Pilgrim Fathers)	20(s)		
SLOGAN POSTMARKS				
(23)	Plymouth Mayflower 70, 2 May-30 September — Plymouth	35(s)		
(24)	Boston Lincs. Mayflower 70, May-September — Boston, Lincs.	35(s)		

SET of single stamp covers with appropriate postmarks......from 8

3rd June 1970 — LITERARY ANNIVERSARIES
4 × 5d Dickens characters; 1s 6d Wordsworth

SPECIAL HANDSTAMPS					
(1)	E78 Chigwell, Essex	40	40	*Chigwell*	
(2)	Dickens Fellowship Broadstairs Branch, Broadstairs, Kent	30	40	*Broadstairs*	
(3)	Dickens Centenary Year Old Curiosity Shop, London WC2	15	30	*Cameo (g)*	
(4)	Dickens Centenary Pickwick, Corsham, Wilts.	45	60	*Corsham*	
(5)	David Copperfield Dickens Winterbourne, Bonchurch, Ventnor	40	50	*Winterbourne*	
(6)	Living Exhibition '70 May 27-June 6, Sheffield	n.k.	10(s)	*Exhib.*	
ORDINARY F.D.I. POSTMARKS					
(7)	British Philatelic Bureau, Edinburgh 1	3			
(8)	Broadstairs (Dickens lived here at 'Bleak House')	6			
(9)	Cambridge (Wordsworth educated at St. John's College, Cambs.)	9			
(10)	Cockermouth (birthplace of Wordsworth in 1770)	25			
(11)	Portsmouth (Dickens born at Landport, Portsmouth in 1812)	7			
(12)	Rochester (Dickens died at Gadshill, Rochester in 1870)	7			
(13)	Any other office	3			
C.D.S. POSTMARKS					
(14)	Ambleside (Wordsworth lived at Rydal Mount, Ambleside)	150			
(15)	Grasmere (Wordsworth lived at Dove Cottage, Grasmere)	150			
(16)	Portsmouth (Dickens born here in 1812)	80			
SLOGAN POSTMARKS					
(17)	First Day of Issue — Broadstairs, Kent	90			
(18)	International Stamp Exhibition (4×5d only)	25			

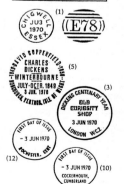

PAIR of covers (4 × 5d on one, 1s 6d on the other) with
appropriate postmarks............from 3

PLEASE READ THE GENERAL NOTES
AT THE BEGINNING OF THIS CATALOGUE
These often provide the answers to enquiries received.

15th July 1970 — IXth BRITISH COMMONWEALTH GAMES EDINBURGH

5d Runners; 1s 6d Swimmers; 1s 9d Cyclists

	ordinary covers £	official covers £	
SPECIAL HANDSTAMPS			
(1) Centenary RCT 1870-1970 BF 1123 PS	150	5(s)	*Forces*
(2) Enterprise Exhibition Philatelic Stand, Nottingham	150	20(s)	*Nott. Fest.*
(3) Thos. Becket 1170-1970, Canterbury, Kent	150	8(s)	*Cant. Cath.*
(4) Cardigan Secondary School Summer Fair, Cardigan	150	100	*Card. Sch.*
(5) IXth Assembly of European Municipalities, London SE1	150	—	*n.o.c.*
(6) Great Yorkshire Show, Harrogate	150	10(s)	*G.Y. Show*
(7) Victoria Cross BF 1210 PS	150	5(s)	*Forces*
(8) Rorke's Drift BF 1211 PS	150	5(s)	*Forces*
ORDINARY F.D.I. POSTMARKS			
(9) British Philatelic Bureau, Edinburgh 1	2		
(10) Edinburgh 1	4		
(11) Any other office	1		
C.D.S. POSTMARKS			
(12) Edinburgh Mobile Post Office	110		
SLOGAN POSTMARKS			
(13) The National Postal Museum	30		
(14) First Day of Issue – Edinburgh, Great Britain	55		
(15) Edinburgh – wavy line	25		

18th September 1970 — INTERNATIONAL STAMP EXHIBITION 'PHILYMPIA'

5d (1d Black); 9d (1s Green); 1s 6d (4d Carmine)

SPECIAL HANDSTAMPS			
(1) British Post Office Philatelic Bureau, Edinburgh	2	—	*Post Office*
(2) Philympia Day, London	4	—	*Post Office*
(3) First Flight, Philympia First Day, Calne-IOW, Calne, Wilts.	150	15(s)	*B.N.I.**
(4) First Flight, Philympia First Day, IOW-Calne, Bembridge, IOW	150	15(s)	*B.N.I.**
(5) 25th Anniv. 23 Base Workshop REME BF 1136 PS	50	40	*Forces*
*B.N.I. = Britten Norman Islander.			
ORDINARY F.D.I. POSTMARKS			
(6) London W1 (local F.D.I. for Philympia)	3		
(7) Any other office	1		
C.D.S. POSTMARKS			
(8) Olympia W14	200		
SLOGAN POSTMARKS			
(9) International Stamp Exhibition 18-26 Sept Philympia 70	500		

25th November 1970 — CHRISTMAS

4d, 5d, 1s 6d The Nativity

SPECIAL HANDSTAMPS			
(1) British Post Office Philatelic Bureau, Edinburgh 1	1	—	*Post Office*
(2) First Day of Issue — Bethlehem, Llandeilo, Carms	2	—	*Post Office*
(3) Lilleshall Parish Church AD670-1970, Lilleshall, Salop	90	110	*Lill. PCh.*
ORDINARY F.D.I. POSTMARKS			
(4) Any office	1		
SLOGAN POSTMARKS			
(5) First Day of Issue — Bethlehem, Llandeilo, Carms	100		
(6) See the Christmas Illuminations during Dec. Cheltenham	40(s)		

With effect from the decimal issues the Ordinary F.D.I. postmarks have only been listed where they are relevant to the stamp issue.

16th June 1971 — ULSTER '71 PAINTINGS

3p, 7½p, 9p Landscapes

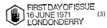

SPECIAL HANDSTAMPS			
(1) First Day of Issue — Philatelic Bureau	2	—	*Post Office*
(2) First Day of Issue — Belfast	4	—	*Post Office*
(3) First Day of Issue — Londonderry	30	—	*Post Office*
(4) First Day of Issue — Coleraine	90	—	*Post Office*
(5) First Day of Issue — Newry	90	—	*Post Office*

Ulster Paintings (contd.)

		ordinary covers £	official covers £	
(6)	First Day of Issue — Ballymena	90	—	*Post Office*
(7)	First Day of Issue — Armagh	90	—	*Post Office*
(8)	First Day of Issue — Portadown	90	—	*Post Office*
(9)	First Day of Issue — Cookstown	90	—	*Post Office*
(10)	First Day of Issue — Omagh	90	—	*Post Office*
(11)	First Day of Issue — Enniskillen	90	—	*Post Office*
(12)	Ulster 71 Exhibition Botanic Gardens Belfast	50	—	*n.o.c.*
(13)	53rd Philatelic Cong. of G.B. Ulster Paintings Day Norwich	40	50	*Phil Congress*

C.D.S. POSTMARKS

(14)	Dungiven, Londonderry (3p)	these C.D.S. are from Post		
(15)	Hilltown, Down (7½p)	Offices situated close to the		
(16)	Newcastle, Down (9p)	scenes depicted on each stamp	75	(set of three)
(17)	Northern Parliament, Belfast		50	

ULSTER '71
EXHIBITION

16 JUN 1971

BOTANIC GARDENS
BELFAST (12)

28th July 1971 — LITERARY ANNIVERSARIES
3p Keats; 5p Gray; 7½p Scott

SPECIAL HANDSTAMPS

(1)	First Day of Issue — Philatelic Bureau	4	—	*Post Office*
(2)	First Day of Issue — London EC	6	—	*Post Office*
(3)	John Keats Shanklin 1819 Shanklin Isle of Wight	80	100	*Shank Library*
(4)	1771-1971 Thomas Gray Bicentenary Stoke Poges Bucks	30	100	*Stoke Court*
(4a)	Ditto with "Carried by Mailcoach" cachet	40	100	*Stoke Court*
(5)	First National Collectors Fair Royal Horticultural Hall SW	130	—	*n.o.c.*
(6)	Ulster 71 Exhibition Botanic Gardens Belfast	125	—	*n.o.c.*

ORDINARY F.D.I. POSTMARKS

(7)	Edinburgh — birthplace of Sir Walter Scott	6	

C.D.S. POSTMARKS

(8)	Melrose (7½p) — Sir Walter Scott died at Abbotsford, Melrose	5(s)	

SET of three single stamp covers with appropriate postmarks 6

JOHN KEATS
SHANKLIN 1819 (3)

28th JULY 1971
SHANKLIN, ISLE OF WIGHT

25th August 1971 — GENERAL ANNIVERSARIES
3p British Legion; 7½p City of York; 9p Rugby Football Union

SPECIAL HANDSTAMPS

(1)	First Day of Issue — Philatelic Bureau	3	—	*Post Office*
(2)	First Day of Issue — Twickenham	15	—	*Post Office*
(3)	First Day of Issue — Maidstone	15	—	*Post Office*
(4)	First Day of Issue — York	15	—	*Post Office*
(5)	Rugby Football Union Centenary Twickenham	150	150	*R.F.U.*
(6)	Rugby Football Union Centenary Year Rugby Warwickshire	175	175	*Rugby School*
(7)	The Royal British Legion 50th Anniv 1921-1971 BF 1182 PS	175	10(s)	*Brit. Leg. 5*
(8)	70th Anniversary Royal Aero Club BF 1170 PS	175	10(s)	*RAF Museum*
(9)	Ulster 71 Exhibition Botanic Gardens Belfast	150	—	*n.o.c.*
(10)	Sir Walter Scott Bicentenary Abbotsford	150	—	*n.o.c.*

C.D.S. POSTMARKS

(11)	Any Field Post Office	10	

SET of three single stamp covers with appropriate postmarks
— usually (2), (3) and (4) 6

22nd September 1971 — BRITISH ARCHITECTURE
MODERN UNIVERSITY BUILDINGS
3p Aberystwyth; 5p Southampton; 7½p Leicester; 9p Essex

SPECIAL HANDSTAMPS

(1)	First Day of Issue — Philatelic Bureau	3	—	*Post Office*
(2)	First Day of Issue — Aberystwyth	13	—	*Post Office*
(3)	First Day of Issue — Colchester	13	—	*Post Office*
(4)	First Day of Issue — Leicester	13	—	*Post Office*
(5)	First Day of Issue — Southampton	13	—	*Post Office*
(6)	Opening of the Postal Management College Rugby	150	150	*P. Man. Coll.*
(7)	Sir Walter Scott Bicentenary Abbotsford	150	—	*n.o.c.*

SET of four single stamp covers with appropriate postmarks
— usually (2), (3), (4) and (5) 6

*Note: Welsh bilingual F.D.I. cancellations for the first time were used at the following offices:-
Cardiff, Caernarvon, Carmarthen, Colwyn Bay, Haverfordwest, Llandudno, Llanelli,
Newport, Monmouthshire, Pontypridd, Rhondda, Rhyl, Swansea. These will only be
included and priced in the catalogue if relevant to an issue.*

SOUTHAMPTON (5)

LEICESTER (4)

FIRST DAY OF ISSUE
22 SEP 1971

FIRST DAY OF ISSUE
22 SEP 1971

DIWRNOD
YMDDANGOSIAD
CYNTAF

COLCHESTER

FIRST DAY OF ISSUE
ABERYSTWYTH
22 SEPT 1971 (2)

FIRST DAY OF ISSUE
22 SEP '71 (3)

13th October 1971 — CHRISTMAS
2½p, 3p, 7½p Stained Glass at Canterbury Cathedral

		ordinary covers	official covers	
SPECIAL HANDSTAMPS		£	£	
(1)	First Day of Issue — Philatelic Bureau	4	—	*Post Office*
(2)	First Day of Issue — Bethlehem, Llandeilo, Carms	6	—	*Post Office*
(3)	First Day of Issue — Canterbury	6	—	*Post Office*
(4)	Commonwealth Postal Conf. Marlborough House London SW1	125	—	*n.o.c.*
(5)	1900th Anniv. Cremation of Emperor Serverus York	125	150	*Emp. Serv.*

16th February 1972 — BRITISH POLAR EXPLORERS
3p Ross; 5p Frobisher; 7½p Hudson; 9p Scott

SPECIAL HANDSTAMPS				
(1)	First Day of Issue — Philatelic Bureau	7	—	*Post Office*
(2)	First Day of Issue — London WC	8	—	*Post Office*
ORDINARY F.D.I. POSTMARKS				
(3)	Plymouth	10		
C.D.S. POSTMARKS				
(4)	Reykjavik, Iceland BFPS (Backstamped) FPO 376	400		
(5)	Gravesend, Kent (7½p)	10(s)		
(6)	Greenwich B.O., S.E.10	10(s)		

SET of four single stamp covers with appropriate postmarks
— usually (2), (3), (5) and (6) 9

26th April 1972 — GENERAL ANNIVERSARIES
3p Tutankhamun; 7½p HM Coastguard; 9p Ralph Vaughan Williams

SPECIAL HANDSTAMPS				
(1)	First Day of Issue — Philatelic Bureau	3	—	*Post Office*
(2)	First Day of Issue — London EC	4	—	*Post Office*
(3)	Treasures of Tutankhamun Exhibition London WC	20	30	*Tut. Exhib.*
(4)	Vaughan Williams Centenary Down Ampney Gloucestershire	20	10(s)	*D. Ampney*
(5)	Treasures of Tutankhamun 1822-1972 Hartland Point Bideford Devon	20	40	*Philart*
(6)	5th Anniversary 200 Hovercraft Trials BF 1270 PS	100	100	*Hovercraft*
SLOGAN POSTMARKS				
(7)	Treasures of Tutankhamun British Museum — London WC (3p)	25(s)		

SET of three single stamp covers with appropriate postmarks
— usually (3), (4) and (5) 6

21st June 1972 — BRITISH ARCHITECTURE — VILLAGE CHURCHES
3p Greensted; 4p Earls Barton; 5p Letheringsett; 7½p Helpringham; 9p Huish Episcopi

SPECIAL HANDSTAMPS				
(1)	First Day of Issue — Philatelic Bureau	5	—	*Post Office*
(2)	First Day of Issue — Canterbury	6	—	*Post Office*
(3)	World's Oldest Wooden Church, Greensted Ongar Essex	20	50	*St. Andrew's*
(4)	Village Churches AD 970 Earls Barton Northampton	17	40	*Earls Barton*
(5)	First Day of Issue Exhibition Huish Episcopi Langport	20	40	*St. Mary's*
(6)	Village Churches Helpringham Sleaford Lincs	20	40	*Helpringham*
(7)	Village Churches Letheringsett Holt Norfolk	25	—	*n.o.c.*
(8)	Parish Church of St. Mary, Langley Slough	150	150	*Philart*
(9)	St. Augustine's Church Centenary Celebrations, Kilburn NW6	150	150	*St. Augustine's*
(10)	Festival of Berkswell Coventry	150	150	*Berkswell*
(11)	Treasures of Tutankhamun Exhibition London WC	100	—	*n.o.c.*
(12)	Royal Engineers Pioneers Military Aeronautics BF 1312 PS	125	125	*Royal Eng. 3*
C.D.S. POSTMARKS				
(13)	Earls Barton, Northampton	100		
(14)	New Romney, Kent on St. Nicholas New Romney Cover	60		

SET of five single stamp covers with appropriate postmarks
— usually (3), (4), (5), (6) and (7) 12

> PLEASE READ THE GENERAL NOTES
> AT THE BEGINNING OF THIS CATALOGUE
> These often provide the answers to enquiries received.

13th September 1972 — B.B.C. & BROADCASTING HISTORY
3p, 5p, 7½p BBC; 9p Marconi/Kemp Experiments

	ordinary covers	official covers	
	£	**£**	
SPECIAL HANDSTAMPS			
(1) First Day of Issue — Philatelic Bureau	4	—	*Post Office*
(2) First Day of Issue — London W1	8	—	*Post Office*
(3) Marconi-Kemp Wireless Experiments 1897 Chelmsford Essex	25	35	*Mar Phil Soc*
(4) Royal Engineers 75th Anniv Army Wireless BF 1326 PS	50	60	*Royal Eng. 4*
(5) 75th Anniv Marconi's First Wireless Flatholm Island, Cardiff	20	60	*Barry College*
(6) BBC Radio Leicester 5th Anniversary Year Leicester	50	75	*Radio Leics*
(7) 21st Anniv 1st Relay T.V. Network Opened Gloucester	45	60	*British Relay*
(8) Humberside's Own Home Service Philatelic Display Hull	45	60	*Radio Hull*
(9) BBC 50th Anniversary Pebble Mill Birmingham	400	*	*Pebble Mill*
(10) John Knox Quatercentenary — Philatelic Bureau	150	—	*n.o.c.*
(11) Manchester City FC Re-enter Europe Kick-Off in UEFA Cup	150	200	*Dawn*
(12) Treasures of Tutankhamun Exhibition London WC	150	—	*n.o.c.*

*Pebble Mill official covers: Two types exist — covers with BBC logo only @ £150; illustrated covers @ £350.

SLOGAN POSTMARKS

(13) Medium Wave BBC Radio Brighton 202 Metres — Brighton	350	

PAIR of covers (3p, 5p, 7½p on one, 9p on the other) with
appropriate postmarks........from 5

18th October 1972 — CHRISTMAS
2½p, 3p, 7½p Angels

SPECIAL HANDSTAMPS

(1) First Day of Issue — Philatelic Bureau	3	—	*Post Office*
(2) First Day of Issue — Bethlehem, Llandeilo, Carms	4	—	*Post Office*
(3) Treasures of Tutankhamun Exhibition London WC	100	—	*n.o.c.*
(4) Rowntree's Philatelic Exhibition Scarborough Yorkshire	150	—	*n.o.c.*
(5) John Knox Quatercentenary British Philatelic Bureau	125	—	*n.o.c.*
(6) Borough Jubilee 1922-1972 Watford Herts	150	150	*Watford B.C.*

20th November 1972 — SILVER WEDDING ANNIVERSARY
3p, 20p

SPECIAL HANDSTAMPS

(1) First Day of Issue — Philatelic Bureau	2	—	*Post Office*
(2) First Day of Issue — Windsor	5	—	*Post Office*
(3) Royal Silver Wedding Westminster Abbey London SW1	7	9	*Philart ACC 6*
(4) Commemorating the Royal Silver Wedding BF 1307 PS	20	20	*RAF M/Batten*
(5) 16th/5th The Queens Royal Lancers 50 years BF 1922 PS	25	30	*R. Lancers*
(6) The Royal Regiment of Artillery BF 1340 PS	25	6(s)	*R.R.A.*
(7) Corps of Royal Engineers Military Tanks BF 1338 PS	25	40	*Royal Eng. 7*
(8) Charlton Athletic FC Silver Jubilee FA Cup Winners	100	110	*Phil. Prom.*
(9) Fiftieth Anniv of the BBC 1922-1972 London W1	100	—	*n.o.c.*
(10) Treasures of Tutankhamun Exhibition London WC	100	—	*n.o.c.*
(11) John Knox Quatercentenary British Philatelic Bureau	100	—	*n.o.c.*

C.D.S. POSTMARKS

(12) Buckingham Palace, S.W.1	125	
(13) House of Commons, S.W.1	20	
(14) House of Lords, S.W.1	25	
(15) Windsor Castle, Windsor, Berks	125	

3rd January 1973 — EUROPEAN COMMUNITIES
3p, 2 × 5p Maps of Europe (jig-saw design)

SPECIAL HANDSTAMPS

(1) First Day of Issue — Philatelic Bureau	4	—	*Post Office*
(2) Commissioning of New Parcel Office Southampton	35	45	*I.D.C.*
(3) Corps of Royal Engineers Brennan Torpedo BF 1343 PS	30	35	*Royal Eng. 8*

ORDINARY F.D.I. POSTMARKS

(4) Dover, Kent	6	
(4a) Dover, Kent with PAQUEBOT markings	35	
(5) Folkestone, Kent	6	
(5a) Folkestone, Kent with PAQUEBOT markings	25	
(6) Harrow & Wembley (Services 'Fanfare for Europe' cover)	25	

```
PRICES & CONDITION — PLEASE READ GENERAL NOTES
```

48

1973 European Communities (contd.)

		ordinary covers £	official covers £
C.D.S. POSTMARKS			
(7)	Calais with PAQUEBOT markings	30	
(8)	Conseil de l'Europe Strasbourg (stamps cancelled Phil Bureau)	8	
(9)	Harwich, Essex on Harwich Gateway to Europe covers	20	
(10)	House of Commons, S.W.1	45	
(11)	House of Lords, S.W.1	55	
(12)	Harrow & Wembley (with Britain v. EEC Football cachet)	20	

28th February 1973 — BRITISH TREES — THE OAK
9p

SPECIAL HANDSTAMPS				
(1)	First Day of Issue — Philatelic Bureau	3	—	*Post Office*
(2)	Stampex 73 Royal Horticultural Hall London SW1	7	10	*Stampex*
(3)	Hatfield Broad Oak Plant a Tree Exhib. Bishops Stortford	7	—	*n.o.c.*
(4)	Tree Planting Year Westonbirt Arboretum Tetbury Glos	7	10	*Cotswold (g)*

18th April 1973 — BRITISH EXPLORERS
2 × 3p Livingstone & Stanley; 5p Drake; 7½p Raleigh; 9p Sturt

SPECIAL HANDSTAMPS				
(1)	First Day of Issue — Philatelic Bureau	5	—	*Post Office*
(2)	Sir Walter Raleigh Exhib. Budleigh Salterton Devon	15	—	*n.o.c.*
(3)	Drake's Island Adventure Centre Plymouth Devon	15	50	*Cotswold*

ORDINARY F.D.I. POSTMARKS			
(4)	Plymouth, Devon	8	
(5)	Blantyre, Glasgow — birthplace of Livingstone	20	
(6)	Denbigh — birthplace of Stanley	18	
(7)	Gloucestershire – Sturt buried here	5(s)	

C.D.S. POSTMARKS			
(8)	Mildenhall, Marlborough, Wilts on Scientific Expl. Soc. cover	110	
(9)	Livingstone, W. Lothian	90	

SET of 4 or 5 single stamp covers with appropriate postmarks   8

16th May 1973 — CENTENARY OF COUNTY CRICKET
3p, 7½p, 9p W.G. Grace

SPECIAL HANDSTAMPS				
(1)	First Day of Issue — Philatelic Bureau	2	—	*Post Office*
(2)	First Day of Issue — Lord's London NW	6	—	*Post Office*
(3)	100 years of English County Cricket Exhib Lord's London NW8	8	10	*TCCB**
(4)	County Cricket Centenary Chelmsford Essex	25	30	*TCCB**
(5)	Headquarters Surrey C.C.C. The Oval Kennington SE11	25	30	*TCCB**
(6)	Headquarters Sussex C.C.C. Hove Sussex	25	30	*TCCB**
(7)	The Birthplace of English County Cricket Hambledon Hants	45	60	*Porton Serv*
(8)	Downend Cricket Club Exhibition W.G. Grace Downend Bristol	15	18	*Cotswold (g)*
(9)	Yorkshire v. Hampshire, Headingley Leeds	25	30	*TCCB**
(10)	IBRA Exhibition Munich Great Britain Day BF 1400 PS	45	90	*BFPS*

ORDINARY F.D.I. POSTMARKS			
(11)	Derby — Derbyshire C.C.C.	7	
(12)	Cardiff — Glamorgan C.C.C.	7	
(13)	Bristol — Gloucestershire C.C.C.	7	
(14)	Southampton — Hampshire C.C.C.	7	
(15)	Canterbury — Kent C.C.C.	7	
(16)	Manchester — Lancashire C.C.C.	7	
(17)	Leicester — Leicestershire C.C.C.	7	
(18)	Northampton — Northamptonshire C.C.C.	7	
(19)	Nottingham — Nottinghamshire C.C.C.	7	
(20)	Taunton — Somerset C.C.C.	7	
(21)	Birmingham — Warwickshire C.C.C.	7	
(22)	Worcester — Worcestershire C.C.C.	7	

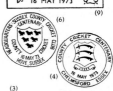

Note: Stamp Publicity of Worthing produced a set of 18 covers for the TCCB (Test & County Cricket Board). The set of covers are valued at around £200.

4th July 1973 — BRITISH PAINTINGS

3p, 7½p Sir Joshua Reynolds; 5p, 9p Sir Henry Raeburn

	ordinary covers £	official covers £	
SPECIAL HANDSTAMPS			
(1) First Day of Issue — Philatelic Bureau	3	—	*Post Office*
(2) 250th Birthday Sir Joshua Reynolds Royal Academy London W1	6	30	*R. Academy*
(3) Douglas Isle of Man	30	25	*Post Office*
(4) Whitehaven Cumberland	30	3(s)	*Post Office*
(5) The Championships 1973 A.E.L.T.C. Wimbledon	110	—	*n.o.c.*
(6) Monarchy 1000 Bath	100	—	*n.o.c.*
(7) 30th Anniv. Death of General Sikorski Exhib. London SW7	100	—	*n.o.c.*
(8) 27th Llangollen International Musical Eisteddfod	100	—	*n.o.c.*
(9) 1923-1973 Aero Philatelic Exhibition APEX 1973 Manchester	70	60	*APEX*
(10) Royal Show Stoneleigh Coventry	100	—	*n.o.c.*

15th August 1973 — INIGO JONES — 400th ANNIVERSARY

3p St. Paul's, Covent Garden; 3p Court Masque Costumes;
5p Prince's Lodging, Newmarket; 5p Court Masque Stage Scene

(1) First Day of Issue — Philatelic Bureau	3	—	*Post Office*
(2) Inigo Jones Exhibition Wilton House Salisbury Wilts	8	25	*Cotswold (g)*
(3) 400th Anniversary of Inigo Jones Newmarket Suffolk	8	40	*Rotary*
(4) 1873-1973 Livestock Market Centenary Northampton	120	—	*n.o.c.*
(5) Monarchy 1000 Bath	120	—	*n.o.c.*
(6) Third International Orthodontic Congress London SE	120	100	*I.O.C.*

ORDINARY F.D.I. POSTMARKS

(7) London W.C.	5		

SLOGAN POSTMARKS

(8) Inigo Jones Banqueting House (on 2 covers)	425		

12th September 1973 — 19th COMMONWEALTH PARLIAMENTARY CONFERENCE

8p 10p Palace of Westminster

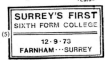

SPECIAL HANDSTAMPS			
(1) First Day of Issue — Philatelic Bureau	3	—	*Post Office*
(2) Commonwealth Parl. Conf. Houses of Parliament London SW1	5	—	*n.o.c.*
(3) Monarchy 1000 Bath	125	—	*n.o.c.*
(4) British Pharmaceutical Conference 1973 London WC	125	—	*n.o.c.*
(5) Surrey's First Sixth Form College Farnham Surrey	125	80	*Farn. Coll.*

C.D.S. POSTMARKS

(6) House of Commons S.W.1	65		
(7) House of Lords S.W.1	85		

14th November 1973 — ROYAL WEDDING

3½p, 20p Princess Anne and Captain Mark Phillips

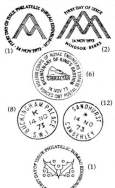

SPECIAL HANDSTAMPS			
(1) First Day of Issue — Philatelic Bureau	2	—	*Post Office*
(2) First Day of Issue — Windsor	6	—	*Post Office*
(3) First Day of Issue — Westminster Abbey	6	—	*Post Office*
(4) Royal Wedding Celebrations Great Somerford Chippenham Wilts	12	—	*n.o.c.*
(5) The Queens Dragoon Guards The Royal Wedding BF 1434 PS	15	3(s)	*Dragoons*
(6) Royal Engineers Kings Bastion Gibraltar BF 1387 PS	15	20	*Royal Eng. 17*
(7) The Chinese Exhibition London W1	20	35	*Ch. Exhib.*

C.D.S. POSTMARKS

(8) Buckingham Palace, S.W.1	100		
(9) Great Somerford, Chippenham, Wilts	20		
(10) House of Commons, S.W.1	15		
(11) House of Lords, S.W.1	20		
(12) Sandhurst, Camberley	15		
(13) Windsor Castle, Windsor, Berks	135		

28th November 1973 — CHRISTMAS

5 × 3p; 3½p 'Good King Wenceslas'

SPECIAL HANDSTAMPS			
(1) First Day of Issue — Philatelic Bureau	2	—	*Post Office*
(2) First Day of Issue — Bethlehem, Llandeilo, Carms	5	—	*Post Office*
(3) The Chinese Exhibition London W1	50	60	*Ch. Exhib.*
(4) 141st Anniv. Birth of Lewis Carroll 1832 Daresbury Warrington	125	125	*Ches. Hist. 3*

> **PRICES & CONDITION** – PLEASE READ GENERAL NOTES

27th February 1974 — BRITISH TREES — THE HORSE CHESTNUT

10p

	ordinary covers £	official covers £	
SPECIAL HANDSTAMPS			
(1) First Day of Issue — Philatelic Bureau	3	—	*Post Office*
(2) Stampex London 1974 Royal Horticultural Hall SW1	6	10	*Stampex*

24th April 1974 — 200th ANNIVERSARY OF FIRST FIRE SERVICE LEGISLATION

3½p, 5½p, 8p, 10p Early Fire Engines

SPECIAL HANDSTAMPS			
(1) First Day of Issue — Philatelic Bureau	4	—	**Post Office*
(2) Binns Philatelic & Fire Services Exhibition Sunderland	35	—	*n.o.c.*
(3) First Open Day Avon County Fire Brigade Bristol	18	25	*Cotswold (g)*
(4) Cambridgeshire Fire & Rescue Service Inaugural Ceremony	25	75	*Cambs C.C.*
(5) Lansing Bagnall 25 Years at Basingstoke Hampshire 1949-1974	175	200	*Lan. Bag.*
(6) MCC v Hampshire Champion County 1973 London NW8	175	175	*S.P.*

*Note — Some PO covers with Bureau handstamp are known to be overprinted 'Merryweather — the first name in firefighting' and 'Science Museum Souvenir — firefighting collection' and are valued at £5 and £15 respectively.

ORDINARY F.D.I. POSTMARKS	
(7) London S.E.1 — H.Q. London Fire Brigade	10

C.D.S. POSTMARKS	
(8) Burnt House Lane, Exeter Devon	450
(9) Hose, Melton Mowbray	150
(10) House of Commons, S.W.1	30
(11) House of Lords, S.W.1	30
(12) Tooley Street, S.E.1 — first fire fought by Ins. Co. brigade	250

SLOGAN POSTMARKS	
(13) The Fire Brigade Needs Men of Courage	550
(slogan in use at Belfast, Coleraine, Portadown, Lurgan, Ballymena and Londonderry)	

12th June 1974 — CENTENARY OF UNIVERSAL POSTAL UNION

3½p P&O Packet Steamer; 5½p First Official Air mail; 8p Air mail Blue Van and Postbox; 10p Imperial Airways Flyingboat

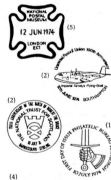

SPECIAL HANDSTAMPS			
(1) First Day of Issue — Philatelic Bureau	4	—	*Post Office*
(1a) Ditto with "Great Britain Day INTERNABA 1974" cachet	7	—	*Post Office*
(2) U.P.U. 100th Anniv. Imperial Airways Flying Boat Southampton	7	45	*Imp. Air.*
(3) Visit of Golden Hind II London E.C.	125	—	*n.o.c.*
(4) Centenary Exhibition Churchill Somerset House London WC	125	—	*n.o.c.*
(5) National Postal Museum (on reprinted 1890 Jubilee cover)	45	—	*n.o.c.*

10th July 1974 — GREAT BRITONS

4½p Robert the Bruce; 5½p Owain Glyndwr; 8p Henry V; 10p Edward of Woodstock

SPECIAL HANDSTAMPS			
(1) First Day of Issue — Philatelic Bureau	4	—	*Post Office*
(2) 700th Anniv. Robert the Bruce National Trust Bannockburn	25	35	*Scot N.T.*
(3) Robert the Bruce Dunfermline Abbey, Dunfermline Fife	25	70	*Dun. Abbey*
(4) Owain Glyndwrs Parliament House Machynlleth Powys	20	45	*Ow. Glyn.*
(5) Royal Tournament BF 1974 PS	60	60	*Royal T.*
(6) Visit of Golden Hind II London EC	125	—	*n.o.c.*
(7) Centenary Exhibition Churchill Somerset House London WC	125	—	*n.o.c.*
(8) 103rd British Open Golf Championship Lytham St. Annes	125	—	*n.o.c.*
(9) Trustee Savings Bank 150th Anniv. 1824-1974 Sunderland	150	20(s)	*T.S.B.*

ORDINARY F.D.I. POSTMARKS	
(10) Canterbury, Kent	12
(11) Windsor, Berks	12
(12) Gwent Dydd Cyhoeddiad Cyntab	12
(13) Dunfermline	12

C.D.S. POSTMARKS	
(14) Calais with PAQUEBOT markings	75
(15) Cardross — where Robert the Bruce died (4½p)	15(s)
(16) Glyndyfrdwy — home of Owain Glyndwr (5½p)	15(s)
(17) House of Commons, S.W.1	15
(18) House of Lords, S.W.1	17
(19) Woodstock — Edward of Woodstock (10p)	20(s)

9th October 1974 — CENTENARY OF THE BIRTH OF WINSTON CHURCHILL

4½p, 5½p, 8p, 10p Portraits of Churchill

	ordinary covers £	official covers £	
SPECIAL HANDSTAMPS			
(1) First Day of Issue — Philatelic Bureau	4	—	*Post Office*
(2) First Day of Issue — Blenheim, Woodstock, Oxford	5	—	*Post Office*
(3) First Day of Issue — House of Commons, London SW1	5	—	*Post Office*
(4) Churchill Centenary 1874-1974 Woodford Green Action This Day	15	25	*See Note**
(5) Sir Winston Churchill's First Constituency Oldham	20	20	*Old. Conserv.*
(6) Sir Winston Churchill RAF Honington BF 1874 PS	20	5(s)	*RAF 12 Squad*
(7) Centenary Exhibition Churchill Somerset House London WC	25	50	*Som. Hse.*
(8) Universal Postal Union 1874 Clitheroe Lancs	100	—	*n.o.c.*
(9) Oldest Post Office In Britain 1763 Sanquhar Dumfriesshire	80	80	*Sanq. PO*
(10) Rotary Club of Paddington Golden Jubilee London W2	125	125	*Padd. R.C.*
(11) Gold Jubilee of Local Radio Nottingham 1924-1974	125	—	*n.o.c.*

*Two covers exist for this handstamp:- (a) Wanstead & Woodford Synagogue
(b) Wanstead & Woodford Conservative Association

ORDINARY F.D.I. POSTMARKS		
(12) Tunbridge Wells, Kent with "Posted at Chartwell" cachet	30	
(13) Medway (HMS Churchill Submarine cover)	25	

C.D.S. POSTMARKS		
(14) Bladon, Oxford — Churchill is buried here	135	
(15) Churchill, Bristol	100	
(16) Churchill, Oxford	100	
(17) House of Commons, S.W.1	80	
(18) House of Lords, S.W.1	110	
(19) Marlborough, Wilts — Churchill related to the Marlboroughs	175	
(20) Normandy, Guildford	50	
(21) Sandhurst, Camberley — Churchill went to Sandhurst	75	
(22) Winston, Darlington	200	

27th November 1974 — CHRISTMAS

3½p York Minster; 4½p St. Helens, Norwich; 8p Ottery St. Mary; 10p Worcester Cathedral

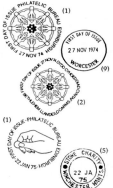

SPECIAL HANDSTAMPS			
(1) First Day of Issue — Philatelic Bureau	3	—	*Post Office*
(2) First Day of Issue — Bethlehem, Llandeilo, Carms	6	—	*Post Office*
(3) St. Helen's Church 1249-1974 Great Hospital Norwich	10	25	*Gt. Hosp.*
(4) The Collegiate Church Exhibition Ottery St. Mary Devon	10	25	*St. Mary*
(5) The Salvation Army Christmas Supermarket Tunbridge Wells	90	20(s)	*Sal. Army*
(6) The Oldest Post Office In Britain 1763 Sanquhar	60	75	*Sanq. PO*
(7) Winston Churchill County Secondary School Woking Surrey	90	90	*W.C. Sch.*

ORDINARY F.D.I. POSTMARKS		
(8) York — York Minster "roof boss" featured on 3½p value	15	
(9) Worcester — Cathedral "roof boss" featured on 10p value	15	

22nd January 1975 — CHARITY

4½p + 1½p donation to charities

SPECIAL HANDSTAMPS			
(1) First Day of Issue — Philatelic Bureau	3	—	*Post Office*
(2) The Oldest Post Office In Britain 1763 Sanquhar	15	25	*Sanq. PO*

ORDINARY F.D.I. POSTMARKS		
(3) Kettering (on Winged Fellowship Trust Holiday Homes cover)	5	
(4) Oxford (Oxfam HQ)	10	

C.D.S. POSTMARKS		
(5) Stoke Charity Winchester Hants	200	

SLOGAN POSTMARKS		
(6) Menphys Love the Handicapped (Leicester or Wigston, Leics)	80	
(7) Tenovus Cares Cardiff	200	
(8) Barnardo's Cares About Children, Hounslow	200	

19th February 1975 — BRITISH PAINTINGS: J. M. W. TURNER

4½p 'Peace: Burial at Sea'; 5½p 'Snowstorm – Steamer off a Harbour's Mouth';
8p 'The Arsenal, Venice'; 10p 'St. Laurent'

	ordinary covers £	official covers £	
SPECIAL HANDSTAMPS			
(1) First Day of Issue — Philatelic Bureau	4	—	*Post Office*
(2) First Day of Issue — London WC	6	—	*Post Office*
(3) The Oldest Post Office in Britain 1763 Sanquhar	30	30	*Sanq. PO*
(4) Worksop & District Chamber of Trade 1875-1975 Worksop	90	—	*n.o.c.*
(5) Up Helly — AA Lerwick Shetland	100	—	*n.o.c.*
C.D.S. POSTMARKS			
(6) Petworth — Turner did much of his painting here	125		
(7) Turner's Hill, Crawley Sussex	110		
(8) Harwich, Essex — relevant to the 5½p value	20(s)		
SLOGAN POSTMARKS			
(9) Turner: Royal Academy (only known on plain cover)	10(s)		

23rd April 1975 — EUROPEAN ARCHITECTURAL HERITAGE YEAR

2 × 7p Charlotte Square, Edinburgh & The Rows Chester; 8p The Royal Observatory, Greenwich;
10p St. George's Chapel, Windsor; 12p The National Theatre, London

SPECIAL HANDSTAMPS			
(1) First Day of Issue — Philatelic Bureau	5	—	*Post Office*
(2) 500 Years St. George's Chapel Windsor Berks	12	—	*see 2(a)*
(2a) Ditto with "Carried by Coach" cachet	12	20	*St. G. Ch.*
(3) National Trust for Scotland EAHY 7 Charlotte Sq. Edinburgh	30	50	*Scot N.T.*
(4) Corinium 1900 Heritage Cirencester	30	50	*Corin. Mus.*
(5) Chester Heritage City	20	40	*Chester EAHY*
(6) Wilton House Open Day Wilton Salisbury Wilts	30	30	*Cotswold*
(7) The Oldest Post Office in Britain 1763 Sanquhar	40	40	*Sanq. PO*
(8) Opening of Meriden Junior School Pool Watford Herts	125	15(s)	*Meriden Sch.*
ORDINARY F.D.I. POSTMARKS			
(9) Chester or Edinburgh .... *each*	5		
(10) London S.E.1 — FDI P.O. for Observatory & Nat. Theatre	5		
(11) Windsor	5		
C.D.S. POSTMARKS			
(12) Greenwich B.O. (Branch Office) London S.E.10	175		
(13) Dartmouth Row, Greenwich S.E.10	200		
(14) Windsor Castle, Windsor, Berks	125		
SLOGAN POSTMARKS			
(15) Chester Heritage City, Chester	225		
(16) European Architectural Heritage Year 1975 Leicester	325		

11th June 1975 — SAILING

7p Dinghies; 8p Keel Boats; 10p Yachts; 12p Multihulls

SPECIAL HANDSTAMPS			
(1) First Day of Issue — Philatelic Bureau	3	—	*Post Office*
(1a) Ditto with "British Post Office Arphila 75 Paris" cachet	7	—	*Post Office*
(2) Royal Dorset Yacht Club centenary 1875-1975 Weymouth	7	20	*R.D.Y. Club*
(3) Royal Thames Yacht Club Bi-centenary London SW	7	20	*R.T.Y. Club*
(4) The Oldest Post Office in Britain 1763 Sanquhar	20	25	*Sanq. PO*
ORDINARY F.D.I. POSTMARKS			
(5) Hastings — Rye Harbour Sailing Club	10		
(6) Newport, I.O.W. — famous for yachting	10		
(7) Plymouth, Devon — sailing traditions	10		
(8) Southampton — International Boat Show cover	12		
(9) Weymouth, Dorset — centre for yachting	10		
(10) Woking, Surrey — Royal Yachting Association's headquarters	12		
C.D.S. POSTMARKS			
(11) Cowes, I.O.W. — yachting centre	80		
(12) Burnham-on-Crouch, Essex — yachting centre	60		
(13) House of Commons S.W.1 — H of C Yacht Club — 25th Anniv.	35		
(14) Lytham, Lancs — Ribble Cruising Club — 25th Anniv.	75		
(15) Rye Harbour — Rye Harbour Sailing Club — 50th Anniv.	75		
(16) West Wittering — W. Wittering Sailing Club — 25th Anniv.	75		

PRICES & CONDITION – PLEASE READ GENERAL NOTES

13th August 1975 — 150th ANNIVERSARY FIRST PUBLIC STEAM RAILWAY

7p Stephenson's Locomotion; 8p Waverley class;
10p Caerphilly Castle; 12p High Speed Train

		ordinary covers £	official covers £	
SPECIAL HANDSTAMPS				
(1)	First Day of Issue — Philatelic Bureau	4	—	*Post Office*
(2)	First Day of Issue — Stockton-on-Tees	6	—	*Post Office*
(3)	First Day of Issue — Darlington	6	—	*Post Office*
(4)	First Day of Issue — Shildon	6	—	*Post Office*
(5)	Railway Festival Wylam Northumberland George Stephenson	20	40	*Round Table*
(6)	Royal Engineers 70th Anniv. Longmoor Railway BF 1396 PS	18	25	*Royal Eng. 27*
(7)	Return of Steam 10th Anniversary Buckfastleigh Devon	10	10	*Cotswold*
(8)	Torbay Steam Railway 25th Anniv. Paignton Devon	15	20	*Cotswold*
(9)	The Story of a Cathedral Exhibition Canterbury Kent	100	—	*n.o.c.*
(10)	Royal Shakespeare Theatre Centenary Stratford-upon-Avon	100	—	*n.o.c.*
ORDINARY F.D.I. POSTMARKS				
(11)	Bournemouth (on Big Four Railway Museum cover)	20		
(12)	Brighton (on Bluebell Railway cover)	20		
(13)	Crewe — railway centre	10		
(14)	Derby — B.R. Technical/Research Centre	10		
(15)	Paddington	10		
(16)	York — Railway Museum	10		
(17)	Swindon (on official British Rail Works cover)	20		
C.D.S. POSTMARKS (inc. T.P.O. CANCELS)				
(18)	Caerphilly, Mid Glam — Caerphilly Castle on 10p value	50		
(19)	Welshpool (on Llanfair Light Railway cover)	30		
(20)	Porthmadog (on Festiniog Railway Co. cover)	20		
(21)	Wylam (birthplace of George Stephenson)	75		
(22)	N.E.T.P.O. — The most appropriate for this issue	30		
(23)	Other T.P.O. (travelling post office) cancellations from	30		
SLOGAN POSTMARKS				
(24)	S & D Rly Jubilee Shildon Co. Durham	250		
(25)	150th S & D Rly Anniversary Darlington	250		
(26)	Ravenglass & Eskdale Rly. Centenary Year Carlisle	25(s)		

3rd September 1975 — INTER-PARLIAMENTARY UNION CONFERENCE

12p

		£	£	
SPECIAL HANDSTAMPS				
(1)	First Day of Issue — Philatelic Bureau	2	—	*Post Office*
(2)	62nd Inter-Parliamentary Conference Royal Festival Hall SE1	3	4	*I.P. Conf*
(3)	The Story of a Cathedral Exhibition Canterbury Kent	85	—	*n.o.c.*
(4)	Stockton & Darlington Rly 1825-1975 Darlington	75	—	*n.o.c.*
C.D.S. POSTMARKS				
(5)	House of Commons, S.W.1	45		
(6)	House of Lords, S.W.1	50		
(7)	Parliament Street B.O. S.W.1	35		

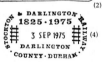

22nd October 1975 — BICENTENARY OF JANE AUSTEN

8½p Emma and Mr. Woodhouse; 10p Catherine Moorland;
11p Mr. Darcy; 13p Mary and Henry Crawford

		£	£	
SPECIAL HANDSTAMPS				
(1)	First Day of Issue — Philatelic Bureau	3	—	*Post Office*
(2)	First Day of Issue — Steventon	3	—	*Post Office*
(2a)	Ditto with "Despatched by Mailcoach" cachet	7	—	*Post Office*
(3)	Jane Austen 1775-1975 Bi-centenary Exhibition Bath	7	15	*City of Bath*
(4)	The Story of a Cathedral Exhibition Canterbury Kent	60	—	*n.o.c.*
C.D.S. POSTMARKS				
(5)	Alton, Hants	75		
(6)	Chawton, Alton, Hants — Jane Austen lived here	90		
(7)	Steventon, Basingstoke — Jane Austen's birthplace	75		
SLOGAN POSTMARKS				
(8)	Jane Austen Bi-centenary 1775-1975 Hampshire	225		
	(slogan in use at Alton, Basingstoke, Southampton and Winchester)			

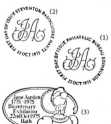

PRICES & CONDITION – PLEASE READ GENERAL NOTES

26th November 1975 — CHRISTMAS
6½p, 8½p, 11p, 13p Angels

		ordinary covers £	official covers £	
SPECIAL HANDSTAMPS				
(1)	First Day of Issue — Philatelic Bureau	2	—	*Post Office*
(2)	First Day of Issue — Bethlehem, Llandeilo, Dyfed	3	—	*Post Office*
C.D.S. POSTMARKS				
(3)	Angel Hill, Sutton, Surrey	100		

10th March 1976 — CENTENARY OF THE INVENTION OF THE TELEPHONE
8½p, 10p, 11p, 13p The Telephone in the Community

SPECIAL HANDSTAMPS				
(1)	First Day of Issue — Philatelic Bureau	2	—	*Post Office*
(2)	Post Office Telecommunications Museum, Taunton	6	—	*n.o.c.*
ORDINARY F.D.I. POSTMARKS				
(3)	Boston, Lincs. — place in USA where invention made	12		
(4)	Edinburgh — birthplace of Alexander Graham Bell	12		
(5)	Hull — independent telephone service	12		
(6)	Worcester — with Centenary Exhibition overprint	8		
C.D.S. POSTMARKS				
(7)	Hope St. Edinburgh — nearest P.O. to Bell's birthplace	100		
SLOGAN POSTMARKS				
(8)	The Samaritans Distress Despair Phone Bognor 25555, Bognor Regis..	225		

28th April 1976 — SOCIAL PIONEERS & REFORMERS
8½p Thomas Hepburn — miners' union 1831; 10p Robert Owen — improved working conditions; 11p Lord Shaftesbury — child labour reform; 13p Elizabeth Fry — prison reform

SPECIAL HANDSTAMPS				
(1)	First Day of Issue — Philatelic Bureau	3	—	*Post Office*
(2)	World of Islam Festival London SW7	25	40	*Pilgrim*
(3)	1776 Exhibition National Maritime Museum Greenwich SE10	40	30	*Pilgrim*
ORDINARY F.D.I. POSTMARKS				
(4)	Durham — National Union of Mineworkers	9		
(5)	Folkestone — Lord Shaftesbury died here	8		
(6)	Norwich — birthplace of Elizabeth Fry	7		
(7)	Rochdale, Lancs — Robert Owen's workers formed first Co-op	7		
C.D.S. POSTMARKS				
(8)	House of Commons, S.W.1	25		
(9)	House of Lords, S.W.1	35		
(10)	Magdalen St., Norwich — nearest P.O. to Fry's birthplace	40		
(11)	Newton, Powys — birthplace of Robert Owen	30		
(12)	Parkhurst, I.O.W. — famous top security prison	50		
(13)	New Lanark — Robert Owen's experiment	100		
(14)	Lanark — Robert Owen's experiment	70		
(15)	Pelton, Durham — Hepburn's birthplace	100		
(16)	Shaftesbury, Dorset	90		
(17)	Wimborne St. Giles — family seat of Earl of Shaftesbury	75		

2nd June 1976 — BICENTENARY OF INDEPENDENCE OF THE U.S.A.
11p Benjamin Franklin

SPECIAL HANDSTAMPS				
(1)	First Day of Issue — Philatelic Bureau	2	—	*Post Office*
(1a)	Ditto with "Interphil 76 British Post Office" cachet	5	—	*Post Office*
(2)	Bicentennial Am. Independence June Campaign BF 1776 PS	5	8	*BFPS*
(3)	USA Independence Bicentenary Washington Tyne & Wear.	5	15	*Wash. Old Hall*
(4)	1776 Exhibition National Maritime Museum Greenwich SE10	6	15	*Pilgrim*
(5)	American Bicentennial 1776-1976 American Museum Bath	4	5	*Clav. Manor*
(6)	58th Philatelic Congress of G.B. Plymouth Devon	15	20	*Phil. Cong.*
(7)	World of Islam Festival London SW7	15	35	*Pilgrim*

> PLEASE READ THE GENERAL NOTES
> AT THE BEGINNING OF THIS CATALOGUE
> These often provide the answers to enquiries received.

		ordinary covers £	official covers £
ORDINARY F.D.I. POSTMARKS			
(8)	Boston, Lincs	5	
(9)	Plymouth, Devon — sailing of Pilgrim Fathers	5	
C.D.S. POSTMARKS			
(10)	Bunker's Hill, Lincoln	90	
(11)	Dallas, Forres, Morayshire	90	
(12)	Denver, Downham Market, Norfolk	90	
(13)	House of Commons, S.W.1	25	
(14)	House of Lords, S.W.1	35	
(15)	New York, Lincoln	100	
(16)	Northborough (Manor) — Claypole family — links with U.S.A.	20	
(17)	Sulgrave, Banbury — home of ancestors of George Washington	50	
(18)	Washington, Pulborough, West Sussex	60	

30th June 1976 — CENTENARY OF ROYAL NATIONAL ROSE SOCIETY

8½p Elizabeth of Glamis; 10p Grandpa Dickson; 11p Rosa Mundi; 13p Sweet Briar

SPECIAL HANDSTAMPS				
(1)	First Day of Issue — Philatelic Bureau	3	—	*Post Office*
(2)	Year of the Rose Northampton		20	*N'ton Ph Soc*
(3)	Year of the Rose Bath	5	20	*City of Bath*
(4)	The Royal National Rose Society 1876-1976 Oxford	5	—	*n.o.c.*
(5)	The Royal National Rose Society 1876-1976 St. Albans	5	—	*n.o.c.*
(6)	Royal Norfolk Show Norwich	10	60	*Daniels*
(7)	The Mothers' Union Centenary London SW1	45	65	*Mothers Un.*
(8)	The Championships A.E.L.T.C. 1976 Wimbledon	70	—	*n.o.c.*
(9)	USA Independence Bicentenary Washington Tyne & Wear	70	—	*n.o.c.*
(10)	Warton Bicentennial Commem. 1776-1976 Warton Carnforth	70	—	*n.o.c.*
(11)	1776 Exhibition National Maritime Museum Greenwich SE10	70	—	*n.o.c.*
(12)	50th Anniv. First Flight Britain to Australia BF 1536 PS	70	—	*n.o.c.*
ORDINARY F.D.I. POSTMARKS				
(13)	Tunbridge Wells, Kent with "Sissinghurst Castle" cachet	15		
C.D.S. POSTMARKS				
(14)	Glamis, Forfar — "Elizabeth of Glamis" featured on 8½p value	85		
(15)	Kew Gardens, Richmond, Surrey	125		
(16)	Rose, Truro, Cornwall	125		
(17)	Rose Cottage, Hull, North Humberside	125		
(18)	Rosebush, or Rosebank	75		

4th August 1976 — BRITISH CULTURAL TRADITIONS

8½p & 13p Eisteddfod; 10p Morris Dancing; 11p Highland Gathering

SPECIAL HANDSTAMPS				
(1)	First Day of Issue — Philatelic Bureau	3	—	*Post Office*
(2)	First Day of Issue — Cardigan	4	—	*Post Office*
(3)	Eisteddfod Genedlaethol Frenhinol Cymru 1176-1976 Cardigan	5	60	*Philart*
(4)	Bristol Morris Men 25th Anniversary Bristol	5	50	*Bristol MM*
(5)	1776 Exhibition National Maritime Museum Greenwich SE10	60	—	*n.o.c.*
(6)	USA Independence Bicentenary Washington Tyne & Wear	60	—	*n.o.c.*
(7)	The Story of a Cathedral Exhibition Canterbury Kent	30	—	*n.o.c.*
(8)	Colchester Tattoo BF 1542 PS	75	—	*n.o.c.*
(9)	Europa 6 Cantat Leicester	75	75	*Contat 6*
ORDINARY F.D.I. POSTMARKS				
(10)	Exeter District with 'Sidmouth Folk Festival' cachet	20		
C.D.S. POSTMARKS				
(11)	Abbots Bromley, Rugeley, Staffs — horn dancing	20		
(12)	Abingdon, Oxon — famous morris team	20		
(13)	Bampton, Oxon — famous morris team	20		
(14)	Britannia, Bacup, Lancs — famous morris team	20		
(15)	Chipping Campden — famous morris team	15		
(16)	Headington Quarry, Oxford — famous morris team	30		
(17)	Padstow — famous for its "Hobby Horse"	15		
(18)	Thaxted, Dunmow — the Morris Ring meet here annually	20		
(19)	Caerwys, Clwyd — famous eisteddfod	15		
(20)	Carmarthen, Dyfed — famous eisteddfod	15		
(21)	Corwen, Clwyd — famous eisteddfod	20		
(22)	Llangollen, Clwyd — International Musical Eisteddfod	30		
(23)	Braemar — Royal Highland Gathering	30		
(24)	Dunoon — Cowal Highland Gathering	15		

29th September 1976 — WILLIAM CAXTON 500th ANNIVERSARY OF PRINTING IN ENGLAND

1976

8½p 'Canterbury Tales'; 10p Caxton's type-faces;
11p Game of Chess; 13p Printing Press

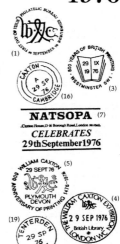

		ordinary covers £	official covers £	
SPECIAL HANDSTAMPS				
(1)	First Day of Issue — Philatelic Bureau	3	—	*Post Office*
(2)	First Day of Issue — London SW1	4	—	*Post Office*
(3)	500 Years of British Printing Westminster SW1	6	8	*Br Pr Ind Fed*
(4)	William Caxton Exhibition British Library London WC	6	25	*BL 1*
(5)	500th Anniv. Printing 1476-1976 William Caxton Plymouth	6	25	*Ply. Coll.*
(6)	Paper & Printing Study Group 500 Years Printing SE1	6	18	*Philart*
(7)	NATSOPA Caxton House 13-16 Borough Road London SE1	6	8	*NATSOPA*
(8)	Raithby Lawrence Centenary De Montfort Press Leicester	10	30	*DeM. Press*
(9)	British Philatelic Exhibition London W1	6	10	*B.P.E.*
(10)	First School Centenary 1876-1976 Stoke Poges Bucks	25	40	*S.P. Sch.*
(11)	1776 Exhibition National Maritime Museum Greenwich SE10	25	—	*n.o.c.*
(12)	Royal Charter Quincentenary 1476-1976 Stow-on-the-Wold	25	40	*S-o-t-W Sch.*
(13)	Manchester United v. Ajax UEFA Cup Manchester	70	—	*n.o.c.*
ORDINARY F.D.I. POSTMARKS				
(14)	Canterbury — Caxton printed 'Canterbury Tales'	6		
C.D.S. POSTMARKS				
(15)	Abingdon — first printing in England for Abbot of Abingdon	75		
(16)	Caxton, Cambridge	65		
(17)	Fleet St. B.O., E.C.4 — home of British printing today	75		
(18)	House of Commons (Caxton buried in St. Margaret's Chapel)	40		
(19)	Tenterden, Kent — presumed birthplace of William Caxton	50		

NATSOPA (7)
.Caxton House,13-16 Borough Road,London SE1 OAL
CELEBRATES
29th September 1976

24th November 1976 — CHRISTMAS

6½p, 8½p, 11p, 13p Embroideries

SPECIAL HANDSTAMPS				
(1)	First Day of Issue — Philatelic Bureau	3	—	*Post Office*
(2)	First Day of Issue — Bethlehem, Llandeilo, Dyfed	3	—	*Post Office*
(3)	Pompeii AD79 Exhibition Royal Academy of Arts London W1	8	20	*Pomp. Exhib.*
(4)	Tonic to the Nation Victoria & Albert Museum SW7	8	20	*H.R.*
(5)	75th Anniversary 1st British Corps Bielefeld BF 1923 PS	20	35	*BFPS*
(6)	75th Anniversary 1st British Corps Aldershot BF 1901 PS	20	35	*BFPS*
(7)	William Caxton Exhibition British Library London WC	40	—	*n.o.c.*
C.D.S. POSTMARKS				
(8)	Angel Hill, Sutton, Surrey	10		
(9)	Pincushion, Boston, Lincs — embroideries	20		

12th January 1977 — RACQUET SPORTS

8½p Lawn Tennis; 10p Table Tennis; 11p Squash; 13p Badminton

SPECIAL HANDSTAMPS				
(1)	First Day of Issue — Philatelic Bureau	3	—	*Post Office*
(2)	The Badminton Association Badminton Avon	6	30	*Badm. Assoc.*
(3)	The Squash Rackets Association Harrow Founded 1928	6	40	*Philart*
(4)	Pompeii AD 79 Exhibition Royal Academy of Arts London W1	30	—	*n.o.c.*
(5)	William Caxton Exhibition British Library London WC	30	—	*n.o.c.*
ORDINARY F.D.I. POSTMARKS				
(6)	Battersea, S.W.11 — Head P.O. for Wimbledon	6		
(7)	Birmingham — World Table Tennis Championships held at NEC	6		
(8)	Hastings — Headquarters of English Table Tennis Association	6		
(9)	Warwick & Leamington — first Tennis Club founded in 1872	6		
C.D.S. POSTMARKS				
(10)	Wimbledon S.D.O., S.W.19	125		
(11)	Wimbledon Park, Wimbledon S.W.19	150		
(12)	Woodside Parade, Wimbledon S.W.19	125		

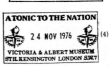

A. G. BRADBURY
The top name in cover and postmark design.
Write for my latest colour leaflets.
3 LINK ROAD, STONEYGATE, LEICESTER LE2 3RA

2nd March 1977 — BRITISH ACHIEVEMENT IN CHEMISTRY
8½p Steroids; 10p Vitamin C; 11p Starch; 13p Salt

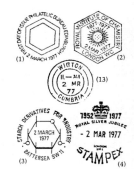

		ordinary covers £	official covers £	
SPECIAL HANDSTAMPS				
(1)	First Day of Issue — Philatelic Bureau	3	—	*Post Office*
(2)	Royal Institute of Chemistry London WC 1877-1977	6	12	*RI of Chem.*
(3)	Starch Derivatives for Industry Battersea S.W.11	6	12	*Garton Ltd*
(4)	1952-1977 Royal Silver Jubilee Stampex London S.W.1	6	12	*Stampex*
(5)	Pompeii AD 79 Exhibition Royal Academy of Arts London W1	20	25	*Pomp. Exh.*
(6)	Tonic to the Nation Victoria & Albert Museum	25	40	*H.R.*
	ORDINARY F.D.I. POSTMARKS			
(7)	Liverpool — birthplace of R.L.M. Synge	5		
	C.D.S. POSTMARKS			
(8)	Barton, Preston or Richmond — Barton featured on 8½p val.	25		
(9)	Gravesend, Kent — birthplace of D.H.R. Barton	30		
(10)	Haworth, Keighley — Haworth featured on 10p value	25		
(11)	Martin, Lincoln — Martin featured on 11p value	25		
(12)	Martin, Hants — Martin featured on 11p value	25		
(13)	Wigton, Cumbria — birthplace of W. H. Bragg	30		

11th May 1977 — THE SILVER JUBILEE OF THE QUEEN'S ACCESSION
8½p, 10p, 11p, 13p

SPECIAL HANDSTAMPS				
(1)	First Day of Issue — Philatelic Bureau	3	—	*Post Office*
(2)	First Day of Issue — Windsor	3	—	*Post Office*
(3)	Jubilee Exhibition Bath England	6	25	*City of Bath*
(4)	A Royal Jubilee Exhibition British Library London WC	6	25	*BL 2*
(5)	Croydon Celebrates Queen's Silver Jubilee Croydon Surrey	7	30	*Croydon*
(6)	Stamp Collecting Prom. Council Silver Jubilee London SE1	8	—	*n.o.c.*
(7)	Queen Elizabeth II Silver Jubilee Special RHDR Hythe	6	25	*RHDR 1*
(8)	St. Martin-in-the-Fields Queen's Silver Jubilee London WC2	8	40	*St. M-i-t-F*
(9)	Hayling Island Philatelic Soc. Silver Jubilee Havant	25	35	*HI Phil Soc*
(10)	The Duke of Edinburgh's Award 1956-1977 London SW1	4	7	*DoE A. Scheme*
(11)	The Stamp of Royalty Exhibition Glasgow	6	15	*Pal. of Art*
(12)	Weymouth & Portland Dorset Philatelic Exhibition	15	40	*W & P Exhib*
(13)	Tenth Conference Dixieme Congress London W1	10	40	*ICTWO*
(14)	Exercise Makefast XXV Chatham BF 1952 PS	8	20	*Royal Eng.*
(15)	Bristol Bordeaux 30th Anniversary Bristol	12	30	*BB Assoc*
(16)	Milton Keynes Arts Association Milton Keynes	12	40	*MK Festival*
	ORDINARY F.D.I. HANDSTAMPS			
(17)	Aberdeen with "Posted near Balmoral Castle" cachet	12		
(18)	King's Lynn, Norfolk with "Estate Office Sandringham" cachet	20		
(19)	Portsmouth — Review of the Fleet	20		
	C.D.S. POSTMARKS			
(20)	Buckingham Palace, S.W.1	140		
(21)	House of Commons, S.W.1	20		
(22)	House of Lords, S.W.1	25		
(23)	Jubilee Crescent, Coventry	20		
(24)	Jubilee Oak, Braintree or Jubilee Fields, Durham....*each*	20		
(25)	Queen Elizabeth Avenue, Walsall	25		
(26)	Queen's Parade, Cleethorpes or Queen's Head, Oswestry....*each*	20		
(27)	Silver Link, Tamworth	20		
(28)	Windsor Castle, Windsor, Berks	150		
	SLOGAN POSTMARKS			
(29)	Queen's Silver Jubilee Appeal, Belfast	45		
(30)	Queen's Silver Jubilee Philatelic Exhibition, Cardiff	45		
(31)	Queen's Silver Jubilee Philatelic Exhibition, Edinburgh	45		
(32)	Queen's Silver Jubilee Philatelic Exhibition NPM, London EC	45		
(33)	Review of Fleet (with Jubilee logo) Portsmouth & Southsea	70		

PLEASE READ THE GENERAL NOTES
AT THE BEGINNING OF THIS CATALOGUE
These often provide the answers to enquiries received.

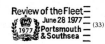

8th June 1977 — COMMONWEALTH HEADS OF GOVERNMENT MEETING

13p 'Gathering of Nations'

	ordinary covers	official covers	
	£	£	
SPECIAL HANDSTAMPS			
(1) First Day of Issue — Philatelic Bureau	2	—	*Post Office*
(2) First Day of Issue — London SW	2	—	*Post Office*
(3) Girl Guides Association Jubilee Open Days London SW1	8	20	*Girl Guides*
(4) St. Martin-in-the-Field Queens Silver Jubilee London WC2	5	15	*St. M-i-t-F*
(5) A Royal Jubilee Exhibition British Library London WC	5	—	*n.o.c.*
(6) Croydon Celebrates Queens Silver Jubilee Croydon Surrey	5	15	*Croydon*
(7) British Genius Exhibition Battersea London SW11	5	—	*n.o.c.*
(8) 50th Anniversary 6000 King George V Hereford	8	—	*n.o.c.*
(9) City of Leicester Silver Jubilee EIIR	5	—	*n.o.c.*
(10) Jubilee Exhibition North Devon	5	—	*n.o.c.*
(11) Royal Image Exhibition City of Bristol Museum & Art Gallery	5	—	*n.o.c.*
(12) The Prince of Wales Division Beating Retreat BF 8677 PS	5	10	*BFPS*
(13) The Queens Silver Jubilee Celebrations 1977 Windsor	5	—	*n.o.c.*
(14) Inaugural run of Silver Jubilee Train Newcastle-upon-Tyne	5	—	*n.o.c.*
(15) The Queen's Silver Jubilee Merseyside Police Liverpool	5	—	*n.o.c.*
(16) Silver Jubilee Festival Canon Hill Park, Birmingham	5	—	*n.o.c.*
C.D.S. POSTMARKS			
(17) House of Commons, S.W.1	40		
(18) House of Lords, S.W.1	60		
(19) Buckingham Palace, S.W.1	65		
SLOGAN POSTMARKS			
(20) House of Commons S.W.1 (wavy line cancel)	10		

15th June 1977 — THE SILVER JUBILEE OF THE QUEEN'S ACCESSION

9p

SPECIAL HANDSTAMPS			
(1) First Day of Issue — Philatelic Bureau	2	—	*Post Office*
(2) First Day of Issue — Windsor	2	—	*Post Office*
(3) Borough of Blackburn Silver Jubilee Lancashire	5	35	*Blackburn B.C.*
(4) Jubilee Exhibition North Devon	5	10	*N. Devon*
(5) Silver Jubilee Exhibition Trafalgar Square London WC2	5	—	*n.o.c.*
(6) Royal Jubilee Exhibition British Library London WC	5	20	*BL 2*
(7) City of Leicester Silver Jubilee EIIR Leicester	5	8	*City of Leics*
(8) Nuneaton Borough Council Silver Jubilee 1952 EIIR 1977	5	15	*Nuneaton BC*
(9) Croydon Celebrates the Queen's Silver Jubilee Croydon	5	15	*Croydon*
(10) Royal Image Exhibition City of Bristol Museum & Art Gallery	5	15	*Royal Image*
(11) British Genius Exhibition Battersea SW11	5	—	*n.o.c.*
ORDINARY F.D.I. POSTMARKS			
(12) Portsmouth – Review of Fleet	5		
C.D.S. POSTMARKS			
(13) Buckingham Palace, S.W.1	75		
(14) House of Commons, S.W.1	8		
(15) House of Lords, S.W.1	10		
(16) Jubilee Oak; Jubilee Cresc.; Jubilee Fields *each*	12		
(17) Silver Link; Queens Head; Queens Parade *each*	12		
(18) Queen Elizabeth Avenue, Walsall, West Midlands	12		
(19) Windsor Castle, Windsor, Berks	75		
SLOGAN POSTMARKS			
(20) The Queen's Silver Jubilee Appeal (various offices)	15		
(21) Review of the Fleet (incorporates Jubilee logo) Portsmouth	20		
(22) Queen's Silver Jubilee Philatelic Exhibition Cardiff	15		
(23) Queen's Silver Jubilee Philatelic Exhibition Edinburgh	15		
(24) Silver Jubilee International Air Tattoo – various	30		
(25) Portsmouth & Southsea (S.J. logo) Portsmouth	30		
(26) St. Neots Jubilee Riverside Festival	100		

11th May & 15th June 1977 — THE SILVER JUBILEE (DOUBLE DATED COVERS)

Many double-dated covers exist and it would be unwieldy to list all possible combinations, especially as the postmarks and covers have already been listed above. Therefore values can be summarised as follows:

(1) spec. handstamp (11th May) + FDI postmark (15th June)	20	30	
(2) spec. handstamp (11th May) + spec. handstamp (15th June)	25	35	
(3) appropriate CDS (11th May) + appropriate CDS (15th June)	35		

5th October 1977 — BRITISH WILDLIFE

5 × 9p: Hedgehog, Hare, Red Squirrel, Otter, Badger

		ordinary covers	official covers	
		£	£	
SPECIAL HANDSTAMPS				
(1)	First Day of Issue — Philatelic Bureau	3	—	*Post Office*
(2)	Badger Beer Blandford Dorset 200th Anniversary	5	10	*Hall & Woodhse*
(3)	SCT (Shropshire Conservation Trust) Bear Steps Shrewsbury	5	10	*SCT*
(4)	Norfolk Wildlife in Trust Norwich Norfolk	5	5	*Markton (NNT)*
(5)	Educational Open Day Port Lympne Wildlife Sanctuary Hythe	5	7	*RHDR 3*
(6)	11-13 Broad Court Covent Garden WC2	5	5	*Garden Studio*
(7)	1827 Darley's 1977 150 Years of Print Burton-on-Trent	15	20	*Darley's*
(8)	Sir Francis Drake Exhibition British Library London WC	25	—	*n.o.c.*
(9)	British Genius Exhibition Battersea London SW11	25	—	*n.o.c.*
(10)	Army & Navy Victoria Official Opening London SW1	25	3(s)	*A. & N.*
(11)	Manchester United FA Cup Winners Into Europe Manchester	40	4(s)	*Dawn*
C.D.S. POSTMARKS				
(12)	Badgers Mount, Sevenoaks, Kent	20		
(13)	Forest Row, East Sussex	15		
(14)	Foxton, Leics.	20		
(15)	Haresfield, Stonehouse, Glos, or Harewood, Leeds	2Λ		
(16)	Hedge End, Southampton	15		
(17)	Nettleham — HQ Society Promotion Nature Conservation	2Λ		
(18)	Otterburn, Newcastle-upon-Tyne	₋0		
(19)	Otter Ferry, Tighnabruaich	20		
(20)	Squirrels Heath, Romford, Essex	25		

23rd November 1977 — CHRISTMAS

5 × 7p; 9p 'The Twelve Days of Christmas'

SPECIAL HANDSTAMPS				
(1)	First Day of Issue — Philatelic Bureau	3	—	*Post Office*
(2)	First Day of Issue — Bethlehem, Llandeilo, Dyfed	3	—	*Post Office*
(3)	Silver Jubilee Christmas Greetings from Blackpool	12	2(s)	*Blackpool*
(4)	Sir Francis Drake Exhibition British Library London WC	6	15	*Br. Lib.*
(5)	40th Anniversary First Mail Flight Lerwick Shetland	6	—	*n.o.c.*
(6)	40th Anniversary First Mail Flight Dyce Aberdeen	6	—	*n.o.c.*
ORDINARY F.D.I. POSTMARKS				
(7)	Cambridge — 12 Days of Christmas original manuscript found at Trinity College	15		
C.D.S. POSTMARKS				
(8)	House of Lords — "Lords a-leaping"	35		
(9)	Partridge Green Horsham, West Sussex	30		
(10)	Pear Tree, Derby, Rugeley or Welwyn Garden City	25		
SLOGAN POSTMARK				
(11)	Collect through Philatelic Bureau	25		

25th January 1978 — ENERGY

9p Oil; 10½p Coal; 11p Gas; 13p Electricity

SPECIAL HANDSTAMPS				
(1)	First Day of Issue — Philatelic Bureau	5	—	*Post Office*
(2)	KW Claymore "A" Project Management Team Peterhead	35	50	*Claymore*
(3)	Institute of Fuel Golden Jubilee Year London W1	8	8	*Cotswold (g)*
(4)	Coal is Precious Save It South Leicester Colliery Ellistown	7	*3(s)	*Greens of MH*
(5)	Oil is Precious Save It Stathern Field Melton Mowbray	7	*3(s)	*Greens of MH*
(6)	British Speedway 50th Anniv. Gulf Oil League London W4	10	—	*n.o.c.*
(7)	SEAGAS a part of British Gas Croydon, Surrey	8	—	*n.o.c.*
(8)	Forties Field Aberdeen BP Contribution to Britain's Energy	8	12	*BOCS 1*
(9)	West Sole Field Hull BP Contribution to Britain's Energy	8	12	*BOCS 1*
(10)	21 Years British Nuclear Electricity Dungeness, Kent	8	10	*RHDR 4*

Note: Greens of Market Harborough sponsored these two handstamps. A set of four single value FDCs were produced — the 9p and 10½p values were cancelled with the special handstamps whilst the other two values received the Leicester FDI handstamp. The set is valued @ £6.

C.D.S. POSTMARKS			
(11)	Bacton — North Sea gas pipeline comes ashore here	30	
(12)	Coalville, Leics, Coal Aston, or Coalpit Heath	30	
(13)	Cruden Bay — Forties Field oil pipeline comes ashore here	35	
(14)	Seascale — Britain's first nuclear power station — Calder Hall	40	
(15)	Selby — site of major U.K. coalfield	40	
SLOGAN POSTMARK			
(16)	Collect through Philatelic Bureau	25	

BADGER BEER

5th OCTOBER 1977 — BLANDFORD DORSET (2)

200th ANNIVERSARY

1827 DARLEY'S 1977
150 YEARS OF PRINT
- 5 OCT 1977 (7)
BURTON-ON-TRENT STAFFS

5 OCT 77 BROAD COURT COVENT GARDEN WC2 (6)

Educational Open 5th October 1977 Port Lympne Wildlife Sanctuary (5)

(10)

Army & Navy
VICTORIA
OFFICIAL OPENING OCT. 10
5th Oct 1977 LONDON S.W.1

(1)

First Day of Issue
Dydd Cyhoeddiad Cyntaf
Bethlehem
Llandeilo Dyfed (2)
23 November 1977

COLLECT
THROUGH THE
BRITISH
PHILATELIC BUREAU (11)

COAL IS PRECIOUS SAVE IT (4)
Celebrating 101 years of Mining at South Leicester Colliery 1877-1978
JANUARY 25th 1978
ELLISTOWN • LEICESTER

OIL IS PRECIOUS SAVE IT (5)
Commemorating 25 yrs. Oil Production in the Heart of England, Leicestershire's Stathern Field, 1953-1978
JANUARY 25th 1978
MELTON MOWBRAY LEICS.

25 Jan 78 CROYDON SURREY
SEGAS a part of British Gas
Gas-the fuel for the future (7)

(14) SEASCALE 25 JA 78 CUMBRIA

West Sole Field B.P. Hall North Humberside Contribution to Britain 8 Jan 78 (9)

THE INSTITUTE OF FUEL
GOLDEN JUBILEE YEAR
25 JAN 1978 LONDON W.1 (3)

60

1st March 1978 — BRITISH ARCHITECTURE — HISTORIC BUILDINGS

9p Tower of London; 10½p Holyroodhouse;
11p Caernarvon Castle; 13p Hampton Court

		ordinary covers £	official covers £	
SPECIAL HANDSTAMPS				
(1)	First Day of Issue — Philatelic Bureau	2	—	*Post Office*
(2)	First Day of Issue — London EC	2	—	*Post Office*
(3)	Her Majesty's Tower of London 1078-1978 BF 9000 PS	4	15	*Tower of Lon*
(4)	British Architecture The British Library London WC	4	20	*BL 5*
(5)	Britain's Royal Heritage Hampton Court Palace Kingston	4	8	*BOCS 2*
(6)	Hampton Court England's Oldest Tennis Court Kingston	4	25	*S.P.*
(7)	Wells Cathedral 800th Anniversary Wells Somerset	7	15	*Cotswold (g)*
(8)	1953-1978 Stampex Silver Jubilee London SW1	5	10	*Stampex*
(9)	Portland 900th Portland Dorset	10	25	*Portland*
(10)	Northwest Genius Manchester Evening News	50	—	*n.o.c.*
ORDINARY F.D.I. POSTMARKS				
(11)	Dydd Cyhoeddiad Cyntaf, Caernarfon, Gwynedd	4		
C.D.S. POSTMARKS				
(12)	Holyrood, Edinburgh 8	30		

1st March 1978 — BRITISH ARCHITECTURE — HISTORIC BUILDINGS

Miniature Sheet

SPECIAL HANDSTAMPS				
(1)	First Day of Issue — Philatelic Bureau	4	—	*Post Office*
(2)	First Day of Issue — London EC	4	—	*Post Office*
(3)	Her Majesty's Tower of London 1078-1978 BF 9000 PS	8	20	*Tower of Lon*
(4)	British Architecture The British Library London WC	8	25	*BL 5*
(5)	Britain's Royal Heritage Hampton Court Palace Kingston	8	35	*BOCS 2d*
(6)	Hampton Court England's Oldest Tennis Court Kingston	8	—	*n.o.c.*
(7)	Wells Cathedral 800th Anniversary Wells Somerset	10	30	*Cotswold (g)*
(8)	1953-1978 Stampex Silver Jubilee London SW1	10	20	*Stampex*
(9)	Portland 900th Portland Dorset	12	—	*n.o.c.*
(10)	Northwest Genius Manchester Evening News	50	—	*n.o.c.*
ORDINARY F.D.I. POSTMARKS				
(11)	Dydd Cyhoeddiad Cyntaf, Caernarfon, Gwynedd	10		
C.D.S. POSTMARKS				
(12)	Earl's Court SW5 — venue of London 1980	30		
(13)	Holyrood, Edinburgh 8	35		

31st May 1978 — 25th ANNIVERSARY OF THE CORONATION

9p State Coach; 10½p St. Edward's Crown; 11p The Orb; 13p Imperial State Crown

SPECIAL HANDSTAMPS				
(1)	First Day of Issue — Philatelic Bureau	3	—	*Post Office*
(2)	First Day of Issue — London SW	3	—	*Post Office*
(3)	1953 Coronation 1978 The British Library London WC	4	20	*BL 7*
(4)	Cameo Stamp Centre Coronation Exhibition London WC2	4	10	*Cameo*
(5)	25th Anniv Coronation Q.E.II RAF Wattisham BF 1953 PS	4	10	*RAF Watt.*
(6)	Queen Elizabeth II 25th Anniv Coronation RHDR Hythe	4	5	*RHDR 6*
(7)	Caernarfon (depicting castle) Gwynedd	15	—	*n.o.c.*
(8)	Official Opening HRH Prince of Wales Newcastle-upon-Tyne	10	25	*Freeman Hosp.*
(9)	60th British Philatelic Fed. Congress Worthing	10	15	*B.P.F.*
(10)	Union of PO Workers 59th Annual Conference Blackpool	25	25	*U.P.O.W.*
(11)	25th Anniversary RAF Hospital Wegberg BF 1612 PS	20	20	*BFPS*
(12)	Lewis's Celebrate 21 Years in Bristol	20	20	*Lewis's*
(13)	Mint Sutton Surrey	15	25	*Mint*
(14)	The Gatwick Park Opens 16th June 1978 Horley Surrey	15	30	*G. Park Hotel*
(15)	Assoc. Dairies Benton Royal Opening Newcastle-upon-Tyne	15	—	*n.o.c.*
(16)	Visit of HRH Prince of Wales Newton Aycliffe Durham	15	25	*Newton Aycl.*
(17)	Temple of Jerusalem 1128-1978 850th Anniv Leicester	15	—	*n.o.c.*
ORDINARY F.D.I. POSTMARKS				
(18)	Windsor, Berks	10		
(19)	King's Lynn with "Estate Office Sandringham" cachet	15		

PRICES & CONDITION – PLEASE READ GENERAL NOTES

Coronation (contd.)	ordinary covers £	official covers £	
C.D.S. POSTMARKS			
(20) Buckingham Palace, S.W.1	140		
(21) Coronation Road, Halifax, West Yorks	12		
(22) Coronation Road, Wednesbury, West Midlands	15		
(23) Coronation Square, Reading, Berks	12		
(24) House of Commons, S.W.1	20		
(25) House of Lords, S.W.1	25		
(26) Queen Elizabeth Avenue, Walsall, West Midlands	12		
(27) Scone — Stone of Scone now an integral part of Coronation Chair	150		
(28) Windsor Castle, Windsor, Berks	150		

5th July 1978 — HORSES — CENTENARY OF SHIRE HORSE SOCIETY
9p Shire Horse; 10½p Shetland Pony; 11p Welsh Pony; 13p Thoroughbred

SPECIAL HANDSTAMPS

(1)	First Day of Issue — Philatelic Bureau	3	—	*Post Office*
(2)	First Day of Issue — Peterborough	3	—	*Post Office*
(3)	Horses on Stamps Exhib. Havering Park Riding School	5	15	*Havering (f)*
(4)	Tribute to the Horse Market Weighton School York	5	20	*MW School*
(5)	Horses of Britain The British Library London WC	5	20	*BL 8*
(6)	Courage Shire Horse Centre Centenary Maidenhead	5	35	*BOCS 4*
(7)	The Royal Show 1878-1978 Kenilworth Warwickshire	6	30	*S.P.*
(8)	The Sport of Kings Brighton	6	25	*B Racecourse*
(9)	Shetland Pony Stud Book Society Haroldswick Shetland	9	25	*Pilgrim*
(10)	Home of the Derby Epsom Derby	7	—	*Post Office*
(11)	World Dressage Championships Goodwood Chichester	7	25	*W Dressage*
(12)	700th Anniversary of the Cinque Ports Hythe Kent	7	9	*RHDR 7*
(13)	RNLI Clacton 1878-1978 Clacton-on-Sea Essex	6	30	*Pilgrim*
(14)	Ars Gratia Artis London W1	8	40	*MGM*
(15)	The Royal Scots Dragoon Guards 1678-1978 BF 1678 PS	10	—	*n.o.c.*
(16)	Royal Irish Rangers 10th Anniversary BF 1621 PS	10	30	*Roy. Ir. Rang.*
(17)	1978 Lawn Tennis Championships Wimbledon	20	—	*n.o.c.*
(18)	The Salvation Army International Congress Wembley	20	15(s)	*S. Army (HR)*
(19)	Sutton-on-Trent Comprehensive School Centenary Newark	15	30	*Sutton Sch*
(20)	LMSR 41st Anniv LNER Big Four Rly Museum Bournemouth	20	—	*n.o.c.*
(21)	Llangollen International Musical Eisteddfod	15	15(s)	*L.I.M. Eisteddfod*
(22)	Caernarfon (depicting castle) Gwynedd	15	—	*n.o.c.*

ORDINARY F.D.I. POSTMARKS

(23) Aberystwyth with "Welsh Pony Express" cachet on special cover	15	
(24) King's Lynn with "The Royal Studs Sandringham" cachet	25	

C.D.S. POSTMARKS

(25) Aintree, Liverpool 9 — famous racecourse	50
(26) Ascot, Berks — famous racecourse	75
(27) Blackhorse, Bristol	15
(28) Darley — "The Darley Arabian" one of the three great sires	40
(29) Godolphin Cross — "Goldolphin Arabian" — do —	40
(30) Epsom Downs, Epsom, Surrey — home of the Derby	50
(31) Great Yarmouth on Anna Sewell (Black Beauty) House cover	25
(32) Horsefair, Kidderminster, Worcs	15
(33) Lerwick — Shetland pony	18
(34) Riding Mill, Northumberland	12
(35) Shireoaks, Worksop, Notts	15
(36) Studlands, Newmarket, Suffolk, or Newmarket	25

2nd August 1978 — CYCLING CENTENARY
9p Penny Farthing; 10½p Touring Bicycles; 11p Modern Bikes; 13p Road Racers

SPECIAL HANDSTAMPS

(1)	First Day of Issue — Philatelic Bureau	3	—	*Post Office*
(2)	First Day of Issue — Harrogate	3	—	*Post Office*
(3)	BCF Centenary International Meeting Leicester Sports Centre	4	15	*City Council*
(4)	TI Raleigh Largest Bicycle Manufacturer Nottingham	4	15	*BOCS 5*
(5)	TI Raleigh Tour de France Winners 1978 Nottingham	4	6	*BOCS 5*
(6)	1953 Coronation 1978 The British Library London WC	12	20	*B. Library*
(7)	Colchester Searchlite Tattoo BF 1606 PS	20	5(s)	*C.S. Tattoo*
(8)	Self-righting Lifeboat Exhib. Science Museum London SW7	30	—	*n.o.c.*
(9)	Caernarfon (depicting castle) Gwynedd	12	—	*n.o.c.*
(10)	700th Anniversary of the Cinque Ports Hythe Kent	20	25	*RHDR 7*

Cycling (contd.)	ordinary covers	official covers
ORDINARY F.D.I. POSTMARKS	£	£
(11) Dumfries — Kirkpatrick MacMillan of Dumfries invented bicycle	25	
C.D.S. POSTMARKS		
(12) Charlbury — it was here that the Tandem Club was founded .	45	
(13) Godalming — National office of Cylists' Touring Club	45	
(14) Meriden — site of Cyclists' War Memorial..........................	45	
(15) Raleigh, Torpoint, Cornwall...	125	
SLOGAN POSTMARKS		
(16) Driver — Mind that Bike Reading, Berks	50	
(17) Driver — Mind that Bike, Sussex Coast (Brighton)..............	50	

22nd November 1978 — CHRISTMAS
7p, 9p, 11p, 13p Carols

SPECIAL HANDSTAMPS

(1) First Day of Issue — Philatelic Bureau	2	—	*Post Office*
(2) First Day of Issue — Bethlehem, Llandeilo, Dyfed..............	2	—	*Post Office*
(3) Carols for Christmas The British Library London WC.........	3	15	*BL 9*
(4) 50 Years Broadcasting Carols Kings College Cambridge	3	4	*BOCS 6*
(5) Parish of Dalgety 1178-1978 Dalgety Bay Dunfermline	3	3	*Dal Parish*
(6) London Borough of Havering Music for All Romford	3	5	*Havering (f)*
(7) History of Philately Exhibition Warwick............................	4	20	*W & W*
(8) Meet Your Post Office Dunfermline Fife	4	—	*n.o.c.*
(9) 50 Years of Rotary in Clacton-on-Sea Essex	4	15	*Rotary*
(10) The Gold of Eldorado The Royal Academy of Arts London W1	4	20	*Pilgrim*
(11) Croeso Cymru I'r Crysau Duon Cardiff	4	60	*All Blacks*

ORDINARY F.D.I. POSTMARKS

(12) Oxford — Boars Head Carol sung each year at Queens College	5	

C.D.S. POSTMARKS

(13) Boars Head, Wigan — Boars Head Carol featured on 13p value	25	
(14) Fairy Cross, Bideford, Devon	12	
(15) Fir Tree, Crook, Co. Durham	12	
(16) Hollybush, Blackwood, Gwent	10	
(17) Nasareth, Caernarfon, Gwynedd	15	

7th February 1979 — DOGS
9p Old English Sheepdog; 10½p Welsh Springer Spaniel; 11p West Highland Terrier; 13p Irish Setter

SPECIAL HANDSTAMPS

(1) First Day of Issue — Philatelic Bureau	2	—	*Post Office*
(2) First Day of Issue — London SW	2	—	*Post Office*
(3) Spillers Congratulate Kennel Club Crufts Exhib. London EC4	3	6	*BOCS 7*
(4) New Zealand The Second Pictorial Issue Exhibition Warwick......	5	15	*W & W*
(5) The Gold of Eldorado The Royal Academy of Arts London W1.....	5	20	*Pilgrim*
(6) England v. N. Ireland European Championships Wembley ...	8	2(s)	*Dawn*

ORDINARY F.D.I. POSTMARKS

(7) Battersea — Battersea Dogs Home	8	
(8) Brighton on Coral Brighton & Hove Stadium cover	20	
(9) Redhill on P.D.S.A. (Peoples Dispensary for Sick Animals) cover ...	20	

C.D.S. POSTMARKS

(10) Barking, Essex	15	
(11) Battersea Park Road — nearest P.O. to Battersea Dogs Home	30	
(12) Black Dog, Crediton	30	
(13) Dog & Gun, Liverpool 11	60	
(14) Dog Kennel Lane, Oldbury, Warley, West Midlands	75	
(15) Dogsthorpe, Peterborough	20	
(16) Hounds Hill, Blackpool, Lancs	35	
(17) Isle of Dogs, London E14	90	

21st March 1979 — BRITISH FLOWERS
9p Primrose; 10½p Daffodil; 11p Bluebell; 13p Snowdrop

SPECIAL HANDSTAMPS

(1) First Day of Issue — Philatelic Bureau	2	—	*Post Office*
(2) Royal Botanic Gardens Kew Richmond Surrey	2	20	*Botanic Gdns*
(3) Bath Floral City Exhibition...	3	4	*Cotswold (g)*
(4) Nat. Assoc. Flower Arrangers Soc. 20th Anniv St. Marys.....	3	4	*BOCS 8*
(5) Nat. Assoc. Flower Arrangers Soc. 20th Anniv Penzance	3	4	*BOCS 8*

Flowers (contd.)

		ordinary covers £	official covers £	
(6)	20th Anniv. Founders Day Bluebell Rly Uckfield E. Sussex .	3	10	*RHDR 8*
(7)	Rural Blisworth Exhibition Northampton	5	15	*Blisworth*
(8)	W.I. Canterbury Kent (Women's Institute)	5	25	*W.I.*
(9)	Egypt Postage Stamp Exhibition Warwick	5	20	*W & W*

C.D.S. POSTMARKS
(10)	Blue Bell Hill, Huddersfield, West Yorks	30
(11)	Botanic Gardens, Belfast	30
(12)	Flowery Field, Hyde, Cheshire	25
(13)	Kew Gardens, Richmond, Surrey	75
(14)	Primrose, Jarrow, Tyne & Wear	35
(15)	Spring Gardens, Lytham St. Annes, Lancs	30

SLOGAN POSTMARKS
(16)	Bath Europe's Floral City, Bath, Avon	55
(17)	21st Spalding Flower Parade 12th May 1979, Spalding, Lincs	45

9th May 1979 — DIRECT ELECTIONS TO EUROPEAN ASSEMBLY
9p, 10½p, 11p, 13p Flags of Member Nations

SPECIAL HANDSTAMPS
(1)	First Day of Issue — Philatelic Bureau	3	—	*Post Office*
(2)	First Day of Issue — London SW	3	—	*Post Office*
(3)	Strasbourg — European Assembly Leicester's Twin City	4	8	*City Council*
(4)	First British European Parliamentary Elections London SW 1	4	8	*BOCS 10*
(5)	Entente Cordiale, Stowmarket	200	100	*Stow. Tie. Com.*
(6)	National Stamp Week Europa Day Cameo Stamp Centre WC2	3	6	*Cameo*
(7)	Inst. of Gas Engineers 50 Years Royal Charter London SW	4	10	*Gas Eng.*
(8)	Worth Valley Rly Letter Service Keighley West Yorks	4	15	*W V Rly*
(9)	Lions Holiday 79 District Hayling Island Hants	6	15	*Lions*
(10)	Barbados Postage Stamps Exhibition Warwick	4	15	*W & W*
(11)	Nat. Assoc. Flower Arrangers Northern Lights Blackpool	5	5	*BOCS 8*
(12)	Derby 200 Exhibition Royal Academy W1	5	5	*BOCS 9*
(13)	British Chess Federation 1904-1979 Norwich	5	15	*Chess Fed*

ORDINARY F.D.I. POSTMARKS
(14)	Folkestone, Kent — Gateway to Europe	4

C.D.S. POSTMARKS
(15)	Blackrod, Bolton	12
(16)	Dover or Harwich — Gateways to Europe	8
(17)	House of Commons, S.W.1	20
(18)	House of Lords, S.W.1	25
(19)	Newhaven, East Sussex — Gateway to Europe	8
(19a)	Ditto with PAQUEBOT markings	12
(20)	Dieppe with PAQUEBOT markings	12
(21)	Parliament Street B.O., S.W.1	12
(22)	Weymouth, Dorset — Gateway to Europe	8

SLOGAN POSTMARKS
(23)	Are you on the Voters List — Check Now, Lincoln	475
(24)	Bath — Europe's Floral City	100

6th June 1979 — HORSE RACING
9p The Derby; 10½p Aintree; 11p Newmarket; 13p Windsor

SPECIAL HANDSTAMPS
(1)	First Day of Issue — Philatelic Bureau	3	—	*Post Office*
(2)	First Day of Issue — Epsom, Surrey	3	—	*Post Office*
(3)	Headquarters of the Jockey Club Newmarket	4	20	*S.P.*
(4)	Derby 200 Exhibition Royal Academy London W1	4	4	*BOCS 9*
(5)	Derby 200 Epsom Surrey	4	4	*BOCS 11*
(6)	England's Oldest Horse Race Kiplingcotes Mkt Weighton York	4	10	*MW School*
(7)	Derbyshire Festival Matlock	4	20	*Derbys Fest.*
(8)	Newbury Show Newbury Berks	5	5	*New. Ag. Soc*
(9)	Chigwell School 1629-1979 Chigwell Essex	6	15	*Chigwell Sch*
(10)	Nauru 1906-1942 Postal History Exhibition NPC Warwick	8	20	*W & W*
(11)	Norwich Union First Class Insurance Service Norwich	7	20	*Norwich Union*
(12)	35th Anniversary of "D" Day Southampton	6	—	*n.o.c.*
(13)	35th Anniversary D Landings Operation Neptune BF 3544 PS	6	—	*n.o.c.*
(14)	First Collection Edinburgh Eurocrest Hotel	6	35	*Euro Hotel*
(15)	First Collection Glasgow Eurocrest Hotel	6	35	*Euro Hotel*

Horse Racing (contd.)

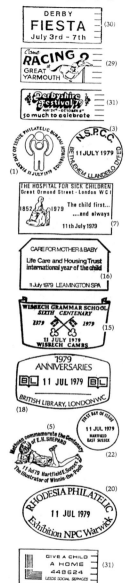

1979

	ordinary covers	official covers
ORDINARY F.D.I. POSTMARKS		
(16) Derby or Doncaster ....*each*	4	
(17) King's Lynn, Norfolk with "Royal Studs Sandringham" cachet ...	6	
(18) Liverpool	3	
(19) Windsor, Berks — Dorsett Ferry, Windsor featured on 13p value .	4	
C.D.S. POSTMARKS		
(20) Aintree, Liverpool 9 — famous racecourse	40	
(21) Ascot, Berks — famous racecourse...................................	25	
(22) Derby	15	
(23) Epsom Downs, Epsom, Surrey — famous racecourse	50	
(24) Horse Fair, Kidderminster, Worcs	15	
(25) Newmarket, Suffolk	30	
(26) Stud Farm, Polegate, East Sussex	25	
(27) Studlands, Newmarket — horse breeding & training centre.	25	
(28) Tattenham Corner, Epsom — part of Epsom racecourse	50	
SLOGAN POSTMARKS		
(29) Come Racing at Great Yarmouth.....................................	50	
(30) Derby Fiesta July 3rd-7th, Derby	50	
(31) Derbyshire Festival — Much to Celebrate	100	

11th July 1979 — YEAR OF THE CHILD
9p Peter Rabbit — Beatrix Potter; 10½p Wind in the Willows — Kenneth Grahame; 11p Winnie the Pooh — A. A. Milne; 13p Alice — Lewis Caroll

SPECIAL HANDSTAMPS			
(1) First Day of Issue — Philatelic Bureau	2	—	*Post Office*
(2) 40th Anniversary Yardley Primary School Chingford..........	7	25	*Walth. Forest*
(3) NSPCC Bethlehem Llandeilo Dyfed.................................	3	5	*BOCS Sp 1*
(4) Kent & East Sussex Rly Childrens Day Tenterden Kent	3	4	*RH 9*
(5) Methuen Commem E.H. Shephard Winnie the Pooh Hartfield....	3	6	*BOCS 12*
(6) Beatrix Potter 1866-1943 Lived in Near Sawrey Ambleside .	7	—	*Post Office*
(7) Hospital for Sick Children Great Ormonde Street London WC1...	7	—	*n.o.c.*
(8) Palitoy Diamond Jubilee 1919-1979 Leicester....................	10	150	*Palitoy*
(9) New Parks Boys School Jubilee 1954-1979 Leicester	5	15	*NPB School*
(10) Lewis Carroll Society Daresbury Warrington	6	12	*L.C. Soc*
(11) Alice in Wonderland Inspired by our town Llandudno	6	20	*Llan Town C*
(12) 1979 Year of the Child & Cub Country Year Birkenhead	5	15	*Dawn*
(13) Year of the Child Wokingham Berks	5	8	*Rotary*
(14) IYC Westminster Cathedral London SW1	6	20	*Cotswold*
(15) Wisbech Grammar School 6th Centenary 1379-1979 Wisbech.....	6	30	*Wisbech GS*
(16) Care for Mother & Baby Life Care & Housing Trust Leamington .	—	15	*LIFE*
(17) Royal Tournament 1979 BF 1979 PS	6	20	*BFPS*
(18) 1979 Anniversaries British Library London WC	6	20	*BL 10*
(19) Home International Bowls Tournament Pontypool Gwent ...	10	25	*Pilgrim*
(20) Rhodesia Philatelic Exhibition NPC Warwick	10	20	*W & W*

ORDINARY F.D.I. POSTMARKS		
(21) Edinburgh — birthplace of Kenneth Graham.....................	3	
(22) Hartfield — home of A. A. Milne	4	
(23) Oxford — Lewis Carroll spent most of his life at Christ Church	4	
(24) Stourbridge — home of Adrian Cresswell (designer of PO cover)..	4	

C.D.S. POSTMARKS		
(25) Child Okeford, Blandford Forum....................................	30	
(26) Child's Hill, London N.W.2	25	
(27) Far Sawrey, Ambleside, Cumbria — home of Beatrix Potter	40	
(28) Hartfield, East Sussex — home of A. A. Milne....................	15	
(29) Playing Place, Truro, Cornwall.....................................	30	

SLOGAN POSTMARKS		
(30) Barnardo's Care about Children — Ilford or Edinburgh	50	
(31) Give a Child a Home Leeds Social Services — Leeds	75	

Note — The date of issue was originally planned for 18th July 1979, but due to a shortage of stocks of definitive stamps at many Post Offices — resulting from an industrial dispute at the Post Office Supplies Dept. — the date was brought forward by one week, to allow these commemorative stamps to be used.

PLEASE READ THE GENERAL NOTES
AT THE BEGINNING OF THIS CATALOGUE
These often provide the answers to enquiries received.

22nd August 1979 — CENTENARY OF THE DEATH OF SIR ROWLAND HILL

10p Sir Rowland Hill; 11½p General Post c. 1839;
13p London Post c. 1839; 15p Uniform Postage 1840

	ordinary covers £	official covers £	
SPECIAL HANDSTAMPS			
(1) First Day of Issue — Philatelic Bureau	2	—	*Post Office*
(2) First Day of Issue — London EC	2	—	*Post Office*
(3) London EC Chief Office (Rowland Hill Statue)	4	—	*n.o.c.*
(4) National Postal Museum (Red Maltese Cross) London EC4	4	—	*n.o.c.*
(5) Bruce Castle Museum Tottenham N17	5	15	*Haringey*
(6) Sir Rowland Hill Kidderminster Art Gallery Wyre Forest DC	5	—	*n.o.c.*
(7) Bath Postal Museum Rowland Hill Centenary Exhib. Bath	3	5	*BP Museum*
(8) Sir Rowland Hill Commem Mail Coach Run Kidderminster	3	4	*BOCS 13*
(9) Sir Rowland Hill Commem Mail Coach Run Birmingham	3	4	*BOCS 13*
(10) Rowland Hill Centenary Commemorative Delivery Rayleigh	5	50	*Wiggins Teape*
(11) Rowland Hill 1795-1879 Coventry (some with Mailcoach cachet)	3	—	*n.o.c.*
(12) Rowland Hill 1795-1879 Stratford (some with Mailcoach cachet)	3	—	*n.o.c.*
(13) Rowland Hill 1795-1879 Warwick (some with Mailcoach cachet)	3	—	*n.o.c.*
(14) Rowland Hill First Day of Issue Kidderminster	3	—	*n.o.c.*
(15) 1979 Anniversaries British Library London WC	5	15	*BL 11*
(16) Military Tattoo Edinburgh	6	20	*M Tattoo*
(17) York Races Tote Ebor Handicap York	6	5(s)	*S.P.*
(18) Pier Centenary 1880-1980 Bournemouth	6	20	*Philatex*
(19) Skirrid Energy Drive in aid of Barnardos London SW1	6	20	*Skirrid*
(20) Haddo House & Country Park Now Open Aberdeen	6	8	*Scot N.T.*
ORDINARY F.D.I. POSTMARKS			
(21) Sanquhar — Britain's oldest Post Office	6		
C.D.S. POSTMARKS			
(22) Belsize Park B.O., N.W.3 — near to where Rowland Hill died	25		
(23) Hampstead Heath N.W.3 — near to where Rowland Hill died	18		
(24) Hampstead S.D.O., N.W.3 — near to where Rowland Hill died	18		
(25) Bruce Grove N.17 — Rowland Hill lived here at Bruce Castle	15		
(26) House of Commons, S.W.1	10		
(27) House of Lords, S.W.1	12		
(28) Kidderminster, Worcs — birthplace of Rowland Hill	7		
(29) Newhaven or Dieppe PAQUEBOT — introduced by Rowland Hill	12		
(30) Rowlands Castle, Hants	12		
SLOGAN POSTMARKS			
(31) International Stamp Exhibition Earls Court London 1980, EC	70		
(32) Datapost D — a new postal service Enfield, Middx	90		

26th September 1979 — 150th ANNIVERSARY OF THE FOUNDING OF THE METROPOLITAN POLICE FORCE

10p Local 'bobby'; 11½p Traffic Control; 13p Mounted police; 15p Police Launch on the Thames

SPECIAL HANDSTAMPS			
(1) First Day of Issue — Philatelic Bureau	2	—	*Post Office*
(2) First Day of Issue — London SW	2	—	*Post Office*
(3) New Scotland Yard Metropolitan Police	3	8	*Cotswold*
(4) Port of London Police London E16	6	75	*Port London*
(5) Devon & Cornwall Constabulary Exhibition Exeter	4	20	*D & C Const.*
(6) West Yorks Metropolitan Police 150 Years Wakefield	3	4	*BOCS 14*
(7) Sir Robert Peel Commemoration Tamworth Staffs	4	—	*n.o.c.*
(8) Royal Air Force Police Bruggen BF 1665 PS	4	25	*RAF Police*
(9) 1979 Anniversaries The British Library London WC	6	20	*BL 12*
(10) 40th Anniv Shooting First Enemy Aircraft BF 1662 PS	6	—	*n.o.c.*
(11) Zeppelin Mail Exhibition NPC Warwick	6	15	*W & W*
(12) 40th Anniversary Sir John Gielgud at Blackpool	6	20	*Blk Theatre*
ORDINARY F.D.I. POSTMARKS			
(13) Bolton & Bury on Greater Manchester Police cover	10		
C.D.S. POSTMARKS			
(14) Bow Street, Dyfed — Bow Street Runners	40		
(15) Bury, Lancs — birthplace of Sir Robert Peel	20		
(16) Constable Burton, Leyburn, North Yorks	30		
(17) Constable Road, Sheffield 14	30		

```
PRICES & CONDITION – PLEASE READ GENERAL NOTES
```

Police (contd.)

	ordinary covers £	official covers £
(18) Crook, Co. Durham	25	
(19) Hendon, N.W.4 — Police Training School	15	
(20) House of Commons, S.W.1	15	
(21) House of Lords, S.W.1 — highest court in the land	20	
(22) Law, Carluke, Lanarkshire	20	
(23) Tamworth — Home of Sir Robert Peel	10	
(24) Wapping, E.1 — headquarters of River Police (on 15p value)	25	
(25) Eynsham on. Police Training Centre — Eynsham Hall cover	20	
(26) Field Post Office 999 on North Yorks Police cover	40	

SLOGAN POSTMARKS

(27) Durham 800 Years a City (Durham prison)	60	

24th October 1979 — CENTENARY OF THE DEATH OF SIR ROWLAND HILL

Miniature sheet

SPECIAL HANDSTAMPS

(1) First Day of Issue — Philatelic Bureau	2	—	*Post Office*
(2) First Day of Issue — London EC	2	—	*Post Office*
(3) London EC Chief Office (Rowland Hill Statue)	4	—	*n.o.c.*
(4) National Postal Museum (Red Maltese Cross) London EC	4	—	*n.o.c.*
(5) Bruce Castle Museum, Tottenham N17	15	40	*Haringey*
(6) Sir Rowland Hill London & Brighton Rly Co 1845-46 Brighton	3	4	*BOCS 16*
(7) Cartoonists Club Honour Sir Rowland Hill Gatwick Airport	3	4	*BOCS Sp 2*
(8) 1979 Anniversaries The British Library London WC	4	20	*BL 11a*
(9) PUC 1929 Exhibition NPC Warwick	4	—	*n.o.c.*

ORDINARY F.D.I. POSTMARKS

(10) Kidderminster — birthplace of Rowland Hill	4	
(11) Sanquhar — Britain's oldest Post Office	6	

C.D.S. POSTMARKS

(12) Hampstead N.W.3 — P.O. near to where Rowland Hill died	12	
(13) House of Commons, S.W.1	10	
(14) House of Lords, S.W.1	12	
(15) Kidderminster, Worcs — birthplace of Rowland Hill	8	
(16) Rowlands Castle, Hants	15	

SLOGAN POSTMARKS

(17) International Stamp Exhibition Earls Court London 1980, EC	45	

22nd August & 24th October 1979 — CENTENARY OF THE DEATH OF SIR ROWLAND HILL (DOUBLE DATED COVERS)

Some double-dated covers exist with both the set of four stamps postmarked 22nd August and the miniature sheet postmarked 24th October.

		£
(1) spec. handstamp (22nd Aug) + spec. handstamp (24th Oct)	from	30
(2) appropriate CDS (22nd Aug) + appropriate CDS (24th Oct)		40

21st November 1979 — CHRISTMAS

8p, 10p, 11½p, 13p, 15p The Nativity

SPECIAL HANDSTAMPS

(1) First Day of Issue — Philatelic Bureau	2	—	*Post Office*
(2) First Day of Issue — Bethlehem, Llandeilo, Dyfed	2	—	*Post Office*
(3) Christmas The British Library London WC	3	15	*BL 13*
(4) 1954-1979 Christmas 25th Anniv After the Ball Blackpool	3	10	*Blk Theatre*
(5) RHDR Salutes Cheriton & Morehall Traders Christmas Lights	3	6	*CM Traders*
(6) Father Christmas Special Kent & E. Sussex Rly Tenterden	3	4	*RH 10*
(7) Centenary of the War Cry 1879-1979 London EC4	3	25	*H.R.*
(8) Rotary Club of Swansea Diamond Jubilee West Glamorgan	3	10	*Rotary*
(9) Year of the Child Stamp & Coin Exhibition Coventry	3	8	*D.F.*
(10) Official Naming Ceremony new Margate Lifeboat Margate	3	8	*Pilgrim*
(11) Air Mails 1920-1950 NPC Warwick	5	15	*W & W*
(12) BIPEX London SW	5	—	*n.o.c.*
(13) England v. Bulgaria Wembley	5	2(s)	*Dawn*

C.D.S. POSTMARKS

(14) Nasareth, Caernarfon, Gwynedd	25	

In addition, covers are known with the following CDS postmarks: Angel Hill, Holy Island, Kings Road, Star, Starcross, Shepherds Bush. Prices range from £6 each.

SLOGAN POSTMARKS

(15) Milton Keynes Xmas Shopping As It Should Be, M. Keynes	55	

In addition: Barnardos Cares About Children. Prices range from £30.

16th January 1980 — BRITISH BIRDS
10p Kingfisher; 11½p Dipper; 13p Moorhen; 15p Yellow Wagtail

	ordinary covers £	official covers £	
SPECIAL HANDSTAMPS			
(1) First Day of Issue — Philatelic Bureau	2	—	*Post Office*
(2) First Day of Issue — Sandy, Beds	2	—	*Post Office*
(3) 1880-1980 Essex Field Club Centenary Chelmsford	3	5	*Havering 5*
(4) Leics. & Rutland Ornithological Society 40th Year Leicester	3	10	*LFDC (t)*
(5) West Midlands Bird Club 51st Anniversary Birmingham	3	4	*P.P.S.*
(6) Wildfowl Trust Arundel West Sussex	3	4	*BOCS 17*
(7) Wildfowl Trust Washington Tyne & Wear	3	4	*BOCS 17*
(8) Wildfowl Trust Peakirk Peterborough	3	4	*BOCS 17*
(9) Wildfowl Trust Martin Mere Liverpool	3	4	*BOCS 17*
(10) Wildfowl Trust Slimbridge Gloucester	3	4	*BOCS 17*
(11) Pioneers in Bird Protection RSPB Sandy Beds	3	8	*R.S.P.B.*
(12) Hull Natural History Society Centenary Year 1880-1980 Hull	3	8	*MW School*
(13) NNT Celebrates 1880 Wild Birds Protection Act Norwich	3	4	*Markton*
(14) 10th Anniv. Cotswold Wildlife Park Burford	3	5	*Cotswold (g)*
(15) Wintertime The British Library London WC	9	25	*BL 14*
(16) The Salvation Army 100 Harwich Essex Harwich Corps	9	40	*H.R.*
(17) The Royal Image Exhibition NPC Warwick	9	20	*W & W*
(18) Queens School Rheindahlen 25 Years BF 1671 PS	9	50	*Queens Sch*
C.D.S. POSTMARKS			
(19) Fair Isle, Shetland — famous bird observatory	30		
(20) House of Commons, S.W.1 — Wild Bird Protection Act	15		
(21) House of Lords, S.W.1 — Wild Bird Protection Act	18		
(22) Sandy, Beds. — R.S.P.B. Headquarters	40		

In addition, covers are known with the following CDS postmarks: Birds Edge, Cley, Eagle, Heron Cross, Hickling, Holme, Partridge Green, Ranworth, Swallownest, Wing, Wren's Nest. Prices range from £10 each.

SLOGAN POSTMARKS

(23) Do it at the Dovecot Arts Centre (depicting dove), Stockton	250		

In addition: Collect British Stamps £20.

12th March 1980 — 150th ANNIVERSARY OF THE OPENING OF THE LIVERPOOL & MANCHESTER RAILWAY
5 × 12p 'The Rocket' and various railway carriages

SPECIAL HANDSTAMPS			
(1) First Day of Issue — Philatelic Bureau	2	—	*Post Office*
(2) First Day of Issue — Manchester	2	—	*Post Office*
(3) First Day of Issue — Liverpool	2	—	*Post Office*
(4) Great Railway Exposition Liverpool Rd. Station Manchester	3	—	*n.o.c.*
(5) Main Line Steam Trust Celebrates 150 Years Mail by Rail Leics	3	7	*LFDC (t)*
(6) Newton-le-Willows Earlstown Merseyside 150 years	3	20	*Newton 150*
(7) 80th Anniversary Rother Railway Tenterden Kent	3	10	*RH 11*
(8) The Railway Age 150th Anniversary Coventry	3	10	*D.F.*
(9) To London 1980 by Rail BF 1682 PS	4	2(s)	*R.A.F.*
(10) Havering's own Railway Celebrates 150 Years Mail by Rail	3	5	*Havering 6*
(11) Bressingham Steam Museum Diss Norfolk	3	5	*Markton*
(12) T.P.O. Exhibition Crewe	4	10	*Dawn*
(13) Manchester (sponsored by Kelloggs)	5	15	*Kelloggs*
(14) Austro-Hungarian Postal History Collection Warwick	10	15	*W & W*
(15) Volvo Diplomat Sales Consult the Experts London W1	12	50	*Volvo*
(16) LSP Ammeraal 1880-1980 Century of Service Ware Herts	12	50	*LSP*
(17) Wintertime The British Library London WC	12	30	*BL 16*
(18) Daily Mail 1980 Ideal Home Exhib. Earls Court London SW5	15	15	*Pilgrim*
(19) Codesort Comes to Manchester, OR Liverpool ....*each*	15	—	*Post Office*
C.D.S. POSTMARKS (inc. T.P.O. CANCELS)			
(20) Crowthorne Station — one of the few station Post Offices	15		
(21) Rainhill, Prescot, Merseyside — 'Rainhill Trials'	25		
(22) The Rocket, Liverpool	35		
(23) North Western T.P.O. Night Down — the most appropriate	15		
(24) Other T.P.O. (travelling post office) cancellations ....from	15		
(25) T.P.O. "A.M." postmarks — these are more rare as they have to be handed over early on the morning of the stamp issue ....from	20		
SLOGAN POSTMARKS			
(26) Liverpool to Manchester 150 Years of Mail by Rail — Manchester	30		
(27) Liverpool to Manchester 150 Years of Mail by Rail — Liverpool	30		

PRICES & CONDITION – PLEASE READ GENERAL NOTES

9th April 1980 — LONDON 1980 INTERNATIONAL STAMP EXHIBITION

50p Montage of London Buildings

SPECIAL HANDSTAMPS	ordinary covers £	official covers £	
(1) First Day of Issue — Philatelic Bureau	2	—	*Post Office*
(2) First Day of Issue — London S.W.	2	—	*Post Office*
(3) Stampway to London 1980 Cameo Stamp Centre London WC2	3	5	*Cameo*
(4) London Tourist Board Visit London 1980 Victoria London SW1	3	4	*BOCS 4*
(5) West Country-Liverpool Inaugural Flight Royal Mail Exeter	4	10	*Royal Mail Air*
(6) Manchester (sponsored by Kelloggs)	4	—	*n.o.c.*
(7) Trafalgar Square Branch Office (Nelson's Column)	6	—	*n.o.c.*
(8) G.B. Major Errors Exhibition Warwick	6	10	*W & W*
(9) Springtime British Library London WC	6	10	*BL 17*
(10) C.S./R.I.C. Annual Congress Durham	6	15	*CS/RIC*

C.D.S. POSTMARKS		
(11) Earls Court B.O., London S.W.5	40	
(12) House of Commons, S.W.1	12	
(13) House of Lords, S.W.1	15	

SLOGAN POSTMARKS		
(14) Collect British Stamps World's Greatest Hobby	30	
(15) Int. Stamp Exh. Earls Court London 1980 — Leeds MLO	45	

7th May 1980 — LONDON 1980 INTERNATIONAL STAMP EXHIBITION

50p Miniature Sheet

SPECIAL HANDSTAMPS			
(1) First Day of Issue — Philatelic Bureau (Eros)	2	—	*Post Office*
(2) First Day of Issue — Philatelic Bureau (London 1980 logo)	2	—	*Post Office*
(3) First Day of Issue — Kingston-upon-Thames	2	—	*Post Office*
(4) First Day of Issue — London SW	2	—	*Post Office*
(5) Stamps Magazine pays tribute to London 1980 Brentwood	3	—	*n.o.c.*
(6) Supersonically to London 1980 BF 7580 PS	3	8	*BOCS 20*
(7) 1880-1980 Centenary Appeal London Union of Youth Clubs	3	—	*n.o.c.*
(8) Leicester Philatelic Society Celebrates 75th Anniv Leicester	3	30	*LFDC Sp 1*
(9) London Stamp Fair London SW1	3	3	*Showpiece*
(10) Post Office Day London 1980 Int. Stamp Exhibition London SW	3	3	*PO Comm Ctr*
(11) Royal Opera House Covent Garden London WC	3	—	*n.o.c.*
(12) Warwick Penny Post Postal History Exhibition Warwick	8	—	*n.o.c.*
(13) Festival Fringe Brighton	8	—	*n.o.c.*
(14) Salvation Army 1880-1980 Belfast	8	10	*Sal Army*
(15) 25th Anniv. Freedom of Plymouth Royal Marines BF 1694 PS	8	—	*n.o.c.*
(16) Manchester (sponsored by Kelloggs)	8	—	*n.o.c.*
(17) Parish Church Anniv. 1130-1980 Hampton-in-Arden Solihull	15	—	*n.o.c.*
(18) Springtime British Library London WC	10	15	*B. Lib. 17a*

C.D.S. POSTMARKS		
(19) Earl's Court B.O., London S.W.5	45	
(20) Earl's Court Exhibition B.O., S.W.5	50	
(21) House of Commons, S.W.1	12	
(22) House of Lords, S.W.1	15	
(23) Little London, Basingstoke, Hants	20	

SLOGAN POSTMARKS		
(24) Collect British Stamps – World's Greatest Hobby, Norwich	25	

9th April & 7th May 1980 — LONDON 1980 INTERNATIONAL STAMP EXHIBITION (DOUBLE DATED COVERS)

Some double-dated covers exist with both the 50p stamp postmarked 9th April and the miniature sheet postmarked 7th May. It would be unwieldy to list all possible combinations, especially as the postmarks and covers have already been listed over. Prices range from £25.

7th May 1980 — LONDON LANDMARKS
10½p Buckingham Palace; 12p Albert Memorial;
13½p Royal Opera House; 15p Hampton Court;
17½p Kensington Palace

	ordinary covers £	official covers £	
SPECIAL HANDSTAMPS			
(1) First Day of Issue — Philatelic Bureau (Eros)	2	—	*Post Office*
(2) First Day of Issue — Philatelic Bureau (London 1980 logo) ...	2	—	*Post Office*
(3) First Day of Issue — Kingston-upon-Thames	2	—	*Post Office*
(4) First Day of Issue — London SW	3	—	*Post Office*
(5) Stamps Magazine pays tribute to London 1980 Brentwood ...	3	—	*n.o.c.*
(6) Supersonically to London 1980 BF 7580 PS	3	2(s)	*RAF Mus.*
(7) 1880-1980 Centenary Appeal London Union of Youth Clubs	3	—	*n.o.c.*
(8) Leicester Philatelic Society Celebrates 75th Anniv Leicester	3	6	*LFDC 1*
(9) London Stamp Fair London SW1	3	4	*Showpiece*
(10) Post Office Day London 1980 Int. Stamp Exhibition London SW ..	3	4	*PO Commem Cvr*
(11) Royal Opera House Covent Garden London WC	3	10	*Cotswold*
(12) Warwick Penny Post Postal History Exhibition Warwick	5	10	*W & W*
(13) Festival Fringe Brighton	6	3(s)	*Brighton FF*
(14) Salvation Army 1880-1980 Belfast	6	10	*S. Army*
(15) 25th Anniv. Freedom of Plymouth Royal Marines BF 1694 PS	6	3(s)	*R. Marines*
(16) Manchester (sponsored by Kelloggs)	6	—	*n.o.c.*
(17) Parish Church Anniv. 1130-1980 Hampton-in-Arden Solihull	6	20	*H-i-A Church*
(18) Springtime British Library London WC	6	10	*BL 18*
C.D.S. POSTMARKS			
(19) Buckingham Palace, S.W.1	80		
(20) Earl's Court — posted at the Exhibition	50		
(21) Little London, Basingstoke, Hants or Piccadilly, Tamworth ..	15		

9th July 1980 — FAMOUS PEOPLE
12p Charlotte Brontë — Jane Eyre; 13½p George Eliot — Mill on the Floss;
15p Emily Brontë — Wuthering Heights; 17½p Mrs Gaskell — North & South

SPECIAL HANDSTAMPS			
(1) First Day of Issue — Philatelic Bureau	2	—	*Post Office*
(2) First Day of Issue — Haworth, Keighley, W. Yorks	2	—	*Post Office*
(3) International Society Commemorates Mrs Gaskell Manchester ...	3	6	*Int. Society*
(4) Elizabeth Gaskell Chelsea London SW3	3	23	*Hawkwood*
(5) Leicester Writers' Club Celebrates its 27th Year Leicester	3	6	*LFDC 2*
(6) The Elms Rickmansworth Country Home of George Eliot ...	3	6	*The Elms*
(7) George Eliot Centenary Nuneaton Warwickshire	3	6	*D.F.*
(8) Dent Commemorate Charlotte & Emily Bronte Haworth ...	3	6	*BOCS 22*
(9) World's Women Christian Temperance Union Sheffield	6	—	*n.o.c.*
(10) Rush & Tompkins Golden Jubilee Swindon Wilts	6	50	*R & T*
(11) Summertime British Library London WC	6	20	*BL 19*
(12) William Shakespeare Stratford-upon-Avon Warwickshire ...	10	—	*n.o.c.*
(13) Manchester (sponsored by Kelloggs)	5	—	*n.o.c.*
(14) Channel Isles Occupation Exhibition Warwick	5	10	*W & W*
(15) Llangollen International Musical Eisteddfod Llangollen Clwyd....	5	15	*Eist 2 cvrs*
(16) The Royal Tournament Centenary 1880-1980 BF 1980 PS	5	15	*BFPS*
ORDINARY F.D.I. POSTMARKS			
(17) Altrincham with official Knutsford P.O. cachet	8		
C.D.S. POSTMARKS			
(18) Chilvers Coton, Nuneaton — birthplace of George Eliot	18		
(19) Cranford, Kettering, Northants — Mrs Gaskell's famous book	15		
(20) Haworth, Keighley, W. Yorks — home of Bronte sisters	15		
(21) Inkpen, Newbury, Berks	18		
(22) Knutsford, Cheshire — Mrs Gaskell's 'Cranford'	15		
(23) Thornton, Bradford, W. Yorks — birthplace of Bronte sisters	18		
SLOGAN POSTMARKS			
(24) Knutsford Mrs Gaskell's Cranford — An historic town, Altrincham	30		
(25) Central Library & Museum Sunderland Centenary, Sunderland ...	100		

PLEASE READ THE GENERAL NOTES
AT THE BEGINNING OF THIS CATALOGUE
These often provide the answers to enquiries received.

4th August 1980 — 80th BIRTHDAY HER MAJESTY QUEEN ELIZABETH THE QUEEN MOTHER

12p

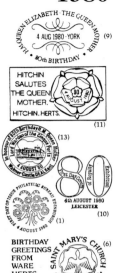

		ordinary covers £	official covers £	
SPECIAL HANDSTAMPS				
(1)	First Day of Issue — Philatelic Bureau	2	—	*Post Office*
(2)	First Day of Issue — Glamis, Forfar	2	—	*Post Office*
(3)	The Queen Mother's 80th Birthday BF 8080 PS	4	10	*BFPS*
(4)	The Queen Mother's 80th Birthday Clarence House London SW1	3	4	*Havering 11*
(5)	St. Paul's Walden Flower Festival Hitchin Herts	3	8	*Hawkwood*
(6)	St. Mary's Church 1380-1980 Birthday Greetings Ware Herts	3	15	*St. Mary's*
(7)	A Royal Birthday 1900-1980 Grand Theatre Blackpool	3	10	*Blk Theatre*
(8)	The Queen Mother's 80th Birthday Windsor Berks	3	15	*Sumner*
(9)	The Queen Mother's 80th Birthday York	3	15	*Sumner*
(10)	First Day Covers of Royalty Exhibition Leicester	3	4	*LFDC 3*
(11)	Hitchin Salutes the Queen Mother Hitchin Herts	5	—	*n.o.c.*
(12)	The Queen Mother Happy Birthday British Library WC	3	20	*BL 20*
(13)	The Queen Mother Lord Warden of Cinque Ports Walmer Deal	3	4	*BOCS 25*
(14)	The Queen Mother's 80th Birthday St. Paul's Walden Hitchin	3	15	*Sumner*
(15)	100 Years of GMT Greenwich London SE10	3	10	*GMT*
(16)	Poppy Appeal cares all year Richmond Surrey	3	6	*Poppy Appeal*
(17)	Forces Help Society & Lord Roberts Workshops London SW3	3	6	*Cotswold*
(18)	Hull Kingston Rovers RL Cup Winners 1980 Hull	3	6	*MW School*
(19)	RNLI Station Calshott 10th Anniversary Southampton	3	6	*Pilgrim*
(20)	Great Railway Exposition Liverpool Rd Station Manchester	3	—	*n.o.c.*
(21)	Paramins 50 Years 1930-1980 Southampton	5	35	*Paramins*
(22)	80th Anniversary of Rother Railway Tenterden	3	3	*RH 11*
(23)	1980 Promenade Concerts Royal Albert Hall London SW7	6	—	*n.o.c.*
(24)	Recro '80 Royal Showground Kenilworth Warwickshire	6	20	*D.F.*
(25)	Manchester (sponsored by Kelloggs)	6	—	*n.o.c.*
(26)	Anglo-Boer War 1899-1902 Exhibition Warwick	6	15	*W & W*
(27)	Rochdale Toad Lane, Posted in the Box	6	—	*n.o.c.*
(28)	British Chess Federation Congress Brighton	6	6	*Chess Fed*
ORDINARY F.D.I. POSTMARKS				
(29)	King's Lynn with "Estate Office Sandringham" cachet	10		
C.D.S. POSTMARKS				
(30)	Bowes, Barnard Castle — Bowes-Lyon is Queen Mothers family	15		
(31)	Buckingham Palace, S.W.1	110		
(32)	Glamis, Forfar, Angus — Queen Mother's ancestral home	20		
(33)	House of Commons, S.W.1	15		
(34)	House of Lords, S.W.1	20		
(35)	Mey, Thurso — Castle of Mey belongs to Queen Mother	15		
(36)	Queen Elizabeth Avenue, Walsall	9		
(37)	Windsor Castle, Windsor, Berks	130		
SLOGAN POSTMARKS				
(38)	Isle of Man Queen Mother Crowns Minted in Sutton	15		

*In addition covers are known with the following slogan pmks: Elizabethan Banquets;
Post Code It. Prices range from £20.*

10th September 1980 — BRITISH CONDUCTORS

*12p Sir Henry Wood; 13½p Sir Thomas Beecham;
15p Sir Malcolm Sargent; 17½p Sir John Barbirolli*

SPECIAL HANDSTAMPS				
(1)	First Day of Issue — Philatelic Bureau	2	—	*Post Office*
(2)	First Day of Issue — London SW	2	—	*Post Office*
(3)	Royal Opera House Covent Garden British Conductors WC2	3	10	*Cotswold*
(4)	Guildhall School of Music & Drama Centenary London EC2	3	3	*Benham*
(5)	Leicester Symphony Orchestra honour Sir Malcolm Sargent	3	6	*LFDC 4*
(6)	Famous British Conductors Bedford	3	10	*Bed Music Club*
(7)	Conductors of the Hallé Manchester	3	5	*P.P.S.*
(8)	1980 Promenade Concerts Royal Albert Hall London SW7	3	4	*BOCS 24*
(9)	50th Anniv BBC Symphony Orchestra Royal Albert Hall SW7	3	4	*BOCS 24*
(10)	Royal Philharmonic Orchestra Royal Festival Hall London SE1	3	12	*S.P.*
(11)	Anaesthesia 1980 Royal Festival Hall London SE1	3	6	*Hawkwood*
(12)	Sir Malcolm Sargent Cancer Fund for Children London SW3	3	4	*Havering 12*
(13)	Birthplace Sir Thomas Beecham St. Helens	3	15	*Th Beecham*
(14)	CBSO (City of Birmingham Symphony Orch) Diamond Jubilee	3	3	*C.B.S.O.*
(15)	T1 Commemorates CBSO Diamond Jubilee Birmingham	3	12	*C.B.S.O.*

PRICES & CONDITION – PLEASE READ GENERAL NOTES

Conductors (contd.)	ordinary covers £	official covers £	
(16) Sir Thomas Beecham Rossall School Fleetwood Lancs	4	1½(s)	Benham 'silk'
(17) Fairfield Croydon	3	8	Fairfield
(18) Manchester (sponsored by Kelloggs)	5	—	n.o.c.
(19) Summertime British Library London WC	5	25	BL 21
(20) Sponne School 550th Anniv 1430-1980 Towcester Northants	6	10	Sponne Sch
(21) National Festival of Flower Arrangement Nottingham........	6	12	NFFA
(22) Moorlands Festival Leek.....................................	5	15	Festival
(23) From Tom-Tom to Telex Exhibition NPC Warwick	6	12	W & W
(24) Sir Geoffrey De Havilland First Flight 70th Anniv Hatfield .	8	15	Mosquito Mus
(25) England v. Norway World Cup Wembley......................	10	15	Dawn
(26) Great Railway Exposition Liverpool Rd Station Manchester	10	—	n.o.c.

C.D.S. POSTMARKS

(27) Hitchin, Herts — Sir Henry Wood died here	10	
(28) Marylebone, W.1 — nearest P.O. to Royal Academy of Music	10	
(29) New York, Lincoln — Barbirolli, Conductor of N.Y. Philharmonic	10	
(30) Southampton Row B.O., W.C.1 — birthplace of Barbirolli	10	
(31) Stamford, Lincs — birthplace of Sir Malcolm Sargent	10	
(32) St. Helens, Merseyside — birthplace of Sir Thomas Beecham.....	10	

SLOGAN POSTMARK
B.P.E. Wembley. Prices range from £40.

10th October 1980 — SPORTING ANNIVERSARIES
12p Athletics; 13½p Rugby; 15p Boxing; 17½p Cricket

SPECIAL HANDSTAMPS

(1) First Day of Issue — Philatelic Bureau	2	—	Post Office
(2) First Day of Issue — Cardiff	2	—	Post Office
(3) W.R.U. Centenary Cardiff Arms Park	4	15	W.R.U.
(4) The Saints 1880-1980 Northampton............................	4	15	Saints RFC
(5) King Henry VIII Rugby Centenary Coventry	3	10	D.F.
(6) Leicester Football Club Centenary 1880-1980 Leicester	3	6	LFDC 5
(7) Norfolk County Football Assoc Centenary Season Norwich	3	4	Markton
(8) Middlesex CCC 1980 County Champions Gillette Cup NW8	3	4	Havering 13
(9) Post Office XI v Cricket Writers/Vic Lewis XI Lord's NW8 .	3	45	S.P.
(10) Centenary Tour Centenary Test 1880-1980 Lord's London NW8 ..	3	45	S.P.
(11) A Century of Tests England v Australia Kennington Oval SE11...	3	12	Hawkwood
(12) London Union of Y.C. Salutes London Sportsmen London SE5 ...	5	—	n.o.c.
(13) 100th Anniv Amateur Athletic Assoc Crystal Palace SE19..	3	4	BOCS 23
(14) 100th Anniv Amateur Boxing Assoc Wembley Middlesex...	3	6	BOCS Sp 3
(15) St. John Ambulance 1880-1980 Manchester Centre	6	15	Cotswold
(16) Autumntime British Library London WC	5	25	BL 22
(17) New Zealand Exhibition National Philatelic Centre Warwick	5	10	W & W
(18) Manchester (sponsored by Kelloggs)	6	—	n.o.c.
(19) Post Office Philatelic Centre Opened Plymouth.................	6	—	n.o.c.
(20) 10th Anniversary 1970-1980 Nearest & Dearest Blackpool .	6	15	Blk Theatre

ORDINARY F.D.I. POSTMARKS

(21) Oxford — Amateur Athletics Assoc founded here	4
(22) Rugby — Rugby Football originated here..........................	5
(23) Twickenham — English Rugby Union ground	5

C.D.S. POSTMARKS

(24) Hambledon, Portsmouth, Hants — birthplace of English cricket .	30
(25) Kennington, London S.E.11..	20
(26) Llanelli, Dyfed — one of the founding WRU members	12
(27) Marylebone B.O., W.1 — Marylebone Cricket Club (MCC) ..	25
(28) Murrayfield — Scottish Rugby Football ground..................	25
(29) Neath, West Glamorgan — Welsh Rugby Union formed here	25

In addition covers are known with the following C.D.S. postmarks: Boycott, Bowling, Box, Brecon, Lampeter, Jump, Llandovery, Rugby, The Oval, Wells. Prices range from £10.

SLOGAN POSTMARKS
Leicester Speedway. Prices range from £125.

A. G. BRADBURY
The top name in cover and postmark design.
Write for my latest colour leaflets.
3 LINK ROAD, STONEYGATE, LEICESTER LE2 3RA

19th November 1980 — CHRISTMAS

10p, 12p, 13½p, 15p, 17½p Christmas decorations

1980

	ordinary covers £	official covers £	
SPECIAL HANDSTAMPS			
(1) First Day of Issue — Philatelic Bureau	2	—	*Post Office*
(2) First Day of Issue — Bethlehem, Llandeilo, Dyfed	3	—	*Post Office*
(3) 950 Years of Worship Rejoice Waltham Abbey Essex	3	8	*Hawkwood*
(4) 1980 Christmas British Library London WC	3	10	*BL 23*
(5) The Regent Street Assoc wish you a Very Happy Christmas W1	3	3½	*Havering 14*
(6) Christmas Carols Ivybridge Devon	4	—	*n.o.c.*
(7) Merry Christmas Hollybush Ledbury Herefordshire	4	—	*n.o.c.*
(8) Norway's Christmas Gift Trafalgar Square Christmas Tree WC	3	4	*BOCS 26*
(9) Commonwealth Christmas Stamps Exhibition NPC Warwick	4	10	*W & W*
(10) Leics. Fire Service Annual Charity Appeal Leicester	3	6	*LFDC 6*
(11) Salvation Army Opening of Mount Cross Complex Bramley	8	35	*H.R.*
(12) England v. Switzerland World Cup Wembley	8	10	*Dawn*
(13) W.R.U. Centenary Cardiff Arms Park	8	15	*W.R.U.*
(14) Manchester (sponsored by Kelloggs)	10	—	*n.o.c.*

C.D.S. POSTMARKS			
(15) Bethlehem, Llandeilo, Dyfed	20		
(16) Glastonbury — first conversions to Christianity in Britain	13		
(17) Nasareth, Caernarfon, Gwynedd	15		

In addition, covers are known with the following CDS Postmarks: Fairy Cross, Holly Bush, Holly Hall, Holy Island, Ivybridge, Ivychurch, Magdalen, Star. Prices range from £8 each.

SLOGAN POSTMARKS

Shopping By Post. Prices range from £30.

6th February 1981 — FOLKLORE

14p St. Valentine's Day; 18p Morris Dancers; 22p Lammastide; 25p Medieval Mummers

SPECIAL HANDSTAMPS

(1) First Day of Issue — Philatelic Bureau	2	—	*Post Office*
(2) First Day of Issue — London WC	2	—	*Post Office*
(3) My Valentine Lover Salisbury Wilts	3	4	*Cotswold (g)*
(4) Valentines at the British Library London WC	3	25	*BL 25*
(5) Newarke Houses Museum Valentines Card Exhibition Leicester	3	13	*LFDC 7*
(6) English Folk Song & Dance Society Folk Festival London SW1	3	4	*Hawkwood*
(7) Centuries of Tradition Headington Morris Dancers Oxford	3	7	*Hawkwood*
(8) 70th Anniv Thaxted Morris Men Thaxted Essex	3	10	*Havering 15*
(9) The Dunmow Flitch Little Dunmow Essex	3	10	*Havering Sp 1*
(10) Folklore Robin Hood Society Exhibition Nottingham	3	10	*Bradbury*
(11) Radley College St. Helens School Scantour '81 Abingdon	3	15	*Radley Coll*
(12) Royal Mail Stampede Hornsea Pottery Lancaster	6	—	*n.o.c.*
(13) 70 Years of Aviation History at Hendon BF 1725 PS	8	8	*RFDC 1*
(14) Orient F.C. Centenary 1881-1981 Leyton London E10	8	15	*Hawkwood*
(15) The Victoria Cross Exhibition National Postal Museum EC1	10	—	*n.o.c.*
(16) George VI Died at Sandringham 6.2.1952 King's Lynn Norfolk	10	—	*n.o.c.*
(17) W.R.U. Centenary Cardiff Arms Park	10	20	*W.R.U.*

C.D.S. POSTMARKS		
(18) Gretna Green, Carlisle	35	
(19) Headington Quarry, Oxford (Morris Dancers)	15	
(20) Lover, Salisbury	20	
(21) Thaxted, Dunmow, Essex — the Morris Ring meet here annually	18	

In addition, covers are known with the following CDS postmarks: Bampton, Chipping Campden, Davey Place, Honiton, Padstow, Robin Hood, St. George's, Tintagel, Widecombe-in-the-Moor. Prices range from £9 each.

25th March 1981 — INTERNATIONAL YEAR OF DISABLED PEOPLE

14p Guide Dog; 18p Sign Language; 22p Wheelchair; 25p Foot Artist

SPECIAL HANDSTAMPS

(1) First Day of Issue — Philatelic Bureau	2	—	*Post Office*
(2) First Day of Issue — Windsor	2	—	*Post Office*
(3) Year of Disabled People Oaklands PH School Salford Lancs	4	20	*Oaklands*
(4) Guide Dogs Jubilee Wallasey	3	4	*BOCS (2) 2*
(5) Menphys Celebrate IYDP Leicester	3	15	*LFDC 8*
(6) MS Exeter & District Branch Exeter	4	15	*Exeter MS*
(7) IYDP Toynbee Hall D.I.G. London E1	3	4	*Havering 16*
(8) Leicestershire Committee Commemorates IYDP Leicester	3	6	*P.P.S.*
(9) Le Court: First Cheshire Home Petersfield Hants	3	10	*Cotswold*
(10) Cambridge & District Hard of Hearing 1960-1981 Cambridge	3	15	*Cam. HHA*

Disabled (contd.)

	ordinary covers £	official covers £	
SPECIAL HANDSTAMPS			
(11) Arthritis Care International Year of Disabled London SW1 .	5	50	*Arlington*
(12) RAF Headley Court Medical Rehabilitation Unit BF 1726 PS.....	3	7	*RFDC 2*
(13) Stoke Mandeville Hospital National Spinal Unit Aylesbury .	3	6	*Hawkwood*
(14) Coventry Sports Association for the Disabled Charity Walk	3	8	*D.F.*
(15) DDMC Disabled Drivers Motor Club London W3	3	10	*D.D.M.C.*
(16) The Royal British Legion Diamond Jubilee London SW1 ...	3	45	*Brit. Leg.*
(17) Stars for the Disabled Exhibition Peterborough...................	3	10	*Stars*
(18) Carters (J & A) Commemorates IYDP Westbury Wilts	6	15	*P.P.S.*
(19) Donington Park 1931-1981 Derby	4	20	*Don. Park*
(20) W.R.U. Centenary Cardiff Arms Park	4	20	*W.R.U.*
(21) Daily Mail 1981 Ideal Home Exhibition Earls Court SW5 ...	5	10	*Pilgrim*
(22) Official Opening Swansea West Glam Philatelic Counter	6	25	*Cotswold*
(23) March Philatelic Displays British Library London WC	7	20	*BL 24*
(24) Victoria Cross Exhibition National Postal Museum London EC1 .	7	—	*n.o.c.*
C.D.S. POSTMARKS			
(25) King Edward VII Hospital, Midhurst, W. Sussex................	25		
(26) Stoke Mandeville, Aylesbury — Spinal Injury Unit	25		
(27) The Orthopaedic Hospital, Oswestry, Salop	25		

In addition, covers are known with the following CDS Postmarks: Bethesda, Guide, St. Dunstans, Stoke Charity, Tredegar, Wallasey. Prices range from £8 each.

SLOGAN POSTMARKS

(28) 1981 IYDP "Can Disabled People Go Where You Go" Dumfries ..	35		
(29) 1981 IYDP St. Loyes College Exeter	50		
(30) The British Deaf Association Cares, Carlisle Cumbria	35		

13th May 1981 — BUTTERFLIES

14p Small Tortoiseshell; 18p Large Blue; 22p Peacock; 25p Chequered Skipper

SPECIAL HANDSTAMPS			
(1) First Day of Issue — Philatelic Bureau	2	—	*Post Office*
(2) First Day of Issue — London SW	2	—	*Post Office*
(3) British Butterflies Conservation Soc Large Blue Quorn Leics	4	4	*BOCS (2) 3*
(4) British Butterflies Conservation Chequered Skipper Bourton.....	4	4	*BOCS (2) 3*
(5) British Butterflies Conservation Soc Peacock Sherborne Dorset .	4	4	*BOCS (2) 3*
(6) Wildfowl Trust Slimbridge Gloucester...............................	4	4	*BOCS (2) 3*
(7) World Wide Butterflies 21st Anniv Compton House Sherborne...	4	4	*Havering Sp 2*
(8) Nottingham Trust for Nature Conservation Eakring Meadows....	4	4	*Bradbury*
(9) Margaret Fountaine Exhibition Castle Museum Norwich	4	5	*Markton*
(10) Leics. Museums Service British Butterflies Exhib. Leicester......	4	5	*LFDC 9*
(11) British Naturalist Assoc 75th Year Woodwalton Huntingdon	4	8	*Hawkwood*
(12) National Butterfly Museum Small Tortoiseshell Bramber ...	4	10	*S.P.*
(13) 40th Anniv No 20 Mtce Unit Conservamus BF 1738 PS	4	8	*RFDC 3*
(14) 25 Years Freedom 1956-1981 RAF Locking Weston-super-Mare .	5	2(s)	*RAF*
(15) National Federation of Sub-Postmasters Conf Scarborough........	5	—	*n.o.c.*
(16) Victorian Postbox Postcards First Day of Sale Liverpool......	5	—	*n.o.c.*
(17) Victorian Postbox Postcards First Day of Sale Keswick	5	—	*n.o.c.*
(18) Victorian Postbox Postcards First Day of Sale Buxton	5	—	*n.o.c.*
(19) Re-introduction of Rochdale's Unique Pillar Box Rochdale ..	5	—	*n.o.c.*
(20) May Philatelic Displays British Library London WC..........	5	20	*BL 26*
(21) Inauguration of Wood Green Shopping N22 by HM the Queen	5	10	*Havering 17*
(22) 25th Christian Aid Week Preston	6	10	*Chr. Aid*
(23) Ynys Pyr Caldey Island Tenby Dyfed Museum 81	6	10	*Caldey Isl.*
C.D.S. POSTMARKS			
(24) Peacock Cross, Hamilton..	15		
(25) Quorn, Leics — HQ British Butterflies Conservation Society	15		

In addition, covers are known with the following CDS postmarks: Castle Acre, Dousland, Kings Norton, Nettlebed, Nettleham, Spring Gardens. Prices range from £7 each.

SLOGAN POSTMARKS

(26) National Butterfly Museum First Year at Bramber, Brighton	30	

24th June 1981 — NATIONAL TRUSTS
14p Glenfinnan; 18p Derwentwater; 20p Stackpole Head;
22p Giant's Causeway; 25p St. Kilda

	ordinary covers	official covers	
SPECIAL HANDSTAMPS	**£**	**£**	
(1) First Day of Issue — Philatelic Bureau	3	—	Post Office
(2) First Day of Issue — Keswick	4	—	Post Office
(3) First Day of Issue — Glenfinnan	4	—	Post Office
(4) National Trust Derwentwater Keswick	4	4	BOCS (2) 4
(5) National Trust for Scotland Glenfinnan Inverness-shire	4	4	BOCS Sp 4
(6) National Trust for Scotland St. Kilda Western Isles	4	5	BOCS Sp 5
(7) National Trust Stackpole Head Pembroke Dyfed	4	2(s)	Benham 'Silk'
(8) National Trust Giants Causeway Bushmills Co Antrim	4	2(s)	Benham 'Silk'
(9) N.T. Leicester Sir Robert Shirley's Church Staunton Harold	4	20	LFDC 10
(10) Oakham Castle 800 Years Rutland Oakham Leics	4	8	Oakham Castle
(11) Lingholm Gardens Open Day Keswick Cumbria	5	8	Hawkwood
(12) Inst. Geog. Sciences Geology of Causeway Coast Nottingham	4	10	Bradbury
(13) Robin Hood Society Exhibition Nottingham Castle Nottingham	4	10	Bradbury
(14) St. Kilda 25 Years BF 1750 PS	4	10	BFPS
(15) The N.T. Scotland 50th Anniv Charlecote Warwick	4	10	Charlecote
(16) London International Stamp Centre Opening London WC2	5	10	Stamp Centre
(17) Lyke Wake Walk National Trust RAF Fylingdales BF 1739 PS	5	8	RFDC 4
(18) Friends of the Earth 10th Anniv 1971-1981 Olympia W14	5	5	Havering 18
(19) Jaguar Drivers Club 1956-1981 Luton Beds	5	8	Jaguar DC
(20) Crane Schools Golden Jubilee Nottingham	5	10	Crane Sch.
(21) Bygones Exhibition Holkham Hall Wells-next-the-Sea Norfolk	5	5	Markton
(22) The Lawn Tennis Museum All England Club Wimbledon SW19	5	10	Lawn Tennis
(23) 1350th Anniversary Christianity in Otley Leeds	5	8	Parish Church
(24) June Philatelic Displays British Library London WC	5	20	BL 27
(25) Scottish Council for Spastics Upper Springland Perth	5	20	Spastics
(26) Ynys Pyr Caldey Island Tenby Dyfed Museum 81	5	10	Caldey Isl.
(27) 30 Years ANTAR Service in BAOR BF 1724 PS	6	1(s)	Army
(28) Humber Bridge Hull Open to Traffic	9	—	n.o.c.

C.D.S. POSTMARKS
(29) Alfriston — clergy house was first building acquired by N.T.	10	
(30) Barmouth — it was here that the NT acquired its first site	10	
(31) Buckland Monachorum — Buckland Abbey (N.T.), home of Drake	8	
(32) Culross — castle was first building acquired by N.T. for Scotland	10	
(33) Glenfinnan, Inverness-shire, Stackpole, or Causeway Head	10	
(34) Tintagel — Tintagel PO belongs to National Trust	12	
(35) Haslemere — home of Sir Robert Hunter (founder of N.T.)	10	
(36) Lower Shiplake — birthplace of Canon Rawnsley (founder N.T.)	10	
(37) Wisbech — birthplace of Octavia Hill (founder of N.T.)	15	
(38) Land's End & John O' Groats — pair of covers	60	

SLOGAN POSTMARKS
Bluebell Railway; Gawsworth Hall. Prices range from £75.

22nd July 1981 — ROYAL WEDDING
14p, 25p Prince of Wales and Lady Diana Spencer

SPECIAL HANDSTAMPS			
(1) First Day of Issue — Philatelic Bureau	2	—	Post Office
(2) First Day of Issue — London EC	2	—	Post Office
(3) First Day of Issue — Caernarfon	2	—	Post Office
(4) Royal Wedding Celebrations Leicester	4	15	LFDC 11
(5) Royal Wedding 800th Anniv of Chingford Old Church London E4	4	6	Hawkwood
(6) Royal Wedding St. Paul's Cathedral London EC4	3	4	Havering 19
(7) Royal Wedding Stamp Exhibition Exeter	4	5	Ex Stamp Centre
(8) Royal Wedding Celebrations Cameo Stamp Centre London WC2	4	8	Cameo
(9) First Prince of Wales Proclaimed at Lincoln Cathedral Lincoln	5	30	Lin. Cath
(10) Loyal Greetings from Watton-at-Stone Hertford	5	15	Watton Church
(11) Marriage of Prince of Wales & Lady Diana Spencer Caernarfon	3	9	BOCS (2) 6
(12) Royal Wedding Greetings Canterbury	6	—	n.o.c.
(13) Canoe 81 Championships the Royal Wedding Nottingham	3	10	Bradbury
(14) The Royal Wedding RAF St. Clement Danes BF 1932 PS	4	15	RFDC 5
(15) Commemorating the Royal Wedding Althorp Northampton	4	15	Althorp

> **PLEASE READ THE GENERAL NOTES**
> **AT THE BEGINNING OF THIS CATALOGUE**
> These often provide the answers to enquiries received.

NATIONAL TRUST
LEICESTER CENTRE
Restoration of
Sir Robert Shirley's
Church
LEICESTER -24th JUNE 1981

ROBIN HOOD SOCIETY
EXHIBITION
Nottingham Castle
24th JUNE 1981
NOTTINGHAM

ROYAL WEDDING

ST. PAUL'S
CATHEDRAL
LONDON EC4
22-7-81

(9)
FIRST
PRINCE OF WALES
PROCLAIMED AT
LINCOLN CATHEDRAL IN 1301
22ND JULY 1981 — LINCOLN

Royal Wedding (contd.)

		ordinary covers £	official covers £	
(16)	Loyal Greetings from Lullingstone Silk Farm Sherborne.....	4	75	Benham L1
(17)	Royal Wedding St. Pauls London EC4 (with changeable date)	3	15	H.R.
(18)	Congratulations from East of England Show Peterborough .	4	15	S.P.
(19)	Congratulations 1931-1981 Todd Scales Cambridge	4	12	Todd Scales
(20)	The Royal Tournament BF 1805 PS	4	12	BFPS
(21)	1981-1982 Mayors Charity City of Exeter........................	4	6	Mayors Charity
(22)	Centenary Postcard First Day of Sale Cornhill P.O. Ipswich..	8	—	n.o.c.
(23)	Keswick Commemorates the National Trust	8	—	n.o.c.
(24)	South Lakeland Commemorates the National Trust...........	8	—	n.o.c.
(25)	July Philatelic Displays British Library London WC	8	20	BL 28
(26)	East Midlands CBI Council Meeting Head Post Office Leicester .	8	—	n.o.c.
(27)	Lifeboat Week 1981 Lyme Regis Dorset	8	10	Pilgrim
(28)	Ynys Pyr Caldey Island Tenby Dyfed Museum 81	8	10	Caldey Isl.
(29)	Gredington Jamboree Whitchurch Shropshire...................	20	25	Jamboree
(30)	Port Sunlight Liverpool...	8	40	Lever Bros
(31)	Windsor, Berks	9	—	n.o.c.

ORDINARY F.D.I. POSTMARKS
(32)	Chester — HRH Prince Charles is Earl of Chester..............	4	
(33)	Gloucestershire — on Highgrove House Tetbury special cover.....	4	
(34)	King's Lynn, Norfolk — on Sandringham Estate special cover	9	

C.D.S. POSTMARKS
(35)	Buckingham Palace, S.W.1	150
(36)	House of Commons, S.W.1	25
(37)	House of Lords, S.W.1	30
(38)	Prince Charles Avenue, Derby or Prince of Wales Ave Reading....	15
(39)	Princetown	15
(40)	Romsey — honeymoon started at Broadlands, Romsey........	35
(41)	Tetbury, Glos — Highgrove House.....................................	25
(42)	Windsor Castle, Windsor, Berks	175

In addition, covers are known with the following CDS postmarks: Caernarfon, Charlestown, Dartmouth, Diss, Duffus, Highgrove, Sevenoaks, Spencers Wood, St. Paul's, Trinity Street. Prices range from £8 each.

SLOGAN POSTMARKS
(43)	Prince Charles Lady Diana Isle of Man Crowns — Sutton, Surrey	25
(44)	Exhibition of Royal Pagentry TSB Hagley Hall — Dudley ...	50
(45)	Royal Westminster Exhibition in Parliament Sq. — London SW ..	70

In addition: The Pantiles. Prices range from £25.

*NOTE: Some **double dated covers** exist with 22nd July handstamp together with 29th July (Wedding Day) handstamp. Each handstamp cancelling both stamps.*   *Prices range from £12*
*In addition there were some **triple dated covers** serviced with 22nd July, 28th July (Royal Wedding Fireworks) and 29th July (Wedding Day) handstamps. Each handstamp cancelling both stamps.*   *Prices range from £15*

Doubt has arisen over the authenticity of some of these covers — particularly those which bear all London handstamps. Whilst the covers have genuine handstamps, it is understood that many were unofficially back-dated.

12th August 1981 — 25th ANNIVERSARY OF THE DUKE OF EDINBURGH'S AWARD SCHEME
14p Expeditions; 18p Skills; 22p Service; 25p Recreation

SPECIAL HANDSTAMPS
(1)	First Day of Issue — Philatelic Bureau	2	—	Post Office
(2)	First Day of Issue — London W2	3	—	Post Office
(3)	Duke of Edinburgh's Award 1956-1981 Belfast..................	3	10	Cotswold
(4)	Duke of Edinburgh's Award 1956-1981 Cardiff..................	3	10	Cotswold
(5)	Duke of Edinburgh's Award 1956-1981 Edinburgh..............	3	10	Cotswold
(6)	Duke of Edinburgh's Award 1956-1981 London EC4	3	10	Cotswold
(7)	Duke of Edinburgh's Award 1956-1981 London SW1	3	10	Cotswold
(8)	Duke of Edinburgh's Award County of Devon South Devon..	3	3	Devon DoEAS
(9)	Duke of Edinburgh's Award 85th ATC Winchmore Hill N24	3	4	Havering 20
(10)	Duke of Edinburgh's Award RAF Canadian Rockies BF 1740 PS	3	9	RFDC 6
(11)	25th Anniversary of Duke of Edinburgh's Award Hull	3	6	Hull DoEAS
(12)	Leics Girl Guides Assoc Celebrate 25th Anniv of D of E Scheme .	3	7	LFDC 12
(13)	August Philatelic Displays British Library London WC.......	4	20	BL 29
(14)	Royal Mail House Official Opening Wakefield West Yorks...	4	8	Wakefield PS
(15)	Cardiff Searchlight Tattoo BF 1747 PS	4	12	BFPS

(21)

(11)

(15)

(8)

Royal

Wedding Celebrations
22nd JULY 1981 LEICESTER

(4)

(25)

(20)

(45)

(5)

The **25th Anniversary** *of the Duke of Edinburgh's Award*
12 AUG 1981·HULL

(11)

(8)

(7)

(10)

Duke of Edinburgh Awards (contd.)	ordinary covers £	official covers £	
(16) Stoke Mandeville Hospital Games 30th Year Aylesbury Bucks....	6	10	*Hawkwood*
(17) Military Tattoo Edinburgh	6	20	*M Tattoo*
(18) Ynys Pyr Caldey Island Tenby Dyfed Museum 81	6	10	*Caldey Isl.*
(19) Keswick Commemorates the National Trust	7	—	*n.o.c.*
(20) South Lakeland Commemorates the National Trust...........	7	—	*n.o.c.*
(21) Port Sunlight Liverpool..	8	—	*n.o.c.*
(22) Royal Wedding St. Pauls Cathedral London EC4	6	25	*H.R.*

C.D.S. POSTMARKS

(23) Buckingham Palace, S.W.1	100	
(24) Pathfinder Village, Exeter..	20	
(25) Windsor Castle, Windsor, Berks	100	

In addition, covers are known with the following CDS postmarks: Calshot, Duffus, Edinburgh, Gateshead, Holyrood, House of Lords, Okehampton, Phillipstown. Prices range from £7 each.

SLOGAN POSTMARKS

(26) Duke of Edinburgh's Award Crowns Minted in Sutton — Sutton ..	25	

23rd September 1981 — FISHING
14p Cockle dredging; 18p Hauling in a Trawl Net;
22p Lobster Potting; 25p Hoisting a Seine Net

SPECIAL HANDSTAMPS

(1) First Day of Issue — Philatelic Bureau	2	—	*Post Office*
(2) First Day of Issue — Hull...	3	—	*Post Office*
(3) International Fisheries Exhibition Catch '81 Falmouth	3	10	*Catch '81*
(4) Manchester Weather Centre 21 Years Service to Fishing Ind	3	10	*Dawn*
(5) Royal Nat. Mission Deep Sea Fishermen Centenary Aberdeen....	3	4	*BOCS (2) 5*
(6) In the Heart of Scotland's Fishing Industry Buckie Banffshire	3	12	*Fish.Mut.Ass.*
(7) Fishing Fleets of Brixham South Devon............................	3	10	*Pandora Press*
(8) Leics. & Dist. Amalgamated Society of Anglers 75th Anniv.......	3	15	*LFDC 13*
(9) Centuries of Trading Billingsgate London EC3..................	3	10	*Hawkwood*
(10) Ocean Tapestry 1500th Patrol BF 1741 PS RAF St. Mawgan......	5	10	*RFDC 7*
(11) Fisherman's Year 1981 Fishmonger's Company London EC4	3	3½	*S. Petty 1*
(12) September Philatelic Displays British Library London WC	7	20	*Bl. 30*
(13) The Transporter Bridge Newport Gwent 75th Anniversary .	7	25	*Newport BC*
(14) Travelling Tram Post Office in Blackpool	7	—	*n.o.c.*
(15) Langley Slough 25 Silver Jubilee LGS Langley Grammar ...	8	10	*Langley Sch*
(16) Port Sunlight Liverpool..	8	—	*n.o.c.*

ORDINARY F.D.I. POSTMARKS

(17) Grimsby or Lowestoft — principal fishing ports	5

C.D.S. POSTMARKS

(18) Lighthouse, Fleetwood	40
(19) Six Bells, Abertillery or The Wharf, St. Ives, Cornwall	15

In addition, covers are known with the following CDS Postmarks: Crab Lane, Dousland, Eyemouth, Fisherie Turriff, Fisherow, Fisher's Pond, Fishpool, Fishguard, Fleetwood, The Harbour, Hull, Milford Haven, Stafford, St. Peter's St., The Salmon Leap, Whale Hill, Whiting Bay. Prices range from £7 each.

SLOGAN POSTMARKS

(20) Hastings — A resort for all seasons (depicts boat)	50

18th November 1981 — CHRISTMAS
11½p, 14p, 18p, 22p, 25p Childrens Paintings

SPECIAL HANDSTAMPS

(1) First Day of Issue — Philatelic Bureau	2	—	*Post Office*
(2) First Day of Issue — Bethlehem, Llandeilo, Dyfed	3	—	*Post Office*
(3) Children First Canterbury Kent	3	4	*BOCS (2) 8*
(4) Children's Christmas Book Show Blackwells Oxford..........	3	12	*Hawkwood*
(5) Assoc of Friends of Leicester Cathedral Merry Christmas...	3	15	*LFDC 14*
(6) Christmas 1981 Church of St. Mary-at-Hill London EC3 ...	3	7	*S. Petty 2*
(7) Greetings from Stamp Magazine Link House Croydon Surrey	3	1(s)	*Benham 'silk'*
(8) Very Happy Xmas from Big C Appeal Norwich Norfolk	3	8	*Big C Appeal*
(9) Seasons Greetings to Princess of Wales Regent St. London W1 ...	3	4	*Havering 22*
(10) Pillar Box Postcards — First Day of Sale Preston	3	—	*n.o.c.*

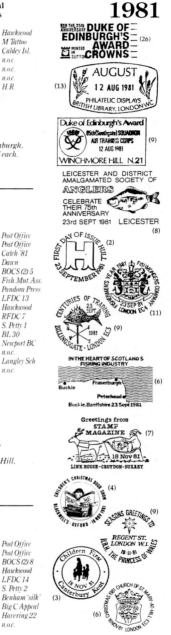

1981 Christmas (contd.)

	ordinary covers £	official covers £	
(11) Pillar Box Postcards — First Day of Sale Oldham	4	—	*n.o.c.*
(12) Pillar Box Postcards — First Day of Sale Manchester	4	—	*n.o.c.*
(13) Pillar Box Postcards — First Day of Sale Blackpool	4	—	*n.o.c.*
(14) November Philatelic Displays British Library	7	20	*BL 31*
(15) Manchester (sponsored by Kelloggs)	7	8	*Kelloggs*
(16) England v. Hungary World Cup Xmas 1981 Wembley	7	10	*Dawn*
(17) Port Sunlight Liverpool	7	—	*n.o.c.*

C.D.S. POSTMARKS

(18) Bethlehem, Llandeilo, Dyfed	12	
(19) Nasareth, Gwynedd	8	
(20) Rhoose, Glamorgan; Ramridge, Luton; Clutton, Bristol; Horsham; Fulwood, Preston — homes of stamp designers ....each	6	

In addition, covers are known with the following CDS Postmarks: Angel Hill, Holy Island, Kings Road, Star, Starcross, St. Nicholas, Trinity. Prices range from £5 each.

10th February 1982 — CHARLES DARWIN
15½p Giant Tortoises; 19½p Iguanas; 26p Finch; 29p Skulls

SPECIAL HANDSTAMPS

(1) First Day of Issue — Philatelic Bureau	2	—	*Post Office*
(2) First Day of Issue — Shrewsbury	2	—	*Post Office*
(3) Darwin Centenary RSPB Protects Wild Birds, Sandy Beds	3	5	*R.S.P.B.*
(4) Maer Hall Tribute to Charles Darwin, Newcastle Staffs	4	40	*Maer Hall*
(5) Charles Darwin 1809-1882 Slimbridge, Gloucester	3	4	*BOCS(2)9*
(6) Charles Darwin 1809-1882 Cambridge	3	4	*BOCS(2)9*
(7) Charles Darwin 1809-1882 Shrewsbury	3	4	*BOCS(2)9*
(8) Down House The Charles Darwin Memorial, Downe Orpington	3	4	*S. Petty 3*
(9) Charles Darwin Westminster Abbey London SW1	3	6	*Hawkwood*
(10) The Voyage of HMS Beagle 150th Anniversary, Plymouth	3	4	*BLS 1*
(11) Charles Darwin Centenary Man of Vision London SW7	3	6	*Havering 23*
(12) HMS Beagle 150th Anniv of the Great Voyage BF 1762 PS	3	7	*RFDC 9*
(13) 1809-1882 Charles Darwin Centenary London NW1	4	18	*London Zoo*
(14) Leicester University Jubilee Year 1981-82 Leicester	7	10	*LFDC 15*
(15) February Philatelic Displays British Library London WC	7	20	*BL 32*
(16) Valentines at Harrods London SW1	6	20	*Pilgrim*
(17) Manchester (sponsored by Kelloggs)	8	—	*n.o.c.*
(18) Port Sunlight, Liverpool	8	—	*n.o.c.*

C.D.S. POSTMARKS

(19) Downe, Orpington, Kent — Darwin's home (he also died here)	12	
(20) Frankwell, Shrewsbury — nearest P.O. to Darwin's birthplace	30	
(21) The Lizard, Cornwall — lizards featured on 19½p value	15	

In addition, covers are known with the following CDS postmarks: Atcham, Falmouth, Frog Island, Oxford, Piltdown, Sandown, Shrewsbury, Slimbridge, Stonehouse (Plymouth), Whipsnade. Prices range from £7 each.

24th March 1982 — YOUTH ORGANISATIONS
15½p Boys' Brigade; 19½p Girls' Brigade; 26p Scouts; 29p Girl Guides

SPECIAL HANDSTAMPS

(1) First Day of Issue — Philatelic Bureau	2	—	*Post Office*
(2) First Day of Issue — Glasgow	2	—	*Post Office*
(3) First Day of Issue — London SW	2	—	*Post Office*
(4) Scouts Anniversary St. Mary's 8th Hendon London NW4	3	5	*Havering 24*
(5) The Year of the Scout Celebrations, Peterborough	3	10	*Petch. Scouts*
(6) Lord Baden Powell Memorial Westminster Abbey, London SW1	3	4	*Hawkwood*
(7) Loughborough District Celebrate Year of Scout Loughborough	3	8	*Loughb. Scouts*
(8) 1982 Year of Scout British Movement W. Europe BF 1742 PS	3	8	*Forces*
(9) 75th Anniversary of Scouting, Glasgow	3	8	*Glasgow Scouts*
(10) Scouting for Boys by BP — Baden-Powell House London SW7	3	8	*Scouts Council*
(11) 75th Anniversary of Scouting 1907-1982 Caterham Surrey	3	10	*Cat'm Scouts*
(12) The Girls Brigade London SW6	3	7	*BOCS(2)10b*
(13) Girl Guides Association London SW1	3	10	*Cotswold*
(14) First for Boys London SW6	3	7	*BOCS(2)10a*
(15) Youth Organisations Young Enterprise Folkestone Kent	3	10	*S. Kent Coll.*
(16) National Association of Youth Clubs 70th Anniversary Leicester	3	20	*Bradbury*
(17) Eighteen in '82 National Youth Bureau Leicester	3	9	*LFDC 16*
(18) 1982 (Huyton) Sqd ATC 40th Anniversary BF 5282 PS	8	8	*RFDC 10*

PRICES & CONDITION – PLEASE READ GENERAL NOTES

Youth (contd.)

		ordinary covers £	official covers £	
(19)	Youth Activities St. Donats Castle Llantwit Major S. Glamorgan .	8	10	*S. Petty 4*
(20)	Yorkshire County Bowling Assoc. 50th Anniv. Youth Sport, York .	8	10	*Yorks CBA*
(21)	Opening of Motorway Sub Post Office Rank M6 Forton, Lancaster	8	35	*Rank M6*
(22)	First Postbus in Yorkshire Masham Ripon Harrogate N. Yorks	8	—	*n.o.c.*
(23)	Four Marks Golden Jubilee Four Marks Alton Hants...........	8	20	*Four Marks PO*
(24)	March Philatelic Displays British Library London WC........	8	20	*BL 33*
(25)	Norwich Union Royal Mail Coach to Rayleigh — Norwich	8	10	*Norwich Un.*
(26)	Daily Mail 1982 Ideal Home Exhibition Earls Court SW5	8	10	*Pilgrim*
(27)	Manchester (sponsored by Kelloggs)	8	—	*n.o.c.*
(28)	Port Sunlight, Liverpool..	8	—	*n.o.c.*

C.D.S. POSTMARKS

(29)	Bentley, Farnham, Surrey — home of Baden-Powell...........	9
(30)	Euston Centre B.O. — nearest P.O. birthplace Baden-Powell	6
(31)	Fleur-de-lis, Blackwood, Gwent — the scout's emblem	75
(32)	Guide, Blackburn, Lancs	15
(33)	Pathfinder Village, Exeter, Devon	20
(34)	The Camp, St. Albans, Herts	12
(35)	West Hampstead, London NW — location of guide on 29p value ..	15

In addition, covers are known with the following CDS postmarks: Chingford, Pinkneys Road, Poole, Sandbanks, Scouthead, coul Hill, Thurso. Prices range from £6 each.

SLOGAN POSTMARKS

(36)	Scouts help others — Chingford, London E4 (Gilwell Park)..	15
(37)	Scouts help others — London SW1 (HQ of scouts and guides)	15
(38)	Scouts help others — used at other offices	12

28th April 1982 — BRITISH THEATRE

15½p Ballet; 19½p Harlequin; 26p Drama; 29p Opera

SPECIAL HANDSTAMPS

(1)	First Day of Issue — Philatelic Bureau	2	—	*Post Office*
(2)	First Day of Issue — Stratford-upon-Avon	2	—	*Post Office*
(3)	John Gay 250th Death Anniv Westminster Abbey London SW1 ..	3	5	*Hawkwood*
(4)	50th Anniversary Royal Shakespeare Theatre, Stratford	3	7	*BOCS (2) 11*
(5)	250th Anniv Royal Opera House Covent Garden London WC	3	4	*BLS 3*
(6)	Arts Theatre Cambridge 1936-82	3	15	*Arts Theatre*
(7)	Theatre Royal Bath Restoration Project, Bath	3	15	*Cotswold*
(8)	Queens Theatre Stamp Exhibition Hornchurch Essex	3	7	*Havering 25*
(9)	Tavistock Repertory Co London N1 Golden Jubilee 1932-1982 ...	3	10	*Tav. Rep.*
(10)	Leicester Drama Society Diamond Jubilee 1922-1982 Leicester ..	3	45	*LFDC 17*
(11)	Theatre Royal 225 Years Norwich Norfolk	3	20	*Th. Royal*
(12)	Mercury Theatre Tenth Anniversary Colchester Essex........	3	15	*Mercury Th.*
(13)	Shakespeare Memorial at Southwark Cathedral London SE1	3	5	*S. Petty 5*
(14)	New Theatre Hull 150th Anniv. of our Historic Building Hull	3	15	*New Theatre*
(15)	Worthing Operatic Society Founded 1902 Worthing W. Sussex ...	3	15	*S.P.*
(16)	Barbican Centre where the Arts come to life London EC2	3	40	*Barbican*
(17)	S.C.D.A. Golden Jubilee Festival Final Pitlochry Perthshire........	3	8	*S.C.D.A.*
(18)	Theatr Clwyd Ebrill Yr Wyddgrug Mold Clwyd....................	6	—	*n.o.c.*
(19)	William Shakespeare Stratford-upon-Avon, Warwicks	10	—	*n.o.c.*
(20)	The Royal Air Force Central Band 62nd Anniv BF 1773 PS........	8	8	*RFDC 11*
(21)	Centenary 1882-1982 British Forces Postal Service BF 8282 PS ..	8	10	*Forces*
(22)	Army Bag (Post Office at War Exhib) National Postal Museum ...	8	—	*n.o.c.*
(23)	The Rating & Valuation Association 1882-1982 London SW1 ...	8	18	*Bradbury*
(24)	Centenary of Queen Victoria's Visit of Epping Forest London E4 .	8	5	*Hawkwood*
(25)	Manchester (sponsored by Kelloggs)	10	—	*n.o.c.*
(26)	Port Sunlight, Liverpool..	10	—	*n.o.c.*

C.D.S. POSTMARKS

(27)	Barnstaple, Devon — birthplace of John Gay	6
(28)	Ben Jonson Road, London E1	7
(29)	Great Yarmouth — site of first theatre..........................	10
(30)	Shakespeare Street, Padham, Burnley, Lancs	5
(31)	Stratford-upon-Avon...	6
(32)	The Harlequin, Radcliffe-on-Trent — harlequin on 19½p value ...	10

In addition, covers are known with the following CDS postmarks: Aldeburgh, Amesbury, Barbican, Bishopgate, Blackfriars, Broadway, Globe Road, Hereford, Macduff, Shoreditch, Stafford, The Circle. Prices range from £6 each.

SLOGAN POSTMARKS

(33)	Eden Court, Inverness — The Theatre of the Highlands......	25
(34)	Dickens Festival — Rochester 3rd-6th June	75

In addition: Dunfermline Abbey Festival; Congleton Carnival. Prices range from £60.

16th June 1982 — MARITIME HERITAGE

15½p Henry VIII/Mary Rose; 19½p Admiral Blake/Triumph;
24p Lord Nelson/HMS Victory; 26p Lord Fisher/HMS Dreadnought;
29p Viscount Cunningham/HMS Warspite

	ordinary covers £	official covers £	
SPECIAL HANDSTAMPS			
(1) First Day of Issue — Philatelic Bureau	3	—	*Post Office*
(2) First Day of Issue — Portsmouth	3	—	*Post Office*
(3) Birthplace of Horatio Nelson, Burnham Thorpe, King's Lynn	5	8	*Hawkwood*
(4) National Maritime Museum, Greenwich London SE10	5	4	*BLS 4*
(5) Lloyds Register of Shipping London EC3	5	8	*S. Petty 6*
(6) Over 250 Years of Maritime Heritage Lloyds of London, EC3	5	10	*Cotswold*
(7) Britannia's Maritime Heritage Dartmouth South Devon	5	25	*B.R.N.C.*
(8) National Maritime Heritage Year Stamp Exhibition Exeter	5	7	*Exeter Crs*
(9) Maritime England Year Poole Dorset	5	20	*Poole Mar Tr*
(10) Nottinghamshire Lifeboat Appeal Nottingham	5	10	*Pilgrim*
(11) Axe Valley Maritime 82 Seaton Devon	5	12	*Fire Ser NBF*
(12) Weymouth & Portland Chamber of Commerce Dorset	5	15	*Ch. of Comm.*
(13) 180th Anniv of Capt Matthew Flinders Discovery Port Lincoln	5	25	*Lincoln Cath 2*
(14) Captain Cook's Endeavour Salutes Nelson's Victory Whitby	5	6	*B. Travers*
(15) Royal Mail Maritime Heritage Cruise Penarth South Glamorgan	5	6	*Post Office*
(16) Maritime England Year Stratford The Missions to Seamen	5	20	*Eng. T. Board*
(17) Historic Ships Collection St. Katherines Dock E1	5	8	*Havering 26*
(18) Missions to Seamen Serving Seafarers Since 1856 Portsmouth	5	20	*S.P.*
(19) Cinque Ports Exhibition, Dover Kent	5	10	*Cinque Ports*
(20) The Mountbatten Memorial Trust Broadlands Romsey	5	4	*S. Petty 7*
(21) Leicester Sea Cadets Maritime Heritage Year Leicester	5	20	*LFDC 18*
(22) 35th Anniversary Formation RAF Marine Branch BF 1779 PS	10	10	*RFDC 12*
(23) Peru Joint Services Hovercraft Expedition BF 1956 PS	10	10	*Forces*
(24) Worshipful Co. of Shipwrights Bicentenary of Grant of Livery EC	10	7	*BOCS (2) 12*
(25) Army Bag (Post Office at War Exhib) National Postal Museum	10	—	*n.o.c.*
(26) Centenary 1882-1982 British Forces Postal Service BF 8282 PS	10	10	*Forces*
(27) Trafalgar Square Philatelic Counter (Nelson's Column)	12	—	*n.o.c.*
(28) Philatelic Counter Official Opening Coventry	12	—	*n.o.c.*
(29) Royal Shakespeare Co at the Barbican Centre London EC2	12	30	*Barbican*
(30) Ynys Pyr Caldey Island Tenby Dyfed Pope John Paul Wales 1982	12	20	*Caldey Isl.*
(31) Manchester (sponsored by Kelloggs)	10	—	*n.o.c.*
C.D.S. POSTMARKS			
(32) Bridgwater — birthplace of Blake	7		
(33) Buckingham Palace, S.W.1	65		
(34) Burnham Thorpe, King's Lynn — birthplace of Horatio Nelson	14		
(35) Castle Rd, Southsea — where Henry VIII saw Mary Rose sink	14		
(36) Devonport, Plymouth	25		
(37) Falkland	12		
(38) Flotta, Orkney — Scapa Flow (anchorage of Home Fleet)	11		
(39) F.P.O. — Fleet Mail Office Portsmouth or Devonport	35		
(40) Greenwich, London S.E.10	10		
(41) House of Lords, SW1	15		
(42) Marazion (birthplace of Sandy Woodward)	25		
(43) Naval Barracks, Chatham	12		
(44) Nelson, Portsmouth	10		
(45) The Quarterdeck, Millwall E.14	13		
(46) Trafalgar	10		
(47) Victory Street, Devonport	8		
(48) Westward Ho!, Bideford, Devon	8		

In addition, covers are known with the following CDS Postmarks: Blakes Corner, Blake Street,
Bridgwater, Britannia, The Chart, Clyde Submarine Base, Cunningham Crescent, Dartmouth,
Deptford High Street, The Docks (Bridgwater), Fleet, Henry St., Marton-in-Cleveland, Nelson
(Lancs), Portsmouth, Portsmouth Dock Yard, St. Andrews Cross (Plymouth), Tavistock.
Prices range from £8 each.

SLOGAN POSTMARKS

(49) See the Spectacular Tall Ships in Southampton	25
(50) Maritime Bristol The Start of Many an Adventure this Summer	45
(51) Tower Bridge Open to the Public — London E.C.	55

1988 SPORTS

Lawn Tennis official cover

Amateur Gymnastics official cover

Wimbledon CDS

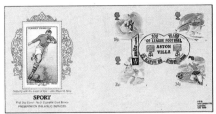

Aston Villa special handstamp

Manchester United official cover

Liverpool F.C. official cover

Wolverhampton Wanderers official cover

Preston North End official cover

Arsenal official cover

Tottenham Hotspur official cover

These "money off" vouchers are a special promotion for this edition, which if successful may be repeated in future yea
For addresses of participating dealers, please refer to their advertisements.

CONDITIONS

(1) Each voucher can only be redeemed once, i.e. vouchers will **NOT** be accepted from the purchase of a second catalo
(2) Photocopies will **NOT** be accepted

DEDUCT **£2** THE NEXT TIME YOU SPEND £25 OR MORE WITH

Peter Middleton

PLEASE INCLUDE VOUCHER
WITH YOUR ORDER
For Conditions
See Above

DEDUCT **£2**
NEXT TIME
SPEND £25
MORE W

*Daw
Cover*

PLEASE INCLUDE V(
WITH YOUR OR
For Conditio
See Above

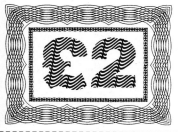

DEDUCT **£2** THE NEXT TIME YOU SPEND £25 OR MORE WITH

West End Stamp Co.

PLEASE INCLUDE VOUCHER
WITH YOUR ORDER
For Conditions
See Above

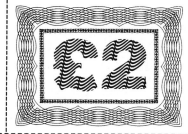

DEDUCT **£2**
NEXT TIME
SPEND £25
MORE WI

*Steve
Scott*

PLEASE INCLUDE V(
WITH YOUR OR
For Conditio
See Above

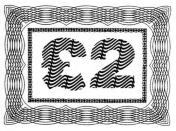

DEDUCT **£2** THE NEXT TIME YOU SPEND £25 OR MORE WITH

Mark Grimsley

PLEASE INCLUDE VOUCHER
WITH YOUR ORDER
For Conditions
See Above

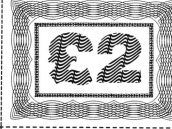

DEDUCT **£2**
NEXT TIME
SPEND £25
MORE WI

*John (
Rice*

PLEASE INCLUDE V(
WITH YOUR ORI
For Conditio
See Above

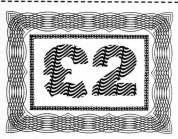

DEDUCT **£2** THE NEXT TIME YOU SPEND £25 OR MORE WITH

Brian Reeve

PLEASE INCLUDE VOUCHER
WITH YOUR ORDER
For Conditions
See Above

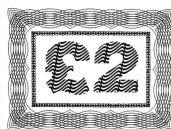

DEDUCT **£2**
NEXT TIME
SPEND £25
MORE WI

*London
Stamp*

PLEASE INCLUDE V(
WITH YOUR ORI
For Conditio
See Above

DEDUCT **£2** THE NEXT TIME YOU SPEND £25 OR MORE WITH

Sajal Philatelics

PLEASE INCLUDE VOUCHER
WITH YOUR ORDER
For Conditions
See Above

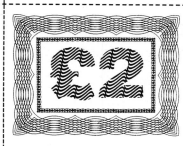

DEDUCT **£2**
NEXT TIME Y
SPEND £25
MORE WI

*Greenbe
& Port*

PLEASE INCLUDE V(
WITH YOUR ORI
For Conditio
See Above

DEDUCT **£5** THE
NEXT TIME YOU
SPEND £50 OR
MORE WITH

*Sajal
Philatelics*

PLEASE INCLUDE VOUCHER
WITH YOUR ORDER
For Conditions
See Above

DEDUCT **£5** THE
NEXT TIME YOU
SPEND £50 OR
MORE WITH

*London Rd.
Stamps*

PLEASE INCLUDE VOUCHER
WITH YOUR ORDER
For Conditions
See Above

DEDUCT **£5** THE
NEXT TIME YOU
SPEND £50 OR
MORE WITH

*Brian
Reeve*

PLEASE INCLUDE VOUCHER
WITH YOUR ORDER
For Conditions
See Above

DEDUCT **£5** THE
NEXT TIME YOU
SPEND £50 OR
MORE WITH

*John G.
Rice*

PLEASE INCLUDE VOUCHER
WITH YOUR ORDER
For Conditions
See Above

DEDUCT **£5** THE
NEXT TIME YOU
SPEND £50 OR
MORE WITH

*Breedon
Covers*

PLEASE INCLUDE VOUCHER
WITH YOUR ORDER
For Conditions
See Above

DEDUCT **£5** THE
NEXT TIME YOU
SPEND £50 OR
MORE WITH

*Mark
Grimsley*

PLEASE INCLUDE VOUCHER
WITH YOUR ORDER
For Conditions
See Above

DEDUCT **£5** THE
NEXT TIME YOU
SPEND £50 OR
MORE WITH

*Greenberg
& Porter*

PLEASE INCLUDE VOUCHER
WITH YOUR ORDER
For Conditions
See Above

DEDUCT **£5** THE
NEXT TIME YOU
SPEND £50 OR
MORE WITH

Rushstamps

PLEASE INCLUDE VOUCHER
WITH YOUR ORDER
For Conditions
See Above

DEDUCT **£5** THE
NEXT TIME YOU
SPEND £50 OR
MORE WITH

*Dawn
Covers*

PLEASE INCLUDE VOUCHER
WITH YOUR ORDER
For Conditions
See Above

DEDUCT **£5** THE
NEXT TIME YOU
SPEND £50 OR
MORE WITH

*Peter
Middleton*

PLEASE INCLUDE VOUCHER
WITH YOUR ORDER
For Conditions
See Above

1988 TRANSPORT & COMMUNICATIONS

'Jessop Collection' official cover

RMS 'Queen Elizabeth' handstamp

'Fools Play on Railway Lines' slogan

Garden Festival CDS

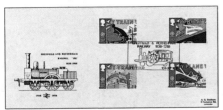

Sheffield & Rotherham official cover

Spilsby Post Box official cover

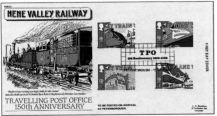

Nene Valley Railway official cover

NPM 'Railways & the Post' handstamp

Fleet Air Arm Museum official cover

Cunard official cover

23rd July 1982 — BRITISH TEXTILES

15½p 'Strawberry Thief' (Morris); 19½p 'Scarlet Tulips' (Steiner);
26p 'Cherry Orchard' (Nash); 29p 'Chevrons' (Foster)

(2)

	ordinary covers £	official covers £	
SPECIAL HANDSTAMPS			
(1) First Day of Issue — Philatelic Bureau	3	—	*Post Office*
(2) First Day of Issue — Rochdale	3	—	*Post Office*
(3) William Morris Exhibition Water House Lloyd Park London E17	4	8	*Hawkwood*
(4) Sir Richard Arkwright 250th Anniv Arkwright House Preston	4	5	*BOCS (2) 13*
(5) Hockley Mill World's First Mechanised Cotton Mill Nottingham	4	6	*Cotswold (g)*
(6) The Textile Institute 1910-1982 Manchester	4	6	*Pilgrim*
(7) School of Textiles 99 Years in Leicester	4	50	*Bradbury*
(8) Textile Exhibition Bradford Industrial Museum Bradford	4	6	*Peter Scot*
(9) Leek Centre of Textile Industry Leek Staffs	4	15	*Staffs C.C.*
(10) Polytechnic Huddersfield Textile Design Education Huddersfield	4	12	*Hudd. Poly*
(11) Textiles on Stamps Exhibition at Liberty Regent Street W1	4	5	*Benham 'silk'*
(12) Coldharbour Mill Uffculme — Cullompton Devon	4	12	*Coldhbr. Mill*
(13) Leicester & District Knitting Industry Association Leicester	4	50	*LFDC 19*
(14) Royal School of Needlework 25 Princes Gate London SW7	4	5	*S. Petty 8*
(15) 60th Anniversary No. 2 Squadron RAF Regiment BF 1781 PS	6	8	*RFDC 13*
(16) 1732-1982 Arkwright Anniv Cromford Mills Matlock Derby	4	8	*Ark. Soc.*
(17) British Philatelic Federation 64th Congress Southampton	6	6	*B.P.F.*
(18) European Floral City 1981/82 Exeter	6	10	*Exeter C.C.*
(19) Centenary British Forces Postal Service BF 8282 PS	7	10	*Forces*
(20) BAE (Post Office at War Exhibition) National Postal Museum	7	—	*n.o.c.*
(21) Travelling Tram Post Office in Blackpool	8	10	*Blackpool*
(22) Papal Visits in Philately Westminster Cathedral Hall SW1	8	10	*Bradbury*
(23) Royal Tournament BF 1840 PS	8	10	*Forces*
(24) International Scout Camp Blair Atholl Pitlochry	8	8	*Scot Scouts*
(25) Life Boat Week 1982 Lyme Regis Dorset	8	10	*Pilgrim*
(26) The First Ever Open Days 1982 RNLI HQ Poole Dorset	8	10	*Pilgrim*
(27) Ynys Pyr Caldey Island Tenby Dyfed Pope John Paul Wales 1982	10	10	*Caldey Isl.*

(3) 1943 ... 1982

HOCKLEY MILL (13)

C.D.S. POSTMARKS

(28) Cherry Orchard, Worcester — 'Cherry Orchard' featured on 26p	5	
(29) Forest Rd. Walthamstow E17 — birthplace of Wm. Morris	9	
(30) Hall-ith-Wood (later named Spinning Mule)	12	
(31) Hammersmith W6 — London home of Wm. Morris	7	
(32) Preston, Lancs — birthplace of Richard Arkwright	8	
(33) Silk Street, Paisley, Renfrewshire	7	
(34) Stanhill — birthplace of James Hargreaves ('Spinning Jenny')	15	
(35) Walthamstow B.O. E17 — birthplace of Wm. Morris	7	

(16)

(5)

In addition, covers are known with the following CDS Postmarks: All Saints (Derby), Arkwright Town, Axminster, Bobber's Mill, Coggeshall, Cotton Tree, Draperstown, Fair Isle, Harris, Lechlade, Merton, Milltown, New Invention, Shaftesbury, Tweed Road, Weaver Lodge, Wilton, Wool, Worstead. Prices range from £6 each.

SLOGAN POSTMARKS

Collect British Stamps, Hull. Prices from £10.

(10)

(22)

8th September 1982 — INFORMATION TECHNOLOGY

15½p History of Communications; 26p Technology Today

SPECIAL HANDSTAMPS

(1) First Day of Issue — Philatelic Bureau	2	—	*Post Office*
(2) First Day of Issue — London WC	2	—	*Post Office*
(3) 2nd Anniversary Intelpost Head Post Office London E1	3	5	*Hawkwood*
(4) Computertown Croydon Surrey	3	7	*Croy. Lib.*
(5) ITY — The National Electronics Centre — World Trade Centre	3	3	*Havering 28*
(6) Information Technology Year Bedford	3	7	*Texas Instr.*
(7) 10th Anniv. RAF Supply Centre BF 1787 PS	3	6	*RFDC 14*
(8) Best of Prestel 1st Year P.O. Research Centre Martlesham	3	4	*Prestel*
(9) 25 Years of Artificial Earth Satellites — Jodrell Bank Macclesfield	3	4	*BLS 6*
(10) Information Technology Year UMIST Manchester	3	5	*BOCS (2) 14*
(11) University of Leicester Celebrates Information Tech Leicester	3	25	*LFDC 20*
(12) Ashville College Joins the Computer Age Exhibition Harrogate	5	—	*n.o.c.*
(13) Centenary British Forces Postal Service BF 8282 PS	6	7	*Forces*
(14) Centenary Celebrations Exercise British Prince 82 BF 1882 PS	6	7	*Forces*
(15) Travelling Tram Post Office in Blackpool	6	7	*Blackpool*
(16) Open Days Broadlands Romsey Hants	6	6	*S. Petty 9*
(17) 6th European Cong Anaesthesiology Royal Festival Hall SE1	6	7	*Assoc Anaesth*
(18) 1982 Museum of the Year Award Museum & Art Gallery Stoke	7	7	*Stoke Museum*

(4)

ASHVILLE COLLEGE JOINS THE COMPUTER AGE EXHIBITION HARROGATE NORTH YORKSHIRE (12)

(5)

(1)

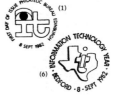

(6)

PLEASE READ THE GENERAL NOTES
AT THE BEGINNING OF THIS CATALOGUE
These often provide the answers to enquiries received.

Information Technology (contd.)

		ordinary covers £	official covers £	
(19)	Military Tattoo Edinburgh	7	8	*Mil. Tattoo*
(20)	Round Britain Trishaw Marathon Dartford Kent Fire Brigade.....	7	8	*Kent Fire B.*
(21)	60th Anniversary of the King's Cup Air Race BF 1788 PS ...	7	8	*Mosquito Mus.*
(22)	Manchester (sponsored by Kelloggs)	7	—	*n.o.c.*

(11) (18)

C.D.S. POSTMARKS

(23)	Helston, Mawgan or Mullion — Goonhilly Downs..........*each*	9	
(24)	Martlesham, Woodbridge — British Telecom Research Centre....	20	
(25)	New Invention, Willenhall, West Midlands	8	

In addition, covers are known with the following CDS postmarks: Bletchley, Bracknell, Caversham, Cheltenham, Edinburgh, Felixstowe, Helensburg, Lovelace Road (Norwich), Mount Pleasant, National Insurance Blgs (Newcastle), Newton Street (Manchester), Oldland Common, Oxford, The Rocket, Rosetta, South Kensington, Stock Exchange, Taunton, Telephone House, Totnes, Walworth Road. Prices range from £6 each.

8 SEPT 1982
City Museum & Art Gallery
Stoke-on-Trent

SLOGAN POSTMARKS

Radio Gwent; Beat Crime Dial 999; Collect British Stamps; any Postcode slogans; Senders Name & Address etc. Prices range from £15.

6th EUROPEAN CONGRESS OF ANAESTHESIOLOGY
ROYAL FESTIVAL HALL
LONDON SE1

13th October 1982 — BRITISH MOTOR CARS

15½p Metro & Austin Seven; 19½p Ford Escort & Model T; 26p Jaguar XJ6 & SS1; 29p RR Silver Spirit & Silver Ghost

SPECIAL HANDSTAMPS

(1)	First Day of Issue — Philatelic Bureau	3	—	*Post Office*
(2)	First Day of Issue — Birmingham	3	—	*Post Office*
(3)	First Day of Issue — Crewe	3	—	*Post Office*
(4)	National Motor Museum Beaulieu Hampshire	5	5	*Beaulieu*
(5)	2nd Anniversary Metro World Trade Centre London E1	5	6	*Havering 29*
(6)	Year of the Car 1982 Motoring Anniversaries Woodford Green....	5	15	*Havering*
(7)	Ford Motor Co Halewood Liverpool Millionth New Ford Escort ..	5	6	*Ford*
(8)	45th Anniversary of Nuffield College, Oxford	5	8	*Univ. Covers*
(9)	70th Anniv. of Motor Transport Royal Flying Corps BF 1789 PS..	5	12	*RFDC 15*
(10)	Worshipful Company of Coachmakers London WC	5	6	*S. Petty 10*
(11)	Ford Sierra Launch Day Ford Chippenham Wilts	5	20	*Cotswold*
(12)	Motor Cycle & Car Museum Stanford Hall Leicester	5	25	*LFDC 21*
(13)	60th Anniversary Austin 7 Brooklands Weybridge Surrey...	5	5	*BLS 7*
(14)	Transport Centenary 1882-1982 Chesterfield Derbyshire....	5	6	*Dawn*
(15)	Heritage Collection Car Design Exhibition Syon Park Brentford .	5	6	*Hawkwood*
(16)	Dagenham Home Ford & Dagenham Motors Model T to Sierra...	5	25	*Dag. Motors*
(17)	Sixty Years of Jaguar Cars Coventry	5	5	*BOCS (2) 15*
(18)	35 Years of Silverstone Circuit Silverstone Towcester Northants ..	5	8	*Silverstone*
(19)	Rolls-Royce Enthusiasts' Club 1957 1982 Paulerspury Towcester	5	30	*Bradbury*
(20)	Manchester (sponsored by Kelloggs)	8	—	*n.o.c.*
(21)	Centenary British Forces Postal Service BF 8282 PS	8	10	*Forces*
(22)	Wootton Bassett Swindon Wilts Welcomes Wiltshire Radio..	8	10	*Wilts Radio*
(23)	Tile Hill Wood School Jubilee Coventry	8	10	*Tile Hill*

(10)
DAGENHAM HOME OF DAGENHAM | FROM MODEL T TO SIERRA (16)
DAGENHAM-ESSEX - 13th OCT 1982

(15) (9) (1) (32)

ORDINARY F.D.I. POSTMARKS

(24)	Manchester — meeting place of Charles Rolls and Henry Royce ..	6

C.D.S. POSTMARKS

(25)	Amersham, Bucks — birthplace of Sir Herbert Austin	6	
(26)	Alwalton, Peterborough — birthplace of Henry Royce	10	
(27)	Austin, Plymouth	7	
(28)	Brighton & Knightsbridge – veteran car rally	20	(pair)
(29)	Dagenham, Essex — Dagenham Motors (Ford)	9	
(30)	Foleshill, Coventry — site of original Jaguar SS production..	7	
(31)	Ford, Liverpool	7	
(32)	Halewood, Liverpool — Ford Escort	9	
(33)	Leyland, Preston, Lancs — birthplace of Leyland Motors	9	
(34)	Longbridge, Birmingham — Mini Metro	10	
(35)	Mount Street, W1 — birthplace of Charles Rolls	10	
(36)	N.E.C. Birmingham — Motor Show	45	
(37)	R.A.C. London SW1	300	
(38)	Rank Forton Services — first motorway Post Office	50	
(39)	Trafford Park, Manchester — site of U.K. assembly for Model T ...	35	

In addition, covers are known with the following CDS postmarks: Allesley, Beaulieu, Bentley, Crewe, Dunlop, Hulme (Manchester), Lanchester, Lewisham, Milton, Rockfield, Saltley (Birmingham), Silverstone, Sparkbrook (Birmingham), St. James' St., Tooting, Vauxhall, Walthamstow. Prices range from £7 each.

FORD MOTOR COMPANY LIMITED,
HALEWOOD, LIVERPOOL
COMMEMORATING THE MILLIONTH NEW FORD ESCORT
(7) 13 OCTOBER 1982

TRANSPORT CENTENARY 1882-1982
(14) 13 OCT 1982
CHESTERFIELD DERBYSHIRE

SLOGAN POSTMARKS

(40)	Hella of Banbury Motor Show Exhibition 20-31 Oct — Banbury ..	30
(41)	Hella of Banbury Motor Show Exhibition 20-31 Oct — Oxford	30

45th Anniversary (8)
of Nuffield College
13 October 1982
OXFORD

HELLA OF BANBURY MOTOR SHOW EXHIBITION (40) (41)
20-31st OCTOBER

17th November 1982 — CHRISTMAS

12½p, 15½p, 19½p, 26p, 29p Christmas Carols

		ordinary covers £	official covers £	
SPECIAL HANDSTAMPS				
(1)	First Day of Issue — Philatelic Bureau	3	—	*Post Office*
(2)	First Day of Issue — Bethlehem	3	—	*Post Office*
(3)	We Three Kings Christmas 1982 Star, Glenrothes, Fife	4	4	*BLS 8*
(4)	I Saw Three Ships Exhibition (Cinque Port of) Hythe, Kent.	4	4	*BOCS (2) 16*
(5)	Good King Wenceslas Christmas 1982 Salisbury Wilts	4	4	*Benham*
(6)	Seasons Greetings Norwich Cathedral Norwich Norfolk	4	6	*Nor. Cath.*
(7)	Seasons Greetings Cutty Sark Greenwich SE10 Christmas 1982 .	4	7	*Havering 30*
(8)	Salvation Army Leicester Region Wish You a Happy Christmas ..	4	15	*LFDC 22*
(9)	Christmas Carol Exhibition Dickens House London WC1 ...	4	10	*Hawkwood*
(10)	St. John Ambulance 1882-1982 City of Leicester Area	4	10	*St. John Am.*
(11)	Sir Christopher Wren Born 1632 East Knoyle Salisbury	8	15	*S. Petty 11*
(12)	1st Highams Park Girl Guides Brigade Co Golden Jubilee E4	8	15	*Girls Brig.*
(13)	Centenary of British Forces Postal Service BF 8282 PS	8	10	*Forces*
(14)	North Atlantic Assembly 28th Annual Session London SW.	8	—	*n.o.c.*
(15)	HMS Brilliant Freedom of Tunbridge Wells Kent	8	10	*H.R.*
(16)	Manchester (sponsored by Kelloggs)	8	—	*n.o.c.*
(17)	BAE (Post Office at War Exhibition) National Postal Museum	8	—	*n.o.c.*
C.D.S. POSTMARKS				
(18)	Bethlehem, Llandeilo, Dyfed	7		
(19)	Nasareth, Caernarfon, Gwynedd	7		

In addition, covers are known with the following CDS postmarks: Chipping Campden, East Grinstead, Fleet Street, Holly Bank, Hollybush, Holy Island, Holytown, Ivy Bush, Ivychurch, Kingsway, Kingsworthy, London SE1, Noel Road, Orient Road, St. Erth, St. Nicholas, St. Stephen, Shepherds Hill, Shepherdswell, Star, Starcross, Theobalds Road BO, Three Kingham. Prices range from £6 each.

26th January 1983 - BRITISH RIVER FISH
Izaak Walton 'The Compleat Angler' 1593-1683

15½p Salmon; 19½p Pike; 26p Trout; 29p Perch

SPECIAL HANDSTAMPS				
(1)	First Day of Issue — Philatelic Bureau	2	—	*Post Office*
(2)	First Day of Issue — Peterborough	2	—	*Post Office*
(3)	Fishing the Teign Newton Abbot Devon	5	—	*Post Office*
(4)	Display of River Fish Salisbury Wilts	5	—	*Post Office*
(5)	400 years of Fishing Tackle Redditch	5	—	*Post Office*
(6)	Make the most of Waterways 1963-1983 British Waterways Board	4	6	*D. Taylor*
(7)	Cinque Ports Angling Society 60th Anniversary Hythe Kent	4	5	*BOCS (2) 17*
(8)	The Pike Anglers Club Izaak Walton Tercentenary Norwich	5	6	*Pike Anglers*
(9)	London Anglers Association 1884-1983 Walthamstow E17	4	6	*Havering 1*
(10)	Izaak Walton Tercentenary River Itchen Winchester Hants .	5	6	*S. Petty 12*
(11)	40th Anniversary RAF Stafford Angling Club BF 1798 PS..	4	10	*RFDC 17*
(12)	14th Anniversary Tisbury Fish Farm Noak Hill Romford Essex ..	6	7	*Havering*
(13)	National Anglers Council Izaak Walton Tercentenary NAC EC4..	4	6	*NAC*
(14)	History of House of Hardy Exhibition Pall Mall London SW1	4	7	*Hawkwood*
(15)	Celebrating the Return of the Salmon Thames Water London EC	5	10	*Thames Water*
(16)	Over 100 years of Salmon Fishing Salmon Leap Coleraine...	4	4	*BLS (83) 1*
(17)	Douglas Bader Angling Club 1970-1983 Leicester	6	20	*Bradbury*
(18)	Birmingham Anglers Association Ltd 1883-1983 Birmingham....	6	20	*Bradbury*
(19)	Izaak Walton Tercentenary Stafford	6	10	*Staff. Museum*
(20)	Izaak Walton 1593-1683 Stafford	5	10	*LFDC 23*
(21)	I.E.W. National Postal Museum	6	—	*n.o.c.*
C.D.S. POSTMARKS				
(22)	Fleet Street BO, EC4 — 'The Compleat Angler' published here ..	6		
(23)	Itchen, Southampton — Izaak Walton's favourite fishing spot	6		
(24)	Kingsgate St., Winchester — nearest PO to Walton's burial place .	7		
(25)	The Salmon Leap, Coleraine, Co. Londonderry	5		
(26)	Stafford — Izaak Walton's birthplace	5		
(27)	Troutbeck, Windermere or Penrith	5		
(28)	Walton, Stafford	5		
(29)	Winchester, Hants	5		

In addition covers are known with the following CDS postmarks: Alnwick, Angle, Bream, Coldstream, Fishbourne, Fishguard, Fishers Pond, Fishlake, Fishponds, Freshwater, Hook, Lochawe, Newton Solney, Norton Bridge, Oulton Broads, Pike Hill, Pike Road, River, Potters Heigham, Romsey, Salmon Lane, Walton-on-Thames. Prices range from £4.

PRICES & CONDITION – PLEASE READ GENERAL NOTES

9th March 1983 — COMMONWEALTH
15½p Tropical Island; 19½p Arid Desert;
26p Temperate Climate; 29p Mountainous Region

	ordinary covers	official covers	
	£	£	
SPECIAL HANDSTAMPS			
(1) First Day of Issue — Philatelic Bureau	2	—	*Post Office*
(2) First Day of Issue — London SW	2	—	*Post Office*
(3) Commonwealth Institute 1962-1983 First Twenty one Years W8 ...	3	15	*LFDC 24*
(4) 215th Anniv. Capt. Cook's Voyages of Discovery Whitby	3	6	*B. Travers*
(5) Wilberforce Council — William Wilberforce 150th Anniv Hull	3	8	*Wilb. Council*
(6) 35th Commonwealth Anniversary World Trade Centre E1	3	4	*Havering 2*
(7) Royal Commonwealth Society Founded 1863 London WC2 ..	3	5	*D. Taylor*
(8) Romsey Hants Mahatma Gandhi 1869-1948	3	6	*S. Petty 13*
(9) 68th Anniversary Formation of No 24 Squadron BF 1799 PS	4	8	*RFDC 18*
(10) British Airways Flight BA494 London Airport W. Sussex	4	4	*BOCS (2) 18*
(11) Geographical Magazine 48 years Window on the World London ...	4	5	*Hawkwood*
(12) Association of Cricket Umpires 30 years 1953-1983 Leicester	8	8	*Assoc. C.U.*
(13) Dunsmore Boy's School 25 years 1958-83 Rugby Warwicks .	8	8	*Dunsmore Sch.*
(14) Daily Mail Ideal Home Exhibition London SW	8	10	*Pilgrim*
(15) I.E.W. National Postal Museum	8	—	*n.o.c.*
(16) Sixty years of Jaguar Cars Coventry	8	7	*Benham*
C.D.S. POSTMARKS			
(17) Buckingham Palace	65		
(18) Gleneagles Hotel, Perthshire — 1977 'Gleneagles Agreement'	50		
(19) House of Commons	25		
(20) House of Lords	30		
(21) Parliament Street BO, SW1	13		
(22) Marldon (birthplace of Sir Humphrey Gilbert)	10		

In addition, covers are known with the following CDS postmarks: The Beach, Blantyre, Dartmouth, Falklands, Forest Town, Hull, India Street, Kensington High Street, Marton-in-Cleveland, Melbourne, Mountain Ash, Queen Elizabeth Avenue, Queen Victoria Road, Romsey, Toronto, Windsor, Whitby. Prices range from £6.

25th May 1983 — BRITISH ENGINEERING ACHIEVEMENTS
16p Humber Bridge; 20½p Thames Barrier; 28p Energy Support Vessel — Iolair

SPECIAL HANDSTAMPS			
(1) First Day of Issue — Philatelic Bureau	2	—	*Post Office*
(2) First Day of Issue — Hull	2	—	*Post Office*
(3) Institution of Civil Engineers 1828-1983 London SW1	3	15	*LFDC 25*
(4) Ten years of Eng. Achievement Thames Flood Barrier SE7	3	7	*G & P*
(5) Commemorating the CTH Joint Venture Thames Flood Barrier SE7	3	6	*Havering 3*
(6) GLC Thames Barrier Protecting London Woolwich Reach SE7	3	6	*Des. Enc.*
(7) Celebrating Engineering Achievements AUEW London SE15	3	10	*AUEW*
(8) British Shipbuilders Iolair first of her type built in UK SW7	3	3	*Benham*
(9) BP Contribution Iolair Engineering Achievement Aberdeen	3	4	*BOCS (2) 19*
(10) Taking Technology to greater depths UDI Aberdeen	4	8	*UDI*
(11) Humber Bridge Hull Longest Single Span 2 Years a Tribute	3	6	*Hawkwood*
(12) Humber Bridge Opened 17 July 1981 Barton on Humber	3	4	*BLS (83) 3*
(13) Institute of Mechanical Engineers 1847-1983 London SW1	4	10	*Pilgrim*
(14) Printing Shares the fruits of Human Genius, Slough, Berks..	4	8	*Havering*
(15) 25th Anniv No 2 Sch. Tech Training RAF Cosford BF 1806 PS	3	6	*RFDC 19*
(16) The Harrier Birthplace Kingston upon Thames Surrey	4	8	*S. Petty 14*
(17) 30 Years experience 1953-1983 Dan Air London Airport	3	10	*Benham*
(18) Post Office Philatelic Counter Grimsby S. Humberside	5	—	*n.o.c.*
(19) Telecom Technology Showcase London EC4	6	—	*n.o.c.*
(20) Chester-le-Street Co. Durham Commemorate 1100 years	6	5	*C. leS. Council*
(21) The Wilberforce Council 150th Anniversary Year Hull	6	6	*Wilb. Council*
(22) Children's Hospital Radio Lollipop, Rotary Chippenham, Wilts	6	6	*Rotary*
(23) I.E.W. National Postal Museum	6	—	*n.o.c.*
C.D.S. POSTMARKS			
(24) Coalbrookdale, Telford, Salop — birthplace of Ind Revolution	8		
(25) Eagle, Lincoln — Iolair is gaelic for eagle	8		
(26) Hessle and Barton — north and south end of the Humber Bridge ..	12	(pair)	
(27) Ironbridge, Telford, Salop — the world's first iron bridge	12		
(28) New Bridge Road, Hull	13		
(29) Port Glasgow — Iolair was built here	35		
(30) Silvertown & Woolwich (or Charlton) — north & south of Barrier ..	12	(pair)	

PRICES & CONDITION – PLEASE READ GENERAL NOTES

Engineering (contd.)

	ordinary covers £	official covers £

GLC THAMES BARRIER — (31) — (32)
PROTECTING LONDON

In addition, covers are known with the following CDS postmarks: Bacton, Bridge, Clydebank, Cleveland, Cruden Bay, Dundee, Hatfield, Langholm. Portsmouth, Rigside, Rotherham, Saltash, Telford. Prices range from £5.

SLOGAN POSTMARKS

(31)	GLC Thames Barrier Protecting London — Charlton SE7 ...	13
(32)	GLC Thames Barrier Protecting London — Woolwich SE18	13
(33)	Collect British Stamps your Humberside Philatelic Link — Hull..	25

In addition: Middlesbrough Philatelic Counter; Royal Mail Helping Business on Merseyside; World Communications Year. Prices range from £20.

6th July 1983 — THE BRITISH ARMY
16p The Royal Scots; 20½p Royal Welch Fusiliers; 26p Royal Green Jackets; 28p Irish Guards; 31p Parachute Regiment

SPECIAL HANDSTAMPS

(1)	First Day of Issue — Philatelic Bureau	3	—	Post Office
(2)	First Day of Issue — Aldershot..	3	—	Post Office
(3)	Regimental Stamp Display Philatelic Counter Glasgow.......	6	—	Post Office
(4)	The British Army Series BF 1983 PS	6	10	Army
(5)	The Royal Scots (The Royal Regt.) 1633-1983 BF 0350 PS ..	6	10	Army
(6)	The Royal Welch Fusiliers 1689-1983 BF 0294 PS	6	10	Army
(7)	The Royal Greenjackets 1966-1983 BF 1800 PS................	6	10	Army
(8)	The Irish Guards 1900-1983 BF 1900 PS	6	10	Army
(9)	The Parachute Regiment 1942-1983 BF 2000 PS	6	10	Army
(10)	75th Anniversary of the TA in Wales BF 1908 PS	6	40	Forces
(11)	Rheindahlen Allied Marches BF 1810 PS	6	15	Forces
(12)	Royal Military Academy Serving to Lead for 200 Yrs Sandhurst ..	6	12	G & P
(13)	The Queen's Own Hussars Silver Jubilee Warwick	6	20	LFDC 26
(14)	Duke of York's Royal Military School 180th Anniversary Dover ...	6	7	Benham L2
(15)	Blenheim Palace Woodstock Oxford................................	6	10	Havering 4
(16)	Soldier Print Soc. Paintings of Military Uniforms Worthing	6	15	S.P.
(17)	12th Anniversary National Army Museum 1971-1983 SW3	6	7	BOCS (2) 20
(18)	Ensign Miniatures Model Soldier Exhib. Kirton Boston Lincs	6	10	Hawkwood
(19)	Duke of Edinburgh's Royal Regimental Museum Salisbury .	6	10	S. Petty 15
(20)	Ancient Order of Foresters Memorial Plaque Rugeley	6	15	A.O.F.
(21)	Richard III 500th Anniv Celebrations Middleham N. Yorks.	6	20	R III Soc
(22)	Llangollen International Eisteddfod	8	15	Eist'd
(23)	Telecom Technology Showcase London EC4	8	15	Brit Tele
(24)	Royal Show Kenilworth Warwickshire..............................	8	—	n.o.c.

C.D.S. POSTMARKS

(25)	Aldershot — Regimental HQ of the Parachute Regiment	10
(26)	Battle, or Battlefield	12
(27)	Broadway, SW1 — Regimental HQ of the Irish Guards	10
(28)	Buckingham Palace, SW1...	65
(29)	Catterick Garrison, N. Yorks..	13
(30)	Duke of York's School, Dover (Military School).................	20
(31)	Edinburgh — Regimental HQ of the Royal Scots................	10
(32)	Hightown, Wrexham — Regimental HQ Royal Welch Fusiliers	10
(33)	Marlborough, Wilts	10
(34)	Sandhurst, Camberley — Royal Military Academy.............	15
(35)	Wilton, Salisbury – HQ – UK Land Forces......................	10
(36)	Winchester — Regimental HQ of the Royal Greenjackets	10
(37)	Army POs (e.g. Bassingbourn, Crookham Camp, Worthy Down)..	12
(38)	Any Field or Forces Post Office cancellations	15

In addition, covers are known with the following CDS postmarks: Athelstaneford, Bannockburn, Barracks, Brunswick Road (Pirbright Camp), Bunkers Hill, Chelsea Royal Hospital, Falkland, Guard House, Gunhill, Huntingdon, Montgomery, Naseby, St. Andrews, Sentry Corner, Terriers, Tidworth, Waterloo, Wellington, Woodstock, Woolwich, York, Yorktown. Prices range from £7.

SLOGAN POSTMARKS

(39)	Join Territorial Army 1908-1983 75th Anniv. — Northampton.....	450
(40)	The Army 1914-82 National Army Museum — London SW	20

24th August 1983 — BRITISH GARDENS
'Capability' Brown, Landscape Gardener 1716-1783
16p Sissinghurst; 20½p Biddulph Grange; 28p Blenheim; 31p Pitmedden

	ordinary covers £	official covers £	
SPECIAL HANDSTAMPS			
(1) First Day of Issue — Philatelic Bureau	3	—	*Post Office*
(2) First Day of Issue — Oxford	3	—	*Post Office*
(3) Capability Brown at Bowood 220th Anniv. Bowood Calne Wilts	6	—	*Post Office*
(4) The Queen's Gardens Croydon Surrey	6	—	*Post Office*
(5) Capability Brown 1715-1983 Kew Gardens Richmond Surrey	5	12	*LFDC 27*
(6) The National Trust Sissinghurst Castle Sissinghurst Kent	5	5	*BOCS (2) 21*
(7) League of Friends The Grange Biddulph Stoke-on-Trent	5	8	*League of F*
(8) Blenheim Palace, Woodstock Oxford	5	6	*Havering 5*
(9) The National Trust for Scotland Pitmedden Ellon Aberdeen	5	5	*BLS (83) 5*
(10) Capability Brown 200th Anniversary Esher Surrey Claremont	5	8	*Arlington*
(11) Roses in August Syon Park Brentford Middx	5	5	*Hawkwood*
(12) Lancelot Capability Brown 1716-1783 Fenstanton Huntingdon	5	8	*Fenst Par Ch*
(13) National Trust for Scotland Crathes Castle Banchory	5	7	*Benham L4*
(14) The National Trust Lyme Park Disley Cheshire	5	5	*Benham L3*
(15) Capability Brown 1716-1783 Kirkharle Newcastle-upon-Tyne	5	8	*Landscape Ins.*
(16) Capability Brown GRBS Hampton Court Kingston upon Thames	5	10	*S. Petty 16*
(17) A Celebration of English Gardens London SW1	5	4	*DGT*
(18) 30th Anniv RAF Memorial Gardens at Runnymede BF 1814 PS	10	10	*RFDC 21*
(19) International camp BB 83 Perth	10	30	*Boys Brig.*
(20) Travelling Tram Post Office in Blackpool	10	—	*n.o.c.*
(21) Military Tattoo Edinburgh	10	10	*Mil. Tattoo*
(22) Bicentenary Hornchurch Cricket Club Hornchurch Essex	20	20	*H.C.C.*
C.D.S. POSTMARKS			
(23) Biddulph, Stoke-on-Trent — featured on 20½p value	10		
(24) Botanic Gardens, Belfast	20		
(25) Fenstanton, Cambs — Capability Brown is buried here	12		
(26) Kew Gardens, Richmond Surrey	30		
(27) Kirkwhelpington, Newcastle — birthplace of Capability Brown	10		
(28) Mayfair BO, W1 — Capability Brown died here	10		
(29) Sissinghurst, Kent — featured on 16p value	7		
(30) Udny, Ellon, Aberdeenshire — PO for Pitmedden (31p value)	8		
(31) Woodstock, Oxford — PO for Blenheim Palace (28p value)	8		

In addition, covers are known with the following CDS postmarks: Garden Suburb, Garden Village, Glamis, Harewood, Headstone Gardens, Petworth, Rake, Royal Hospital Chelsea, Sledmere, The Allotments, Trentham, Welwyn Garden City. Prices range from £6.

SLOGAN POSTMARKS		
(32) Back Beautiful Britain — used at several Post Offices	20	
(33) Chamber of Commerce — Devizes in Bloom 1982 Cup Winners	25	
(34) Your Garden Isle is Beautiful Keep it Tidy — Isle of Wight	30	

In addition: Beautiful Bath. Prices range from £20.

5th October 1983 — BRITISH FAIRS
16p Merry-go-round; 20½p Menageries and rides; 28p Side shows; 31p Early trade and produce fairs

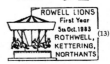

SPECIAL HANDSTAMPS			
(1) First Day of Issue — Philatelic Bureau	③	—	*Post Office*
(2) First Day of Issue — Nottingham	③	—	*Post Office*
(3) Priory Church of St. Bartholomew the Great 1123-1983 EC	5	6	*Havering 6*
(4) Butchers Charitable Institution Bartholomew Fair London EC1	5	6	*Hawkwood*
(5) The Showmen's Guild of GB Honouring British Fairs Staines	5	9	*S. Guild*
(6) Goosie Fair Tavistock Devon	5	15	*S. Petty 17*
(7) Chipperfield's Circus 300 Years London EC	5	5	*BLS (83) 6*
(8) NABMA (Nat. Assoc'n British Market Auth.) Birmingham	5	6	*Des. Enc.*
(9) Fairfield Croydon 21st Birthday Croydon Surrey	5	6	*F. Field Halls*
(10) Turner's Musical Merry-go-Round 1896-1983 Northampton	5	8	*BOCS (2) 22*
(11) Goose Fair 1983 Nottingham	5	25	*LFDC 28*
(12) 80th Anniv. World's First Air Fair BF 1815 PS	7	8	*RFDC 22*
(13) Rowell Lions first year Rothwell Kettering Northants	6	8	*Rothwell Lions*
(14) British Philatelic Federation 65th Congress Bath	9	9	*BPF*
(15) Travelling Tram Post Office Blackpool	8	—	*n.o.c.*
(16) Samuel Pepys 350th Anniversary Cambridge	8	10	*Univ. Covers*
(17) The Boys Brigade Centenary first for boys Cardiff	8	20	*BB Wales*
(18) MMB (Milk Marketing Board) 1933-1983 Newcastle Staffs	8	10	*MMB*
(19) Exhibition Garden City 83 Letchworth Herts	8	—	*n.o.c..*

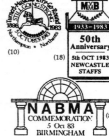

British Fairs (contd.)

	ordinary covers £	official covers £
C.D.S. POSTMARKS		
(20) Borough High Street, S.E.1 (Southwark Fair — one of the 3 great fairs) .	10	
(21) Cambridge or Chesterton (Sturbridge Fair — one of the 3 great fairs)....	10	
(22) Horse Fair, Kidderminster or Rugeley	8	
(23) London Chief Office, (Bartholomew Fair — one of the 3 great fairs)......	10	
(24) St. Giles Oxford — largest surviving wake (uncharted fair) ..	12	
(25) Scarborough, N. Yorks	15	
(26) Tavistock, Devon (Goose Fair)	12	
(27) Widecombe-in-the-Moor, Devon	18	
(28) Winchester, Hants (Bishops Fair — oldest Charter Fair)	7	

In addition, covers are known with the following CDS postmarks: Abingdon, Alford, Appleby-in-Westmorland, Barrus Bridge, Big Top, Brigg, Elephant and Castle, Exeter, Frome, Greenwich, Honiton, Hyson Green, King's Lynn, Marlborough, Market Sidmouth, Mayfair, North End, St. Ives, Stow-on-the-Wold, Stratford-upon-Avon, Ulverston, Warwick, Wookey Hole, Woodkirk, Yarm. Prices range from £8 each.

SLOGAN POSTMARKS
Wonderland of Wales; Magnum World of Entertainment. Prices range from £75.

16th November 1983 — CHRISTMAS
12½p, 16p, 20½p, 28p, 31p Goodwill at Christmas

SPECIAL HANDSTAMPS

(1) First Day of Issue — Philatelic Bureau	3	—	*Post Office*
(2) First Day of Issue — Bethlehem	3	—	*Post Office*
(3) Peace and Goodwill Christmas 1983 Nasareth Caernarfon ..	4	10	*LFDC 29*
(4) 50th Ann. Rededication Minster Gatehouse Sheppey Sheerness .	6	8	*Hawkwood*
(5) Leicestershire Society for the Blind 1858-1983 Leicester	4	10	*L. Blind Soc*
(6) Winchester Cathedral Christmas 1983 Winchester Hants ...	4	8	*S. Petty 18*
(7) Peace on Earth Goodwill Toward Men Christmas 83 Peacehaven .	4	5	*BLS (83) 7*
(8) Christmas Greetings St. Mary le Strand London WC2	4	6	*Havering 7*
(9) Seasons Greetings Telecom Technology Showcase London EC4 ..	4	15	*Brit Tele*
(10) 1350th Ann. Lyminge Parish Church Festival Year Folkestone	4	5	*BOCS (2) 23*
(11) T.C. (Tandy Corporation) Celebration 1973-1983 Walsall	10	35	*T.C.*

C.D.S. POSTMARKS

(12) Bethlehem, Llandeilo, Dyfed	7	
(13) Nasareth, Gwynedd	7	

In addition, covers are known with the following CDS postmarks: Birdsall, Blackbird Leys, Canterbury, Chapel, Chester-le-Street, Christchurch, Dovecot, Dove Holes, Dove House Lane, Holy Island, Kingsworthy, Minster, Peacehaven, Quakers Road, St. Augustine's, St. Nicholas, Star. Prices range from £6 each.

SLOGAN POSTMARKS
(14) Hastings — A Resort for All Seasons (snowmen & Xmas scene) ..   90
In addition: Royal Mail Special Services, Hull. Prices range from £30.

17th January 1984 — HERALDRY
16p College of Arms; 20½p Richard III; 28p The Earl Marshal; 31p City of London

SPECIAL HANDSTAMPS

(1) First Day of Issue — Philatelic Bureau	3	—	*Post Office*
(2) First Day of Issue — London EC	3	—	*Post Office*
(3) Heraldry Guildhall City of London, London EC	6	—	*Post Office*
(4) College of Arms Quincentenary London EC4	5	10	*Cotswold*
(5) The Heraldry Society celebrates The College of Arms WC	5	10	*BOCS (2) 24*
(6) Richard III Society Quincentenary Celebrations Leicester ..	5	30	*LFDC 30*
(7) Richard III Born 1452 Fotheringhay Castle, Peterborough..	5	30	*LFDC 30*
(8) Richard III Celebration, Scarborough N. Yorks	5	15	*Pilgrim*
(9) The City of London The Square Mile Financial Capital EC	5	15	*G&P*
(10) 400th Anniv. Deputy Norroy King of Arms Visit to York	5	10	*Hawkwood*
(11) Friary Meux Kings Arms & Royal Godalming Exhibition....	5	10	*Hawkwood*
(12) Coat of Arms Granted in 1890 Belfast	5	15	*BLS (84) 1*
(13) Coat of Arms Granted in 1906 Cardiff	5	15	*BLS (84) 1*
(14) Coat of Arms Granted in 1975 Edinburgh	5	15	*BLS (84) 1*
(15) Spencer Anthorp Commemorating 475 Years Northampton	5	10	*Althorp*
(16) Heirlooms, 1 Hayhill, Berkeley Square, London W1	7	10	*Havering*
(17) The Arthurian Legend Camelot Tintagel Cornwall.............	8	12	*S. Petty 19*
(18) 65th Anniv. of Award of 1st RAF Badge BF 1826 PS...........	10	12	*RFDC 24*
(19) NSPCC Centenary Founded 1884 Mansion House London EC4 ..	10	15	*NSPCC*
(20) High Wycombe 50 Years Post Office Stamp Printing..........	10	10	*Harrisons*

Fairfield Croydon (9)

Croydon Surrey 5 Oct 83

(25) (22) (26)

CHRISTMAS GREETINGS (2)

(8)

St-MARY-le-STRAND LONDON W.C.2. (1)

(4)

(4)

LONDON-THE FINANCIAL CAPITAL (9)

THE CITY OF THE WORLD LONDON E.C. 17 JANUARY 1984

(12)

(17)

(11)

(19)

(16)

17th JANUARY 1984 LONDON W.1.

(13)

(10)

PRICES & CONDITION – PLEASE READ GENERAL NOTES

Heraldry (contd.)

		ordinary covers £	official covers £	
(21)	Lincoln Philatelic Counter Opened 17 Jan 1984, Lincoln	15	—	n.o.c.
(22)	Marks & Spencer Baker St. 100 Years of Quality & Value, W1	8	15	DGT
(23)	London FS 1919-1934 Air Mail, National Postal Museum ...	10	—	n.o.c.
(24)	Berkswell Parish Church Rest. of Funeral Hatchments, Coventry	10	15	Par. Ch.
(25)	The Good News People Martins Golden Jubilee Aylesbury	10	35	Martins
(26)	The Story of the Poppy Royal British Legion, Maidstone, Kent ...	10	15	Brit. Leg.
(27)	London SW1 (Buckingham Palace)	10	—	n.o.c.

C.D.S. POSTMARKS

(28)	Arundel, West Sussex — home of the Earl Marshal.............	8	
(29)	Cannon St., London EC4 — nearest PO to College of Arms..	8	
(30)	Fore St., London EC2 — nearest PO to the Guildhall	8	
(31)	Market Bosworth, Nuneaton — Richard III killed at Bosworth ...	10	
(32)	Middleham, Leyburn, N. Yorks — Richard III's castle.........	10	

In addition covers are known with the following CDS postmarks: Barony, Chester, College Town, Coneysthorpe, Fleur-de-Lis, Godalming, Gloucester, Harewood, King Arthur's Way, Leadenhall St., Lombard St., Ludgate Circus, Ludlow, Queen Elizabeth Ave., Richmond, St. Georges Cross, Sloane Square, Stock Exchange, York. Prices range from £7.

6th March 1984 — BRITISH CATTLE
16p Highland Cow; 20½p Chillingham Wild Bull; 26p Hereford Bull; 28p Welsh Black Bull; 31p Irish Moiled Cow

SPECIAL HANDSTAMPS

(1)	First Day of Issue — Philatelic Bureau	4	—	Post Office
(2)	First Day of Issue — Oban Argyll	4	—	Post Office
(3)	Centenary of the Highland Cattle Society, Edinburgh	5	7	BOCS (2) 25
(4)	Chateau Impney Highland Cattle Herd Droitwich Worcs....	15	—	Post Office
(5)	The Last Stronghold of the Chillingham Bull, Chillingham	5	5	BLS (84) 2
(6)	Home of the Chillingham Wild Cattle Chillingham Alnwick	5	10	CWC Assoc
(7)	Hereford Herd Book Society 1846 1st Vol closed 1884 Hereford ..	5	8	DGT
(8)	Welsh Black Cattle Society 1904-1984 Caernarfon, Gwynedd	5	8	DGT
(9)	The Irish Moiled Cattle Society Founded 1926 Ballynahinch...	5	8	DGT
(10)	The British Friesian Cattle Soc. GB & Ireland, Rickmansworth ..	5	8	DGT
(11)	Livestock Show Tring Herts	15	—	Post Office
(12)	Farming the Backbone of Britain, London SW1	5	8	DGT
(13)	Rare Breeds Survival Trust 10th Anniv. Stoneleigh, Kenilworth..	5	7	LFDC 31
(14)	Butcher's Charitable Institute, Smithfield Market, London EC1..	5	6	Hawkwood
(15)	Earl's Court — Home of the Royal Smithfield Show, SW5..........	5	6	Havering
(16)	The Royal Veterinary College, London NW1	6	7	S. Petty 20
(17)	Farmers Weekly Golden Jubilee 1934-1984 Sutton Surrey...	6	20	Des. Enc.
(18)	Dairy Crest Honours British Cattle Crewe	8	15	MMB
(19)	25th Anniv. Freedom of Entry RAF Hereford BF 1828 PS ..	8	10	RFDC 25
(20)	The Martyrs Tolpuddle Dorchester Dorset	10	15	TUC
(21)	Stampex London SW1	10	10	Stampex
(22)	London FS 1919-1984 Air Mail, National Postal Museum ...	10	—	n.o.c.
(23)	Colchester Castle Restoration 1984, Colchester	25	—	n.o.c.
(24)	Daily Mail Ideal Home Exhibition London SW..................	15	18	Pilgrim
(25)	767 Another 1st from Britannia Celebration Flight, Luton Beds ..	20	50	Brit. Airw.

A special handstamp "Maiden Flight Skyship 600, Cardington" was used on 6th March but no covers are known to exist with the British Cattle Stamps affixed.

C.D.S. POSTMARKS

(26)	Ballynahinch, or Saintfield — Irish Moiled Cow ....from	15	
(27)	Black Bull St., Leeds...	15	
(28)	Bull Farm, Mansfield, Notts	15	
(29)	Caernarfon, Gwynedd — Welsh Black Cattle....................	8	
(30)	Cattle Market, Preston	25	
(31)	Chillingham, Alnwick — Chillingham Wild Cattle	10	
(32)	Hereford...	7	
(33)	Kyle, or Kyleakin — Kyloe Highland Cattle	15	
(34)	Oban, Argyll — Highland Cattle	15	
(35)	Red Cow, Exeter	25	

In addition covers are known with the following CDS postmarks: Bull Bay, Bull Brook, Cowplain, Dolgellau, Heriot, Lavenham, Lincoln, Moy, Oxen Park, Royal College Street, Stoneleigh, Terling, Thames Ditton, The Markets, Thirsk. Prices range from £6.

PRICES & CONDITION – PLEASE READ GENERAL NOTES

10th April 1984 — URBAN RENEWAL

16p Liverpool Garden Festival; 20½p Milburngate Centre, Durham;
28p City Docks, Bristol; 31p Commercial St. Redevelopment, Perth

1984

	ordinary covers £	official covers £	
SPECIAL HANDSTAMPS			
(1) First Day of Issue — Philatelic Bureau	3	—	*Post Office*
(2) First Day of Issue — Liverpool	3	—	*Post Office*
(3) International Garden Festival, Liverpool............................	5	7	*BOCS (2) 26*
(4) Abbey National Building Society at the IGF Liverpool '84	5	6	*G&P*
(5) Urban Renewal City of Durham	5	10	*C of Durham*
(6) Laing Development & Constr. Urban Renewal, Durham.......	5	9	*Laing*
(7) Urban Renewal BDP (Business Design Partnership) London W1 ..	5	6	*BDP*
(8) Bush House Arnolfini Gallery Bristol	5	7	*C of Bristol*
(9) Commercial Street Redevelopment Perth	5	8	*G&P*
(10) The Landscape Institute, Int. Garden Festival Liverpool	5	6	*Lans. Inst.*
(11) RIBA 150th Anniv. Festival of Architecture Yorks Region, York ...	5	10	*Cotswold*
(12) RIBA 150 Years Festival of Architecture 1984 London W1 ...	5	10	*Cotswold*
(13) St. John the Evangelist 1834-1984 (RIBA) Stratford E15	5	5	*Hawkwood*
(14) Festival of Arch. Urban Renewal City of London Guildhall EC2	7	—	*Post Office*
(15) The Year of Building 1834-1984 CIOB Ascot Berks..............	5	7	*DGT*
(16) DIADEM Dundee Inst. of Architects Centenary 1984 Dundee	7	10	*D.I.A.*
(17) Letchworth the First Garden City, Letchworth, Herts...........	5	10	*LFDC 32*
(18) London Docklands Enterprise Zone Isle of Dogs London E14	6	9	*Havering*
(19) Covent Garden Market 1634-1984 London WC	6	8	*S. Petty 21*
(20) Bicentenary Cheshire Gibson, Chart. Surv. Birmingham	10	—	*n.o.c.*
(21) The Wigan Pier Project, Wigan	8	10	*Wigan Coun.*
(22) 70th Anniv. First Flight Bristol Scout BF 1835 PS	12	15	*RFDC 26*
(23) London FS 1919-1984 Air Mail National Postal Museum......	15	—	*n.o.c.*
(24) Colchester Castle Restoration 1984, Colchester	25	—	*n.o.c.*
C.D.S. POSTMARKS			
(25) Aigburth, or Cockburn St., Liverpool — nearest POs to the IGF	7		
(26) Ascot, Berks — home of Chararted Inst. of Building............	7		
(27) Brigend, Perth — adjacent to Commercial St. Redevelopment	10		
(28) Letchworth, Herts — the First Garden City	7		
(29) New Buildings, Londonderry	35		
(30) North Road, Durham — nearest PO to Milburngate Centre ...	7		
(31) Prince Street, Bristol — nearest PO to Arnolfini Gallery.......	7		

In addition covers are known with the following CDS postmarks: Fore Street, Isle of Dogs, Red
House, Southampton Street, Telford, Tingley, Welwyn Garden City. Prices range from £6.

SLOGAN POSTMARKS

(32) International Garden Festival Liverpool 84 2nd May-14th Oct.	15		

In addition: Royal Mail Special Services, Hull; Beautiful Bath. Prices range from £20.

15th May 1984 — EUROPA

2 × 16p; 2 × 20½p

SPECIAL HANDSTAMPS			
(1) First Day of Issue — Philatelic Bureau	3	—	*Post Office*
(2) First Day of Issue — London SW	3	—	*Post Office*
(3) European Elections 84 London SW	4	4	*Havering*
(4) Second British European Parliamentary Elections, London SW1 ..	4	4	*BLS (84) 4*
(5) Sealink Britains Bridge with Europe Folkestone, Kent	4	7	*BOCS (2) 27*
(6) 1606-1984 Dover Harbour Board 1606 Dover Kent	4	8	*LFDC 33*
(7) Hawkwood Covers Europa Stamp Exhibition Europe House E1 ...	4	5	*Hawkwood*
(8) D-Day+40 Portsmouth..	4	12	*S. Petty 22*
(9) 35th Anniv. Formation of NATO BF 1949 PS......................	12	12	*RFDC 27*
(10) International Garden Festival Liverpool...........................	8	—	*n.o.c.*
(11) London FS 1919-1984 Air Mail National Postal Museum......	8	—	*n.o.c.*
(12) 1959-1984 25th Anniv. Mosquito Aircraft Museum Hatfield .	10	15	*M.A. Mus.*
(13) Colchester Castle Restoration 1984, Colchester	20	—	*n.o.c.*
C.D.S. POSTMARKS			
(14) Bridge, Kent or Postbridge, Devon	7		
(15) Dover, Folkestone, Harwich, Newhaven or Weymouth ...*each*	7		
(16) House of Commons SW1	15		
(17) House of Lords	20		
(18) Mark Cross, Crowborough...	35		
(19) Newhaven with PAQUEBOT markings	12		
(20) Boulogne, Calais or Dieppe with PAQUEBOT markings	15		
(21) Parliament Street, London SW1 or Burnley	12		

89

Europa (contd.)

	ordinary covers £	official covers £

In addition covers are known with the following CDS postmarks: Felixstowe, Holland Fen, Montgomery, Normandy, Northern Parliament, Portsmouth, Portsmouth Dockyard, York. Prices range from £6.

SLOGAN POSTMARKS
Milk on your Doorstep; Historic Sandwich; Royal Mail Special Services or Collect British Stamps. Prices from £20.

5th June 1984 — LONDON ECONOMIC SUMMIT 1984
31p Lancaster House

SPECIAL HANDSTAMPS

(1)	First Day of Issue — Philatelic Bureau	2	—	*Post Office*
(2)	First Day of Issue — London SW	2	—	*Post Office*
(3)	Economic Summit London SW1	4	5	*LFDC 34*
(4)	London Economic Summit London SW1	4	4	*Havering*
(5)	London Welcomes the Economic Summit London EC1	4	4	*BOCS (2) 29*
(6)	Sterling Travellers Cheques Available at the P.O. Croydon Surrey.	4	—	*Post Office*
(7)	1984 1st Year as TSB England & Wales, Chingford	6	8	*Hawkwood*
(8)	Brit. Phil. Cover Producers Assoc. Economic Summit SW1.	4	5	*BPCPA*
(9)	Institute of London Underwriters Centenary London EC3 ..	4	6	*Cotswold*
(10)	1924 Wembley Exhibition 1984 Grange Museum London NW10.	5	5	*DGT*
(11)	75th Rotary International Convention Birmingham	5	5	*Int. Rotary*
(12)	H.M. The Queen Embarks Britannia for Normandy Portsmouth .	10	20	*Rembrandt*
(13)	UPU Exhibition June-July 1984 National Postal Museum ...	10	—	*n.o.c.*
(14)	International Garden Festival Liverpool	10	—	*n.o.c.*
(15)	Colchester Castle Restoration 1984, Colchester	15	—	*n.o.c.*

C.D.S. POSTMARKS

(16)	Dollar, Clackmannanshire	30	
(17)	Lombard St. B.O., London EC3 — London's "banking street"	15	
(18)	Pound	12	
(19)	St. James's St. B.O., London SW1 — PO for Lancaster House	8	
(20)	Stock Exchange B.O. London EC2	25	
(21)	Summit, Heywood or Littleborough, Lancs.	15	

In addition covers are known with the following CDS postmarks: Bretton, The Forum, Lancaster, Moneyhill, Parliament Street BO. Prices range from £6.

SLOGAN POSTMARKS
Sunderland Loans & Grants; Shopping by Post; Datapost, Express Post etc., Hull; Inverness Conference Capital; Post Code It. Prices range from £30.

26th June 1984 — GREENWICH MERIDIAN
16p Astronomy; 20½p Navigation; 28p The Observatory; 31p Time

SPECIAL HANDSTAMPS

(1)	First Day of Issue 3° 11′ 57″ Longitude — Philatelic Bureau	3	—	*Post Office*
(2)	First Day of Issue 0° 0′ 0″ Greenwich Longitude London SE10 ...	3	—	*Post Office*
(3)	Centenary of the World's Prime Meridian Greenwich SE10	4	5	*BOCS (2) 28*
(4)	Greenwich Mean Time London EC4	8	—	*n.o.c.*
(5)	The Geographical Magazine Longitudinal Obelisk Chingford E4	4	4	*Hawkwood*
(6)	Royal Naval College Greenwich Meridian Centenary London SE .	4	15	*RNC*
(7)	Meridian Road 0° 00′ 00″ Longitude Boston Lincs	6	—	*Post Office*
(8)	Centenary of the Greenwich Meridian, East Lindsey Louth.	4	10	*L. Rotary*
(9)	Royal Naval Staff College 65th Anniversary BF 1838 PS.....	4	9	*RFDC 28*
(10)	1884-1984 Longitude Zero Somersham Huntingdon	6	—	*Post Office*
(11)	Meridian Day Meridian County School Comberton Cambridge ...	4	10	*MCP Sch.*
(12)	Meridian Day Celebrations 0° MG GM Swavesey Cambs ...	4	10	*MG Owners*
(13)	Meridian Centenary Peacehaven Newhaven E. Sussex	4	10	*P'haven PO.*
(14)	British Horological Institute 1858-1984 Newark Notts ...	4	7	*LFDC 35*
(15)	John Longitude Harrison Copley Gold Medallist 1749 Barrow	6	15	*Lincoln Cath.*
(16)	British Astronomical Association London W1	4	8	*DGT*
(17)	The U.K. Time Standard Nat. Physical Lab. Teddington Middx ..	4	10	*NPL*
(18)	Captn. Cook Study Unit — HMS Resolution Whitby	6	10	*B. Travers*
(19)	Lloyds List 1734-1984 Greenwich London SE10	6	12	*Lloyds*
(20)	UPU Exhibition June-July 1984 National Postal Museum EC1 ...	10	—	*n.o.c.*
(21)	Wembley Exhibition 1924-1984 Grange Museum NW10.....	10	12	*DGT*
(22)	National Federation of Women's Institutes London W14.....	10	12	*Arlington*
(23)	Steve Davis Embassy World Professional Champion, Romford	10	12	*Havering*
(24)	1884-1984 Ladies Cent. Year Lawn Tennis Museum Wimbledon .	15	15	*AELTC*
(25)	Colchester Castle Restoration 1984, Colchester	15	—	*n.o.c.*
(26)	International Garden Festival, Liverpool	15	—	*n.o.c.*

Greenwich Meridian (contd.)

	ordinary covers £	official covers £
C.D.S. POSTMARKS		
(27) Alnwick, Northumberland — birthplace of Sir George Airy.	6	
(28) Chingford, London E4 — site of the longitudinal obelisk......	7	
(29) Clock Face, St. Helens	15	
(30) Hartland, Bideford — home of the Magnetic Observatory ...	20	
(31) Herstmonceux, Hailsham — home of new observatory........	7	
(32) Greenwich B.O., SE10 or East Greenwich....................*from*	10	
(33) Meridian Centre, Peacehaven, Newhaven	90	
(34) Playford, Ipswich — home and burial place of Sir George Airy.....	15	
(35) The Chart, Oxted, Surrey	10	

In addition covers are known with the following CDS postmarks: Cleethorpes, Comberton, Globe Road, Great Ayton, Great Portland Street, Louth, Macclesfield, Swavesey, Washington, World's End. Prices range from £5.

SLOGAN POSTMARKS
Magyar Philatelic Society. Prices range from £40.

31st July 1984 — THE ROYAL MAIL
16p The Bath Mail Coach 1784; 16p Attack on Exeter Mail Coach 1816; 16p Norwich Mail Coach in a thunderstorm 1827; 16p Holyhead & Liverpool Mail Coaches 1828; 16p Edinburgh Mail Coach Snowbound 1831

SPECIAL HANDSTAMPS			
(1) First Day of Issue — Philatelic Bureau	3	—	*Post Office*
(2) First Day of Issue — Bristol	3	—	*Post Office*
(3) Bath Mail Coach Commemorative Run, Bath Avon............	3	4	*BOCS (2) 30*
(4) Golden Age of Coaching Bath	3	12	*LFDC 36*
(5) The Interlink Express Parcels Co Commemorative Run Bristol	3	5	*Hawkwood*
(6) Royal Mail Transport 1784-1984 Leicester	3	5	*Mus. of Tech.*
(7) Manchester — Altrincham Mail Coach Run Manchester	3	4	*BLS (84) 7*
(8) Liverpool Mail Coach Liverpool	3	4	*BLS (84) 7*
(9) 65th Anniv. of 1st Regular Brit Airways Mail Service BF 1845 PS	5	10	*RFDC 30*
(10) 1960-1984 The Islington Soc. Protecting & Improving, N1	5	8	*Havering*
(11) Worshipful Company of Coachmakers and Harness Makers WC2	5	8	*Cotswold*
(12) Royal Mail Commemoration The Holyhead Mail Holyhead Gwynedd ..	5	—	*Post Office*
(13) North Eastern Parcel Centre Royal Mail Parcels Washington......	10	—	*Post Office*
(14) Worlds First Post Office Tram Blackpool	10	—	*Post Office*
(15) St. James's Church Piccadilly Tercentenary Year London W1	10	13	*St. J. Church*
(16) Colchester Castle Restoration 1984, Colchester.................	12	—	*n.o.c.*
(17) International Garden Festival Liverpool	10	—	*n.o.c.*
(18) UPU Exhibition June-July 1984 National Postal Museum EC1 ...	12	—	*n.o.c.*
(19) Wembley Exhibition 1924-1984 Grange Museum London NW10	12	15	*DGT*
(20) Island of Portland Heritage Trust Dorset	12	15	*PHT*
(21) International Essex Jamboree 1984 Great Leigh's Chelmsford	15	20	*Scouts*

C.D.S. POSTMARKS		
(22) Bath, Bristol, Edinburgh, Exeter, Holyhead, Liverpool, Norwich....each	7	
(23) Fleet Street, BO, EC4 — 'Bolt-in-Tun' Inn	8	
(24) Holyhead or Dun Laoghaire Paquebots ....each	17	
(25) Islington BO, N1 — 'The Angel Inn'	7	
(26) London Chief Office EC1	7	
(27) Marlborough, Wilts — Inn provided Bath Mail Coach horses	10	
(28) Moffat — scene of 'snowbound' Edinburgh Mail.................	8	
(29) Newmarket — scene of Norwich Mail in thunderstorm........	7	
(30) Thatcham, Newbury — Inn provided Bath Mail Coach horses	12	
(31) Winterslow or Lopcombe Corner — scene of the attack on the Exeter Mail	7	

In addition covers are known with the following CDS postmarks: Black Horse, Coach Road, Devonport. Prices range from £6.

SLOGAN POSTMARKS		
(32) Collect British Stamps, Lincoln or Cleveland	30	
(33) Be Properly Addressed, Post Code It, Hull........................	40	
(34) First Day of Issue (Envelope design), Bristol	8(s)	

> **PLEASE READ THE GENERAL NOTES AT THE BEGINNING OF THIS CATALOGUE**
> These often provide the answers to enquiries received.

25th September 1984 — THE BRITISH COUNCIL

17p Medicine; 22p Arts; 31p Construction; 34p Language

	ordinary covers £	official covers £	
SPECIAL HANDSTAMPS			
(1) First Day of Issue — Philatelic Bureau	3	—	*Post Office*
(2) First Day of Issue — London SW	3	—	*Post Office*
(3) The British Council 50th Anniversary London SW	4	10	*G&P*
(4) Centenary of the Oxford Exhibition Dictionary 1884-1984 Oxford	4	8	*Hawkwood*
(5) 1st Australian Stamp Exhibition Ausipex 84 Melbourne Derby	4	6	*BOCS (2) 31*
(6) Serving Asia, Africa & the Middle East RBPD 1976-84 Sutton	7	9	*Des. Enc.*
(7) Samuel Johnson 1709-1784, Lichfield Staffs	4	8	*LFDC 37*
(8) 44th Anniversary of Battle of Britain BF 1850 PS	6	10	*RFDC 31*
(9) Worlds First Post Office Tram Blackpool	6	—	*Post Office*
(10) St. James's Church Piccadilly Tercentenary Year London W1	5	—	*Post Office*
(11) Colchester Castle Restoration 1984, Colchester	8	—	*n.o.c.*
(12) International Garden Festival Liverpool	8	—	*n.o.c.*
(13) Speed, Regularity & Security Mail Coach Service, N.P.M	10	—	*n.o.c.*
(14) The Beagles Congratulate Daley Thompson & EBAC E13	10	15	*Havering*

C.D.S POSTMARKS

(15) Southampton St. BO, WC2 — 1st meeting of British Council	10	
(16) St. James's St. BO, SW1 — B.C. inaugurated at St. James's Palace	9	
(17) Trafalgar Sq. BO WC2 — nearest PO to British Council	10	
(18) Wadhurst — where Tippett wrote 'The Midsummer Marriage'	10	
(19) Walton St., Oxford — home of Oxford English Dictionary	7	
(20) Westminster Bdg. Rd. — Tippett, Director of Music, Morley Coll.	7	

In addition covers are known with the following CDS postmarks: Aberystwyth, Burgh, Dundee, King Edward VII Hospital, Lichfield, Limpsfield, Lower Broadheath, Melbourne, Oxford. Prices range from £7.

SLOGAN POSTMARKS

Doctor Johnson, Lichfield. Prices range from £15.

20th November 1984 — CHRISTMAS

13p, 17p, 22p, 31p, 34p The Nativity

SPECIAL HANDSTAMPS

(1) First Day of Issue — Philatelic Bureau	3	—	*Post Office*
(2) First Day of Issue — Bethlehem	3	—	*Post Office*
(3) Christian Heritage Year — Durham	5	6	*BOCS (2) 32*
(4) Christian Heritage Year — Ely	5	8	*BOCS (2) 32*
(5) Christian Heritage Year — Norwich	5	4	*BLS (84) 6*
(6) Christian Heritage Year — Liverpool	5	4	*BLS (84) 6*
(7) Christmas Isle of Iona	6	12	*Pilgrim*
(8) Glastonbury Abbey, Glastonbury Somerset	6	15	*Fine Arts 1*
(9) Christmas Greetings 1984 World Trade Centre London E1	6	8	*Havering*
(10) Christmas 1984 Weybridge Surrey	7	15	*S. Petty 25*
(11) Christmas Greetings Theatre Royal 1884-1984 Stratford E15	4	7	*Hawkwood*
(12) Seasons Greetings Telecom Technology Showcase London EC4	8	—	*n.o.c.*
(13) John Wycliffe c.1320-1384 Lutterworth Leics	6	9	*LFDC 38*
(14) The Lindisfarne Gospels Holy Island Berwick on Tweed	6	7	*S. Muscroft*
(15) Samuel Johnson 1709-1784 Lichfield Staffs	8	10	*Bradbury*
(16) Speed, Regularity & Security Mail Coach Service, N.P.M	10	—	*n.o.c.*

C.D.S. POSTMARKS

(17) Bethlehem, Llandeilo, Dyfed	7	
(18) Nasareth, Gwynedd	7	

In addition covers are known with the following CDS postmarks: Canterbury, Glastonbury, Holy Island, Holytown, Horbury Bridge, Jarrow, Lutterworth, Shepherd's Bush, Shepherd's Hill, Three Kingham. Prices range from £5.

SLOGAN POSTMARKS

(19) Hastings — A Resort for All Seasons (snowman and Xmas scene)	30	
(20) Halfpenny Green — Christmas 1984 — Dudley	35	

In addition: Late Night Shopping, Exeter. Prices range from £20.

CHRISTMAS DISCOUNT BOOKLET: Covers bearing pair or block of 4 × 13p Christmas stamps from booklet with relevant postmark 5

> PLEASE READ THE GENERAL NOTES
> AT THE BEGINNING OF THIS CATALOGUE
> These often provide the answers to enquiries received.

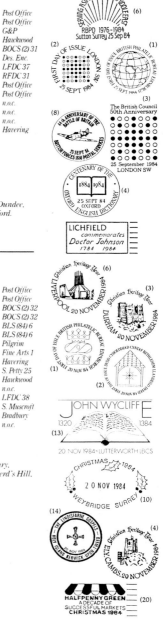

22nd January 1985 — FAMOUS TRAINS

17p Flying Scotsman; 22p Golden Arrow; 29p Cheltenham Flyer;
31p Royal Scot; 34p Cornish Riviera

1985

	ordinary covers	official covers	
SPECIAL HANDSTAMPS	£	£	
(1) First Day of Issue — Philatelic Bureau	5	—	*Post Office*
(2) First Day of Issue — Bristol	5	—	*Post Office*
(3) Steamtown Railway Museum Famous Trains, Carnforth, Lancs....	10	15	*LFDC 39*
(4) Flying Scotsman, Pride of Doncaster, Doncaster	10	15	*LFDC 39*
(5) 150th Anniv. GWR The Flying Scotsman King's Cross, N1 ..	10	15	*Benham L6*
(6) Scotrail, Edinburgh Welcomes the Flying Scotsman, Edinburgh ..	10	—	*n.o.c.*
(7) 150th Anniv. GWR The Golden Arrow 1929-1972 Dover, Kent	10	15	*Benham L8*
(8) Famous Trains Golden Arrow VSOE Victoria Station SW1	10	18	*G&P*
(9) VSOE Stops at Denham Station, Uxbridge, Middx.	10	—	*Post Office*
(10) GWR 150 Paddington Stn., London W2	10	25	*CoverCraft*
(11) Congratulations from the Great Western Hotel, Paddington W2 ...	10	25	*Fine Arts 2*
(12) 150th Anniv. GWR The Cheltenham Flyer, Cheltenham, Glos.	10	60	*B'ham 500 (1)*
(13) Great Western Town 150th Anniv. GWR 1835-1985 Swindon	10	12	*Hawkwood*
(14) 150th Anniversary GWR Didcot, Oxon	10	20	*814 TPO Gp*
(15) GWR Preservation Group Southall Railway Centre, Middx. .	10	12	*DGT*
(16) The Firefly Project Swindon	10	15	*Cotswold*
(17) 150th Anniv. GWR King George V Hereford, Shrewsbury....	10	—	*Post Office*
(18) Scotrail, Glasgow Welcomes The Royal Scot Glasgow	10	—	*n.o.c.*
(19) 150th Anniv. GWR The Royal Scot Euston Station London NW1 ..	10	15	*Benham L7*
(20) 150th Anniv. GWR The Cornish Riviera Paddington Stn., W2......	10	20	*BLCS 1*
(21) 150th Anniv. GWR The Cornish Riviera Penzance, Cornwall	10	20	*BLCS 1*
(22) National Railway Museum Famous Trains, York	10	—	*Post Office*
(23) York Station Rail Riders, Magical World of Trains, York	10	12	*DGT*
(24) N. Staffs Rly Co. Ltd. Tribute to Famous Trains, Leek	10	50	*NSRly*
(25) Railway Loco's The Royal British Legion Maidstone Kent	10	15	*Brit. Leg.*
(26) Battle of Britain Exhibition Hendon Spitfire BF 1857 PS	15	25	*RFDC 33*
(27) Picture Card MPB 15 2-2-2 Loco Rowland Hill 1885, Crewe...	20	—	*Post Office*
(28) National Assoc'n Boys' Clubs 1925-1985, Blenheim, Oxford .	20	30	*NABC*

C.D.S. POSTMARKS (inc. T.P.O. CANCELS)

(29) Carnforth, Lancs. — where Flying Scotsman is housed.........	15
(30) Cheltenham, Penzance or Swindon............................*each*	15
(31) Didcot, Oxon — GWR centre..	15
(32) Doncaster — where the Flying Scotsman was built	15
(33) Euston Centre B.O.; King's Cross B.O.; or Paddington B.O. .....*from*	20
(34) Railway Place, Coleraine	20
(35) Saltash — Brunel's famous GWR bridge	15
(36) Any 'station' postmark (Auchterless, Bosham, Carstairs Junction, Central Stn., Edinburgh, Crowthorne, Martin Mill, Meopham, Murton, Nigg, Nunthorpe, Timperley, Trimdon)...................*from*	20
(37) Any connected T.P.O. as follows (same route or part thereof):	

Flying Scotsman: North Eastern T.P.O. Night Up and Down;
London-York-Edinburgh; Edinburgh-York
Golden Arrow: South Western Night Up and Night Down
Cheltenham Flyer: Midland Going South and North; Bristol-Derby; Derby-Bristol
Royal Scot: Up and Down Specials; Up Special Glasgow Section; North Western Night Down; Crewe-Glasgow Sorting Carriage; Caledonian Up and Day Up Edinburgh Section

Cornish Riviera: Great Western Up and Down ....*from*	20
(38) Any other T.P.O. cancellations ....*from*	15

In addition covers are known with the following C.D.S. postmarks: City of Bristol, Edinburgh, Glasgow, Portsmouth, Silver Link, The Rocket. Prices range from £12.

A. G. BRADBURY
The top name in cover and postmark design.
Write for my latest colour leaflets.
3 LINK ROAD, STONEYGATE, LEICESTER LE2 3RA

93

12th March 1985 — BRITISH INSECTS
17p Buff Tailed Bumble Bee; 22p Seven Spotted Ladybird;
29p Water-Biter Bush-Cricket; 31p Stag Beetle;
34p Emperor Dragonfly

	ordinary covers £	official covers £	
SPECIAL HANDSTAMPS			
(1) First Day of Issue — Philatelic Bureau	4	—	*Post Office*
(2) First Day of Issue — London SW	4	—	*Post Office*
(3) Cent. Royal Entomological Soc. Meadow Bank, Cheshire	5	17	*B'ham 500 (2)*
(4) Centenary of Charter of Royal Ent. Soc., London SW7	5	6	*BLCS 2*
(5) A.E.S. Golden Jubilee 1935-1985 Feltham, Middx.	5	17	*LFDC 40*
(6) Selborne Society Centenary 1885-1985 Gilbert White, Alton	6	10	*Cotswold*
(7) Writhlington School, Radstock, Avon	5	15	*Writh. Sch.*
(8) British Insects British Museum Natural History, London SW7	5	6	*BLCS 2*
(9) 1980-1985 Stamp Bug Club 5th Anniv. High Wycombe, Bucks.	5	25	*SB Club*
(10) Bugford, Dartmouth Devon I AM FIVE 1980-1985	5	30	*SB Club*
(11) Nature Conservation Hummer Sherborne, Dorset	5	—	*Post Office*
(12) The Enfield Butterfly Centre, British Insects Exh., Enfield	5	7	*Hawkwood*
(13) Robert Hooke The Minute Anatomist, Freshwater, I.O.W.	5	15	*Fine Arts 3*
(14) 21st Anniv. Scottish Wildlife Trust, Edinburgh	5	10	*Pilgrim*
(15) 45th Anniv. of Mosquito Aircraft BF 1862 PS	6	8	*RFDC 34*
(16) Pestalozzi Children's Village Trust Hastings E. Sussex	25	—	*n.o.c.*
(17) National Assoc'n Boys' Clubs 1925-1985 Abercrave, Swansea	15	25	*NABC*
C.D.S. POSTMARKS			
(18) Buckfastleigh — Buckfast Abbey monks famous for bee-keeping	7		
(19) Nettleham — HQ of Society for Nature Conservation	8		
(20) St. Bees	7		
(21) St. James' St SW1 — inaugural meetings of R.E.S.	7		
(22) Selborne — Gilbert White's 'Natural History of Selborne'	7		
(23) South Kensington SW7 — Royal Entomological Society	7		

In addition covers are known with the following C.D.S. postmarks: Alexandra Park, Alexandra,
Beeston, Bugthorpe, Church St. Enfield, Dunkeld, Duns, Feltham, Fleet St., Kingsstag, Lady,
Meadow Bank, Northam, Sedgfield, Sheerness, Wickham, Writhlington. Prices range from £6.

14th May 1985 — BRITISH COMPOSERS
17p Handel — Water Music; 22p Holst — The Planets;
31p Delius — The First Cuckoo; 34p Elgar — Sea Pictures

SPECIAL HANDSTAMPS			
(1) First Day of Issue — Philatelic Bureau	3	—	*Post Office*
(2) First Day of Issue — Worcester	3	—	*Post Office*
(3) 300th Anniv. Handel's Birthday Royal Opera House London WC	4	6	*BLCS 3*
(4) George Frideric Handel Westminster Abbey London SW1	4	8	*LFDC 41*
(5) St. Paul's Cathedral 850 Years of Music City of London	4	10	*St. Paul's*
(6) 1975-1985 Holst Birthplace Museum Cheltenham Glos.	4	10	*H.B. Museum*
(7) Gustav Holst European Music Year, Cheltenham Glos.	3	15	*B'ham 500 (3)*
(8) Stagenhoe Park Home of Sullivan, Cent. of Mikado, Hitchin	4	4	*Hawkwood*
(9) Delius Festival St. George's Hall Bradford W. Yorks.	4	4	*P. Scott*
(10) Sir Edward Elgar University of Birmingham. Birmingham	5	—	*n.o.c.*
(11) Sir Michael Tippett 80th Birthday, E.M.Y., Bournemouth	5	8	*Pilgrim*
(12) British Composers G.L.C. Royal Festival Hall London SE1	4	4	*G.L.C.*
(13) European Music Year High Wycombe Bucks.	5	—	*n.o.c.*
(14) Scottish National Orch. SNO Music Week 85 Aberdeen	4	10	*Benham L9*
(15) Scottish National Orch. SNO Proms 85 Dundee	4	10	*Benham L10*
(16) 128th Anniv. Royal Military School of Music BF 2128 PS	4	8	*RFDC 35*
(17) European Music Year National Postal Museum EC1	5	—	*n.o.c.*
(18) Leicester Philharmonic Society Centenary Season Leicester	4	10	*L. PO*
(19) 1st Ruislip Guides Celebrate 75th Anniv. Ruislip, Middx.	6	16	*Ruislip GG*
(20) St. David's Hall, Nat. Concert Hall of Wales, Cardiff	6	10	*Pilgrim*
(21) Haddo House National Trust for Scotland Aberdeen	5	10	*Pilgrim*
(22) Lennon & McCartney, Classic Composers of Today Liverpool	8	10	*Fine Arts 4*
(23) Philatelic Counter — Worcester	8	—	*n.o.c.*
(24) Centenary of SSAFA 1885-1985 London SW1	10	15	*SSAFA*
(25) North Norfolk Railway Poppy Line Trips Sheringham Norfolk	10	15	*NNR*
(26) Royal Visit of HRH The Princess of Wales London E13	10	12	*Havering*
(27) Ultramar Fifty Years London EC	10	50	*CoverCraft*
(28) National Assoc'n Boys' Clubs 1925-1985, Edinburgh	10	25	*NABC*
(29) 700th Mayoral Anniv. 1285-1985 High Wycombe	10	15	*High Wycombe DC*

PRICES & CONDITION – PLEASE READ GENERAL NOTES

British Composers (contd.)	ordinary covers £	official covers £
C.D.S. POSTMARKS		
(30) Chichester — Holst buried in Chichester Cathedral............	7	
(31) Hammersmith — Holst wrote 'Planets' whilst teaching here	7	
(32) Limpsfield, Surrey — Delius is interred here	8	
(33) Lower Broadheath, Worcs. — Elgar's birthplace	10	
(34) Lowesmoor, Worcs. — Elgar died here	9	
(35) Pittville, Cheltenham — Holst's birthplace	9	
(36) South Molton Street W1 — Handel lived here	7	
(37) Thaxted — Holst wrote 'Planets' whilst living here............	10	
(38) University, Bradford — nearest PO to Delius's birthplace	8	
(39) Upper Welland, Malvern, or Malvern — Elgar buried locally	9	

In addition covers are known with the following C.D.S. postmarks: Brigg, Chelsea, Hereford, Whitwell. Prices range from £3½.

SLOGAN POSTMARKS

(40) CBSO Proms 1945-1985 Town Hall B'ham (on two covers)...	30	
(41) The Bradford Delius Festival May 20th-26th (on two covers)	30	

In addition: Hereford Cathedral; North Wiltshire Entertains. Prices range from £50.

18th June 1985 — SAFETY AT SEA

17p Lifeboat; 22p Lighthouse; 31p Satellite; 34p Buoy

SPECIAL HANDSTAMPS

	ordinary	official	
(1) First Day of Issue — Philatelic Bureau	3	—	*Post Office*
(2) First Day of Issue — Eastbourne, E. Sussex	3	—	*Post Office*
(3) The Plimsoll Line, Bristol	4	—	*Post Office*
(4) Spurn Head Lifeboat 175th Year 1810-1985, Hull	4	—	*Post Office*
(5) Lifeboat Dedication Cromer, Norfolk	4	10	*RNLI*
(6) Lifeboat Display Poole, Dorset..	4	10	*RNLI*
(7) Berwick-upon-Tweed Lifeboat Service 1835-1985	4	10	*B.u.T. Lifeboat*
(8) Appledore RNLI Lifeboat Station Bideford, Devon.............	4	10	*Appledore LS*
(9) 200th Anniv. Earliest Lifeboat Design, Lowestoft, Suffolk...	4	15	*B'ham 500 (4)*
(10) Grace Darling Museum Bamburgh, Northumberland	4	6	*LFDC 42*
(11) Lukin's Patent for Lifeboat Design 200th Anniv. Hythe, Kent	4	10	*BLCS 4*
(12) The Lighthouse Club Whitley Bay, Tyne & Wear	4	10	*Light. Club*
(13) Nore Lightship Historic Ship Collection, London E1..........	4	10	*Fine Arts*
(14) Global Maritime Safety at Sea London WC2	4	10	*Global*
(15) 200 Years Safety at Sea Maritime Museum Greenwich, SE10	4	5	*BLCS 4*
(16) Schermuly celebrates Safety at Sea Greenwich SE10.........	4	10	*Schermuly*
(17) Sealion Shipping 1975-1985 Tenth Anniv. City of London....	4	10	*Sealion*
(18) 50th Anniv. The Geographical Magazine, London SW7	5	4	*Hawkwood*
(19) 70th Anniv. Formation No. 22 Squadron RAF BF 1890 PS ..	7	12	*RFDC 36*
(20) British Film Year Bristol..	8	12	*CoverCraft*
(21) The Ashes Tour 1985 London NW8	8	12	*S.P.*
(22) London Welsh Rugby Football Club Cent. Richmond, Surrey......	8	12	*London Welsh*
(23) Re-opening Lawn Tennis Museum Wimbledon SW19.........	8	12	*AELTA*
(24) North Norfolk Railway Poppy Line Trips Sheringham, Norfolk ..	8	12	*NNR*
(25) Nat. Assoc. of Boys' Clubs 1925-1985 River Severn, Worcester	8	25	*NABC*
(26) GWR 150 Exhibition Train Shrewsbury SY1 1AA..............	8	8	*BLCS 4*
(27) Scottish National Orchestra SNO Proms 85 Glasgow	8	—	*n.o.c.*

C.D.S. POSTMARKS

(28) Anstruther or Cromer — site of both lighthouse and lifeboats....	6	
(29) Austhorpe — b/place of Smeaton (Eddystone Lighthouse)..........	6	
(30) Bamburgh — first lifeboat station..................................	6	
(31) Cawsand, Toward Point or Whitley Bay — lighthouses	6	
(32) Daventry — first successful radar experiments	9	
(33) Dover — Britain's first lighthouse — built by the Romans.....	8	
(34) East Dean or Grand Hotel Blgs, Eastbourne — Beachy Head	8	
(35) Hawes, N. Yorks — birthplace of Sir W. Hillary — RNLI founder .	6	
(36) Hythe — Lionel Lukin is buried here	8	
(37) Lighthouse, Fleetwood, Lancs.	10	
(38) Little Dunmow — birthplace of Lionel Lukin....................	9	
(39) Poole — Headquarters of RNLI.....................................	7	
(40) Redcar — The 'Zetland' oldest lifeboat in Redcar RNLI Museum	7	
(41) Richmond — b/place of H. Greathead — builder of 'Zetland'	7	
(42) Seething Lane EC3 — nearest PO to Trinity House............	6	
(43) Culdrose or Yeovilton RN Air Stations (Air-Sea Rescue)......	18	

(1)

(26) London E.3 14-5-1985

(27) ULTRAMAR FIFTY YEARS

London EC 14 May 1985 (15)

SCOTTISH NATIONAL ORCHESTRA PROMS 85 DUNDEE MAY 14th 1985

(14) Safety at Sea 18 June 85 London WC2 GLOBAL MARITIME

(1) FIRST DAY OF ISSUE BRITISH PHILATELIC BUREAU EDINBURGH

(2) FIRST DAY OF ISSUE EASTBOURNE E. SUSSEX 18 JUNE 1985

(6) LIFE-BOAT DISPLAY 18 JUN 85 POOLE DORSET

(5) LIFE-BOAT DEDICATION 18 JUNE 1985 CROMER NORFOLK

(10) GRACE DARLING MUSEUM BAMBURGH 18 JUNE 1985 NORTHUMBERLAND

(13) NORE Historic Ship 18 June 1985 St. Katharine's Dock London, E.1

1810 R N L I 1985 SPURN HEAD LIFEBOAT 175th YEAR HULL 18 JUNE 1985 (4)

(9) 200th ANNIVERSARY EARLIEST LIFEBOAT DESIGN LOWESTOFT SUFFOLK 18 JUNE 1985

(11) PATENT FOR LIFEBOAT DESIGN 200th ANNIVERSARY 18 JUNE 1985 HYTHE KENT

(17) SEA-LION SHIPPING TENTH ANNIVERSARY 1975-1985 18 JUNE 1985 CITY OF LONDON

Safety at Sea (contd.)

	ordinary covers £	official covers £

(44) Any RAF (Air-Sea Rescue) Station — Finningley, Lindholme,
Valley St. Athan Main Site or St. Athan 15

(45) Cottishall, Leuchars, Manston, Portland, or Prestwick Airport —
RN or RAF Stations (Air-Sea Rescue) 12

In addition covers are known with the following C.D.S. postmarks: Beacon, Camborne, Marton-in-Cleveland, Sheerness, Six Bells, The Rocket, Thorpe Esplanade, Yeovil. Prices range from £5.

SLOGAN POSTMARKS

(46) Relax at Sunny Weymouth........................... 75

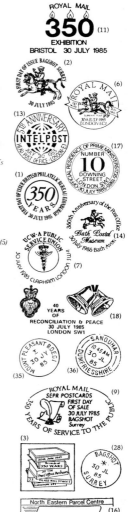

30th July 1985 — 350th ANNIVERSARY OF THE ROYAL MAIL
17p Datapost; 22p Postbus; 31p Parcel Post; 34p Letter Post

SPECIAL HANDSTAMPS

(1) First Day of Issue — Philatelic Bureau .... 3 — *Post Office*
(2) First Day of Issue — Bagshot .... 3 — *Post Office*
(3) Records of 350 Years P.O. Archives, 23 Glass Hill Street, SE1 ...... 4 10 *Fine Arts 6*
(4) Nat. Post. Museum 350 Years Service to the Public London EC1 . 4 — *Post Office*
(5) 350th Anniv. Thomas Witherings Postmaster 1635 Hornchurch.. 4 10 *St. Andrew's*
(6) Royal Mail London Post 350 Years 1635-1985 London EC1.. 4 — *Post Office*
(7) UCWA Public Service Union Clapham London SW4 .... 4 4 *BLCS 5*
(8) Royal Mail 350 Years of Service to the Public London EC .... 4 — *Post Office*
(9) Royal Mail SEPR Postcards First Day of Sale Bagshot, Surrey .... 4 — *Post Office*
(10) Royal Mail SEPR Postcards First Day of Sale Windsor, Berks. .... 4 — *Post Office*
(11) Royal Mail 350 Exhibition Bristol.................................... 4 — *Post Office*
(12) Post Paid 100 Years in the City of London Healey & Wise EC4 ... 4 10 *H & W*
(13) 5th Anniv. Intelpost Head Post Office London E1 .... 4 10 *Hawkwood*
(14) 350th Anniv. of the Post Office, Postal Museum, Bath, Avon .... 4 13 *B'ham 500 (5)*
(15) National Postal Museum, London EC1 (Red Maltese Cross) .... 10 — *Post Office*
(16) North Eastern Parcels Centre Royal Mail Parcels Washington..... 10 — *Post Office*
(17) Official Residence of Prime Ministers 10 Downing Street, SW1 .. 8 35 *LFDC 43*
(18) British Legion 40 Years of Reconciliation & Peace London SW1 .. 9 12 *Brit. Leg.*
(19) The Cardiff Tattoo BF 1879 PS.. 9 14 *Forces*
(20) Norton 100 1885-1985 Leicester....................................... 10 25 *N. Clipper*
(21) GWR 150 Steam Special Swindon — Gloucester, Gloucester .... 10 — *n.o.c.*
(22) M.C.C. Cricket Festival, Uxbridge, Middlesex.................... 10 25 *MCC*
(23) The Ashes Tour 1985 London NW8 .... 10 12 *S.P.*
(24) North Norfolk Railway Poppy Line Trips Sheringham, Norfolk ... 10 14 *NNR*
(25) Nat. Assoc. of Boys' Clubs 1925-1985 Trentham Gdns., Stoke ..... 10 25 *NABC*
(26) Ptarmigan Equipment in Service BF 3254 PS .... 10 10 *RFDC 37*

C.D.S. POSTMARKS

(27) Aberfeldy — postbus 12
(28) Bagshot — where Charles I made his Proclamation............ 7
(29) Buckingham Palace, SW1 40
(30) Cannon Street, EC1 6
(31) Hornchurch — Thomas Witherings, first postmaster buried here 7
(32) Letter, Enniskillen... 12
(33) Llangurig or Llanidloes — world's first ever postbus 20
(34) Lombard Street EC3 — General Letter Office 8
(35) Mount Pleasant — Britain's major sorting office 12
(36) Sanquhar — Britain's oldest Post Office 10
(37) Stock Exchange EC2 — PO for Royal Exchange (on 17p value) 15

In addition covers are known with the following C.D.S. postmarks: Brighton, Dunfermline, Edinburgh, Henfield, House of Commons, Kidderminster, Kingstanding and FPO postmarks. Postbridge. Prices range from £5.

SLOGAN POSTMARKS

(38) Royal Mail 350 Years of Service to the Public — In Business to
serve you — used at several offices...................................... 12
(39) Make any Post Office in Cleveland your first stop, etc. 40

OTHER POSTMARKS

(40) Parcel Post cancellation — known used at Chingford, London E4 . 40

ROYAL MAIL DISCOUNT BOOKLET

Covers bearing pair or block of 4 × 17p 'Datapost' stamps from
booklet with relevant postmark 4

A. G. BRADBURY
The top name in cover and postmark design.
Write for my latest colour leaflets.
3 LINK ROAD, STONEYGATE, LEICESTER LE2 3RA

3rd September 1985 — ARTHURIAN LEGEND

17p King Arthur & Merlin; 22p The Lady of the Lake;
31p Guinever & Lancelot; 34p Sir Galahad

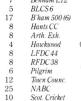

	ordinary covers	official covers	
SPECIAL HANDSTAMPS	£	£	
(1) First Day of Issue — Philatelic Bureau	3	—	*Post Office*
(2) First Day of Issue — Tintagel, Cornwall	3	8	*Post Office*
(3) Arthurian Legend The Sword & The Stone St. Paul's EC4....	5	10	*Fine Arts 7*
(4) Legendary Camelot Old Post Office Tintagel Cornwall	5	7	*Benham L12*
(5) The Legendary Camelot Winchester, Hants.	5	5	*BLCS 6*
(6) Morte D'Arthur Mere Warminster, Wilts.	5	17	*B'ham 500 (6)*
(7) The Great Hall Winchester Hants.	5	8	*Hants CC*
(8) Land of Arthur Exhibition of Celtic Legend Glastonbury	5	8	*Arth. Exh.*
(9) St. Margaret's Church Caxton's Mort D'Arthur London SW1	5	4	*Hawkwood*
(10) King Arthur's Avalon Glastonbury, Somerset	5	8	*LFDC 44*
(11) 80th Anniv. Royal Fleet Auxiliary BF 1880 PS	6	8	*RFDC 38*
(12) 40th Anniv. Leith Hall Nat. Trust for Scotland, Huntly	6	6	*Pilgrim*
(13) Stockton on Tees Town Hall 250th Anniv. Year Cleveland	8	12	*Town Counc.*
(14) Nat. Assoc. of Boys' Clubs 1925-1985 Guildhall London EC3	8	25	*NABC*
(15) BI Centenary Cricket in Scotland Schaw Park Alloa	8	10	*Scot. Cricket*
(16) Nat. Post. Museum 350 Years Service to the Public London EC1 ..	8	—	*Post Office*
(17) North Norfolk Railway Poppy Line Trips Sheringham	8	8	*NNR*
(18) 40th Anniversary 23 BASE WKSP REME, BF 2340 PS	8	10	*Forces*
ORDINARY F.D.I. POSTMARKS			
(19) Cardiff or Newport — Arthur was King of Glamorgan and Gwent ..	6		
C.D.S. POSTMARKS			
(20) Amesbury – Guinevere became a nun and died here	8		
(21) Bamburgh — Lancelot's Castle of 'Joyous Gard'	8		
(22) Bodmin — Dozmary Pool where Excalibur was cast	8		
(23) Camelford — where Arthur was mortally wounded by Mordred	10		
(24) Glastonbury — the legendary 'Isle of Avalon'.	6		
(25) King Arthur's Way, Andover	10		
(26) Lancelot Place, London SW7	10		
(27) Merlin's Bridge, Haverfordwest	12		
(28) Silchester — where Arthur was crowned	8		
(29) South Cadbury — the most probable site of 'Camelot'	10		
(30) Stretton-under-Fosse — birthplace of Malory	9		
(31) Tintagel — birthplace of Arthur	8		
(32) Winchester — the Round Table is housed in the Great Hall ...	8		

In addition covers are known with the following C.D.S. postmarks: Caxton, Corfe Castle, Knight's Road, Tregaron. Prices range from £7.

SLOGAN POSTMARKS
Carlisle — worth a closer look. Prices range from £45.

8th October 1985 — BRITISH FILM YEAR

17p Peter Sellers; 22p David Niven; 29p Charles Chaplin;
31p Vivien Leigh; 34p Alfred Hitchcock

SPECIAL HANDSTAMPS			
(1) First Day of Issue — Philatelic Bureau	4	—	*Post Office*
(2) First Day of Issue — London WC	4	—	*Post Office*
(3) British Film Year MCMLXXXV London W1	6	10	*LFDC 45*
(4) British Film Year Bradford W. Yorkshire	6	15	*BLCS 7*
(5) British Film Year Richmond Surrey	6	30	*B'ham 500 (7)*
(6) British Film Year Leicester Square London WC2 (rectangular)	6	10	*Arlington*
(7) British Film Year Goldcrest London W1	6	12	*G&P*
(8) British Film Year David Niven Campaign MNDA Northampton ...	6	8	*Cotswold*
(9) British Film Year Leicester Sq. London WC2 (circular)	6	20	*BLCS 7*
(10) Equity Celebrates British Film Year Harley St. London W1 ..	6	15	*Fine Arts 8*
(11) 50 Years 1935-1985 National Film Archives London W1	10	13.	*N.F.A.*
(12) 30th Anniv. Dambusters last Operationl Sorties BF 2101 PS	8	20	*RFDC 39*
(13) Alfred Hitchcock Exh. Hitchcock Hotel, Leytonstone E11	8	8	*Hawkwood*
(14) Charrington Pres. Yr. Bass LVNH Denham Village Uxbridge	6	10	*Havering*
(15) National Postal Museum Film Festival London EC1	8	—	*n.o.c.*
(16) Brian Reeve Opening of New Stamp Shop London WC2	8	8	*DGT*
(17) Perth Theatre 50th Season Perth	8	12	*Perth*
(18) EPR Opening Arndale Centre Branch Office Luton	10	—	*n.o.c.*
(19) National Postal Museum London EC1 350 Years Royal Mail .	10	—	*n.o.c.*
(20) Nat. Assoc. of Boys' Clubs 1925-1985 Belfast	12	25	*NABC*

3:9·1985
SCHAW PARK
ALLOA

The David Niven Campaign for the
Motor Neurone Disease Association
8 OCTOBER 85   NORTHAMPTON

PRICES & CONDITION – PLEASE READ GENERAL NOTES

97

Film Year (contd.)

	ordinary covers £	official covers £

C.D.S. POSTMARKS

(21) Bray; Denham; Hammersmith; Shepherd's Bush; St. Margaret's Twickenham; St. Mary's Road, Ealing; Walton; Welwyn; or Wembley — all sites of film studios ....from	10
(22) Castle Road, Southsea — birthplace of Peter Sellers	8
(23) Down Special T.P.O. — Post Office film 'Night Mail'............	25
(24) East Street, Walworth — birthplace of Charles Chaplin	7
(25) Elstree — famous film studios..	12
(26) Hollywood, Birmingham	10
(27) Iver Heath — site of Pinewood film studios.........................	10
(28) Kirriemuir, Angus — home of David Niven	6
(29) Lacock — home of Fox Talbot (inventor photographic negative) ...	6
(30) Leytonstone — birthplace of Alfred Hitchcock	8
(31) Maida Vale — home of Friese Green (inventor of cine)	6
(32) Shepperton, Middx. — famous film studios.........................	15
(33) Victoria Street, SW1 — birthplace of David Niven	15

In addition covers are known with the following C.D.S. postmarks: Chancery Lane, Goonhaven, Queens Rd., Shamley Green, Sloane Square, Star. Prices range from £6.

SLOGAN POSTMARKS
Eden Court, Theatre. Prices from £35.

19th November 1985 — CHRISTMAS
12p, 17p, 22p, 31p, 34p – pantomime characters

SPECIAL HANDSTAMPS

(1) First Day of Issue — Philatelic Bureau	3	—	*Post Office*
(2) First Day of Issue — Bethlehem, Llandeilo, Dyfed	3	—	*Post Office*
(3) Christmas Greetings Telecom Technology Showcase EC4 ...	5	—	*n.o.c.*
(4) Nottingham Theatre Royal Presents Aladdin Nottingham ..	5	6	*LFDC 46*
(5) Traditional Home of the English Pantomime Drury Lane WC2....	5	10	*B'ham 500 (8)*
(6) Peace on Earth Sewardstone Evan. Church Christmas '85 E4......	5	6	*Hawkwood*
(7) Mother Goose Pantomime Goose Green Biddenden Ashford	5	5	*BLCS 8*
(8) Cinderella at the Palladium London W1.............................	5	12	*Fine Arts 9*
(9) National Postal Museum London EC1 350 Years Royal Mail	8	—	*n.o.c.*
(10) Nat. Assoc. of Boys' Clubs 1925-1985 Althorp, Northampton	8	25	*NABC*

C.D.S. POSTMARKS

(11) Bethlehem, Llandeilo, Dyfed	8
(12) Nasareth, Gwynedd	15
(13) Shrewsbury — birthplace of John Weaver (father of pantomime)..	8
(14) The Harlequin, Radcliffe-on-Trent	10

In addition covers are known with the following C.D.S. postmarks: Holy Island, Lilliput, Old Whittington, Robin Hood, Star, The Circle, Whittington. Prices range from £6.

SLOGAN POSTMARKS
Eastgate Shopping; Eden Court Theatre; Exeter Late Shopping; Explorer Bus Tickets. Prices range from £15.

CHRISTMAS BOOKLET: Covers bearing pair or block of 4 × 12p stamps from booklet with special handstamp   5

14th January 1986 — INDUSTRY YEAR
17p Energy; 22p Health; 31p Leisure; 34p Food

SPECIAL HANDSTAMPS

(1) First Day of Issue — Philatelic Bureau	3	—	*Post Office*
(2) First Day of Issue — Birmingham	3	—	*Post Office*
(3) Ironbridge Birthplace of Industry, Telford.........................	5	10	*LFDC 47*
(4) Centenary RTH Rank Taylor Hobson Industry Year, Leicester	5	10	*RTH*
(5) Osram A Leading Light in Industry Year '86 Wembley, Middx	6	100	*G&P*
(6) British Steel, Industry Year 1986, London SE1....................	6	15	*CoverCraft*
(7) Purveyors of Flour Hovis Centenary 1886-1986, Windsor, Berks .	6	100	*CoverCraft*
(8) The Workers Playground Since 1840, Blackpool, Lancs	5	5	*BLCS 9*
(9) Farming the Industry that Feeds the Nation, Wheatacre, Beccles	5	10	*B'ham 500(9)*
(10) British Steel Smelters Assoc'n 1886-1986 ISTC, London WC1	6	8	*BSSA*
(11) 1976 A Breakthrough in Ulcer Therapy, Welwyn, Herts	5	50	*Smith K.F.*
(12) All Industrious People are Happy, Blackwells, Oxford	5	7	*Hawkwood*
(13) Industry Year BP, London EC	5	7	*BP*
(14) World Leading Energy Technology, Aberdeen	7	—	*n.o.c.*
(15) 70th Anniv. Soc. British Aerospace Companies BF 2105 PS	8	10	*RFDC 41*
(16) Goodwill Centenary The Salvation Army Hoxton, London N1	10	12	*H.R.*
(17) Nat. Postal Museum 350 Years Royal Mail, London EC1	10	—	*n.o.c.*

	ordinary covers £	official covers £

C.D.S. POSTMARKS
(18) Aycliffe; Slough or Team Valley Trading Estates 15
(19) Bridgend; Kirby or Treforest Industrial Estates 15
(20) Clydebank — shipbuilding industry 10
(21) Cruden Bay, Peterhead — North Sea oil pipeline 7
(22) Furnace, Inverary or Furnace End, Birmingham 10
(23) Greenock — birthplace of James Watt 7
(24) Ironbridge, Telford — 'Birthplace of Industry' 10
(25) Oxford St., Sunderland — birthplace of Joseph Swan (light bulb) . 7
(26) Steel or Steel City House 15
In addition covers are known with the following C.D.S. postmarks: Bacton, Bakewell, NEC Birmingham, New Invention, Pill. Prices range from £6.

SLOGAN POSTMARKS
Clydebank; Sedgemoor has the Edge; Nissan Sunderland. Prices range from £35.

18th February 1986 — HALLEY'S COMET
17p, 22p, 31p, 34p

SPECIAL HANDSTAMPS
(1) First Day of Issue — Philatelic Bureau .... 4 — *Post Office*
(2) First Day of Issue — London SE10 .... 4 — *Post Office*
(3) Old Royal Observatory, Happy Returns Halley, Greenwich SE10 . 4 5 *BLCS 10*
(4) A Return at Halley's Comet, Winscombe, Avon........... 4 13 *B'ham 500(10)*
(5) Giotto Halley's Comet Interceptor, Bristol......................... 4 10 *CoverCraft*
(6) Halley's Comet Society, London SE10 .... 4 9 *HC Soc.*
(7) Islington Home of Halley Salutes his Comet, London N1 ..... 4 7 *Hawkwood*
(8) The London Planetarium Celebrates Halley's Comet, NW1 .... 4 10 *LFDC 48*
(9) The Return of Halley's Comet Interplanetary Society, SW .... 4 6 *DGT*
(10) Edmund Halley born 1656 Haggerston, London E2 .... 4 12 *Fine Arts*
(11) Halley's Comet Royal Greenwich Observatory, Herstmonceux .... 4 7 *K&D*
(12) Commemorating Skynet 4A Satellite BF 2109 PS .... 4 15 *RFDC 42*
(13) Royal Mail Opening Fiveways Stamp Shop, Tunbridge Wells ...... 8 — *Post Office*
(14) Royal Mail SEPR Postcards First Day of Sale, Brighton ...... 8 — *Post Office*
(15) Ripon 1100 AD886-1986 Ripon, N. Yorks .... 8 8 *Ripon Counc.*
(16) Nat. Postal Museum 350 Years Royal Mail, London EC1 ..... 8 — *n.o.c.*

C.D.S. POSTMARKS
(17) Battle, Sussex — Bayeux Tapestry features Halley's Comet . 6
(18) Filton, Bristol — Giotto Project Team based here 8
(19) Greenwich or Herstmonceux — new and old observatories .. 10
(20) Hartland, Bideford — home of Magnetic Observatory......... 7
(21) Helston, Cornwall — Satellite Earth Station (Goonhilly Downs)... 7
(22) Islington — Home of Edmund Halley.................................. 7
(23) Lower Withington, Macclesfield — Nearest PO to Jodrell Bank ... 6
(24) Macclesfield — Jodrell Bank 8
(25) Seven Sisters or Star 8
(26) Shoreditch — birthplace of Edmund Halley 7

SLOGAN POSTMARKS
Shop at any Post Office; Zone Tickets etc; Industry Year. Prices from £18.

21st April 1986 — H.M. THE QUEEN'S 60th BIRTHDAY
2 × 17p; 2 × 34p

SPECIAL HANDSTAMPS
(1) First Day of Issue — Philatelic Bureau .... 4 — *Post Office*
(2) First Day of Issue — Windsor.. 4 — *Post Office*
(3) Birthday Greetings, London SW1 .... 5 12 *LFDC 49*
(4) HM The Queen's Birthday, Sandringham Norfolk .... 5 5 *BLCS 11B*
(5) HM The Queen's Birthday, London SW1 .... 5 6 *BLCS 11A*
(6) Lombard North Central, 17 Bruton St., Birthplace, London W1 .. 5 5 *G&P*
(7) HM The Queen's Birthday, Windsor, Berks .... 5 17 *B'ham 500(11)*
(8) Radio Times Congratulates HM The Queen, London W1.... 5 10 *Arlington*
(9) Commemorating HM The Queen's 60th Birthday, London SW1.. 5 10 *Arlington*
(10) Southend Salutes Queen's 60th Birthday, Pier Train, Southend ... 5 7 *Hawkwood*
(11) 50th Anniversary of the Queen's Flight BF 2106 PS........... 5 20 *RFDC 43*
(12) HM The Queen's 60th Birthday Bruton St. Happy Returns, W1 .. 5 7 *K&D*
(13) HM The Queen's Birthday Balmoral, Crathie Aberdeenshire ..... 5 18 *Benham S.G. 1*

> PLEASE READ THE GENERAL NOTES
> AT THE BEGINNING OF THIS CATALOGUE
> These often provide the answers to enquiries received.

H.M. The Queen's 60th Birthday (contd.)

		ordinary covers £	official covers £	
(14)	Loyal Greetings the City of London, London EC	5	—	*n.o.c.*
(15)	Many Happy Returns National Postal Museum, London EC1	5	—	*n.o.c.*
(16)	60th Birthday HM The Queen Lord High Admiral BF 2113 PS	5	30	*Royal Navy*
(17)	The Royal British Legion Happy Birthday to our Patron, SW1	5	8	*Brit. Leg.*
(18)	London SW1 (Buckingham Palace) — permanent handstamp	8	—	*n.o.c.*
(19)	Windsor (Castle) Philatelic Counter handstamp	8	—	*n.o.c.*
(20)	Tower Hill (Tower of London) — permanent handstamp	8	—	*n.o.c.*
(21)	Royal Academy of Dancing 1936-1986, London SW11	7	20	*CoverCraft*
(22)	First Day of Issue — N. Ireland £1 Coin Royal Mint, Llantrisant	7	—	*n.o.c.*
(23)	Federation of Women's Institutes Denham College, Chichester	7	8	*Fed. WI*
(24)	Durham County Spastics Society 21 Years of Service, Durham	10	10	*DCSS*
(25)	100th Presidency Licensed Victuallers Soc., Horsham	12	40	*Rum Merchants*
(26)	G&J Swingler Ltd. 1786-1986, Birmingham	10	12	*G&J Sw.*
(27)	BNAI Brith District 15 1926-1986, London WC1	10	15	*B.B.*
(28)	80 Years of Austin Rover, Birmingham	10	25	*A. Rover*
(29)	Open Days Broadlands, Romsey, Hants	10	10	*Broadlands*
(30)	Greetings from the Thames Barrier Visitors Centre, SE18	8	20	*CoverCraft*
(31)	Nat. Postal Museum 350 Years Royal Mail, London EC1	8	—	*n.o.c.*

C.D.S. POSTMARKS

(32)	Aldershot — HM Queen enroled in A.T.S., Aldershot 1944	6	
(33)	Badminton — part of stamp designs depicts HM at Horse Trials	6	
(34)	Buckingham Palace, SW1	100	
(35)	Camberley Surrey	6	
(36)	Crathie, Aberdeenshire – near to Balmoral	8	
(37)	House of Commons SW1	15	
(38)	House of Lords SW1	17	
(39)	Mount Street, W1 — nearest PO to Queen's birthplace	6	
(40)	Romsey, Hants — HM Queen spent honeymoon at Broadlands	6	
(41)	Queen Elizabeth Ave; Queen's Parade; or Queensway ..from	10	
(42)	Windsor, Berks	10	
(43)	Windsor Great Park, Windsor, Berks	10	
(44)	Windsor Castle, Berks	120	

In addition covers are known with the following C.D.S. postmarks: RAF Benson.
Prices range from £10.

20th May 1986 — NATURE CONSERVATION

17p Barn Owl; 22p Pine Marten; 31p Wild Cat; 34p Natterjack Toad

SPECIAL HANDSTAMPS

(1)	First Day of Issue — Philatelic Bureau	4	—	*Post Office*
(2)	First Day of Issue — Lincoln	4	—	*Post Office*
(3)	Caring for the Countryside Ramblers' Assoc'n., London SW8	5	13	*LFDC 50*
(4)	The Barn Owl Endangered Species, Owlsmoor Camberley, Surrey	5	13	*B'ham 500(12)*
(5)	RSPB Endangered Species, Sandy, Beds	5	7	*BLCS 12*
(6)	Life & Landscape on the Norfolk Broads 1886-1986, Norwich	5	10	*Brs.Inf.Ltd*
(7)	The Wildfowl Trust 1946-1986, Slimbridge, Gloucester	5	7	*BLCS 12*
(8)	Friends of the Earth, London EC1	5	6	*F.o.t.E.*
(9)	Royal Society for Nature Conservation, London EC4	5	10	*Arlington*
(10)	Striving to Protect Species at Risk Hants & IOW, Romsey	5	10	*H&IOW NT*
(11)	British Herpetological Soc. Conservation Exhibition, Studland	5	8	*Hawkwood*
(12)	Cornish Wildlife, CTNC, Truro	5	5	*CTNC*
(13)	Royal Society for Nature Conservation, London W1	5	10	*Arlington*
(14)	Species at Risk Lady's Slipper Orchid, Grassington, Skipton	5	12	*Fine Arts*
(15)	1986 National Garden Festival, Stoke on Trent	6	10	*NGF*
(16)	Friends of Arundel Castle CC 1986 Touring Team, Arundel	10	15	*FACCC*
(17)	70th Anniv. First Flight of the Big Ack BF 2111 PS	10	15	*RFDC 44*
(18)	British Naval Anniversary, Plymouth, Devon	10	—	*n.o.c.*
(19)	England v. India 1986 Tour Match, London NW8	10	12	*S.P.*
(20)	Caring & Sharing 1861-1986 Colchester & E. Essex Co-op Soc.	10	30	*Col. Co-op*
(21)	Greetings from the Thames Barrier Visitor Centre, SE18	8	15	*CoverCraft*
(22)	Hawk 200 First Flight Godalming	10	12	*V.A.F.A.*

C.D.S. POSTMARKS

(23)	Aviemore, Kinloch, or Tummel Bridge — habitats of Wildcat ......each	8	
(24)	Beddgelert or Kilnlochewe — habitats of Pine Marten ....each	8	
(25)	Lincoln or Nettleham — HQ of Royal Soc. Nature Conserv.........each	9	

Nature Conservation (contd.)

	ordinary covers £	official covers £
(26) Park Road, Regents Park — Council for Env. Cons. & London Zoo	10	
(27) Selbourne — home of Gilbert White (famous naturalist)	7	

In addition covers are known with the following C.D.S. postmarks: Cheltenham; Ecclestone St., SW1; Eagle; Eaglescliffe; Fair Isle; Frog Island; Isle of Rhum; Otterburn; Otterferry; Owlsmoor; Paddock Wood; Studland and Willsbridge. Prices range from £6.

SLOGAN POSTMARKS

(28) Lincs. & South Humberside Trust Nature Conserv. — Lincoln	70	
(29) Lincs. & South Humberside Trust Nature Conserv. — Doncaster .	70	
(30) Natureland Marine Zoo Skegness 21st Anniv. — Skegness	70	

In addition: Stoke Garden Festival (2 versions). Prices from £40.

17th June 1986 — MEDIEVAL LIFE

17p Serf; 22p Freeman; 31p Knight; 34p Baron

SPECIAL HANDSTAMPS

(1) First Day of Issue — Philatelic Bureau	4	—	*Post Office*
(2) First Day of Issue — Gloucester	4	—	*Post Office*
(3) Domesday Book MLXXXVI, Winchester, Hants...............	5	6	*LFDC 51*
(4) Freemen of England, Oswestry, Shropshire........................	5	8	*Bradbury*
(5) 70th Anniv. Cub Scouts Medieval Pageant, Worthing, Sussex	5	8	*Worthing Cubs*
(6) Crofters Act Achd Nan Croiteran 1886-1986, Inverness	6	20	*Crofters Comm.*
(7) Crofters Act Achd Nan Croiteran 1886-1986, Edinburgh	6	20	*Crofters Comm.*
(8) Medieval Life Stamps designed by Tayburn, Edinburgh....	6	—	*n.o.c.*
(9) Medieval Life Stamps designed by Tayburn, London W14 ..	6	—	*n.o.c.*
(10) Domesday 900th Anniversary 1086-1986 London WC2.......	5	8	*Cotswold*
(11) Charter Celebrations Port of Penryn, Penryn, Cornwall.......	5	10	*Penryn*
(12) Domesday Survey 900 Years, Battle, East Sussex	5	12	*B'ham 500(13)*
(13) Hereward Country, Isle of Ely, Cambridge	5	10	*E.Cambs DC*
(14) Hereward Country, Peterborough	5	10	*E.Cambs DC*
(15) The Great Hall Domesday 900, Winchester, Hants.	5	10	*Winchester CC*
(16) 900th Anniversary of the Domesday Survey, Exeter, Devon .	5	7	*BLCS 13*
(17) Domesday — Chapter House Abbey of St. Peter, Gloucester	5	12	*Fine Arts*
(18) Blackwells Childrens Bookshop Domesday Exhibition, Oxford ...	5	8	*Hawkwood*
(19) Battle, East Sussex (permanent handstamp)......................	10	—	*n.o.c.*
(20) Hastings, East Sussex (permanent handstamp).................	10	—	*n.o.c.*
(21) Ripon 1100 AD 886-1986 Ripon, N. Yorks........................	6	8	*Ripon*
(22) Harrow Heritage Trust, Harrow, Middx.	5	8	*HHT*
(23) 75th Anniv. Start of Restoration of Tattershall Castle BF 2116 PS	8	10	*RFDC 45*
(24) 150th Anniv. 1836 to 1986 Legal & General, London EC4 ...	8	10	*CoverCraft*
(25) Stamplink '86, Portsmouth..	8	10	*Brit. Ferries*
(26) Blair Castle 50th Anniv. Public Opening, Blair Atholl Pitlochry ..	8	10	*Pilgrim*
(27) Commonwealth Games 1986 MAC Edinburgh	8	10	*DGT*
(28) England v. India Tour Match, London NW8	8	10	*S.P.*
(29) Greetings from the Thames Barrier Visitors Centre, SE18	8	20	*CoverCraft*
(30) Friends of Arundel Castle 1986 Touring Team, Arundel............	8	10	*S.P.*
(31) 1986 National Garden Festival, Stoke on Trent	8	10	*NGF*

ORDINARY F.D.I. POSTMARKS

For this issue only, many Post Offices used special F.D.I. postmarks. These were non-pictorial and incorporated both the modern and medieval spelling of the town name. Such covers are valued at £6 each.

C.D.S. POSTMARKS

(32) Battle, Sussex — sites of William's battle with Harold	12	
(33) Bosham — the only Manor reserved by William.................	17	
(34) Braunton or Laxton — sites of ancient methods of farming...each	30	
(35) Chancery Lane WC2 — home of the Domesday Book	12	
(36) Cherbourg, Normandy PAQUEBOT — William was Duke of Normandy	10	
(37) Kingsholm — where William decreed the Domesday survey	35	
(38) Winchester — where the Domesday was compiled	9	

In addition covers are known with the following C.D.S. postmarks: Castle Acre, Castle Rising, Castleton, Chertsey, Egham, Ettington, Guernsey or Jersey Paquebots, Hasting, Knight's Road, Oswestry, The Barony, Westham. Prices range from £6.

SLOGAN POSTMARKS

(39) Hereward Country — Fen Heritage & Legend — Peterborough ...	40	
(40) Hereward Country — Fen Heritage & Legend — Cambridge	40	

In addition: Crofter's Act. Prices range from £35.

PRICES & CONDITION – PLEASE READ GENERAL NOTES

15th July 1986 — SPORTS

17p Athletics; 22p Rowing; 29p Weight Lifting;
31p Shooting; 34p Hockey

	ordinary covers £	official covers £	
SPECIAL HANDSTAMPS			
(1) First Day of Issue — Philatelic Bureau	4	—	*Post Office*
(2) First Day of Issue — Edinburgh.......................................	4	—	*Post Office*
(3) Amateur Rowing Association ARA, London W6	5	6	*LFDC 53*
(4) Home of British Rowing, Henley-on-Thames, Oxfordshire	5	12	*B'ham 500(14)*
(5) Commemorating 21st Anniv. of the Cosford Arena BF 2119 PS	15	15	*RFDC 46*
(6) 6th World Hockey Cup 1986 Willesden Stadium, London NW10 ..	5	6	*Cotswold*
(7) Scottish Brewers Welcome XIII Common. Games to Edinburgh ...	5	6	*DGT*
(8) Legion Youth & Sports The Royal British Legion, London SW1 ...	5	6	*Brit.Leg.28*
(9) Amateur Athletic Association, London SW1	5	6	*DGT*
(10) Commonwealth Games 1986 MAC, Edinburgh	5	6	*DGT*
(11) Waltham Forest salutes London Youth Games, London E17..	5	6	*Hawkwood*
(12) The Royal Tournament BF 2118 PS...............................	8	—	*n.o.c.*
(13) 1986 National Garden Festival, Stoke on Trent	8	10	*NGF*
(14) England v. N. Zealand 1986 Tour Match, London NW8	8	10	*S.P.*
(15) England v. India 1986 Tour Match, London NW8.................	8	10	*SP.*
(16) Medieval Life Stamps designed by Tayburn, Edinburgh	8	—	*n.o.c.*
(17) Medieval Life Stamps designed by Tayburn, London W14....	8	—	*n.o.c.*
(18) Domesday 900th Anniversary 1086-1986, London WC2	8	—	*n.o.c.*
(19) Blair Castle 50th Anniv. Public Opening Blair Atholl, Pitlochry....	8	10	*Pilgrim*
(20) Greetings from the Thames Barrier Visitors Centre, SE18	8	15	*CoverCraft*

C.D.S. POSTMARKS

(21) Edinburgh, Jock's Lodge, Leith Walk, Murrayfield,	
Musselborough, Newbridge, North Motherwell or Norton Park —	
venues of Games events ....each from	9
(22) Bisley — famous shooting venue	10
(23) Gleneagles Hotel, Perthshire — 1977 'Gleneagles Agreement'	20
(24) Henley-on-Thames — the 'Henley Royal Regatta'	10
(25) Mobile Post Office 2 Edinburgh — sited in Games Village.....	100
(26) Willesden — venue of World Hockey Championships	15

In addition covers are known with the following C.D.S. postmarks: Badminton, Bowling Green, Clarkston, Fulham Rd SW6, Gun Hill, and Shooting Common. Prices range from £6.

22nd July 1986 — ROYAL WEDDING

12p, 17p Prince Andrew & Sarah Ferguson

SPECIAL HANDSTAMPS

(1) First Day of Issue — Philatelic Bureau	2	—	*Post Office*
(2) First Day of Issue — London SW1	2	—	*Post Office*
(3) Congratulations Village of Dummer, Royal Wedding, Dummer.....	3	6	*G&P*
(4) Royal Wedding Westminster Abbey, London SW1	3	15	*LFDC 52*
(5) Royal Wedding Greetings, Windsor, Berks.	3	18	*B'ham 500(15)*
(6) Loyal Greetings from York, York	3	14	*Benham S.G.2*
(7) The Royal Wedding, London EC4......................................	3	8	*Arlington*
(8) The Royal Wedding Westminster Abbey, London SW1	3	8	*Arlington*
(9) Loyal Greetings from Lullingstone Silk Farm Sherborne, Dorset ..	3	12	*Benham L14*
(10) Debretts Recording Royal History across the centuries, SW6	20	15	*Fine Arts*
(11) Royal Wedding Westminster Abbey, London SW1	3	3	*Havering*
(12) The Royal Wedding, London EC	3	—	*Post Office*
(13) Congratulations to Prince Andrew & Sarah Ferguson, Dummer ...	3	4	*K&D*
(14) The Lewis Carroll Society Salutes The Royal Wedding, Oxford	3	4	*Hawkwood*
(15) Royal Wedding Congratulations XIII C'wealth Games, Edinburgh	3	4	*DGT*
(16) Woman's Weekly 75th Anniversary Year 1911-1986, SW1	3	4	*DGT*
(17) Woman's Weekly 75th Anniversary Year 1911-1986, SE1	6	20	*CoverCraft*
(18) Open Days Broadlands, Romsey, Hants............................	6	8	*Broadlands*
(19) London SW1 (Buckingham Palace) — permanent handstamp	6	—	*n.o.c.*
(20) Windsor (Castle) Philatelic Counter handstamp..................	6	—	*n.o.c.*
(21) Blair Castle 50th Anniv. Public Opening Blair Atholl, Pitlochry....	6	7	*Pilgrim*
(22) Commonwealth Games 1986 MAC, Edinburgh	6	7	*DGT*
(23) Wednesbury Sport Union Golden Jubilee Wednesbury........	7	9	*Wed.Sports*
(24) Lifeboat Week Lyme Regis Dorset 1986	8	9	*Pilgrim*
(25) 1911 Brooklands Daily Mail Air Race Anniversary, Weybridge	8	20	*V.A.F.A.*
(26) Head Post Office Official Opening, Hemel Hempstead.........	10	45	*H.H.P.O.*

1986 Royal Wedding (contd.)

		ordinary covers £	official covers £	
SPECIAL HANDSTAMPS				
(27)	The Royal Tournament BF 2118 PS	7	—	*n.o.c.*
(28)	1986 National Garden Festival, Stoke-on-Trent	8	9	*NGF*
(29)	England v. N. Zealand 1986 Tour Match, London NW8	8	9	*S.P.*
(30)	England v. India 1986 Tour Match, London NW8	8	9	*S.P.*
(31)	Greetings from the Thames Barrier Visitors Centre, SE18	8	20	*CoverCraft*
(32)	Amateur Athletic Association, London SW1	8	9	*DGT*

C.D.S. POSTMARKS		
(33)	Ascot — Andrew and Sarah both went to schools here	7
(34)	Buckingham Palace, SW1	100
(35)	Dummer — home of Sarah Ferguson	12
(36)	Great Portland St. or Portman Square, W1 — nearest POs to Sarah's birthplace	8
(37)	House of Commons, SW1	12
(38)	House of Lords, SW1	15
(39)	Kelso — where Prince Andrew proposed to Sarah Ferguson	7
(40)	Windsor or Windsor Great Park ....each	15
(41)	Windsor Castle, Berks.	120

In addition covers are known with the following C.D.S. postmarks: Culdrose RNAS, Dartmouth, Duffus, Duke of York's School, Ferguson's Lane, Princetown, Romsey, St. Aldates, St. Andrews, Yeovilton RNAS. Prices range from £6.

SLOGAN POSTMARKS
St. Anne's Church, Naval Base Portsmouth; Collect British Stamps; Victorian Rose Garden. Prices range from £15.

19th August 1986 — COMMONWEALTH PARLIAMENTARY ASSOCIATION CONFERENCE

34p

SPECIAL HANDSTAMPS				
(1)	First Day of Issue — Philatelic Bureau	2	—	*Post Office*
(2)	First Day of Issue — London SW1	2	—	*Post Office*
(3)	Commonwealth Parliament. Conf. Houses of Parliament, SW1	3	4	*LFDC 54*
(4)	Commonwealth Parliament. Association 32nd Conference, SW1	3	6	*BLCS 16*
(5)	St. Margaret's Parish Church of House of Commons, SW1	3	4	*Hawkwood*
(6)	London SW1 (Buckingham Palace) permanent handstamp	5	—	*n.o.c.*
(7)	Dumfries Octocentenary 1186-1986, Dumfries	5	6	*Dumfries*
(8)	World Chess Championship FIDE Park Lane, London W1	7	10	*H.Murray*
(9)	1986 National Garden Festival, Stoke-on-Trent	5	6	*NGF*
(10)	England v. N. Zealand 1986 Tour Match London, NW8	5	6	*S.P.*

C.D.S. POSTMARKS	
(11)	Buckingham Palace, SW1	60
(12)	Gleneagles Hotel, Perthshire — 1977 'Gleneagles Agreement'	15
(13)	House of Commons, SW1	25
(14)	House of Lords, SW1	35
(15)	Huntingdon — birthplace of Oliver Cromwell	12
(16)	Kensington High Street W8 — PO for Commonwealth Institute	7
(17)	Queen Elizabeth Ave., Walsall	7
(18)	Westminster Bridge Rd., SE1 — near to venue of Conference	8

SLOGAN POSTMARKS
Inverness Conference Capital; British Presidency. Prices range from £15.

16th September 1986 — THE ROYAL AIR FORCE

17p Lord Dowding/Hurricane; 22p Lord Tedder/Typhoon; 29p Lord Trenchard/DH 9A; 31p Sir Arthur Harris/Lancaster; 34p Lord Portal/Mosquito

SPECIAL HANDSTAMPS				
(1)	First Day of Issue — Philatelic Bureau	5	—	*Post Office*
(2)	First Day of Issue — Farnborough	5	—	*Post Office*
(3)	46th Anniversary Battle of Britain, Uxbridge, Middx.	7	10	*LFDC 55*
(4)	Hawkinge Aerodrome 50 Years of the Spitfire, Hawkinge	7	35	*B'ham 500(17)*
(5)	50th Anniversary of the RAF Scampton, Lincoln	7	14	*BLCS 17*
(6)	50th Anniversary of the Spitfire 1936-1986, Eastleigh, Hants.	7	12	*Bradbury*
(7)	RAFA Andover, Hants.	7	10	*Cotswold*
(8)	Kenley Aerodrome Salutes the RAF, Kenley, Surrey	8	15	*Fine Arts*
(9)	50th Anniv. Operational Re-organisation of RAF BF 2114 PS	9	15	*RFDC 49*
(10)	46th Anniversary The Battle of Britain BF 2123 PS	9	15	*Forces*

PRICES & CONDITION – PLEASE READ GENERAL NOTES

103

R.A.F. (contd.)

		ordinary covers £	official covers £	
(11)	Newark on Trent Salutes the RAF, Newark, Notts.	7	10	*Newark*
(12)	Duxford Aviation Society Duxford Airfield, Duxford, Cambs......	7	8	*Havering*
(13)	England v. N. Zealand 1986 Tour Match, London NW8	9	10	*S.P.*
(14)	British Philatelic Federation 68th Congress, Norwich	7	—	*n.o.c.*
(15)	Marx Memorial Library Spain 1936-39 Exhibition, London EC1.	7	8	*Hawkwood*
(16)	1986 National Garden Festival, Stoke-on-Trent	7	8	*NGF*
(17)	High Wycombe, Bucks..	7	—	*n.o.c.*

C.D.S. POSTMARKS

(18)	RAF Biggin Hill	150
(19)	Any other RAF station postmark ....from	12
(20)	Any Field or Forces Post Office	15
(21)	House of Lords, SW1	15
(22)	Moffat, Killearn, Taunton, Cheltenham or Hungerford —	
	birthplaces of Commanders featured on stamps ....each	10
(23)	Gravesend, Hawkinge, Digby Aerodrome, Manston, Kenley or	
	Oakington — connected with aircraft featured on stamps ....each	17
(24)	Biggin Hill, Cosford Camp, Cranwell, Duxford, Honington Camp	
	or Leuchars — all having well known RAF connections.............	12

In addition covers are known with the following C.D.S. postmarks: Churchill, Eastleigh, Gatenby, The Hyde, Hendon, Lancaster, Middle Wallop, Northolt, Pathfinder Village, Stanmore. Prices range from £7.

18th November 1986 — CHRISTMAS

13p The Glastonbury Thorn; 18p The Tanad Valley Plygain; 22p The Hebrides Tribute; 31p The Dewsbury Church Knell; 34p The Hereford Boy Bishop

SPECIAL HANDSTAMPS

(1)	First Day of Issue — Philatelic Bureau	3	—	*Post Office*
(2)	First Day of Issue — Bethlehem, Llandeilo, Dyfed	3	—	*Post Office*
(3)	The Hebrides Tribute Christmas Stornaway Isle of Lewis ...	4	10	*B'ham 500(18)*
(4)	The Devil's Knell All Saints Church, Dewsbury W. Yorks....	4	10	*Dewsbury PC*
(5)	Christmas Greetings, Folkestone, Kent	4	6	*Benham L15*
(6)	Christmas Greetings from St. Margaret's Westminster, SW1......	4	5	*Hawkwood*
(7)	The Glastonbury Thorn, Christmas 1986, Glastonbury.......	4	8	*LFDC 56*
(8)	English Folk Dance & Song Soc. Christmas, Sheffield	4	5	*BLCS 18*
(9)	Happy Christmas Telecom Technology Showcase, London EC1 ..	4	—	*n.o.c.*
(10)	Seasons Greetings to all Railway Societies, London WC1	4	—	*n.o.c.*
(11)	Christmas, Hereford	4	5	*BLSC 18*
(12)	NE Parcels Centre Washington, Tyne & Wear	10	—	*Post Office*
(13)	Greetings from the Thames Barrier Visitors Centre, SE18 ..	10	20	*CoverCraft*
(14)	Lloyd's of London New Building Opening, London EC3	10	20	*CoverCraft*
(15)	70th Anniv. Last Day Battle of the Somme BF 2124 PS.......	10	—	*n.o.c.*
(16)	High Wycombe, Bucks...	8	—	*n.o.c.*
(17)	Leicester Circuits 1961-1986 25th Anniversary Year, Leicester....	10	15	*L.Circuits*

C.D.S. POSTMARKS

(18)	Bethlehem, Llandeilo, Dyfed or Nasareth, Gwynedd	8
(19)	Dewsbury, Glastonbury or Hereford ....each	10
(20)	Llanrhaeadr-ym-Mochnant (Welsh Plygain)....................	10
(21)	Lochboisdale or Lochmaddy, Isle of Uist (Hebrides Tribute) each	10

In addition covers are known with the following C.D.S. postmarks: Holy Island, St. Nicholas. Prices range from £6.

SLOGAN POSTMARKS

10th Anniversary Codesort. Prices from £20.

2nd December 1986 — CHRISTMAS

12p The Glastonbury Thorn

SPECIAL HANDSTAMPS

(1)	First Day of Issue — Philatelic Bureau	1	—	*Post Office*
(2)	The Glastonbury Thorn, Christmas 1986, Glastonbury.......	3	3	*LFDC 56*
(3)	The Glastonbury Thorn, Glastonbury SC, Somerset..........	3	3	*Cotswold*
(4)	Christmas Glastonbury, Somerset....................................	3	8	*B'ham 500(19)*
(5)	Happy Christmas Telecom Technology Showcase, London EC1 ..	5	—	*n.o.c.*
(6)	Christmas Greetings from Biggin Hill, BF 2130 PS	3	3	*RFDC 51*
(7)	Greetings from the Thames Barrier Visitors Centre, SE18 ..	4	10	*CoverCraft*
(8)	High Wycombe, Bucks...	4	—	*n.o.c.*
(9)	Launch of the Type 2400 Upholder, Barrow in Furness, Cumbria .	4	10	*Vickers*

PLEASE READ THE GENERAL NOTES
AT THE BEGINNING OF THIS CATALOGUE
These often provide the answers to enquiries received.

	ordinary covers £	official covers £

1986

C.D.S. POSTMARKS
(10) Bethlehem, Llandeilo, Dyfed 5
(11) Nasareth, Gwynedd 5
(12) Glastonbury, Somerset... 5
In addition covers are known with the following C.D.S. postmarks: Holy Island. Prices range from £4.

A HAPPY **Christmas** THE POST OFFICE (13)

SLOGAN POSTMARKS
(13) Happy Christmas The Post Office — used at several offices . 6

THE LAUNCH OF THE
TYPE 2400 CLASS SUBMARINE
UPHOLDER
2 DECEMBER 1986
BARROW-IN-FURNESS
CUMBRIA (9)

Note: On the same day of issue, 2nd December, a special Christmas stamp pack was issued containing 36 × 13p Glastonbury Thorn Christmas stamps. The stamps were printed in sheetlet form — 2 panes of 18 with a central double gutter and star underprint (to indicate the stamps were issued at a discount). In all other respects they were identical to the 18th November 13p issue. Many of the covers produced for this issue bore both 12p and 13p values — the prices quoted above reflect this. Some covers exist with a complete pane of 18 × 13p stamps and are valued at around £10.

(10)

(9)

Some double-dated covers exist with both the set of Christmas stamps postmarked 18th November and 12p value postmarked 2nd December. Prices range from £30.

20th January 1987 — FLOWERS
18p Gaillardia; 22p Echinops; 31p Echeveria; 34p Colchicum

SPECIAL HANDSTAMPS
(1)	First Day of Issue — Philatelic Bureau	4	—	*Post Office*
(2)	First Day of Issue — Richmond, Surrey.............................	4	—	*Post Office*
(3)	Flowers, Flore, Northampton..	5	18	*B'ham 500(20)*
(4)	Nat. Assoc. of Flower Arrangement Societies, London SW1	5	7	*LFDC 57*
(5)	Chelsea Flower Shows Royal Hort. Society, Chelsea, SW3 ..	5	6	*BOCS (3) 1*
(6)	Westminster Shows Royal Hort. Society, Westminster, SW1	5	6	*BOCS (3) 1*
(7)	The Lindley Library Royal Hort. Society, Westminster, SW1	5	6	*BOCS (3) 1*
(8)	Wisley Gardens Royal Hort. Society, Wisley, Woking, Surrey	5	6	*BOCS (3) 1*
(9)	1987 Opening New Conservatory Royal Botanical Gardens, Kew .	5	5	*BLCS 20*
(10)	Stephen Thomas Flora & Fauna Exhibition. Ovingdean......	5	8	*G & P*
(11)	KEB (King Edward Building) Horticultural Society, EC1A .	5	8	*KEB H.S.*
(12)	GQT (Gardeners' Question Time) 1947-1987 BBC Manchester ...	5	15	*CoverCraft*
(13)	Royal College of Art 1837-1987, London SW1	8	25	*CoverCraft*
(14)	50th Anniversary Reformation 77 Squadron BF 2150 PS	10	10	*RFDC 52*
(15)	Bradbury Blinds 1962-1987, Northampton........................	10	15	*Brad Blinds*
(16)	Queen Victoria's Jubilee 1887, National Postal Museum, EC1.....	10	—	*n.o.c.*
(17)	High Wycombe, Bucks...	8	—	*n.o.c.*

(8) FLOWERS 20 JAN 87 WISLEY WOKING SURREY (6) FLOWERS 20 JAN '87 1962 1987 (14)
(15) NORTHAMPTON
(12) (11)

C.D.S. POSTMARKS
(18) Botanic Gardens, Belfast.. 15
(19) Flowery Field or Spring Gardens 10
(20) Kew or Kew Gardens 15
(21) Royal Hospital, Chelsea (Flower Show)............................ 12
(22) Sissinghurst or Ripley (Wisley) 8
In addition covers are known with the following C.D.S. postmarks: Ipswich, Mickleton, Ovingdean, Saffron Walden, St. Bees, Thistle Hill, and Tresco. Prices range from £6.

(20)

(10)

24th March 1987 — SIR ISAAC NEWTON
18p Principia; 22p Motion of Bodies in Ellipses; 31p Optics; 34p The System of the World

SCIENCE MUSEUM ■ LONDON S.W.7

SPECIAL HANDSTAMPS
(1)	First Day of Issue — Philatelic Bureau	3	—	*Post Office*
(2)	First Day of Issue — Woolsthorpe, Lincs	3	—	*Post Office*
(3)	Isaac Newton, Woolsthorpe, Grantham, Lincs...................	4	8	*LFDC 58*
(4)	Sir Isaac Newton 1642-1727 Trinity College, Cambridge.....	4	11	*B'ham 500(21)*
(5)	The Old Royal Observatory, Sir Isaac Newton, Greenwich SE10..	4	5	*BLCS 21*
(6)	25 Jubilee, Weston Favell Upper School, Northampton	4	9	*WF School*
(7)	Isaac Newton, Grantham	4	8	*Maths Assoc*
(8)	The George Celebrates Newton's Tercentenary, Grantham ..	4	10	*George Hotel*
(9)	Apple's Tenth Anniversary Hemel Hempstead, Herts.........	4	30	*Arlington*
(10)	Sir Isaac Newton Science Museum, London SW7..............	4	5	*Cotswold*
(11)	Sir Isaac Newton Pres. Royal Society 1707-1727 Crane Court EC4	4	—	*n.o.c.*
(12)	London College of Music Centenary, London W1	6	10	*CoverCraft*
(13)	190th Anniv. 1st Human Parachute Descent BF 2151 PS	6	8	*RFDC 53*
(14)	Holmfirth Postcard Museum, Wish You Were Here	6	—	*n.o.c.*
(15)	Queen Victoria's Jubilee 1887, National Postal Museum, EC1.....	6	—	*n.o.c.*

APPLE'S TENTH ANNIVERSARY (9)
24th March 1987
Hemel Hempstead Herts.

(4) (5)

THE GEORGE CELEBRATES
· 24 MAR 1987 · (8)
GRANTHAM
NEWTON'S TERCENTENARY

PRICES & CONDITION – PLEASE READ GENERAL NOTES

Sir Isaac Newton (contd.)

	ordinary covers £	official covers £
C.D.S. POSTMARKS		
(16) Colsterworth, Lincs. (nearest P.O. to Woolsthorpe Manor) ...	7	
(17) Grantham, Lincs. (attended King's School, Grantham)........	7	
(18) Greenwich (reflecting telescope — Royal Observatory)........	7	
(19) House of Commons (Newton MP for Cambridge University)	10	
(20) Kensington (where Newton died)	7	
(21) Newton (Cambridge, Swansea or Wisbech)	9	
(22) Regent St., SW1 (Newton's home for many years)...............	7	
(23) Trinity St., Cambridge (nearest P.O. to Trinity College)........	8	

In addition covers are known with the following C.D.S. postmarks: Globe Road, and Seething Lane EC3. Prices range from £6.

12th May 1987 — BRITISH ARCHITECTS IN EUROPE
18p Ipswich (Foster); 22p Paris (Rogers & Piano);
31p Stuttgart (Stirling & Wilford); 34p Luxembourg (Lasdun)

SPECIAL HANDSTAMPS			
(1) First Day of Issue — Philatelic Bureau	3	—	*Post Office*
(2) First Day of Issue — Ipswich	3	—	*Post Office*
(3) British Architects in Europe, London W1	4	5	*LFDC 59*
(4) The Clore Gallary British Architects in Europe, London SW1.....	4	11	*B'ham 500(22)*
(5) Brit. Arch. in Europe RIBA Community Archit. Macclesfield	4	5	*BLCS 22*
(6) R.I.B.A. Royal Charter 1837-1987, London W1	4	15	*CoverCraft*
(7) Willis Faber Heritage & Progress, Ipswich	4	8	*CoverCraft*
(8) Association of Clinical Biochemists, Eastbourne	8	13	*A.C.B.*
(9) 200th Anniv. Royal Warrant Royal Engineers BF 1876 PS ...	8	12	*RFDC 54*
(10) Holmfirth Postcard Museum, Wish You Were Here	8	—	*n.o.c.*
(11) Queen Victoria's Jubilee 1887, National Postal Museum, EC1....	8	—	*n.o.c.*
(12) Presentation of RNLI Gallantry Awards RNLI, London SE1	8	10	*Pilgrim*
(13) London-Venice Simplon Orient Express, Folkestone, Kent ..	8	45	*Benham S.G.3*

C.D.S. POSTMARKS		
(14) Ascot, Berks. (home of Chartered Institute of Building)	6	
(15) Euston Centre BO (near to James Stirling & Associates)	6	
(16) Gt. Portland St. (near to Foster Associates & R.I.B.A.)	6	
(17) Hammersmith W6 (near to Richard Rogers Partnership).....	6	
(18) Ipswich, Suffolk (Willis Faber Building)	6	
(19) New Buildings, Londonderry..	25	
(20) Vauxhall Bridge Rd. (near to Denys, Lasdun & Associates)..	6	

In addition covers are known with the following C.D.S. postmarks: Buxton Road, Macclesfield; Kirkwall; Paris Ave.; Stirling, and Town Centre. Prices range from £5.

SLOGAN POSTMARKS
St. Magnus Cathedral; The Copthorne; Arndale Centre; Collect British Stamps. Prices range from £35.

16th June 1987 — ST. JOHN AMBULANCE
18p Early First Aid Duties 1887; 22p First Aid in Wartime 1940;
31p First Aid at Pop Concert 1965; 34p Transplant Organ Flights 1987

SPECIAL HANDSTAMPS			
(1) First Day of Issue — Philatelic Bureau	3	—	*Post Office*
(2) First Day of Issue — London EC1	3	—	*Post Office*
(3) St. John's Gate SJA Centenary Exhibition, London EC1......	4	7	*LFDC 60*
(4) The World's 2nd Oldest Div. SJA Brigade, Heywood, Lancs......	4	6	*Cotswold*
(5) St. John Ambulance Centenary Hyde Park London SW1	4	11	*B'ham (500)23*
(6) 100th Anniversary St. John Ambulance Stansted, Essex.....	4	6	*BLCS 23*
(7) St. John Ambulance Brigade, London SW1.......................	4	5	*Arlington*
(8) St. Margaret's Hospital, Epping, Essex	4	5	*Arlington*
(9) Greetings from Thames Barrier Visitors Centre, London SE18 ...	7	12	*CoverCraft*
(10) Holmfirth Postcard Museum, Wish You Were Here	7	—	*n.o.c.*
(11) Queen Victoria's Jubilee 1887, National Postal Museum, EC1.....	8	—	*n.o.c.*
(12) 40th Anniversary Maiden Voyage Waverley, Glasgow	7	9	*Benham*
(13) London-Venice Simplon Orient Express, Folkestone, Kent .	8	65	*Benham S.G.3*

A. G. BRADBURY
The top name in cover and postmark design.
Write for my latest colour leaflets.
3 LINK ROAD, STONEYGATE, LEICESTER LE2 3RA

St. John Ambulance *(contd.)*

	ordinary covers £	official covers £

C.D.S. POSTMARKS
(14) Ashford, Kent (Birthplace of founder Sir John Furley)......... 8
(15) Bow; Holbrook Lane; or Ordnance Rd., Coventry (The Blitz) 7
(16) Epping or Stansted, Essex (The Airwing) 10
(17) Farringdon Road or London EC (St. John's Gate) 6
(18) Harrow (First road accident attended by St. John Ambulance)..... 6
(19) Margate, Kent (First Ambulance Corp. formed in 1879) 7
(20) Mount St., W1 (Hyde Park — pop festival) 6
(21) Papworth, Cambridge (Transplant surgery) 9
(22) RAF Benson (First flight of Air Wing) 20
(23) St. John's (Bradford, Ipswich or Worcester)....................... 12
(24) St. John's Chapel, Bishop Auckland 12
(25) Woolwich (First Centre of the Association)......................... 6

In addition covers are known with the following C.D.S. postmarks: GWR TPO 'Up'; House of Commons, House of Lords, Muswell Hill, Oldham, Orthopaedic Hospital, Royal Hospital School, and Windsor Great Park. Prices range from £5.

21st July 1987 — SCOTTISH HERALDRY

18p Lord Lyon King of Arms; 22p HRH The Duke of Rothesay;
31p Royal Scottish Academy; 34p Royal Society of Edinburgh

SPECIAL HANDSTAMPS
(1)	First Day of Issue — Philatelic Bureau	4	—	*Post Office*
(2)	First Day of Issue — Rothesay, Isle of Bute	4	—	*Post Office*
(3)	Tercentenary Revival of the Order of the Thistle, Edinburgh.......	5	13	*B'ham 500(24)*
(4)	Scottish Heraldry Drum Castle, Banchory, Kincardineshire	5	8	*BLCS 24*
(5)	Scottish Heraldry Crathes Castle, Banchory, Kincardineshire	5	8	*BLCS 24*
(6)	Scottish Heraldry, Dunkeld, Perthshire	5	8	*BLCS 24*
(7)	Scottish Heraldry Bannockburn, Stirling	5	8	*BLCS 24*
(8)	Mary Queen of Scots 1542-1587 Fotheringhay, Peterborough	5	9	*LFDC 61*
(9)	Royal Scottish Academy, Edinburgh	5	12	*CoverCraft*
(10)	Lord Cameron of Balhousie Knight of the Thistle BF 2144 PS	5	12	*RFDC 56*
(11)	Glasgow Herald – Scotland's Newspaper Glasgow.............	7	15	*Pilgrim*
(12)	The Visit of the Duke & Duchess of York, York	7	12	*Y. Minster*
(13)	Greetings from the Thames Barrier Visitors Centre, SE18	8	10	*CoverCraft*
(14)	Queen's School Rheindahlen 1955-1987 BF 21787 PS........	9	12	*Queens Sch*
(15)	The Royal Tournament BF 2142 PS	9	12	*Forces*

C.D.S. POSTMARKS
(16) Banff (home of Lord Lyon King of Arms) 8
(17) Bannockburn, Stirling (famous battle)............................... 15
(16) Edinburgh (various connections)..................................... 8
(19) Frederick St., Edinburgh (near to Royal Society of Edinburgh).... 8
(20) Holyrood, Edinburgh (Royal residence in Edinburgh) 16
(21) House of Lords, London SW1 15
(22) Largs or Luncarty (battles leading to adoption of Thistle).... 12
(23) Rothesay (arms of HRH Duke of Rothesay on 22p value) 8
(24) Scone, Perthshire (Scone Palace — home of Scottish monarchs)... 35
(25) St. Andrews, Fife (Patron Saint of Scotland)...................... 14
(26) St. Mary St., Edinburgh (near to Royal Scottish Academy) .. 7
In addition covers are known with the following C.D.S. postmarks: Dingwall, Elgin, Gordon, Kintore, Linlithgow, Prince Charles Avenue, Selkirk, Thistle Hill, Ullapool. Prices range from £6.

SLOGAN POSTMARKS
Etterick & Lauderdale; Aberdeen Youth Festival; Inverness, Conference Capital; St. Magnus Cathedral. Prices range from £20.

8th September 1987 — VICTORIAN BRITAIN

18p Great Exhibition; 'Monarch of the Glen'; Grace Darling
22p 'Great Eastern'; Prince Albert; Mrs. Beeton
31p Albert Memorial; Benjamin Disraeli; Ballot Box
34p Relief of Mafeking; Marconi Wireless; Diamond Jubilee

SPECIAL HANDSTAMPS
(1)	First Day of Issue — Philatelic Bureau	4	—	*Post Office*
(2)	First Day of Issue — Newport, Isle of Wight	4	—	*Post Office*
(3)	N.T. for Scotland for places of Historic Interest, Edinburgh .	5	8	*BLCS 25*
(4)	Victorian Britain VA London SW7	5	8	*BLCS 25*

```
┌─────────────────────────────────────┐
│   PLEASE READ THE GENERAL NOTES      │
│  AT THE BEGINNING OF THIS CATALOGUE  │
│ These often provide the answers to   │
│      enquiries received.             │
└─────────────────────────────────────┘
```

Victorian Britain (contd.)

		ordinary covers £	official covers £	
(5)	Queen Victoria, 1837-1901 London SW1	5	8	*LFDC 62*
(6)	Victorian Britain, Balmoral, Ballater, Aberdeenshire	5	18	*B'ham 500(25)*
(7)	Victorian Britain, Windsor, Berks.	5	6	*Benham*
(8)	Southampton Victorian Post Office	8	—	*Post Office*
(9)	Historic Worcester Postmarks Picture Card, Worcester	8	—	*Post Office*
(10)	Mrs. Beeton's A Great Tradition since 1858 London W1	10	6(s)	*Arlington*
(11)	Calderdale's Victorian Inheritance, Halifax	10	—	*Post Office*
(12)	Marconi Philatelic Society, Wireless Transmission, Chelmsford	5	10	*G & P*
(13)	Victorian Britain CPF Edensor Bakewell, Derbyshire	5	10	*CoverCraft*
(14)	Henry Archer Festiniog Rly Victorian Pioneer, Porthmadog	5	18	*Benham L16*
(15)	National Postal Museum 1966-1987 London EC1	6	—	*n.o.c.*
(16)	125th Anniv. Ballooning in British Army BF 2156 PS	8	9	*RFDC 57*
(17)	Ballymena Rugby Football Club 1887-1987	7	15	*Bally RFC*
(18)	Royal Navy Equipment Exhibition 1987 BF 2187 PS	8	12	*Forces*

C.D.S. POSTMARKS

(19)	Balmoral Castle	275
(20)	Bamburgh — home of Grace Darling	8
(21)	Beaconsfield — Disraeli was MP for (and Lord) Beaconsfield	7
(22)	Buckingham Palace, SW1	100
(23)	East Cowes — nearest Crown P.O. to Osborne House	8
(24)	Fleet St., — 'Relief of Mafeking' on newspaper hoarding	15
(25)	Hatch End, Pinner — home of Isabella Beeton	8
(26)	House of Commons SW1 — The Ballot Act 1872	15
(27)	House of Lords SW1 — Disraeli became Lord Beaconsfield	20
(28)	Hughenden Valley — home and burial place of Disraeli	25
(29)	Kensington — V & A Museum, Albert Memorial etc.	10
(30)	Maida Vale — where Landseer painted 'Monarch of the Glen'	8
(31)	Old Windsor or Windsor Great Park	10
(32)	Prince Consort Rd., Queen Victoria Rd., or Victoria Rd.	15
(33)	St. Margaret's Bay Dover — Marconi's wireless transmission	20
(34)	Theobald's Road — birthplace of Disraeli	7
(35)	West Ferry Rd., Millwall — launch of 'The Great Eastern'	9
(36)	Westow St., Norwood — resited Crystal Palace	8

In addition covers are known with the following C.D.S. postmarks: Britannia, Paddington, Nelson, and Woburn. Prices range from £6.

SLOGAN POSTMARKS
Church of Latter Day Saints. Prices range from £20.

13th October 1987 — STUDIO POTTERY
Pots by: 18p Bernard Leach; 26p Elizabeth Fritsch; 31p Lucie Rie; 34p Hans Cope

SPECIAL HANDSTAMPS

(1)	First Day of Issue — Philatelic Bureau	3	—	*Post Office*
(2)	First Day of Issue — St. Ives, Cornwall	3	—	*Post Office*
(3)	The Craftsmen Potters Assoc'n, London W1	5	7	*LFDC 63*
(4)	Studio Pottery, Potters Corner, Ashford, Kent	5	10	*B'ham 500(26)*
(5)	Studio Pottery VA (Victoria & Albert Museum), London SW7	5	5	*BLCS 26*
(6)	Designed and Photographed by Tony Evans, Shrewsbury	5	10	*Tony Evans*
(7)	Stoke-on-Trent, Philatelic Counter	8	—	*n.o.c.*
(8)	47th Anniversary of the Battle of Britain BF 2154 PS	9	12	*RFDC 58*

C.D.S. POSTMARKS

(9)	Carbis Bay, St. Ives (home of Bernard Leach)	25
(10)	Chelsea, London SW3 (annual Craft Fair)	7
(11)	Frome, Somerset (Hans Coper's studio)	8
(12)	Marble Arch, London W1 (Lucie Rie's pottery — Albion Mews)	7
(13)	Poplar, London E14 (Elizabeth Fritsch's studio)	7
(14)	South Kensington, SW7 (Victoria & Albert Museum)	7
(15)	St. Ives (home of studio pottery)	10
(16)	Stennack, St. Ives (Leach's pottery)	25
(17)	Welwyn Garden City (Elizabeth Fritsch — first workshop)	7
(18)	Whitchurch (birthplace of Elizabeth Fritsch)	7

In addition covers are known with the following C.D.S. postmarks: Barlaston, Bathwick St., Dartington, Digswell, Euston Centre, Leach Lane, Potters Bar, Pottery Road. Prices range from £6.

SLOGAN POSTMARKS
Redhill Philatelic Soc.; Royal Mail Code Show. Prices from £15.

PRICES & CONDITION – PLEASE READ GENERAL NOTES

108

17th November 1987 — CHRISTMAS

13p, 18p, 26p, 31p, 34p A child's view of Christmas

	ordinary covers £	official covers £	
SPECIAL HANDSTAMPS			
(1) First Day of Issue — Philatelic Bureau	4	—	*Post Office*
(2) First Day of Issue — Bethlehem, Llandeilo, Dyfed	4	—	*Post Office*
(3) Christmas Toys Hill, Westerham, Kent	4	10	*B'ham 500(27)*
(4) 175th Anniv. Year of the Birth of Charles Dickens	4	6	*LFDC 64*
(5) Happy Xmas from Hamley's Toy Shop, London W1	5	7	*CoverCraft*
(6) Christmas Common, Christmas, Oxford	5	6	*BLCS 27*
(7) Holy Cross Church, Pattishall, Towcester, Northants	5	10	*HC Church*
(8) Christmas, Christleton, Chester	5	6	*BLCS 28*
(9) Christmas 1987 Star Underprint, Star, Gaerwen, Gwynedd.	5	7	*B'ham500 (28)*
(10) A Merry Christmas Telecom Technology Showcase, EC4	9	—	*n.o.c.*
(11) New Aviation Training Ship RFA Argus BP 2157 PS	10	15	*FAA Museum*
(12) Age of Chivalry Exhibition Royal Academy, London W1	10	15	*Pilgrim*
C.D.S. POSTMARKS			
(13) Bethlehem, Dyfed	20		
(14) Nasareth, Gwynedd	9		
(15) Regent Street, W1 — nearest P.O. to Hamley's	6		

In addition covers are known with the following C.D.S. postmarks: Child Okeford, Childs Hill, Fir Tree, Holy Island, Noel Road, Playing Place, St. Nicholas, Snowshill, Star, Sidmouth. Prices range from £5.

SLOGAN POSTMARKS

(16) Gold Angels for Xmas — Pobjoy Mint — Croydon	10(s)	
(17) The Church of Jesus Christ of Latter Day Saints — various offices	25	
(18) Christmas Shopping is Fun, Nottingham	95	
(19) Gold Angels available from Jewellers — Croydon	10(s)	

CHRISTMAS DISCOUNT 13p MINIATURE SHEET

Covers with gutter pair from sheet and special handstamp	4
Covers with whole miniature sheet and special handstamp	20

19th January 1988 — THE LINNEAN SOCIETY

18p Bull-rout (fish); 26p Yellow Waterlily; 31p Bewick's Swan; 34p Morel (fungus)

	ordinary covers	official covers	
SPECIAL HANDSTAMPS			
(1) First Day of Issue — Philatelic Bureau	3	—	*Post Office*
(2) First Day of Issue — Burlington House, London W1	3	—	*Post Office*
(3) 1788-1988 The Linnean Society, London W1	4	10	*LFDC 65*
(4) British Natural History, Watersle, Darwen, Lancs.	4	14	*B'ham (500) 29*
(5) The Wildfowl Trust, Welney, Wisbech, Cambs.	4	8	*BLCS 29*
(6) The Wildfowl Trust, Swan Lake, Arundel, Sussex	4	7	*BLCS 29*
(7) 100th Birthday of Sir Thomas Sopwith BF 2158 PS	8	10	*RFDC 60*
(8) Age of Chivalry Exhibition at The Royal Academy, London W1	8	10	*Pilgrim*
(9) The Emperor's Warriors Exhibition, London SW1	8	10	*Pilgrim*
(10) Railways and the Post Exhib., National Postal Museum, EC1	8	—	*n.o.c.*
C.D.S. POSTMARKS			
(11) Broadwick St., W1 — near to first meeting places of the Society	7		
(12) Davey Place or St. Stephens, Norwich – B/place of founder Sir J.E. Smith	8		
(13) Fleur-de-lis — flower of the lily	10		
(14) Gotenburg, Sweden PAQUEBOT	35		
(15) Heddon St., Albemarle St.. or Regent St., W1 near Burlington House	7		
(16) Holloway, N7 — B/place of Edward Lear (illustration 31p)	7		
(17) Kew Gardens	10		
(18) Lambeth SE11 — home of James Sowerby (illustration 34p)	7		
(19) Ovingham and Mickley Sq., North'land — Bewick born, lived & buried here	7		
(20) Polperro — home of Dr. Jonathan Couch (manuscript 18p)	20		
(21) Slimbridge, Glos. — famous for its Bewick Swans	10		

In addition covers are known with the following C.D.S. postmarks: Abbotsbury, Badger's Mount, Bosherton, House of Commons, Lillies Leaf, London W1, Nettleham, Selbourne, Swanpool, Waterside and Welney. Prices range from £6.

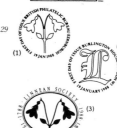

1st March 1988 — THE WELSH BIBLE 1588-1988

18p William Morgan; 26p William Salesbury; 31p Richard Davies; 34p Richard Parry

	ordinary covers	official covers	
SPECIAL HANDSTAMPS			
(1) First Day of Issue — Philatelic Bureau	4	—	*Post Office*
(2) First Day of Issue — Ty Mawr Wybrnant, Gwynedd	4	—	*Post Office*
(3) Bible Society St. David's Day St. Asaph, Clwyd	5	6	*LFDC 66*
(4) The Welsh Bible Caernarfon Castle, Caernarfon, Gwynedd.	5	14	*B'ham (500) 30*
(5) Y Beibl Yn Gymraeg 1588-1988 Llanrhaeadr Ym Mochnant	5	8	*BLCS 30*

Welsh Bible (contd.)

		ordinary covers £	official covers £	
(6)	Translators of Welsh Bible, St. Asaph, Clwyd 1588-1988	5	8	*BLCS 30*
(7)	150th Anniv. Soldiers' & Airmen's Scripture Readers Assoc. BF 2159 PS	6	9	*RFDC 61*
(8)	Y Beibl Cymraeg 1588-1988 Ty Mawr Wybrnant, Gwynedd	6	8	*CoverCraft*
(9)	Spring Stampex, London SW1	8	—	*Post Office*
(10)	Railways and the Post Exhib., National Postal Museum EC1	8	—	*n.o.c.*
(11)	Age of Chivalry Exhibition at The Royal Academy, London W1 ...	8	12	*Pilgrim*

C.D.S. POSTMARKS

(12)	Abergwili, Dyfed — Richard Davies died and was buried here	7
(13)	Bala, Gwynedd — associated with the story of Mary Jones ..	8
(14)	Bethlehem, Dyfed	7
(15)	Conway — birthplace of Richard Davies	6
(16)	Cwm — birthplace of Richard Parry	8
(17)	Dyserth, Clwyd — where Parry worked on his translation ...	6
(18)	House of Commons — Act of 1563 ordered Welsh translation	10
(19)	House of Lords — Act of 1563 ordered Welsh translation	15
(20)	Llandaff, Cardiff — Morgan was Bishop here	6
(21)	Llanrhaeadr Ym, Oswestry — Morgan translated Bible here	6
(22)	Llansanffraid — Richard Davies associations	6
(23)	Llansannan — birthplace of William Salesbury	6
(24)	Penmachno — birthplace of William Morgan......................	6
(25)	St. Asaph — Morgan, Davies and Parry were all Bishops here	6
(26)	St. David's — stamps issued on St. David's Day..................	9
(27)	Welshpool — Morgan was vicar here	6

In addition covers are known with the following C.D.S. postmarks: Ruthin, Trinity St. Prices range from £5.

SLOGAN POSTMARKS

(28)	Jesus is Alive! — used at several offices ....*from*	35

In addition: Oldham Education Week. Prices from £60.

22nd March 1988 — SPORT
18p Gymnastics; 26p Skiing; 31p Lawn Tennis; 34p Association Football

SPECIAL HANDSTAMPS

(1)	First Day of Issue — Philatelic Bureau	4	—	*Post Office*
(2)	First Day of Issue — Wembley..	4	—	*Post Office*
(3)	100 Years Ago Accrington FC, Founder Members of League, Accrington	5	30	*Dawn*
(4)	100 Years of League Football, Aston Villa, Birmingham......	5	30	*Dawn*
(5)	100 Years of League Football, Wolves, Wolverhampton	5	30	*Dawn*
(6)	100 Years of League Football, Everton, Current Champions, Liverpool .	5	30	*Dawn*
(7)	Record Holders, Liverpool FC, 16 Championship Wins, Liverpool	5	30	*Dawn*
(8)	Manchester United, Club with its own Museum, Manchester	5	30	*Dawn*
(9)	Record Holders, Tottenham Hotspur, European Trophy, Tottenham N17	5	8	*BLCS 31*
(10)	Record Holders, Arsenal FC, Division One 1919-1988, N5 ...	5	8	*BLCS 31*
(11)	Preston North End Football Club, Preston	5	7	*LFDC 67*
(12)	130th Anniversary of Lawn Tennis at Edgbaston, Birmingham ...	5	12	*B'ham (500) 31*
(13)	The Lawn Tennis Association 100th Anniv., London W14 ...	5	12	*Cotswold*
(14)	Amateur Gymnastics Assoc., B.A.G.A. 1888-1988 Slough ...	6	12	*Cotswold*
(15)	"A Question of Sport" Celebrates Sport on Stamps, Manchester..	6	7	*CoverCraft*
(16)	128th Anniv. Army Physical Training Corps BF 2161 PS.....	8	10	*RFDC 62*
(17)	Railways and the Post Exhib. National Postal Museum EC1	9	—	*n.o.c.*

C.D.S. POSTMARKS

(18)	Accrington, Blackburn, Bolton, Burnley, Derby, Preston, or Stoke — all founder members of Football League ....*each*	10
(19)	Aviemore, Inverness-shire — ski centre	10
(20)	Deepdale Road, Preston — home of Preston North End FC ..	8
(21)	Eccleston St. SW1 — near to HQ of Ski Association	7
(22)	Edgbaston, Birmingham — first lawn tennis court marked out	10
(23)	Fleet St. — first meeting of Football League (Anderton's Hotel) ..	10
(24)	Inner Park Rd., Wimbledon Park or Wimbledon B.O.....*each*	10
(25)	Leamington Spa — world's first tennis club	8
(26)	Lilleshall, Salop — home of National Gymnastics Centre.....	10
(27)	Liverpool — the most successful League Club of all time	8
(28)	Lytham St. Annes — HQ of the Football League.................	8
(29)	Meadow Lane, Nottingham — home of Notts County FC.....	20
(30)	Slough — HQ of the British Amateur Gymnastics Association	7
(31)	Villa Road — near to Villa Park, home of Aston Villa FC	40
(32)	Wembley B.O.	7
(33)	Wembley Park..	20

In addition covers are known with the following C.D.S. postmarks: Highbury, North End Road W14. Prices range from £8.

10th May 1988 — TRANSPORT AND COMMUNICATIONS

18p 'Mallard' and T.P.O.s; 26p R.M.S. 'Queen Elizabeth';
31p Glasgow Tram; 34p Handley Page

	ordinary covers £	official covers £	
SPECIAL HANDSTAMPS			
(1) First Day of Issue — Philatelic Bureau	3	—	*Post Office*
(2) First Day of Issue — Glasgow	3	—	*Post Office*
(3) Railways and the Post Exhib., National Postal Museum EC1.	6	—	*n.o.c.*
(4) 50th Anniv. World Record, Mallard 88 Nat. Rly. Museum, York	5	9	*BLCS 32*
(5) Mallard 50th Anniversary Rail Riders, York	5	10	*CoverCraft*
(6) T.P.O. 150 Anniversary 1838-1988, Peterborough	5	10	*Nene V. Rly*
(7) The Jessop Collection, Diss, Norfolk	5	6	*P.P.S.*
(8) Sheffield & Rotherham Rly. 1838-1988, Sheffield	5	35	*Br. Rail*
(9) Tenth Anniversary Video Cinecosse Film Ellen, Aberdeenshire ...	5	50	*Cinecosse*
(10) 50th Anniv. Launch of R.M.S. Queen Elizabeth, London SW1	5	7	*Arlington*
(11) 50th Anniv. Year R.M.S. Queen Elizabeth, Southampton	5	8	*LFDC 68*
(12) 71st Anniv. of First Atlantic Convoy, BF 2165 PS	5	10	*FAA Museum*
(13) The Museum of Transport, Glasgow	5	8	*BLCS 32*
(14) 50th Anniv. Imperial Airways Rochester, Kent	5	14	*B'ham 500(32)*
(15) 60th Anniv. Opening Croydon Airport Terminal BF 2162 PS	5	8	*RFDC 63*
(16) National Postal Museum EC1 (depicting AirMail routes)	5	—	*n.o.c.*
(17) TGWU Celebrates Historic Transport Stamps, London SW1	5	8	*CoverCraft*
(18) Laser 15 Years Service 1973-1988, Hythe, Kent	8	10	*G&P*
(19) Illustrated by Andrew Davidson, Bromley, Kent	8	—	*n.o.c.*
(20) Designed by Carroll Dempsey & Thirkell, London WC1	8	—	*n.o.c.*
(21) Lloyd's of London 1688-1988, Tercentenary, London EC3	8	10	*CoverCraft*
(22) 19th Century Post Box Discovery, Spilsby, Lincs.	8	15	*Spilsby C of T*
(23) Transams 10th Anniv. By Technology, London WC1	10	125	*Transams*
(24) W. Indian Tour, 1988, London NW8	10	14	*S.P.*

C.D.S. POSTMARKS (inc. T.P.O. CANCELS)

(25) Berkhamsted — first place to use T.P.O. mail apparatus	7	
(26) Central Station, Edinburgh or Nunthorpe Station	*each*	12
(27) High View, Croydon or Purley — Croydon Airport	*each*	20
(28) Clydebank — where R.M.S. 'Queen Elizabeth' was built	12	
(29) Cricklewood NW2 — Handley Page HP42 was built here	7	
(30) Doncaster — where 'Mallard' was built	7	
(31) Essendine — where 'Mallard' broke the speed record	10	
(32) Garden Festival, Glasgow — Glasgow's trams operated here .	8	
(33) Hong Kong BFPO 1 — resting place of RMS 'Queen Elizabeth'	60	
(34) Mosspark, Glasgow — destination of tram on stamp	10	
(35) Southampton — home port of R.M.S. 'Queen Elizabeth'	7	
(36) Springburn, Glasgow — first trams ran on Springburn route .	7	
(37) Tiverton — where HP42 ended its days	7	
(38) York or Bright Street, York — home of 'Mallard'	7	
(39) Crewe-Peterborough T.P.O. — where 'Mallard' broke record .	15	
(40) Up or Down Special, or N.W. Night Down T.P.O.s — the first T.P.O.s .*each*	15	
(41) London-York-Edin: N.E. Night Up or Down T.P.O.s — route of 'Mallard' ....*each*	15	
(42) Any other T.P.O. postmark	*from*	12

In addition covers are known with the following C.D.S. postmarks: Crich, Forton Services.
Heathrow Airport, Hope St., New York, Queen Elizabeth Ave. Prices range from £5.

SLOGAN POSTMARKS

(43) Only Fools Play on Railway Lines — P'borough, Doncaster or York .*each*	15	
(44) Paisley 500 Paisley Borough Charter (Paisley's last tram No. 146) .	20	
(45) Royal Mail Letters Supports Glasgow Garden Festival	20	
(46) Grampians — Going Places — Aberdeen	30	
(47) West Midlands 100 Great Day Out — Shropshire	35	

In addition: Postcode your Property; Tobormory. Prices from £15.

21st June 1988 — AUSTRALIAN BICENTENARY
(Double Postmarked Covers)

This issue was the first 'joint issue' involving the British Post Office. Arrangements were made for British collectors to send their British first day covers to Australia where the Australia stamps were affixed and cancelled on 21st June 1988. The prices below are in respect of covers with the FULL SET of both British and Australian stamps affixed.

(1) Any British special handstamp + Any Australian handstamp ....*from*	30	
(2) Any British C.D.S. postmark + Any Australian handstamp ....*from*	35	
(3) Any other covers ....*from*	25	

PRICES & CONDITION – PLEASE READ GENERAL NOTES

21st June 1988 — AUSTRALIAN BICENTENARY

18p Historical — Early Settler and Clipper Ship;
18p Constitutional — HM The Queen and Parliament Buildings;
34p Sports — W.G. Grace and Tennis;
34p The Arts — John Lennon, Shakespeare, Sydney Opera House

	ordinary covers £	official covers £	
SPECIAL HANDSTAMPS			
(1) First Day of Issue — Philatelic Bureau	3	—	*Post Office*
(2) First Day of Issue — Portsmouth	3	—	*Post Office*
(3) The Bicentenary of Australia 1788-1988, London SW1	5	8	*LFDC 69*
(4) Australian Bicentenary 1788, Portsmouth, Hants.	5	18	*Benham L17*
(5) Capt. James Cook Museum, Australian Bicen., Marton-in-Cleveland	5	9	*S. Muscroft*
(6) Links with Australia, Amy Johnson, Queen of the Air, Hull	5	20	*Bradbury*
(7) GB Cricketing Links 200 Anniv. Australia, Old Trafford	5	30	*S.P.*
(8) GB Cricketing Links 200 Anniv. Australia, Edgbaston	5	30	*S.P.*
(9) GB Cricketing Links 200 Anniv. Australia, Trent Bridge	5	30	*S.P.*
(10) GB Cricketing Links 200 Anniv. Australia, The Oval, SE11	5	30	*S.P.*
(11) GB Cricketing Links 200 Anniv. Australia, Headingley, Leeds	5	30	*S.P.*
(12) GB Cricketing Links 200 Anniv. Australia, Lords, London NW8	5	7	*S.P.*
(13) Wedgwood, Australian Bicentenary 1788-1988, Barlaston, Stoke	5	8	*Arlington*
(14) Australian Bicentenary, Botany Bay, Enfield, Middx.	5	12	*B'ham (500)33*
(15) 48th Anniv. Bombardment of Bardia BF 2178 PS	8	15	*FAA Museum*
(16) Australian Bicentennial, London EC	7	12	*CoverCraft*
(17) 100 Years of the LTA Lawn Tennis Museum, Wimbledon SW19	9	15	*H.R.*
(18) Railways and the Post Exhib., National Postal Museum EC1	10	—	*n.o.c.*
(19) Greetings from the Thames Barrier Visitors Centre, SE18	10	12	*CoverCraft*
(20) W. Indian Tour 1988, London NW8	10	12	*S.P.*
(21) 50th Anniv. R.A.F. Cottesmore, TTTE BF 2177 PS	10	12	*RFDC 64*

C.D.S. POSTMARKS	
(22) Bathampton — Capt. Arthur Phillip (first Governor of NSW) buried	7
(23) Botany Bay	15
(24) Downend — birthplace of W.G. Grace	8
(25) Hambledon — birthplace of English County Cricket	8
(26) House of Commons SW1	20
(27) House of Lords SW1	35
(28) Penny Lane, Liverpool — famous Beatles' hit record	10
(29) Portsmouth — from where the First Fleet sailed	6
(30) Ryde, Isle of Wight — First Fleet gathered here	6
(31) Stratford-upon-Avon — home of William Shakespeare	6
(32) Whitby — Home of Captain James Cook	6
(33) Windsor	6

In addition covers are known with the following C.D.S. postmarks: Buckingham Palace, Croydon, Headingley, Kennington Park, Marton-in-Cleveland, Melbourne, Queen Elizabeth Ave., St. Bravels, Sydney Road, Wimbledon. Prices range from £5.

SLOGAN POSTMARKS	
(34) 1588-1788-1988 Tobormory 200, Oban	125

In addition: Royal Mail Supports Glasgow G.F.; Ullapool Bicentenary. Prices from £15.

19th July 1988 — THE ARMADA 1588

5 × 18p stamps show the progress of the Armada, viz:
The Lizard; Plymouth; Isle of Wight; Calais; and North Sea

SPECIAL HANDSTAMPS			
(1) First Day of Issue — Philatelic Bureau	3	—	*Post Office*
(2) First Day of Issue — Plymouth	3	—	*Post Office*
(3) Royal Naval College Armada Anniv. Greenwich, London SE10	5	12	*CoverCraft*
(4) The Spanish Armada, Tilbury, Essex (Elizabeth I on horse)	5	15	*Benham SPG 6*
(5) Spanish Armada, Effingham, Leatherhead, Surrey	5	15	*B'ham (500) 34*
(6) 400th Anniv. Sighting of Armada by HM Royal Navy BF 2179 PS	5	9	*RFDC 65*
(7) Armada 400 Plymouth, Devon (circular)	5	9	*PlyPhilSoc*
(8) Armada 400 Years 1588-1988 Plymouth (rectangular)	5	—	
(9) Armada Anniversary, Tavistock, Devon	5	9	*TavBookShop*
(10) First Armada 400 Beacon, The Lizard, Cornwall	5	18	*Benham L19*
(11) Armada 400, The Battle of Gravelines, Dover, Kent	5	7	*S.P.*
(12) The Spanish Armada 1588, Tilbury, Essex (Tudor Rose)	5	10	*LFDC 70*
(13) John Hurleston, Mariner, Chester	5	6	*Havering*
(14) 'The Royal Tournament, Earls Court 1988, BF 2181 PS	8	15	*Forces*
(15) 21st Int. Scout Camp, Blair Atholl, Pitlochry, Scotland	6	12	*Scouts*
(16) 'K' Blackburn, Lancs. (Kellogg's promotion)	8	15	*Kelloggs*
(17) Merriott Mouldings Ltd 50th Anniv. 1938-1988, Merriott	8	15	*Cotswold*
(18) W. Indian Tour 1988, London NW8	10	7	*S.P.*
(19) Greetings from The Thames Barrier Visitors Centre, SE18	8	35	*CoverCraft*
(20) Railways and the Post Exhibition 1988, National Postal Museum	10	—	*n.o.c.*

Merriott Mouldings Limited

50th
ANNIVERSARY
1938 - 1988

MERRIOTT · SOMERSET · 19 JULY 88

(17)

The Armada (contd.)

		ordinary covers £	official covers £
C.D.S. POSTMARKS			
(21)	Altofts, Normanton — birthplace of Sir Martin Frobisher	8	
(22)	Buckland Monachorum — home of Drake	18	
(23)	Calais or Dover + PAQUEBOT markings....................*each*	15	
(24)	Drake, Plymouth	140	
(25)	Effingham — birthplace of Lord Howard of Effingham	9	
(26)	Greenwich — birthplace of Queen Elizabeth I....................	9	
(27)	Maritime Mail I.S. London	90	
(28)	Paquebot, London	50	
(29)	Portland, Southwell (Portland), or Bonchurch (I.O.W.) — battle sites	8	
(30)	Plymouth	15	
(31)	Sandwich — inhabitants prepared to meet invasion on beaches ...	8	
(32)	Santander PAQUEBOT	40	
(33)	St. Mary's Isle of Scilly — first sighting	10	
(34)	Tavistock — birthplace of Sir Francis Drake	8	
(35)	The Lizard and Berwick — first and last beacons ....*each*	12	
(36)	Tilbury — where Elizabeth rallied her troops	8	
(37)	Tobomory, Hope and Fair Isle — wreck sites ....*each*	15	
(38)	West Hoe, Plymouth	20	

In addition covers are known with the following C.D.S. postmarks: Beacon, Drakes Broughton, House of Commons, House of Lords. Prices range from £6.

SLOGAN POSTMARKS

(39)	400th Anniv. of Spanish Armada — Penzance, Truro, or Plymouth	50	
(40)	Tobomory 200 1588-1788-1988 used at Oban..............*from*	200	

In addition: Visit Isle of Skye; Royal Mail Letters Supports G.G.F. Prices from £25.

6th September 1988 — EDWARD LEAR – VERSE FOR CHILDREN

19p 'The Owl and the Pussycat'; 27p Pen Sketch; 32p Alphabet 'C'; 35p Rhyme

SPECIAL HANDSTAMPS

(1)	First Day of Issue — Philatelic Bureau	4	—	*Post Office*
(2)	First Day of Issue — London N7	4	—	*Post Office*
(3)	Cent. of Edward Lear, Foss Rampant Learmouth	5	12	*B'ham (500)35*
(4)	Edward Lear Centenary, Knowsley, Liverpool	5	6	*LFDC 71*
(5)	Hull Schools Reorganization	7	7	*Hull Schools*
(6)	Birthplace of Edward Lear 1812-1888 Holloway, London N7	5	6	*BLCS 35*
(7)	Designed by the Partners Edward Lear 1812-1888, EC1	5	—	*n.o.c.*
(8)	Knowsley from Menagerie to Safari Park, Prescot, Merseyside ...	5	12	*CoverCraft*
(9)	Coeliac Symposium, St. Bartholomew's Hospital, London EC1 ...	9	25	*St. Barts*
(10)	Railways and the Post Exhib., National Postal Museum EC1	9	—	*Post Office*
(11)	Farnborough International 88 BF 2173 PS	9	12	*RFDC 66*
(12)	K Blackburn, Lancs	9	—	*n.o.c.*

C.D.S. POSTMARKS

(13)	Camden Town, or Theobald's Road — homes of Lear ....*each*	6	
(14)	Chester, Gretna, Portree and Ryde — featured in Lear's rhymes ...*each*	6	
(15)	Holloway, N7 — birthplace of Lear	6	
(16)	Knowsley, Prescot — where Lear wrote his nonsense verse .	6	
(17)	Park Rd., Regents Park, and Regents Park Rd. — Lear drew birds and animals at the Zoological Gardens ....*each*	10	

In addition covers are known with the following CDS postmarks: Catsfield, Derry Hill, East Cowes, Foss Mount, Freshwater, Luimneach, Owlsmoor, Petworth, Victoria Street, Winchelsea. Prices range from £5.

SLOGAN POSTMARKS

Visit Isle of Skye; Brighton Guide; Guide Dog Week, Tobomory. Prices from £15.

1988

GUIDE DOG
WEEK
3-9 OCT 1988

27th September 1988 — EDWARD LEAR – VERSE FOR CHILDREN

Miniature Sheet

	ordinary covers £	official covers £	
SPECIAL HANDSTAMPS			
(1) First Day of Issue — Philatelic Bureau	5	—	*Post Office*
(2) First Day of Issue — London N22	5	—	*Post Office*
(3) Cent. of Edward Lear Foss Rampant, Learmouth, Northumberland	6	12	*B'ham (500)36*
(4) Edward Lear Centenary, Knowsley, Liverpool	6	9	*LFDC 72*
(5) Edward Lear Centenary, Stampex London SW	6	10	*BLCS 36*
(6) Birthplace of Edward Lear 1812-1888, Holloway, London N7	6	10	*BLCS 36*
(7) Stampway to the World, Liverpool Museum 466	10	—	*n.o.c.*
(8) Autumn Stampex/BPE, London SW1	9	12	*Stampex*
(9) Royal Mail Exibition Card No.2, Stampex/BPE Exhibition	9	—	*Post Office*
(10) 12th Anniv. Cancer & Leukaemia Childhood Trust BF 2182 PS	9	10	*RFDC 67*
(11) Railways and the Post Exhib., National Postal Museum EC1	9	—	*Post Office*
(12) 150 Wolverton 150 17 Sept. 2 Oct., Milton Keynes	9	—	*n.o.c.*
(13) K Blackburn, Lancs	9	—	*n.o.c.*
(14) 70th Anniv. Eve of Launch of HMS Leamington BF 2189 PS	9	12	*FAA Museum*
(15) 50th Anniv. Launch of RMS Queen Elizabeth Clydebank	9	—	*n.o.c.*
(16) Royal Academy of Arts 1988, Henry Moore, London W1	9	12	*Pilgrim*
C.D.S. POSTMARKS			
(17) Alexandra Park Road, N10 — venue for 'Stamp World 1990'.	10		
(18) Chester, Gretna, Portree, Ryde — featured in Lear's rhymes ..*each*	9		
(19) Holloway, N7 — birthplace of Lear	9		
(20) Knowsley, Prescot — where Lear wrote his nonsense verse...	9		
(21) Park Rd. and Regent's Park — Lear drew birds and animals at the Zoological Gardens ....*each*	12		
(22) Portman Square — home of Lear	9		

In addition covers are known with the following CDS postmarks: Catsfield, Derry Hill, East Cowes, Foss Mount Freshwater, Luimneach, Owlsmoor, Petworth, Victoria St., Winchelsea. Prices range from £5.

SLOGAN POSTMARKS

(23) 'Autumn Stampex/BPE' Royal Horticultural Hall, London SW1 ...	15
(24) 'Have you got your Great Ormonde St. Candle?' — Bournemouth ..	12
(25) British Philatelic Bulletin 25th Anniversary — London EC ...	25

In addition: Visit Isle of Skye; Brighton Guide; Guide Dog Week. Prices from £10.

Some double-dated covers exist with both the set of stamps postmarked 6th September and the miniature sheet postmarked 27th September. Prices range from £30.

15th November 1988 — CHRISTMAS

14p, 19p, 27p, 32p, 35p Christmas Cards

SPECIAL HANDSTAMPS			
(1) First Day of Issue — Philatelic Bureau	4	—	*Post Office*
(2) First Day of Issue — Bethlehem, Llandeilo, Dyfed	4	—	*Post Office*
(3) St. Alban The Martyr, 1938-1988 Northampton	5	10	*Ch. of St. A.*
(4) Christmas Greetings from Guinea Pig Club BF 2184 PS	5	6	*RFDC 68*
(5) York Minister Commemoration	5	8	*CoverCraft*
(6) The Christmas Card Mailcoach Run Box, Corsham, Wilts. ...	5	6	*BLCS 37*
(7) The Christmas Card Mailcoach Run, Luton, Beds	5	9	*BLCS 37*
(8) The Christmas Card Mailcoach Run, Bath	5	5	*BLCS 37*
(9) Victorian Christmas Cards Postling, Hythe, Kent	5	10	*B'ham (500)37*
(10) Saint Dunstan Millennium Year 988-1988, Canterbury	7	8	*LFDC 73*
(11) Cartmel Priory 1188-1988 800 Grange, Cumbria	8	10	*Bradbury*
(12) Happy Christmas, Telecom Technology Showcase, London EC4	10	—	*n.o.c.*
(13) Scanner, HRH Princess Margaret, Christmas 1988, Romford	9	10	*OldchurchHosp*
(14) Royle Royle Royle, London, N1	8	50	*Arlington*
(15) Stampway to the World, Liverpool Museum 466 Stamp Publicity Board .	9	—	*n.o.c.*
(16) Royal Academy of Arts, 1988 Henry Moore, London W1	9	9	*Pilgrim*
(17) The Green Howards 1688-1988, XIX BF 2183 PS	9	25	*Forces*
(18) Railways and the Post Exhib., National Postal Museum EC1	9	—	*Post Office*
(19) Holmfirth Postcard Museum — Wish You Were Here	15	—	*n.o.c.*
C.D.S. POSTMARKS			
(20) Kensington Church Street, W8 — where first Xmas card designed	8		
(21) Nasareth, Gwynedd	9		

In addition covers are known with the following CDS postmarks: Angel Hill, Bath, Holy Island, Lancelot Place SW7, Noel Road W3, St. Nicholas, Shepherds Bush W12, Shepherds Hill and Star. Prices range from £4.

SLOGAN POSTMARKS

| (22) Washington Apples, Bigger Christmas Crunch — various offices .. | 18 |

In addition: Stampway; BBC Children in Need. Prices range from £12.

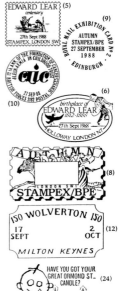

17th January 1989 — SEA BIRDS
19p Puffin; 27p Avocet; 32p Oyster Catcher; 35p Gannet

		ordinary covers £	official covers £	
SPECIAL HANDSTAMPS				
(1)	First Day of Issue — Philatelic Bureau	4	—	*Post Office*
(2)	First Day of Issue — Sandy, Bedfordshire	4	—	*Post Office*
(3)	Britain's Most Famous Gannet Colony, Bass Rock, Firth of Forth	5	10	*Benham S.G. 8*
(4)	Leics. & Rutland Ornithological Society, Leicester	5	12	*LFDC 74*
(5)	Lundy Island, Bristol Channel, Bideford, Devon	5	25	*Lundy P.B.*
(6)	British Sea Birds, Dungeness, Romney Marsh, Kent	5	14	*B'ham (500) 38*
(7)	St. Kilda — Britain's Largest Puffin Colony, Benbecula, W. Isles	5	10	*BLCS 38*
(8)	RSPB Action for Birds, 100 Years, Sandy, Beds.	5	8	*CoverCraft*
(9)	75th Anniv. Formation of No. 201 Squadron, BF 2193 PS	8	12	*RFDC 69*
(10)	HMS Quorn, Ready for Sea, MCMV, BF 2194 PS	8	12	*FAA Museum*
(11)	Royal Academy of Arts, Italian Art in the 20th Century, W1	8	12	*Pilgrim*
C.D.S. POSTMARKS				
(12)	Balivanich, Bempton, Papa Westray or Rathlin Is. — Puffin colonies	12		
(13)	Didsbury Village — where RSPB was founded	9		
(14)	Fair Isle or Ness — homes of the Gannet	15		
(15)	Orford — nearest PO to Minsmere, home of the Avocet	9		
(16)	Sandy — RSPB Headquarters	12		
(17)	Slimbridge — Wildfowl Trust Headquarters	10		
(18)	Snettisham or Westleton — Oystercatcher habitats	10		
(19)	Tring — British Trust for Ornithology Headquarters	35		

In addition covers are known with the following CDS postmarks: Bideford, Birdsedge, Heron Cross, Kinlochleven, Redhill, Swallow's Nest and Wren's Nest. Prices range from £6.

SLOGAN POSTMARK
Visit the Isle of Skye. Prices from £25.

31st January 1989 — GREETING STAMPS
5 designs featuring a rose, cupid, sailing boat, bowl of fruit and teddy bear

SPECIAL HANDSTAMPS				
(1)	First Day of Issue — Philatelic Bureau	8	—	*Post Office*
(2)	First Day of Issue — Lover Salisbury	8	—	*Post Office*
(3)	Greetings from the Teddy Bear Museum, Ironbridge, Telford	10	10	*BLCS 39*
(4)	St. Valentine's Patron Saint of Lovers, Lover Salisbury, Wilts	10	12	*B'ham (500) 39*
(5)	Greetings from Flowery Field, Hyde, Cheshire	10	12	*BLCS 39*
(6)	Commission 'Postes' CEPT Edinburgh	15	—	*n.o.c.*
(7)	75th Anniv. Formation of No. 6 Squadron, BF 2192 PS	15	20	*RDFC 70*
(8)	Royal Academy of Arts, Italian Art in 20th Century, London W1	12	15	*Pilgrim*
(9)	Up-Helly-A Lerwick, Shetland	12	20	*UpHellyA*
C.D.S. POSTMARKS				
(10)	Bearpark or Pudsey	12		
(11)	Cowes or Seaside	12		
(12)	Flowery Field or Kew Gardens	13		
(13)	Greet, Birmingham	15		
(14)	Gretna Green or Lover	13		
(15)	Orchard or Strawberry Hill	12		
(16)	Rose or Rosehearty	12		

In addition covers are known with the following CDS postmark: Greetland. Prices range from £8.

SLOGAN POSTMARK
Visit the Isle of Skye. Prices from £18.

N.B. *Prices quoted above are for covers with a strip of five stamps. These stamps were issued in booklets of ten stamps, i.e. two strips of the same five designs. Covers with the complete pane of ten stamps command a £2/£4 premium.*

7th March 1989 — FOOD & FARMING YEAR
19p Fruit and vegetables; 27p Meat and Fish produce; 32p Dairy produce; 35p Cereal produce

SPECIAL HANDSTAMPS				
(1)	First Day of Issue — Philatelic Bureau	4	—	*Post Office*
(2)	First Day of Issue — Kenilworth, Warwicks	4	—	*Post Office*
(3)	BVA Animal Welfare Foundation, London W1	5	7	*LFDC 75*
(4)	British Food & Farming, Isle of Grain, Rochester, Kent	5	9	*B'ham (500) 40*
(5)	Ministry of Agriculture, Fisheries and Food, SW1	5	15	*CoverCraft*
(6)	50th Anniv. of Women's Land Army, BF 2195 PS	5	8	*RFDC 71*
(7)	150th Anniv. Royal Agricultural Soc. of England, Stoneleigh	5	7	*BLCS 40*
(8)	Purveyors of Flour since 1886, Hovis, Windsor, Berks	5	2(s)	*Arlington*
(9)	Royal Academy of Arts, Italian Art 20th Century, London W1	10	12	*Pilgrim*

PRICES & CONDITION – PLEASE READ GENERAL NOTES

Food and Farming (contd.)

	ordinary covers £	official covers £

C.D.S. POSTMARKS

(10) Bewcastle, Eneclate, Sheepscombe or Rowelton — Farm P.O.s 15
(11) Cheddar, Stilton or Wensley ....*each* 15
(12) Corn Exchange or Market Place ....*each* 8
(13) Farmers, Dyfed 12
(14) Ham or Melton Mowbray (pork pies)...........................*each* 7
(15) Isle of Grain, Rochester, Kent 10
(16) Leek or Bramley ....*each* 8
(17) Ivymeade, High Wycombe (Octagon B.O.) — shopping centre P.O. 15
(18) Savacentre — Supermarket Post Office 30
(19) Stoneleigh — venue Royal Show 12
(20) Tile Farm, Orpington, Kent 10

In addition covers are known with the following CDS postmarks: The Allotments, Bakers Lane, Bakewell, Butterton, Evesham, The Orchard, Wheatley. Prices range from £7.

SLOGAN POSTMARKS

(21) 'Collect British Stamps' — Bradford (features sheep's head) 25

In addition: York Collect British Stamps; Wild about Worcestershire; Hooked on Herefordshire; County Councils; Industry Matters. Prices from £12.

11th April 1989 — ANNIVERSARIES

19p Public Education (150th anniversary);
19p European Parliament (3rd Direct Elections);
35p Postal Telegraph & Telephones Congress;
35p Inter-Parliamentary Union Centenary Conference

SPECIAL HANDSTAMPS

(1)	First Day of Issue — Philatelic Bureau	4	—	*Post Office*
(2)	First Day of Issue — SW London Letter District	4	—	*Post Office*
(3)	Strasbourg — Leicester's Twin City, Leicester	5	9	*LFDC 76*
(4)	26th World Congress PTTI, London W1............................	5	12	*B'ham (500) 41*
(5)	Inter Parliamentary Union Centenary Conference, London SW1.	5	6	*BLCS 41*
(6)	Direct Elections to the European Parliament, Downing St., SW1	5	6	*BLCS 41*
(7)	44th Anniversary Operation Sunfish S.E.A.C., BF 2202 PS .	5	10	*FAA Museum*
(8)	30th Anniversary of RAFLET, BF 2179 PS	7	10	*RFDC 72*
(9)	Centenary Derbyshire County Council 1889-1989, Matlock.	7	20	*DerbysCC*
(10)	Stampway to the World, Manchester Stamp Publicity Board 498........	8	15	*S.P.Board*
(11)	WFUS Weston Favell Upper School, Northampton	8	15	*WFUS*
(12)	Evesham Corps. Centenary Blood & Fire, Evesham, Worcs..	8	12	*H.R.*

C.D.S. POSTMARKS

(13) Brighton — PTTI Conference 7
(14) Brighton Centre, Brighton — venue of PTTI Conference..... 40
(15) Broadway, London SW1 — site of IPU Congress................ 7
(16) Dover or Calais with PAQUEBOT markings................*each* 15
(17) Hope Street, Edinburgh — birthplace Alexander Graham Bell.... 7
(18) House of Commons, SW1.. 20
(19) House of Lords, SW1 30
(20) Mark Cross, Crowborough 17
(21) Northern Parliament, Belfast 15
(22) School pmks: Duke of York's School or Royal Hospital School ......*each* 15
(23) Telephone House, Birmingham.. 10
(24) Temple Hill, Dartford — home of Unwin Pyrotechnics 6
(25) Terminal 4, Heathrow Airport — main UK airport serving Europe 30
(26) University pmks: Bath, Bradford, Essex, Lancaster,
     Liverpool, Norwich and Swansea ....*each* 10

In addition covers are known with the following CDS postmarks: Clapham Common, College Road, Eton, Fareham, Grange Hill, Harwich, Regent Street, Rochdale, Sussex Coast, World's End. Prices range from £7 each.

SLOGAN POSTMARKS

(27) University of Durham 60 Years Dept. of Geography, Darlington... 20
(28) The Mailing and Communications Show, London EC1 20
(29) Liverpool Mechanised Office — use postcodes........................... 20
(30) Remember to use the Postcode — Ipswich 15
(31) Edinburgh International Festival of Science & Technology.......... 20
(32) NATO Fortieth Anniversary... 60

In addition: Lead Free; Derbyshire C.C; Inverness Conference Capital; BBC Wilts Sound; Stampway. Prices from £14.

16th May 1989 — GAMES AND TOYS
19p train and plane; 27p building blocks; 32p board games;
35p boat, robot and doll's house

1989

	ordinary covers £	official covers £	
SPECIAL HANDSTAMPS			
(1) First Day of Issue — Philatelic Bureau	4	—	*Post Office*
(2) First Day of Issue — Leeds	4	—	*Post Office*
(3) Putting Children First NSPCC, London EC	5	7	*CoverCraft*
(4) Lewis Carrol 1832-1898, Oxford	5	15	*Zanders*
(5) The Teddybears' Picnic, Ironbridge, Telford, Salop	5	9	*BLCS 42*
(6) Pollock's Toy Museum, London W1	5	7	*LFDC 77*
(7) Children's Toys and Games, Toys Hill, Westerham, Kent	5	10	*B'ham (500) 42*
(8) Stampway to the World, Manchester Stamp Publicity Board 498	6	12	*S.P.Board*
(9) National Postal Museum Uniform Exhibition, London EC	7	—	*n.o.c.*
(10) Rotary Diamond Charter Celebration, Newcastle, Staffs	8	10	*Rotary*
(11) Guisborough Priory Great Fire 700th Anniv., Guisborough	8	10	*S. Muscroft*
(12) 75th Anniversary Royal Naval Air Service, BF 2200 PS	8	12	*RFDC 73*
(13) Presentation of RNLI Gallantry Awards, London SE1	8	10	*Pilgrim*
(14) History of the Royal Navy Series, Plymouth, Devon	8	—	*n.o.c.*
C.D.S. POSTMARKS			
(15) Fforestfach, Swansea — home of 'Corgi' toys	8		
(16) Hornby or Waddington	12		
(17) Mount Pleasant, Liverpool — birthplace of Frank Hornby	8		
(18) Old Swan, Liverpool — site of 'Hornby' factory	12		
(19) Playing Place, Truro	12		
(20) Regent St., W1— home of Hamley's Toy Shop	8		
(21) Any TPO postmark	10		
(22) Woodlesford or Rothwell, Leeds — home of Waddington Games	8		

In addition covers are known with the following CDS postmarks: Bathampton, Bethnal Green, Bowling, Bunny, Butlin's Holiday Camp, Child's Hill, Ironbridge, Kirton, Market, Mulberry Parade, Paddington, Rothwell. Prices range from £4 each.

SLOGAN POSTMARKS			
(23) 'Chess board' die slogan postmark — Bradford	50		
(24) Save the Children Week, 70 Years of Saving Children	25		

In addition: Medway & Swale Child Safety; 40 Years Council of Europe; Lead Free; Spotless; Robin Hood; Train slogans. Prices range from £12.

4th July 1989 — INDUSTRIAL ARCHAEOLOGY
19p Ironbridge; 27p Tin mine. St. Agnes; 32p New Lanark Mills;
35p Pontcysyllte Aqueduct

SPECIAL HANDSTAMPS			
(1) First Day of Issue — Philatelic Bureau	4	—	*Post Office*
(2) First Day of Issue — Telford	4	—	*Post Office*
(3) Isambard Kingdom Brunel, Industrial Pioneer, Bristol	5	15	*Zanders*
(4) Water Powered Mills at New Lanark, Lanark	5	10	*B'ham (500) 43*
(5) The Pontcysyllte Aqueduct, Llangollen, Clwyd	5	7	*Benham L21*
(6) New Lanark Conservation, Lanark	5	7	*LFDC 78*
(7) Our Industrial Heritage Preserved by National Trust, St. Agnes	5	6	*BLCS 43*
(8) Birthplace of British Industry, Ironbridge Museum, Telford	5	7	*BLCS 43*
(9) Over 300 years of Water Power Aberdulais Falls, W. Glam.	5	6	*CoverCraft*
(10) First Day of Service Penfold Box Waterways Museum, Gloucester	5		*n.o.c.*
(11) Philatelic Counter, Bolton (features the 'Spinning Mule')	12	—	*n.o.c.*
(12) Philatelic Counter, Bradford (features industrial mills)	12	—	*n.o.c.*
(13) Yorkshire Museum, York	7	—	*n.o.c.*
(14) 1689 Killiecrankie 1989 Tercentenary National Trust Scotland	8	—	*n.o.c.*
(15) 65th Anniversary Trenchard-Keyes Agreement BF 2208 PS	9	12	*FAA Museum*
(16) Love All Exhibition at the Lawn Tennis Museum, Wimbledon	9	12	*H.R.*
(17) The Royal Show, Stoneleigh, Warwickshire	9	—	*n.o.c.*
(18) 72nd Anniversary of No. 72 Squadrom BF 2201 PS	9	10	*RFDC 74*
C.D.S. POSTMARKS			
(19) Froncysyllte or Trevor — both ends of the Pontcysyllte aqueduct	10		
(20) Ironbridge, Telford — featured on 19p value	12		
(21) Langholm, Dumfriesshire — birthplace of Thomas Telford	7		
(22) New Lanark, Lanarkshire — featured on 32p value	12		
(23) St. Agnes, Cornwall — featured on 27p value	12		

In addition covers are known with the following CDS postmarks: Arkwright Town, Bolton, Camborne, Chirk, Highway, Illogan, Liverton Mines, Newtown, Preston, Saltaire, Shrewsbury, Stewarton. Prices range from £5.

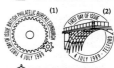

PRICES & CONDITION – PLEASE READ GENERAL NOTES

Industrial Archaeology (contd.)

Aveling Barford (Machines) Ltd (24)

	ordinary covers £	official covers £
SLOGAN POSTMARKS		
(24) Aveling Barford (Machines) Ltd. — The Earthmovers, Leicester..	20	
(25) Collect British Stamps — Bradford (features industrial mills)......	25	

In addition: Marine Engineers; Teesside Talent Ability; Richmond Festival; Post Code; Post Early in the Day. Prices from £10.

25th July 1989 — INDUSTRIAL ARCHAEOLOGY
Miniature Sheet

SPECIAL HANDSTAMPS

(1)	First Day of Issue — Philatelic Bureau...............................	4	—	*Post Office*
(2)	First Day of Issue — New Lanark	4	—	*Post Office*
(3)	Water Powered Mills at New Lanark, Lanark	5	7	*Benham L22*
(4)	The Pontcysyllte Aqueduct, Llangollen, Clwyd	5	14	*B'ham (500) 44*
(5)	Association for Industrial Archaeology, Ironbridge, Telford	5	9	*LFDC 79*
(6)	Our Industrial Heritage Preserved by the National Trust, Pool	5	7	*BLCS 44*
(7)	Ironbridge, Birthplace of British Industry, Telford	5	7	*BLCS 44*
(8)	National Postal Museum SWL90, City of London EC	7	—	*n.o.c.*
(9)	1689 Killiecrankie 1989 Tercentenary National Trust Scotland ...	7	12	*Scot.N.T.*
(10)	International Scout Camp, Discovery 89, Gosford Forest Park	7	20	*Scouts*
(11)	21 Years of Aircraft Archaeology BF 1968 PS	9	12	*RFDC 75*
(12)	Royal Tournament BF 2198 PS	9	12	*Forces*
(13)	Philatelic Counter, Bolton (features 'Spinning Mule')..........	15	—	*n.o.c.*
(14)	Philatelic Counter, Bradford (features industrial mills)	15	—	*n.o.c.*

C.D.S. POSTMARKS

(15)	Froncysyllte or Trevor — both ends of Pontcysyllte aqueduct	12	
(16)	Ironbridge, Telford — featured on 19p value......................	15	
(17)	Langholm, Dumfriesshire — birthplace of Thomas Telford..	8	
(18)	New Lanark, Lanarkshire — featured on 32p value.............	14	
(19)	St. Agnes, Cornwall — featured on 27p value.....................	14	

In addition covers are known with the following CDS postmarks: Alexandra Park Road, Arkwright Town, Camborne, Chirk, Illogen, Liverton Mines, Muswell Hill, Newtown, Preston, Saltaire, Shrewsbury, Stewarton. Prices range from £7.

SLOGAN POSTMARKS

(20)	Aveling Barford (Machines) Ltd. — The Earthmovers, Leicester..	20
(21)	Collect British Stamps — Bradford (features industrialmills).	20

In addition: Marine Engineers; Teesside Talent Ability; Please Post Early in the Day; Post Code. Prices from £10.

Some double-dated covers exist with both the set of stamps postmarked 4th July and the miniature sheet postmarked 25th July. Prices range from £25.

5th September 1989 — MICROSCOPES
19p Snowflake; 27p Blue Fly; 32p Blood Cells; 35p Microchip

SPECIAL HANDSTAMPS

(1)	First Day of Issue — Philatelic Bureau...............................	4	—	*Post Office*
(2)	First Day of Issue — Oxford	4	—	*Post Office*
(3)	Royal Microscopical Society, Oxford.................................	5	15	*Bradbury*
(4)	Year of the Microscope, Royal Microscopical Society 1839-1989 Oxford.	5	7	*Bradbury*
(5)	Cambridge Instruments 25 years Scanning Electron Microscopy	5	20	*Bradbury*
(6)	1989 The Year of the Microscope, London SW7	5	8	*LFDC 80*
(7)	1989 The Year of Microscope Exh. Science Museum, SW	5	7	*BLCS 45*
(8)	The Year of the Microscope, Cambridge	5	10	*B'ham (500) 45*
(9)	Marconi Electronic Devices Microtechnology in Space, Lincoln ..	5	10	*Cotswold*
(10)	Dr. Robert Hooke 1635-1703 Micrographia, Freshwater.......	5	20	*B'ham (Zanders)*
(11)	IMLS 19th Triennial Conference, Warwick University, Coventry.	7	14	*H.R.*
(12)	Stampway to the World, Museum of Science, Newcastle......	7	15	*S.P. Board*
(13)	25th Anniversary of UK North Sea Oil, Aberdeen	7	25	*Arlington*
(14)	21st Anniversary of Jeol (UK), London NW9	7	25	*Arlington*
(15)	Dormeuil The World's Best Cloths, London SW1	10	15	*Dormeuil*
(16)	49th Anniversary of the Battle of Britain BF 2209 PS	10	12	*RFDC 65*
(17)	Inter-Parliamentary Union Centenary Conference, SW1.....	9	9	*BLCS 41*

PLEASE READ THE GENERAL NOTES
AT THE BEGINNING OF THIS CATALOGUE
These often provide the answers to enquiries received.

Microscopes (contd.)

		ordinary covers £	official covers £
C.D.S. POSTMARKS			
(18)	Church, Freshwater — birthplace of Robert Hooke	20	
(19)	Freshwater, Isle of Wight — Robert Hooke	10	
(20)	Regent St., W1 — first meeting of Royal Microscopical Society ...	6	
(21)	St. Clements, Oxford — Royal Microscopical Society HQ	7	
(22)	South Kensington, SW7 — Science Museum	9	
(23)	Whitechapel — first meeting of the Microscopical Society...	8	

In addition covers are known with the following CDS postmarks: Alnwick, Holloway, Houndsditch, Lancaster, London Chief Office, Rotherhithe Lower Road, Royal Hospital School, Snowhill, Stoke Newington and Wollaston. Prices range from £5.

SLOGAN POSTMARKS

(24)	Army — 50 Years of Blood Transfusion — Aldershot	20	
(25)	CARE '89	18	
(26)	Europe Against Cancer Year 1989	20	

In addition: Europe's Universities; Royal Mail in the Community, Winchester; Collect British Stamps. Prices range from £10.

17th October 1989 — THE LORD MAYOR'S SHOW
5 × 20p Scenes from the procession

SPECIAL HANDSTAMPS

(1)	First Day of Issue — Philatelic Bureau	4		*Post Office*
(2)	First Day of Issue — London EC4	4		*Post Office*
(3)	Richard Whittington's Birthplace, Pauntley, Glos	5	20	*Bradbury*
(4)	Dick Whittington Thrice Lord Mayor of London, London EC	5	6	*LFDC 81*
(5)	800th Anniversary Lord Mayor's Show, London EC (trumpet).....	5	15	*Benham SG9*
(6)	800th Anniversary The Lord Mayor City of London, EC (crest)....	5	8	*BLCS 46*
(7)	Exhibition at the Museum of London, EC	6	12	*B'ham (500) 46*
(8)	Stampway to the World, Museum of Science, Newcastle......	6	10	*S.P.Board*
(9)	Royal Mail Open Day Visit Souvenir, London WC1	6	—	*n.o.c.*
(10)	Royal Mail Exhibition Card 3, Stampex/BPE Edinburgh.....	6	—	*n.o.c.*
(11)	Autumn Stampex/BPE 1989, London SW1	6	—	*n.o.c.*
(12)	National Postal Museum SWL90, City of London EC	8	—	*n.o.c.*
(13)	40th Anniversary of the end of the Berlin Airlift BF 2210 PS	9	12	*RFDC 77*
(14)	First Bombardment of Sevastopol, 135th Anniv. BF 1782 PS	9	12	*FAA Museum*
(15)	Town Hall Centenary 1889-1989 Middlesbrough, Cleveland	9	9	*S.Muscroft*
(16)	Royal Academy of Arts, Art of Photography 1839-1989, W1........	9	12	*Pilgrim*

C.D.S. POSTMARKS

(17)	Bovingdon — home of Sir Hugh Bidwell (1989 Lord Mayor)........	9	
(18)	Fore St. EC2; Lombard St. or Stock Exchange EC3; Cannon St. EC4; London Chief Office, EC1; and Fleet St. EC4 — nearest Post Offices to the scenes depicted on the stamps ....*each*	7	
(19)	Ludgate Circus and Moorgate — on the route...............*each*	7	
(20)	Newent or Redmarley, Glos. — birthplace of Dick Whittington	7	
(21)	Wimbledon Park — home of Sir Chris Collet (1988 Lord Mayor)	7	
(22)	Whittington, Lichfield	12	

In addition covers are known with the following CDS postmarks: Richmond, Wickham. Prices range from £5.

SLOGAN POSTMARKS

Autumn Stampex; Stampway; Gloucester Cathedral; Brentford F.C. — Royal Mail; Robin Hood; Aveling Barford; Collect British Stamps. Prices from £15.

14th November 1989 — CHRISTMAS
Ely Cathedral

SPECIAL HANDSTAMPS

(1)	First Day of Issue — Philatelic Bureau	4	—	*Post Office*
(2)	First Day of Issue — Bethlehem, Llandeilo, Dyfed	4	—	*Post Office*
(3)	First Day of Issue — Ely	4	—	*Post Office*
(4)	'Thomas' Invites you to Nene Valley Peterborough	8	9	*N.V.Rly*
(5)	Christmas 1989 Gloucester	6	10	*Bradbury*
(6)	Merry Christmas Telecom Technology Showcase, London EC4...	6	—	*n.o.c.*
(7)	Christmas 1989, Ely, Cambs	6	8	*LFDC 82*
(8)	800th Anniv. the Norman Nave Ely Cathedral, Ely, (Mitre)..	6	12	*B'ham (500) 47*
(9)	800th Anniv. the Norman Nave Ely Cathedral, Ely, (3 Keys)	6	10	*BLCS 47*
(10)	The Christmas Mailcoach Run, Cambridge-Ely Cathedral ..	6	18	*BLCS 47*
(11)	Christmas Greetings HM Ships Abroad, BF 2214 PS.........	6	8	*FAA Museum*
(12)	450th Anniv. of the Dissolution, Whitby Abbey, Whitby........	10	10	*S.Muscroft*
(13)	40th Anniv. Formation RAF Gliding Assoc'n., BF 2212 PS .	10	10	*RFDC 78*
(14)	Stampway to the World Museum of Science, Newcastle	10	15	*S.P.Board*
(15)	Royal Academy of Arts, Art of Photography 1839-1989, W1	10	15	*Pilgrim*

PRICES & CONDITION – PLEASE READ GENERAL NOTES

	ordinary covers £	official covers £
C.D.S. POSTMARKS		
(16) Barnack, Stamford — where the Cathedral stone was quarried....	10	
(17) Ely, Cambs..	12	
(18) Exning, Cambs.–Birthplace of Etheldreda, Founder of the Cathedral ...	10	
(19) Primrose Hill, Tonbridge — Charities Aid Foundation HQ...	12	
(20) Stoke Charity, Winchester..	9	
(21) Walsingham, Norfolk — Alan de Walsingham was the architect ...	8	

In addition covers are known postmarked with the following CDS postmarks: Angel Hill, Canterbury, Holy Island, Nasareth and Northwold. Prices range from £7.

SLOGAN POSTMARKS

(22) Gloucester Cathedral Celebrates 1089-1989	20	
(23) Choose Charity Stamps — show you care — at various offices	20	
(24) Luton Carol Aid '89	40	
(25) BBC Children in Need Appeal	16	

In addition: Unicef Cards; Beautiful Bath; Bath Royal Charter; Liverpool MLO; Collect British Stamps. Prices range from £10.

10th January 1990 — PENNY BLACK ANNIVERSARY
15p, 20p, 29p, 34p, 37p Queen Victoria & Queen Elizabeth II

SPECIAL HANDSTAMPS

(1) First Day of Issue — Philatelic Bureau	4	—	*Post Office*
(2) First Day of Issue — Windsor.....................................	4	—	*Post Office*
(3) Carlisle First Roadside Pillar Box in Mainland Britain, 1853	10	20	*Carlisle P.O.*
(4) National Postal Museum 1840-1990 City of London EC......	7	—	*n.o.c.*
(5) National Postal Museum SWL90 York Paid, Rowland Hill, City of London......	7	—	*n.o.c.*
(6) Unveiling of Victorian Letterbox, Dean Heritage Museum, Glos.	7	35	*CoverCraft*
(7) 150th Anniversary Uniform Penny Post, British Philatelic Federation EC1	6	8	*CoverCraft*
(8) Uniform Penny Postage, 150th Anniv., Rowland Hill, Kidderminster....	6	8	*CoverCraft*
(9) Sir Rowland Hill, Kidderminster.....................................	6	10	*LFDC 83*
(10) 1840-1990 Perkins, Bacon & Co. Printed the Penny Black, Fleet St., EC4	7	20	*Bradbury*
(11) 1840-1990 Uniform Penny Postage, London SW1	8	20	*Bradbury*
(12) Etchingham Stamp Festival..	9	25	*Et'ham P.C.*
(13) 150th Anniversaries SG Plymouth, Devon	8	9	*BLCS 48*
(14) Windsor, Berks. (Maltese Cross)	8	12	*B'ham (500) 48*
(15) Stampway to the World, Museum of Science, Newcastle......	10	15	*S.P.Board*

C.D.S. POSTMARKS

(16) Botchergate, Carlisle — first roadside postbox....................	20	
(16a) Buckingham Palace, SW1	40	
(17) Fleet Street, EC4 — Perkins, Bacon (printers of Penny Black)	15	
(18) House of Commons, SW1 — Postage Act	20	
(19) House of Lords, SW1 — Postage Act	30	
(20) Kidderminster — birthplace of Sir Rowland Hill	10	
(21) Sanquhar — oldest Post Office	15	
(22) Windsor, Berks.	25	
(23) Windsor Castle, Berks.	40	

In addition covers are known with the following CDS postmarks: Arbroath, Bath, Birmingham, Holyrood, London Chief Office, Lordship Lane N17, Queen Elizabeth Avenue, Queensbury, Queen's Parade, Queen Victoria Road, Scone, Seething Lane EC3, Stoke-on-Trent, Victoria Rd. Prices range from £8.

SLOGAN POSTMARKS

(24) Collect British Stamps: Bradford, Lincoln or York Philatelic Counters ..	18	
(25) Collect British Stamps — World's Greatest Hobby	18	
(26) Be Properly Addressed, Postcode It — Leicester	18	
(27) Pass on your Postcode — various offices	18	
(28) Get the Most From Your Post — Post Code It! — Coventry ...	20	
(29) Remember to use the Postcode — various offices	15	
(30) Post Early in the Day — Croydon	20	
(31) Liverpool is a Mechanised Letter Office	15	
(32) Senders Name & Address on the back of envelopes............	15	
(33) Write Now! — Say it Better in a Letter — Nottingham	50	
(34) Stampway to the World – Newcastle	70	

Also available: Great Expectations; Beautiful Bath. Prices from £10.

23rd January 1990 — R.S.P.C.A.
20p Kitten, 29p Rabbit; 34p Duckling; 37p Puppy

SPECIAL HANDSTAMPS

(1) First Day of Issue — Philatelic Bureau	4	—	*Post Office*
(2) First Day of Issue — Horsham......................................	4	—	*Post Office*
(3) Bunny, Nottingham	5	15	*Bradbury*
(4) Battersea, London SW8	5	8	*LFDC 84*
(5) RSPCA 150 Years Caring for Animals, Horsham................	5	10	*CoverCraft*

R.S.P.C.A. *(contd.)*

		ordinary covers £	official covers £	
(6)	RSPCA 150th Anniversary Pett, Hastings, E. Sussex	5	12	*B'ham (500) 49*
(7)	Cats Protection League, Middlesbrough, Cleveland............	5	7	*S. Muscroft*
(8)	Cat World Magazine RSPCA 150th Anniversary, Shoreham.......	5	18	*BLCS 49*
(9)	Provincial Grand Masters 1996 Festival, Hadleigh, Ipswich	7	8	*Masons*
(10)	Arrival at Ekowe of Naval Brigade 111th Anniv., BF 2215 PS......	7	8	*FAA Museum*
(11)	75th Anniversary of No. 24 Squadron BF 2216 PS	7	8	*RFDC 79*

C.D.S. POSTMARKS

(12)	Battersea, or Battersea Park Road, SW8 — Dogs Home*each*	7	
(13)	Bunny, Nottingham	8	
(14)	Dog & Gun, Dog Kennel Lane, or Isle of Dogs, E14 ......*each*	9	
(15)	Horsham, W. Sussex — headquarters of RSPCA	6	
(16)	Sidmouth — birthplace of founder of RSPCA	6	
(17)	Trafalgar Sq, WC2 — near to RSPCA's first meeting	6	

In addition covers are known with the following CDS postmarks: Ballynahinch, Black Dog, Catfield, Catshill, Catsfield, Ducklington, Middlesbrough, Regent St. SW1. Prices range from £5.

SLOGAN POSTMARKS

(18)	Collect British Stamps, Bradford (depicts ram's head)........	15	
(19)	Aveling Barford, the Earthmovers, Leicester (depicts horse).......	70	

Also available: Collect British Stamps; Liverpool MLO; Write Now etc. Prices from £7.

6th February 1990 — GREETINGS STAMPS

10×20p designs featuring famous 'smiles' Teddy Bear; Dennis the Menace, Mr. Punch, Cheshire Cat, Man in the Moon, Laughing Policeman, Clown, Mona Lisa, Queen of Hearts, Stan Laurel.

SPECIAL HANDSTAMPS

(1)	First Day of Issue — Philatelic Bureau	4	—	*Post Office*
(2)	First Day of Issue — Giggleswick, North Yorkshire	8	—	*Post Office*
(3)	Greetings, Clowne, Chesterfield, Derbys	8	10	*Benham D135*
(4)	Greetings, Puncheston, Haverfordwest, Dyfed	8	3(s)	*Benham*
(5)	Greetings, The Teddy Bear Shop, Ironbridge, Salop	8	18	*B'ham (500) 50*
(6)	Greetings, Hartford, Cheshire	8	18	*BLCS 50*
(7)	60th Anniversary No.604 Squadron BF 2217 PS	8	12	*RFDC 80*

C.D.S. POSTMARKS

(8)	Bearpark, Catsfield, or Pudsey ....*each*	10	
(9)	Bow Street, Constable Road, Constable Burton, or Law.......*each*	10	
(10)	Fleet Street, EC4 — where 'Beano' is published	10	
(11)	Giggleswick, North Yorks	12	
(12)	Greet, Birmingham	12	
(13)	Oxford — where Lewis Carrol wrote 'Alice in Wonderland' ..	12	
(14)	Ulverston, Cumbria — birthplace of Stan Laurel.................	12	

In addition covers are known with the following CDS postmarks: Colemore Circus, Greets Green, Big Top, Merry Hill, Laurel Lane, Puncheston, London E.C. Prices from £9.

SLOGAN POSTMARKS

(15)	Take a Bite out of Crime, Newcastle	18	
(16)	Collect British Stamps, Lincoln (depicts the 'Lincoln Imp')..	18	

In addition: Darlington Open Day; Stampex; Collect British Stamps. Prices from £15.

6th March 1990 — EUROPA

20p Alexandra Palace — Stamp World etc; 29p British Philatelic Bureau; Glasgow European City of Culture:- 20p School of Art; 37p Templeton Carpet Factory.

SPECIAL HANDSTAMPS

(1)	First Day of Issue — Philatelic Bureau	4	—	*Post Office*
(2)	First Day of Issue — Glasgow......................................	4	—	*Post Office*
(3)	Cultural Capital of Europe, Glasgow 1990........................	5	10	*Arlington*
(4)	Europa Philatelic Event of the Decade, Stamp World N22 ..	5	7	*BLCS 51*
(5)	First Modern Movement Blg. in Europe, Glasgow School of Art ..	5	10	*B'ham (500) 51*
(6)	British Philatelic Bureau, Edinburgh.............................	5	2(s)	*Bureau*
(7)	Centenary of 1st Int. Stamp Exhibition 1890-1990 BPF N22.......	5	7	*BPF*
(8)	Alexandra Palace, Victorian Heritage London N22............	5	7	*CoverCraft*
(9)	Europa 1990, Edinburgh...	5	7	*LFDC 85*
(10)	Alexandra Palace Europa 1990, London N22	5	15	*Bradbury*
(11)	Britain's Oldest Post Office 1763, Sanquhar, Dumfriesshire.	7	15	*Bradbury*
(12)	Forth Bridge Centennial 1890-1990 S. Queensferry, W. Lothian...	7	15	*Bradbury*
(13)	75th Anniversary No.8 Squadron BF 2219 PS	7	10	*RFDC 81*

PLEASE READ THE GENERAL NOTES
AT THE BEGINNING OF THIS CATALOGUE
These often provide the answers to enquiries received.

Europa (contd.)

	ordinary covers £	official covers £
C.D.S. POSTMARKS		
(14) Alexandra Park Road, N10 — venue of Stamp World..........	7	
(15) Bridgeton, Glasgow — nearest P.O. to Templeton Carpet Factory........	7	
(16) Cowcadden, City Branch, or Hope St. — nearest P.O.s to Glasgow School of Art	8	
(17) Warriston, Edinburgh — nearest P.O. to Philatelic Bureau....	8	

In addition covers are known with the following CDS postmarks: Cove, Craigpark, Duke St., Edinburgh, Glasgow, Helensburgh, London EC1, Paisley and Sanquhar, The Scotlands. Prices range from £5.

SLOGAN POSTMARKS		
(18) There's a lot of Glasgowing on . . . etc., Glasgow	15	
(19) Collect British Stamps — World's Greatest Hobby	18	
(20) Collect British Stamps, Lincoln Philatelic Counter..............	18	
(21) Collect British Stamps, Bradford Philatelic Counter	18	

In addition: Royal Burgh of Lanark; Scottish Blood Transfusion; Liverpool MLO. Prices from £10.

10th April 1990 — QUEEN'S AWARDS TO INDUSTRY
2×20p, 2×37p Export & Technology Award emblems

SPECIAL HANDSTAMPS			
(1) First Day of Issue — Philatelic Bureau	4	—	*Post Office*
(2) First Day of Issue — SW London Letters District................	4	—	*Post Office*
(3) The Queen's Awards to Industry 25th Anniversary, London SW1	5	12	*B'ham (500) 52*
(4) Twice Winner of Queen's Award SAGA Folkestone, Kent	5	7	*BLCS 52*
(5) Laboratory of the Gov. Chemist Queen's Awards, Teddington......	5	7	*CoverCraft*
(6) William Grant & Sons Ltd., Glenfiddich, Dufftown	7	2(s)	*Arlington*
(7) The First 25 Years CBI Silver Jubilee Investing in Success, WC1 .	7	12	*LFDC 86*
(8) Paper for the Penny Black 1840, Northampton..................	7	30	*D.Rutt*
(9) 75th Anniversary of No. 10 Squadron, BF 2220 PS	7	10	*RFDC 82*
(10) Attack on the Konigsberg, 50th Anniversary, BF 2224 PS ...	7	10	*FAA Museum*

C.D.S. POSTMARKS		
(11) Buckingham Palace, SW1	40	
(12) Dover, Gatwick or Heathrow — export 'gateways' ....*each*	10	
(13) Golders Green, NW11 — home of Abram Games (designer of the stamps)	8	
(14) New Invention, Willenhall	10	
(15) Queen Elizabeth Avenue, Walsall	8	
(16) Tufton Street, SW1 — the Queen's Award Office	7	
(17) Turnpike Estate, Newbury — Quantel Ltd., (Computer Graphic artwork for stamps)	11	

In addition covers are known with the following CDS postmarks: Aycliffe Trading Estate, Broadway SW1, Derby, Globe Road E1, House of Commons, Jubilee Crescent, Lombard St., London EC, NEC Birmingham, Newbury, Silver Link, South Lambeth SW8. Prices range from £5.

SLOGAN POSTMARKS		
(18) Invest in Sunderland — Enterprise Zone	20	

In addition: British Steel; Aveling Barford; Hastings Exhibition; Stamp World; Sure Plumber; Collect British Stamps; Penny Black Coin. Prices from £10.

3rd May 1990 — PENNY BLACK ANNIVERSARY
Miniature Sheet: 20p + Facsimile of Penny Black

SPECIAL HANDSTAMPS			
(1) First Day of Issue — Philatelic Bureau	4	—	*Post Office*
(2) First Day of Issue — City of London..................................	4	—	*Post Office*
(3) First Day of Issue + Alexandra Palace, London N22	6	—	*Post Office*
(4) Carlisle First Roadside Pillar Box in Mainland Britain, 1853	6	10	*Carlisle P.O.*
(5) National Postal Museum 1840-1990, City of London EC......	6	—	*n.o.c.*
(6) Royal Mail Exhibition Card No. 4, Stamp World London 90, Edinburgh.	6	—	*n.o.c.*
(7) Int. Stamp Exhibition, Stamp World London 90, Opening Day, N22	6	—	*n.o.c.*
(8) National Postal Museum, SWL90, City of London EC.........	6	—	*n.o.c.*
(9) Penny Black 150th Anniv. Rowland Hill, Kidderminster	6	7	*CoverCraft*
(10) Penny Black 150th Anniv. William Wyon, Birmingham........	6	7	*CoverCraft*
(11) 1d Black 150th Anniversary, Bruce Castle Museum, N17..........	6	7	*CoverCraft*
(12) Honouring Jacob Perkins, Printer of the Penny Black, SE1	6	7	*CoverCraft*
(13) British Philatelic Federation, Stamp World, Alexandra Palace, N22	6	7	*CoverCraft*
(14) Sir Rowland Hill, Kidderminster, Worcs.	6	10	*LFDC 87*
(15) 1840-1990 Perkins Bacon & Co., Printed the Penny Black, Fleet St. EC4	6	15	*Bradbury*
(16) 250th Anniversary 'Rule Britannia' 1740-1990, London SW1......	6	10	*Bradbury*
(17) 150th Anniversary, The Penny Black, Alexandra Palace, N22.....	6	14	*Benham SG10*
(18) The Penny Black, Bath	6	14	*B'ham (500) 53*

PLEASE READ THE GENERAL NOTES
AT THE BEGINNING OF THIS CATALOGUE
These often provide the answers to enquiries received.

Penny Black (miniature sheet) (contd.)

		ordinary covers £	official covers £	
(19)	Stanley Gibbons, Stamp World London 90, London N22	6	18	*BLCS53*
(20)	Perkins, Bacon & Co., Printers 1d Black, Southwark Bridge, SE ..	6	9	*BLCS53*
(21)	Etchingham Stamp Festival...	7	8	*Etc'ham P.C.*
(22)	The First Adhesive Stamp On Cover at Bath — 150th Anniv........	7	8	*S. Muscroft*

C.D.S. POSTMARKS

(23)	Alexandra Park Road, N10 — nearest PO to 'Stamp World' .	7	
(24)	Britannia, Bacup or Porth..	8	
(24a)	Buckingham Palace, SW1	40	
(25)	Fleet Street, EC4 — Perkins, Bacon (printers of Penny Black).....	8	
(26)	House of Commons, SW1 — Postage Act	20	
(27)	House of Lords, SW1 — Postage Act	30	
(28)	Kidderminster — birthplace of Sir Rowland Hill	7	
(29)	Sanquhar — oldest Post Office	8	
(30)	Wood Green, N22 — Mobile Post Office — 'Stamp World' ...	12	
(31)	Windsor, Berks..	65	
(32)	Windsor Castle...	100	

In addition covers are known with the following CDS postmarks: Cobham, Etchingham, Horsefair, London Chief Office, Lordship Lane N17, Queen Elizabeth Ave., South Kensington, Victoria Road. Prices range from £5.

SLOGAN POSTMARKS

(33)	Visit Stamp World, Alexandra Palace — various offices.......	15
(34)	Write Now! Say It Better in a Letter — Nottingham.............	20
(35)	Remember to use the Postcode — Cambridge.....................	30
(36)	Please Post Early in the Day — Croydon	30
(37)	Senders name and address on back of envelopes — Nottingham ..	30
(38)	New Sunday Collections, Royal Mail Serving Birmingham..	15
(39)	Be Properly Addressed Postcode It — Sutton Coldfield	40
(40)	Pass on your Postcode — Leighton Buzzard.......................	20
(41)	Liverpool is a Mechanised Letter Office, Please Use Postcodes ...	20
(42)	Postman of the Year — Radio Two RM 89.1-91.8 — various offices	35
(43)	Queen Victoria School...	20

In addition: Aveling Barford; Cunard; 6 May Code Change. Prices from £7.

5th June 1990 — KEW GARDENS
20p Cycad + Joseph Banks Building; 29p Stone Pine + Princess of Wales Conservatory; 34p Willow Tree + the Palm House; 37p Cedar + the Pagoda

SPECIAL HANDSTAMPS

(1)	First Day of Issue — Philatelic Bureau	4	—	*Post Office*
(2)	First Day of Issue — Kew, Richmond	4	—	*Post Office*
(3)	Arboricultural Assoc. 25 Years of Caring for Trees, Sevenoaks	5	6	*BLCS54*
(4)	150th Anniv. Royal Botanic Gardens, Kew, Richmond.........	5	14	*B'ham (500) 54*
(5)	Royal Botanic Gardens, Kew Given to the Nation 1840, Richmond	5	8	*LFDC 88*
(6)	Royal Botanic Gardens, Kew 1840-1990, Richmond, Surrey	5	8	*LFDC 88*
(7)	Botanical Society of the British Isles, Kew Gardens, SW7 ...	5	7	*CoverCraft*
(8)	The Conservation Trust, 20th Anniversary, Reading............	5	7	*CoverCraft*
(9)	Nat. Garden Festival, Royal Mail Gateshead, (changeable date)...	5	—	*Post Office*
(10)	Nat. Garden Festival, Royal Mail Gateshead, Tyne and Wear	5	—	*Post Office*
(11)	Church in the Wood, 900 Years, St. Leonards on Sea	7	10	*Bradbury*
(12)	Forth Bridge Centennial 1890-1990, South Queensferry......	7	10	*Bradbury*
(13)	10th Anniversary TTTE, BF 2247 PS	7	8	*RFDC 84*

C.D.S. POSTMARKS

(14)	Kew Gardens, Richmond, Surrey	15
(15)	Any 'tree' postmark, e.g. Ash, Beech, Cherry Tree, Elm, Fir Tree, Hatfield Broad Oak, Orange Tree, Pear Tree and Yew Tree ..*each from*	8

In addition covers are known with the following CDS postmarks: Botanic Gardens, Broad Oak, Cedar Road, Chestnut Terrace, Forest Road, The Firs, Glasshouses, Green Willows, Hawkhurst, Pinewoods, Sevenoaks, The Fforest, The Green, The Willows, Wood End, Woodlands. Prices range from £6.

SLOGAN POSTMARKS

(16)	Royal Botanic Gardens, Kew Open 150 Years, Richmond	25
(17)	Richmond, Twin Towns Celebrations 1990, Twickenham	15
(18)	Dronfield & District Feast of Flowers, Sheffield	15

In addition: Steam Rally & Country Show; Royal Mail Derby/ESTF; Royal Mail Uxbridge New Sorting Office, Chester Business Park; Post Code; Collect British Stamps. Prices range from £5.

A. G. BRADBURY
The top name in cover and postmark design.
Write for my latest colour leaflets.
3 LINK ROAD, STONEYGATE, LEICESTER LE2 3RA

Pass on your Postcode (40)

Be properly (39) addressed POSTCODE IT

PLEASE POST EARLY IN THE DAY (36)

National Postal Museum (5)
SWL90 – City of London EC
3 May 1990

NATIONAL GARDEN FESTIVAL
5th JUNE 1990
ROYAL MAIL (10)
GATESHEAD TYNE AND WEAR

ROYAL BOTANIC GARDENS KEW 150 YEARS (16)
CONGRATULATIONS FROM Royal Mail

10th July 1990 — THOMAS HARDY
20p Portrait of Hardy with Clyffe Clump, Dorset

		ordinary covers	official covers	
		£	£	
SPECIAL HANDSTAMPS				
(1)	First Day of Issue — Philatelic Bureau	2	—	*Post Office*
(2)	First Day of Issue — Dorchester	2	—	*Post Office*
(3)	Thomas Hardy Society Ltd., Higher Bockhampton, Dorchester ...	3	5	*LFDC 89*
(4)	Marnhull, Dorset Thomas Hardy's Tess of the D'Urbervilles	3	5	*Bradbury*
(5)	Dorchester, Thomas Hardy's Mayor of Casterbridge	3	5	*Bradbury*
(6)	Thomas Hardy, 1840-1928 Stinsford, Dorset	3	5	*Bradbury*
(7)	150th Anniversary Thomas Hardy, Higher Bockhampton	3	8	*B'ham (500) 55*
(8)	Thomas Hardy 1840-1928 Wessex Poet & Novelist, Dorchester, Dorset..	3	4	*BLCS 55*
(9)	Puddletown, Dorset, Hardy's Weatherbury	3	6	*A. Pearce*
(10)	Thomas Hardy, Dorchester	3	4	*Havering*
(11)	Thomas Hardy, Higher Bockhampton, Dorset	3	5	*CoverCraft*
(12)	Nelson with Capt. Hardy in Amphion BF 2248 PS	4	5	*FAA Museum*
(13)	Gibbons Stamp Monthly 1890-1990 Ringwood, Hants.	4	5	*Benham L24*
(14)	History of the Royal Navy Series, Plymouth, Devon	4	6	*Marriott*
(15)	75th Anniversary of RAF Station Northolt BF 2250 PS	4	5	*RFDC 85*
(16)	Wimbledon 1990 Lawn Tennis Museum	4	7	*H.R.*
(17)	National Garden Festival, Gateshead	4	—	*Post Office*

C.D.S. POSTMARKS
(18) Bere Regis (Hardy's Kingsbere); Dorchester (Hardy's
Casterbridge); Maiden Newton (Hardy's Chalk Newton);
Puddletown (Hardy's Weatherbury); Salisbury (Hardy's
Melchester); Shaftesbury (Hardy's Shaston); Sherborne (Hardy's
Sherton Abbas); Sturminston Newton (Hardy's Stourcastle);
Weymouth (Hardy's Budmouth); Winfrith (Hardy's Haggard
Egden). ....*Prices range from*   7
(19) Harrow Road W2 or Westbourne Park Road — London home   7
(20) Fordington — 'Max Gate' where Hardy wrote many of his works...   8
*In addition covers are known with the following CDS postmarks: Amesbury, Hardy Lane,
Owermoigne, Piddlehinton, Wimborne. Prices from £6.*

SLOGAN POSTMARKS
*Royal Mail Derby/ESTF; Postcode, Dorchester; Say it Better in a Letter; Post Early;
Various Post Code slogans; Uxbridge Sorting Office. Prices range from £7.*

2nd August 1990 — THE QUEEN MOTHER'S 90th BIRTHDAY
*20p Queen Elizabeth The Queen Mother; 29p Queen Elizabeth;
34p Elizabeth Duchess of York; 37p Lady Elizabeth Bowes-Lyon*

SPECIAL HANDSTAMPS				
(1)	First Day of Issue — Philatelic Bureau	4	—	*Royal Mail*
(2)	First Day of Issue — City of Westminster SW1	4	—	*Royal Mail*
(3)	The Queen Mother's 90th Birthday — St. Paul's, Walden, Herts ...	5	10	*LFDC 90*
(4)	The Queen Mother's 90th Birthday — Clarence House, SW1	5	10	*LFDC 90*
(5)	The Queen Mother's 90th Birthday — Glamis, Tayside	5	10	*LFDC 90*
(6)	HM Queen Elizabeth The Queen Mother, 90th Birthday, Clarence House	5	9	*BLCS 56*
(7)	HM Queen Elizabeth The Queen Mother, 90th Birthday, Glamis Castle .	5	12	*B'ham (500) 56*
(8)	HM Queen Elizabeth The Queen Mother, 90th Birthday, Windsor Castle	5	6	*BLCS 56*
(9)	HM Queen Elizabeth The Queen Mother, 90th Birthday, St. Paul's, Hitchin ...	5	12	*Benham SG11*
(10)	The Queen Elizabeth The Queen Mother, Woman & Home, London SE1	5	8	*Benham*
(11)	The British Forces Offer Heartiest Congratulations, BF 1990 PS..	5	10	*RFDC 86*
(12)	Congratulations from Royal Mail, Birmingham	5	15	*RM Bir'ham*
(13)	Congratulations Queen Mother, Bowes Museum, Barnard Castle .	5	6	*S. Muscroft*
(14)	Celebrating the 90th Birthday of HM The Queen Mother, W1	5	15	*CoverCraft (RT)*
(15)	Happy 90th Birthday The Queen Mother, Glamis Castle	5	15	*CoverCraft*
(16)	Happy 90th Birthday The Queen Mother, Clarence House, SW1 ..	5	10	*CoverCraft*
(17)	The Royal Wolverhampton School, The Queen Mother	5	8	*Bradbury*
(18)	Happy Birthday from RNLI, Thurso Lifeboat, RNLB The Queen Mother	5	5	*Pilgrim*
(19)	1815-1990 Royal Doulton, The Potteries, Stoke-on-Trent	5	5	*P.D.Withers*
(20)	National Garden Festival, Gateshead	6	—	*n.o.c.*

C.D.S. POSTMARKS				
(21)	Barnard Castle — Streatham Castle and Bowes Museum	8		
(22)	Bowes — Lady Elizabeth Bowes-Lyon	8		
(23)	Buckingham Palace SW1	90		
(24)	Glamis, Forfar — Queen Mother's ancestral home	15		
(25)	House of Commons SW1	15		
(26)	House of Lords SW1	20		
(27)	Mey, Thurso — Castle of Mey belongs to Queen Mother	12		
(28)	Queen Elizabeth Ave. Walsall or Queen's Rd. Nottingham ...	8		
(29)	Whitwell, Hitchin — home of Bowes-Lyon family	7		

GSM (13)

(12)

(8)

(20)

DORCHESTER
the setting for
Thomas Hardy's (5)
THE MAYOR OF CASTERBRIDGE
10th JULY 1990

MARNHULL, DORSET
one of the settings for
Thomas Hardy's (4)
TESS OF THE D'URBERVILLES
10th JULY 1990

THOMAS HARDY
10 JULY 1990
DORCHESTER (10)

CONGRATULATIONS!
(12) Royal Mail
2 AUGUST 1990

(15)

(18)

(16)

CONGRATULATIONS TO THE
QUEEN MOTHER
ON HER 90th BIRTHDAY
2 AUG 1990 (13)
BOWES MUSEUM
BOWES BARNARD CASTLE

(17)

(24)   (27)

PRICES & CONDITION – PLEASE READ GENERAL NOTES

Queen Mother (contd.)

	ordinary covers £	official covers £
(29) Windsor, Berks., or Windsor Great Park	8	
(30) Windsor Castle, Berks.	100	

In addition covers are known with the following CDS postmarks: Albemarle Street; Crathie; Holyrood; Rose; Royal Botanic Gardens; Scone; Walmer; York. Prices range from £5.

SLOGAN POSTMARKS
Queen Victoria School; Royal Engineers Museum; Cunard; Forres Europe in Bloom; Alder Hey 75th Birthday Appeal; Royal Mail – Car Secure; Royal Botanic Gardens. Prices range from £7.

11th September 1990 — GALLANTRY
20p Distinguished Service Cross and Medal; 20p Distinguished Flying Cross and Medal; 20p Military Cross and Military Medal; 20p Victoria Cross; 20p George Cross

SPECIAL HANDSTAMPS

(1) First Day of Issue — Philatelic Bureau	4	—	*Royal Mail*
(2) First Day of Issue — City of Westminster SW1	4	—	*Royal Mail*
(3) St. George, Bristol	5	15	*Bradbury*
(4) The Spirit of Britain, London SW1	5	8	*LFDC 91*
(5) 50th Anniv. Battle of Britain, B. of B. Museum, Hawkinge, Kent .	5	9	*BLCS 57*
(6) 50th Anniv. Battle of Britain, Westerham, Kent	5	14	*BLCS 57*
(7) The Victoria Cross for Valour, London SW	5	18	*B'ham (500) 57*
(8) The George Cross for Gallantry 50th Anniv., London SW	5	14	*Benham SG 12*
(9) The Military Medal for Bravery, Chichester, W. Sussex	5	7	*Benham L26*
(10) Distinguished Service Medal for Service on the Seas, Liverpool ..	5	7	*Benham L25*
(11) 50th Anniv. of the Battle of Britain, BF 2232 PS	5	10	*Forces*
(12) History of the Royal Navy Series, Plymouth, Devon	5	2(s)	*Marriott*
(13) The Victoria Cross For Valour, Nat. Postal Museum, EC1	5	—	*n.o.c.*
(14) Ending of World War II Far East, 45th Anniv., BF 2251 PS..	5	15	*FAA Museum*
(15) Defence of Rorke's Drift 'B' Coy Regimental Museum, Brecon	5	10	*S. Muscroft*
(16) Battle of Britain 1940, RAF Bentley Priory, Stanmore	5	10	*CoverCraft*
(17) Battle of Britain 1940 BBMF, RAF Coningsby, Lincolnshire	5	10	*CoverCraft*
(18) 50th Anniv. Battle of Britain, RAF Coltishall, Norwich	5	10	*Markton*
(19) George Cross, Island Siege Bell Fund Malta, Brentwood, Essex ..	5	20	*Cam.S.C.*
(20) The Cornwell Scout Badge, Baden-Powell House, London SW7 ..	5	8	*Havering*
(21) Sunderland AFC, 100 Years League Football, Sunderland ..	6	10	*Dawn*

C.D.S. POSTMARKS

(22) High Cross, Ware — birthplace of the first VC and Bar holder	12	
(23) Biggin Hill, Westerham, Kent	20	
(24) Any Field Post Office	15	
(25) Portsmouth — home of Royal Navy	7	
(26) Sandhurst — Royal Military Academy	8	
(27) Royal Hospital Chelsea — Chelsea 'Pensioners'	9	
(28) St. George, Bristol or St. Georges, Telford ....*each*	8	
(29) St. George's Cross, Glasgow	12	
(30) Hawkinge or Duxford ....*each*	8	
(31) Any RAF Station ....*each*	8	
(32) Maritime Mail	30	

In addition covers are known with the following CDS postmarks: Albemarle Street W1, Battle, Battlefield, Battlefield Rd., Battlehill, Buckingham Palace, Churchill, Cove Bay, Duke of York School, Dunkirk, Falklands, Gun End, House of Commons, House of Lords, Immingham Dock, King George, Manor Park, Memorial Road, Mount Ephraim, Normandy, Queen's Cross, Richmond, Sebastopol, Three Crosses, Victoria Road, Walton-on-Thames, Wargrave, Waterloo, Wortley. Prices range from £6.

SLOGAN POSTMARKS

(33) Royal Engineers Museum, Gillingham, Kent	10	
(34) RAF Finningley Air Show, Doncaster or Lincoln	10	

In addition: North Yorks Police; Queen Victoria School. Prices range from £8.

16th October 1990 — ASTRONOMY
22p Armagh Observatory; Jodrell Bank and La Palma telescopes; 26p Moon and tides; Herschel's telescope; 31p Greenwich Old Observatory and early Astronomical equipment; 37p Stonehenge; gyroscope; and navigation by the stars

SPECIAL HANDSTAMPS

(1) First Day of Issue — Philatelic Bureau	4	—	*Royal Mail*
(2) First Day of Issue — Armagh	4	—	*Royal Mail*
(3) Jodrell Bank Science Centre and Tree Park, Macclesfield....	5	6	*LFDC 92*
(4) The Old Royal Observatory, Greenwich, London SE	5	7	*BLCS 58*
(5) The Heavens Declare the Glory of God, Armagh Observatory	5	7	*BLCS 58*
(6) Sir William Herschel Whatsoever Shines etc., Slough	5	14	*B'ham (500) 58*
(7) Woolsthorpe by Colsterworth, Birthplace of Isaac Newton ..	5	20	*CoverCraft*
(8) Astronomical Alignments at Stonehenge, Amesbury, Wilts.	5	15	*Bradbury*

1815 1990
ROYAL DOULTON
2nd AUGUST 1990
THE POTTERIES
STOKE-ON-TRENT (19)

(1) 11 SEPT 1990 / 11 SEPT 1990 (2)

THE GEORGE CROSS
London SW1 11·9·90 (8)

50th ANNIVERSARY
GEORGE CROSS ISLAND SIEGE BELL FUND
MALTA
BRENTWOOD ESSEX 11th SEPT. 1990 (19)

(11)

(10)
THE Distinguished Service on the Seas LIVERPOOL 11·9·90

(9) CHICHESTER W SUSSEX THE MILITARY MEDAL FOR BRAVERY IN THE FIELD

BIGGIN HILL WESTERHAM KENT 11th SEPT 1990 (6)

(12) HISTORY OF THE ROYAL NAVY SERIES

PLYMOUTH DEVON (20)

The CORNWELL SCOUT BADGE
11th September 1990
BADEN-POWELL HOUSE LONDON SW7

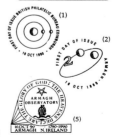

(1)

(2)

ARMAGH OBSERVATORY

16 OCT 90 / 1790-1990 ARMAGH N. IRELAND (5)

Astronomy (contd.)

		ordinary covers £	official covers £	
(9)	Old Royal Observatory, Greenwich	5	15	*Arlington*
(10)	British Astronomical Association, Burlington House, W1 ...	5	15	*Cam.S.C.*
(11)	British Astronomical Assoc., Royal Observatory, Cambridge	5	15	*Cam.S.C.*
(12)	Autumn Stampex/BPE, London SW1	6	—	*Royal Mail*
(13)	Royal Mail Exhibition Card No. 4 Stampex/BPE 1990, Edinburgh	6	—	*Royal Mail*
(14)	50th Anniversary No. 249 Squadron BF 2253 PS...............	6	8	*RFDC 88*

C.D.S. POSTMARKS

(15)	Armagh — Armagh Observatory	9
(16)	Chelford, Goostrey, Macclesfield or Siddington — Jodrell Bank ...	7
(17)	Greenwich, Hertmonceux or Cambridge — Old Royal Observatory	8
(18)	Larkhill or Amesbury — Stonehenge...............................	9
(19)	Albemarle St., W1 — near to Burlington House (Astronomical Assoc.) .	7
(20)	Meridian Centre, Peacehaven	12

In addition covers are known with the following CDS postmarks: Archer Road, Barnard Castle, Blackford Avenue Edinburgh, Ceres, Comberton, The Crescent, Crown View, Denby, Five Points, Globe Rd., Helston, Moore, Newton, North Pole, Oldland Common, The Rocket, Seven Sisters, Southern Cross, Starcross. Prices range from £6.

SLOGAN POSTMARKS

Post Office Mercurycard; Autumn Stampex; New World Domestic Appliances; N. Yorks Police, Royal Mail Car Secure; Smugglers Adventure; Visit Isle of Skye; Royal Society of Chemistry. Prices range from £6.

13th November 1990 — CHRISTMAS

17p Children building snowman; 22p Bringing home the Christmas tree; 26p Carol singers; 31p Tobogganing; 37p Skating

SPECIAL HANDSTAMPS

(1)	First Day of Issue — Philatelic Bureau	4	—	*Royal Mail*
(2)	First Day of Issue — Bethlehem, Llandeilo, Dyfed	4	—	*Royal Mail*
(3)	Central Council of Church Bell Ringers, St. Paul's, London EC4 ..	5	10	*Bradbury*
(4)	Central Council of Church Bell Ringers Centenary, Duffield	5	20	*Bradbury*
(5)	Birmingham Cathedral in Need	5	7	*Bradbury*
(6)	25 Years British Christmas Stamps, Bethlehem, Llandeilo ..	5	15	*LFDC 93*
(7)	Congratulations Royal Mail 150 Years of Stamps, Nasareth .	5	8	*CoverCraft*
(8)	Congratulations Royal Mail 150 Years of Stamps, London EC1....	5	8	*CoverCraft*
(9)	Nat. Postal Museum, Post Early for Christmas, City of London ...	5	—	*n.o.c.*
(10)	25th Christmas Benham, First Day Covers, Folkestone	5	7	*BLCS 59*
(11)	The Christmas Mailcoach Run, Windsor, Berks.	5	6	*BLCS 59*
(12)	Christmas Tradition Snowdown, Dover, Kent	5	10	*B'ham (500) 59*
(13)	125th Anniv. Stanley Gibbons Catalogue 1865-1990, Ringwood ..	5	9	*Benham L27*
(14)	Christmas 1990, Cambridge	5	15	*Cam.S.C.*
(15)	Stampway to the World Museum of Transport, Glasgow 131	6	—	*n.o.c.*
(16)	450th Anniv. Bishop Vesey's Grammar School, Sutton Coldfield ..	6	12	*BVGS*
(17)	Blood & Fire in Darkest England and The Way Out, EC1	6	8	*S.Army*
(18)	History of the Royal Navy Series, Plymouth, Devon	6	—	*n.o.c.*

C.D.S. POSTMARKS

(19)	Church, Freshwater	9
(20)	Hollybush or Fir Tree ....*each from*	7
(21)	Nasareth, Caernarfon, Gwynedd....................................	8
(22)	Playing Place, Truro	8

In addition covers are known with the following CDS postmarks: Aviemore, Churchfield, Church Village, Holy Island, Jericho, Jerusalem St., Merry Hill, Noel Road, St. Nicholas, Trafalgar Square, Winter Hey. Prices range from £6.

SLOGAN POSTMARKS

(23)	Birmingham Cathedral Appeal 021-212-1579	14
(24)	Happy Christmas — Please Post Early, Liverpool	40
(25)	Nadolig Llawen — Happy Christmas	40

In addition: Stampway to the World; Candlelighters Fighting Children's Cancer; Please Control your Dog; Coventry Forward in Friendship; Alder Hey. Prices range from £8.

CHRISTMAS BOOKLET

Covers bearing pair or block of 4×17p stamps from booklet with special handstamp (these have straight edges at top and bottom) ....*from*	5
Full pane of ten stamps on cover ....*from*	20

A. G. BRADBURY
The top name in cover and postmark design.
Write for my latest colour leaflets.
3 LINK ROAD, STONEYGATE, LEICESTER LE2 3RA

8th January 1991 — DOGS

Five paintings by George Stubbs: 22p King Charles Spaniel; 26p A Pointer;
31p Two Hounds in a Landscape; 33p A Rough Dog; 37p Fino and Tiny

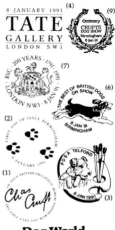

	ordinary covers £	official covers £	
SPECIAL HANDSTAMPS			
(1) First Day of Issue — Philatelic Bureau	4	—	*Royal Mail*
(2) First Day of Issue — Birmingham...................................	4	—	*Royal Mail*
(3) PDSA Telford (People's Dispensary for Sick Animals)........	5	6	*LFDC 94*
(4) Tate Gallery London SW1	5	6	*Bradbury*
(5) Birmingham Dogs Home..	5	6	*Bradbury*
(6) The Best of British Dogs on Show, Birmingham	5	10	*Bradbury*
(7) RVC 200 Years 1791-1991 NW1 (Royal Veterinary College).	5	8	*Bradbury*
(8) Crufts Dog Show Centenary 1891-1991 Birmingham (badge)	5	6	*BLCS 60*
(9) Centenary Crufts Dog Show, Birmingham	5	11	*B'ham (500) 60*
(10) Pawprints, Stoke-on-Trent	5	6	*P. Withers*
(11) Birthplace of George Stubbs 1724-1806, Liverpool............	5	8	*CoverCraft*
(12) National Canine Defence League, A Dog is for Life, NW1 ...	5	8	*CoverCraft*
(13) Dog World Congratulate Crufts NEC Birmingham	5	7	*R. Skinner*
(14) 50th Anniversary Police Guard Dog School BF 2257 PS......	6	7	*RFDC 90*
(15) Stampway to the World, Museum of Transport Glasgow 131	6	—	*n.o.c.*
C.D.S. POSTMARKS			
(16) Barking, Essex or Black Dog, Crediton ....*each from*	6		
(17) Battersea, or Battersea Park Road (Dogs' Home) ..*each from*	6		
(18) Dog & Gun, Liverpool...	8		
(19) Dog Kennel Lane, Oldbury, Warley	10		
(20) Isle of Dogs, London E14	10		
(21) NEC Birmingham — venue for Crufts Centenary Show	10		
(22) Odiham — RVC founded by Odiham Agricultural Soc..........	7		
(23) Portman Square — Stubb's studio	6		
(24) Royal College St. NW1 — home of the Royal Veterinary College ..	7		
(25) Stubb's Cross	8		

In addition covers are known with the following CDS postmarks: Airedale; Corn Exchange;
Dogsthorpe; Houndsditch and Newmarket. Prices from £5.

SLOGAN POSTMARKS

(26) Pawprints Appeal 0782-577282 Stoke-on-Trent	15		
(27) Take a Bite out of Crime, Newcastle...............................	15		

In addition: Stampway to the World. Prices from £8.

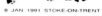

5th February 1991 — GREETINGS STAMPS

10 designs of '1st Class' stamps featuring good luck symbols

SPECIAL HANDSTAMPS			
(1) First Day of Issue — Philatelic Bureau	5	—	*Royal Mail*
(2) First Day of Issue — Greetwell, Lincs.	5	—	*Royal Mail*
(3) Good Luck Charms, Rainow, Macclesfield, Cheshire..........	6	8	*BLCS61*
(4) Good Luck Greetings, Good Easter, Chelmsford, Essex	6	10	*B'ham (500) 61*
(5) Good Luck Greetings, Wishford, Salisbury, Wilts.	6	8	*Benham D158*
(6) Good Luck, Star, Glenrothes, Fife	6	8	*BLCS61*
(7) Good Luck Greetings, Magpie, Yelverton, Devon...............	6	3(s)	*Benham*
(8) Good Luck, Luckington, Chippenham, Wilts.....................	6	8	*Bradbury*
(9) 50th Anniversary Rescue Services BF 2258 PS	7	8	*RFDC91*

C.D.S. POSTMARKS

(10) Acorn St., Bell Green, Boot, Branch End, Bridge, Catsfield,
Clover Rd., Cross Keys, Drakes Broughton, Ducklington, Frog
Island, Frogpool, Greet, Greetland, Jacob's Well, Keyworth,
Klondyke, Luckington, Merlin's Bridge, Primrose Hill,
Silverwell, Sky Crescent, Starcross, Swallow's Nest, Well, Wing,
Wren's Nest – each associated with stamp designs............*each* 10

(11) Goldenacre, Gretna Green, and Luckington ....*each* 10

POSTMARK SLOGANS

Pawprints Appeal; The Samaritans; Alder Hey; Magic of British Music; Royal Mail/Post Code
slogans. Prices range from £15.

5th March 1991 — SCIENTIFIC ACHIEVEMENTS

22p Michael Faraday — electricity; 22p Charles Babbage — computers;
31p Robert Watson-Watt — radar; 37p Frank Whittle — jet engine

SPECIAL HANDSTAMPS			
(1) First Day of Issue — Philatelic Bureau	4	—	*Royal Mail*
(2) First Day of Issue — South Kensington, London SW7	4	—	*Royal Mail*
(3) Charles Babbage Bi-centenary Science Museum, London SW7 ..	5	10	*Bradbury*
(4) Royal Society of Chemistry 1841-1991 Burlington House, W1	5	7	*Bradbury*
(5) 75th Anniv. Year, Society British Aerospace Companies, SW1	5	10	*Bradbury*

Science (contd.)

		ordinary covers £	official covers £	
(6)	The Royal Institution of Great Britain, London W1.............	5	10	*Bradbury*
(7)	Sir Frank Whittle, Jet Engine, Loughborough, Leics.	5	6	*LFDC 95*
(8)	Radar Systems, Marconi, Chelmsford..............................	5	7	*Bradbury*
(9)	Michael Faraday 1791-1991 Pioneer of Electrical Discovery, SW.	5	11	*B'ham (500) 62*
(10)	A.E.U. General Office, London SE15.................................	5	6	*R. Skinner*
(11)	Loughborough University of Technology 1966-1991..........	5	6	*S. Muscroft*
(12)	Michael Faraday 1791, Charles Babbage IEE Founded 1871, WC2	5	25	*Cam.S.C.*
(13)	Industrial Society Official Opening Peter Runge House, SW1.....	5	6	*P. Withers*
(14)	54th Anniv. First Aircraft Turbo Jet Engine BF 2260 PS	5	10	*Forces*
(15)	50th Anniv. First Flight of Jet Aircraft, Cranwell BF 2259 PS	5	10	*RFDC 92*
(16)	Computer Innovation 21 Years, Wembley, Middlesex..........	6	2(s)	*Arlington*
(17)	Electricity, Hove, East Sussex	6	2(s)	*Arlington*
(18)	Royal Signals & Radar Establishment, Malvern, Worcs.......	6	2(s)	*Arlington*
(19)	RMA Woolwich 1741-1991, Sandhurst, Camberley, Surrey .	6	2(s)	*Arlington*

C.D.S. POSTMARKS

(20)	Albermarle Street, W1 — home of the Royal Institution	7
(21)	Cranwell — first official flight of the jet engine	7
(22)	Daventry — BBC transmitter station in radar experiments	8
(23)	Exhibition Road, SW7 — Science Museum	7
(24)	Hucclecote — where the Gloster Meteor was built	17
(25)	Lutterworth — where the jet engine was built	17
(26)	New Invention..	12
(27)	Weedon, Northants — where radar was first successfully demonstrated	17

In addition covers are known with the following CDS postmarks: Alderton, Banbury, Brechin, Brockworth, Broomfield Road, Caversham, Earlsden, Elephant & Castle, Faraday Street, Loughborough, Seascale, Southcliff, Totnes, Trinity St., Cambridge and Walworth Road. Prices range from £4½.

SLOGAN POSTMARKS

(28)	Philips — a hundred years ahead	10
(29)	Loughborough University of Technology 1966-1991...........	10

In addition: Sunderland Enterprise Zone £8.

26th March 1991 — GREETINGS STAMPS
Same 'smiles' designs as for 6th February 1990 — values changed from 20p to '1st Class'

SPECIAL HANDSTAMPS

(1)	First Day of Issue — Philatelic Bureau	5	—	*Royal Mail*
(2)	First Day of Issue — Laughterton, Lincs.	5	—	*Royal Mail*
(3)	Puncheston, Haverfordwest, Dyfed	6	8	*Benham D159*
(4)	Greetings, The Teddy Bear Shop, Ironbridge, Salop	6	3(s)	*Benham*
(5)	Greetings, Clowne, Chesterfield, Derbys.	6	8	*BLCS 63*
(6)	Greetings, Hartford, Cheshire	6	10	*B'ham (500) 63*
(7)	Birthplace of Stan Laurel, Ulverston, Cumbria	6	10	*Bradbury*
(8)	50th Anniv. Battle of Cape Matapan BF 2262 PS	8	—	*n.o.c.*

C.D.S. POSTMARKS

(9)	Bearpark, or Catsfield ....*each from*	9
(10)	Constable Road, or Fleet Street.....................*each from*	9
(11)	Giggleswick, Greet or Laughterton.................*each from*	9
(12)	Puncheston, Clowne or Queen's Head ....*each from*	9
(13)	Ulverston — birthplace of Stan Laurel	10

SLOGAN POSTMARKS

(14)	Take a Bite out of Crime	12

In addition: The Samaritans; Alder Hey. Prices from £7.

23rd April 1991 — EUROPE IN SPACE
2×22p Man looking into space; 2×37p Space looking at man

SPECIAL HANDSTAMPS

(1)	First Day of Issue — Philatelic Bureau	4	—	*Royal Mail*
(2)	First Day of Issue — Cambridge	4	—	*Royal Mail*
(3)	25th Anniv. Soft Moon Landing Jodrell Bank, Macclesfield.	5	6	*BLCS 64*
(4)	30th Anniv. Vostok 1 Yuri Gargarin The Rocket, Liverpool.	5	6	*BLCS 64*
(5)	30th Anniv. First Man in Space, Harwell, Didcot, Oxon	5	10	*B'ham (500) 64*
(6)	Kettering Boys School, Northants......................................	5	6	*P. Withers*
(7)	Space: The Final Frontier London W1, England, Planet Earth....	5	12	*Bradbury*
(8)	The Hubble Space Telescope, Cambridge, England	5	15	*Bradbury*
(9)	125th Anniversary Year, Royal Aeronautical Society, W1	5	10	*Bradbury*
(10)	The British Interplanetary Society, London SW8 1SZ........	5	7	*Bradbury*

PRICES & CONDITION – PLEASE READ GENERAL NOTES

Space (contd.)	ordinary covers £	official covers £	
(11) BNSC — Britain's Space Agency, London SW1	5	6	*LFDC 96*
(12) Jodrell Bank Science Centre 1966-1991 25 Years, Macclesfield....	5	15	*CoverCraft*
(13) 25th Anniv. VC10 in Military Service BF 2272 PS	6	9	*RFDC 93*
(14) Centre for Crop Circle Studies, Guildford	6	7	*S. Muscroft*
(15) Visit of Prince & Princess of Wales to Brazil BF 2271 PS	6	40	*Forces*
(16) The Salvation Army Match Factory Centenary 1891-1991, E3	6	15	*S.Army*

C.D.S. POSTMARKS

(17) Comberton — Mullard Radio Astronomical Observatory	6	
(18) Greenwich or Cambridge — The Royal Greenwich Observatory ..	6	
(19) Helston — Goonhilly Downs Earth Station	6	
(20) The Rocket	8	
(21) Siddington, Goostrey or Macclesfield — Jodrell Bank	6	
(22) South Lamberth Road — British Interplanetary Soc.	6	
(23) Surbiton — home of Helen Sharman, Britain's first astronaut	8	

In addition covers are known with the following CDS postmarks: Chilton, Eye, Farnborough, Neville's Cross, Oldland Common, South Wonston, Upton Lea. Prices range from £5.

SLOGAN POSTMARKS

Loughborough University, BBC Radio, The Samaritans, Sunday Collections, Please Control your Dog, Beat the Burglar, If it moves Postcode it. Prices range from £6.

11th June 1991 — SPORTS

22p Fencing; 26p Hurdling; 31p Diving (World Student Games) and 39p Rugby World Cup

SPECIAL HANDSTAMPS

(1) First Day of Issue — Philatelic Bureau	4	—	*Royal Mail*
(2) First Day of Issue — Sheffield	4	—	*Royal Mail*
(3) Rugby Football Union 'Glam Slam' 1991 Twickenham	5	7	*Sajal Phil*
(4) If it's on, it's in Radio Times Sport '91 London W1	5	20	*Radio Times*
(5) Home of Welsh Rugby, Cardiff Arms Park	5	7	*BLCS 65*
(6) Home of Scottish Rugby, Murrayfield, Edinburgh	5	7	*BLCS 65*
(7) Home of English Rugby, Twickenham, Middx	5	7	*BLCS 65*
(8) 1991 Year of Sport, Sheffield	5	11	*B'ham (500) 65*
(9) Rugby School Celebrates Rugby World Cup, Rugby, Warks .	5	8	*LFDC 97*
(10) William Webb Ellis: Innovator of the Game of Rugby, Rugby	5	10	*Brad. VP No 59*
(11) Birmingham Welcomes the 97th Session of the Inter. Olympic Cttee.	5	7	*Bradbury*
(12) Sport for All, Wembley	5	10	*Bradbury*
(13) World Student Games, Sheffield	5	10	*WSGames*
(14) Avon Pride 1977-1991 Bristol, Avon	10	40	*Avon Pride*
(15) New Modern Gallery at Lawn Tennis Museum, Wimbledon SW19	5	10	*AELT*

C.D.S. POSTMARKS

(16) The Hayes (Cardiff); Kingsholm (Gloucester); Kneller Rd. (Twickenham); Murrayfield (Edinburgh); Ravenhill Park (Belfast); Sandygate (Llanelli); Welford Rd. (Leicester); Otley; Pontypool; Pontypridd – all venues for Rugby World Cup....*each*	10
(17) Cardiff, Gloucester, Leicester, Twickenham ....*each*	8
(18) Rugby — Rugby School where the game started	7
(19) Sheffield B.O. and various sub offices — World Student Games....	7

In addition covers are known with the following CDS postmarks: The University Bath, Fence, Jump, First Lane, Loughborough, University Bradford. Prices range from £6.

SLOGAN POSTMARKS

(20) Birmingham Welcomes 97th Session of IOC Committee	12
(21) Cardiff Just Capital	10
(22) Federation Cup, Nottingham Tennis Centre	12

In addition: Loughborough University; Convention Centre B'ham; Cub Scouting. Prices from £6.

16th July 1991 — ROSES

22p Silver Jubilee; 26p Mme. Alfred Carriere; 31p Rosa Moyesii; 33p Harvest Fayre; 37p Rosa Mutabilis

SPECIAL HANDSTAMPS

(1) First Day of Issue — Philatelic Bureau	4	—	*Royal Mail*
(2) First Day of Issue — Belfast	4	—	*Royal Mail*
(3) The Royal National Rose Society, St. Albans, Herts	5	8	*LFDC 98*
(4) Royal Botanic Gardens, Kew, Richmond, Surrey	5	6	*Bradbury*
(5) World Rose Convention, Belfast	5	7	*Brad. VP No 60*
(6) O, My Luve's Like a Red, Red Rose, Robert Burns, Alloway .	5	10	*Bradbury*
(7) Roses on Stamps, Rose, Truro	5	15	*Bradbury*
(8) The Gardener, A Rosier Outlook, Chelsea SW3	5	7	*BLCS 66*
(9) Rosebush, Clynderwen, Dyfed	5	14	*B'ham (500) 66*
(10) The Rose Garden, Drum Castle, Banchory, Kincardineshire	5	7	*BLCS 66*
(11) Henry VIII 500th Anniversary, Hampton Court, East Molesey	5	12	*Benham SG13*

Roses (contd.)

		ordinary covers £	official covers £	
(12)	Hampton Court Palace Int. Flower Show Surrey	5	15	*CoverCraft*
(13)	National Gallery NG Sainsbury Wing, London WC2	5	15	*CoverCraft*
(14)	The Royal Tournament, Earls Court BF 2292 PS	6	10	*Forces*
(15)	London Economic Summit, Lancaster House SW1	6	20	*Arlington*

C.D.S. POSTMARKS

(16)	Botanic Gardens, Belfast	8	
(17)	Kew Gardens, Richmond, Surrey	10	
(18)	Newtonards — 'Harvest Fayre' bred here	7	
(19)	Rose, Truro	10	
(20)	Rosebush or Rosemarket	*each* 8	
(21)	Roseacre, Rosebank, Rosedale Abbey, Rosehearty, Rose Hill, Roseland or Roses Lane Ends	*each* 7	
(22)	Royal Hospital, Chelsea — Chelsea Flower Show	10	

In addition covers are known with the following CDS postmarks: Chipping Campden, Glamis, Leaves Green. Prices range from £5.

SLOGAN POSTMARKS

(23)	Beechwood Place — Shopping in full bloom	8

In addition: Belfast 1991; Please control your dog; Mansfield Show. Prices from £6.

20th August 1991 — DINOSAURS

22p Iguanodon; 26p Stegosaurus; 31p Tyrannosaurus; 33p Protoceratops; 37p Triceratops

SPECIAL HANDSTAMPS

(1)	First Day of Issue — Philatelic Bureau	4	—	*Royal Mail*
(2)	First Day of Issue — Plymouth 150 Years of Word Dinosaur	4	—	*Royal Mail*
(3)	The Dinosaur Museum, Dorchester	5	6	*BLCS 67*
(4)	The Last Dinosaur? The Loch Ness Monster, Inverness	5	6	*BLCS 67*
(5)	Iguanodon Mantelli at the Maidstone Museum, Maidstone	5	6	*Benham L28*
(6)	150th Anniv. First use of Word Dinosaur, Oxford	5	10	*B'ham (500) 67*
(7)	First Discovery of Iguanodon, Cuckfield, Sussex	5	10	*Brad VP No 61*
(8)	The Natural History Museum, Dinosaurs, London SW7	5	6	*LFDC 99*
(9)	150th Anniv. First use of Word Dinosaur, Plymouth	5	12	*Bradbury*
(10)	Farewell Shackletonsaurus, BF 2299 PS	5	9	*RFDC 96*
(11)	City of Plymouth Museums & Art Gallery	6	10	*Arlington*
(12)	125 Years of Quality Franklin & Andrew, London EC4	6	10	*Arlington*

C.D.S. POSTMARKS

(13)	Camel's Head Plymouth, or Plymouth — first use of Word 'Dinosaur'	7
(14)	Cuckfield, Lyme Regis, Maidstone, Stonesfield or Tilgate — locations where dinosaur remains found	*each* 7
(15)	Dorchester — Dinosaur Museum	7
(16)	Exhibition Rd., S. Kensington — Natural History Museum	7
(17)	The Lizard	8

In addition covers are known with the following CDS postmarks: Lancaster, Lewes, Ness, Stonewell, Sydenham. Prices range from £6.

SLOGAN POSTMARKS

Pawprints Appeal; Control Your Dog; Royal Mail Cambridge; Guide Dogs. Prices from £10.

17th September 1991 — MAPS

24p, 28p, 33p, 39p — The Village of Hamstreet, Kent as depicted on Ordnance Survey maps in 1816, 1906, 1959 and present day.

SPECIAL HANDSTAMPS

(1)	First Day of Issue — Philatelic Bureau	4	—	*Royal Mail*
(2)	First Day of Issue — Southampton	4	—	*Royal Mail*
(3)	Visit the Nene Valley Railway, Peterborough	5	8	*N.V. Rly.*
(4)	Maps and the Post Office, NPM City of London EC	5	—	*n.o.c.*
(5)	Sir George Everest, Surveyor, Greenwich	6	15	*Bradbury*
(6)	Birthplace of Tourism, Leicester	6	10	*Bradbury*
(7)	Bicentenary of the Ordnance Survey RICS, London SW1	5	7	*Bradbury*
(8)	Ordnance Survey, Hamstreet, Kent	5	8	*LFDC 100*
(9)	150th Anniv. Ordnance Survey Act, Westminster SW1	5	10	*Brad VP No 62*
(10)	Bicentenary of Ordnance Survey, Hamstreet (oast house)	5	14	*B'ham (500) 68*
(11)	Hamstreet D 490, Hamstreet, Kent	5	6	*BLCS 68*
(12)	Darling Buds of May, Yorkshire Television, Hamstreet	5	6	*BLCS 68*
(13)	Ordnance Survey Bicentenary OS 1791-1991, Southampton	5	20	*CoverCraft*
(14)	50th Anniv. Royal Observer Corps BF 2301 PS	5	10	*RFDC 97*
(15)	Tower of London Ordnance Survey Bicentenary EC3	5	8	*Sunday Mag.*
(16)	Salvation Army Social Campaign Hadleigh, Benfleet	5	10	*S. Army*

PRICES & CONDITION – PLEASE READ GENERAL NOTES

	ordinary covers £	official covers £

C.D.S. POSTMARKS

(17) Hamstreet, Ashford, Kent	8	
(18) House of Commons, SW1 — Ordnance Survey Act 1841	10	
(19) House of Lords, SW1 — Ordnance Survey Act 1841	15	
(20) John O'Groats/Land's End *pair*	20	
(21) Maybush, Southampton — Ordnance Survey HQ	8	
(22) Newlyn, Cornwall — OS Tidal Observatory	12	
(23) Pathfinder Village, Exeter	10	
(24) Seething Lane — Tower of London — original HQ of OS	7	

In addition covers are known with the following CDS postmarks: The Chart, Cross Roads, Hereford, Marshfield, Richmond, Roman Way, The Triangle, Tingley and World's End. Prices range from £5.

SLOGAN POSTMARKS

(24) See the World with the Royal Scottish Geographical Society	9	

In addition: New Postage Rates; Yellow Brick Road; Royal Mail in the Community; Please Control Your Dog. Prices range from £7.

(15)

(3)

12th November 1991 — CHRISTMAS
18p, 24p, 28p, 33p, 39p Illuminate Manuscripts from books housed in the Bodleian Library.

SPECIAL HANDSTAMPS

(1) First Day of Issue — Philatelic Bureau	4	—	*Royal Mail*
(2) First Day of Issue — Bethlehem, Llandeilo, Dyfed	4	—	*Royal Mail*
(3) The Dean & Chapter Library, Durham Cathedral	5	6	*LFDC 101*
(4) Holy Island, Berwick upon Tweed	5	10	*Bradbury*
(5) Illuminated Manuscripts from the Bodleian Library, Oxford	5	15	*Bradbury*
(6) Christmas Illuminated Manuscripts, Bethlehem, Dyfed	5	10	*Brad VP No 63*
(7) The Second Cadfael Omnibus Christmas, Shrewsbury	5	6	*BLCS 69*
(8) Christmas Manuscripts Fountain's Abbey, Ripon	5	10	*B'ham (500) 69*
(9) Christmas Greetings Jerusalem Skellingthorpe, Lincoln	5	6	*C. Cooke*
(10) The Lindisfarne Gospels, Holy Island, Berwick upon Tweed	5	6	*S. Muscroft*
(11) Happy Christmas Royal Mail, City of London EC1	5	—	*n.o.c.*
(12) National Postal Museum Post Early for Christmas EC	5	—	*n.o.c.*
(13) Christmas 1991, Cambridge	5	15	*Cam. S.C.*
(14) Joy to the World, The Salvation Army, London SW1	5	6	*S. Army*
(15) 25 Christmastides with the Hercules BF 2304 PS	5	6	*RFDC 98*
(16) 500th Anniversary Henry VIII, Greenwich, London SE1	5	6	*BLCS 69*
(17) Naming New Hoylake Lifeboat, Liverpool	5	6	*Pilgrim*

(13)

(6)

(10)

(7)

C.D.S. POSTMARKS

(18) Exeter — birthplace of Sir Thomas Bodley	8	
(19) Holy Island — the Lindisfarne Gospels	7	
(20) Littlewoods P.O., Oxford, or Oxford — Bodleian Library	8	

In addition covers are known with the following CDS postmarks: Angel Hill, Bolton Abbey, Caldey Island, Jerusalem Street, Kings Road, Nasareth, St. Nicholas and Threekingham. Prices range from £5.

SLOGAN POSTMARKS

100 Years of Brewing Newcastle Brown; Clatterbridge Superscan Appeal; JVC Send a Video Letter; Northsound Charity Auction; Please Control Your Dog; Pulse Trust Appeal; Shopping in Full Bloom; The Glasgow Court Hall; Alder Hey; Write Now etc. Prices range from £7.

(17)

(16)

CHRISTMAS BOOKLET: Covers bearing pair or block of 4×18p stamps from booklet with special handstamp (these have straight edges at top and bottom) .... *from* 3

Full pane of ten stamps on cover .... *from* 15

(5)

14th January 1992 — WINTERTIME
18p Deer; 24p Hare; 28p Fox; 33p Redwing; 39p Welsh Sheep.

SPECIAL HANDSTAMPS

(1) First Day of Issue — Philatelic Bureau	3	—	*Royal Mail*
(2) First Day of Issue — Brecon	3	—	*Royal Mail*
(3) Emmerdale, Arncliffe, Skipton, N. Yorks	5	—	*n.o.c.*
(4) Wintertime, Richmond Park, London	4	10	*B. Reeve 1*
(5) Wintertime, Owlsmoor, Camberley	4	6	*LFDC 102*
(6) Wintertime, Haresfield, Stonehouse, Glos.	4	10	*Bradbury*
(7) Wintertime, Lyndhurst, Hants New Forest	4	7	*Brad VP No 64*
(8) The Monarch of the Glen, Glenbuck, Cumnock, Ayrshire	4	10	*B'ham (500) 70*
(9) Wildlife in Winter, Thrushwood, Keswick, Cumbria	4	5	*BLCS 70*
(10) Wild About Animals, London EC	4	5	*Benham*
(11) World Wide Fund for Nature, Godalming, Surrey	4	5	*BLCS 70*
(12) British Wintertime, Brecon, Powys	4	5	*BLCS70*
(13) Wildlife in Winter, Foxearth, Suffolk (or Sufflok)	4	10	*Benham SG 14*

(11)

(1)

(6)

Wintertime (contd.)

		ordinary covers £	official covers £	
(14)	Sittingbourne's New Postbus, Sittingbourne	4½	—	*Royal Mail*
(15)	First Day of Issue — Europe '92, City of London	4	—	*Royal Mail*
(16)	Chester Cathedral the 9th Century, Chester	4½	—	*n.o.c.*
(17)	BMEWS Radar Update, RAF Fylingdales BF 2281 PS	4½	7	*RFDC 99*

C.D.S. POSTMARKS
(18)	Deerpark, New Deer or Old Deer ....*each*	6	
(19)	Harefield, Harehills or Harewood ....*each*	6	
(20)	Foxhole or Fox Lane ....*each*	6	
(21)	Sheepridge or Sheepwash ....*each*	7	
(22)	Sheepscombe — farm Post Office	15	
(23)	Brecon, Powys — design of sheep stamp set in Brecon area..	7	

In addition covers are known with the following CDS postmarks: Brecon, Coldridge, Frosterley, Freezywater, Godalming, Lairg, Lindhurst, Nettleham, Wing, Winterbourne, Winter Hey, Winter Road. Prices range from £5.

SLOGAN POSTMARKS
Please control your dog; Ynys Mon Isle of Anglesey; Pawprints. Prices from £6.

28th January 1992 — GREETINGS STAMPS
10 designs of 1st Class stamps on the theme of memories.

SPECIAL HANDSTAMPS
(1)	First Day of Issue — Philatelic Bureau	5	—	*Royal Mail*
(2)	First Day of Issue — Whimsey, Gloucestershire	5	—	*Royal Mail*
(3)	The Good Old Days, London Colney, St. Albans, Herts.	6	9	*Benham D182*
(4)	The Good Old Days, Surbiton, Surrey	6	12	*B'ham (500) 71*
(5)	The Good Old Days, Brighton, Sussex	6	9	*BLCS 71*
(6)	The Good Old Days, Kings Cross, London N1	6	9	*BLCS 71*
(7)	The Good Old Days, Oxford	6	9	*BLCS 71*
(8)	Harrogate, Yorks	6	9	*BLCS 71*
(9)	Portobello Road, London W11	6	9	*Bradbury*
(10)	Chester Cathedral, The 9th Century, Chester	8	—	*n.o.c.*
(11)	Up Helly AA Lerwick, Shetland	8	20	*A. Moncrief*
(12)	Centenary of Eastbourne Judgement, Salvation Army	7	8	*S. Army*
(13)	First Day of Issue — Europe '92, City of London	7	—	*Royal Mail*

C.D.S. POSTMARKS
(14)	Bala — featured on the map on two of the stamps	10	
(15)	Greet, Birmingham...	10	
(16)	Letter, Enniskillen — open letter features on stamps	12	
(17)	Lover, Sailsbury	10	
(18)	Portobello Road, London — famous antiques market	10	
(19)	Rose, Truro	10	
(20)	Seaside — bucket and spade feature prominently on stamps	12	

In addition covers are known with the following CDS postmarks: Cargreen, Keyford, Kings Road, Chelsea, Market Place, Maypole, Ordnance Road, Penny Lane. Prices range from £7.

SLOGAN POSTMARKS
(21)	Southend on Sea Borough Centenary 1892-1992	17½	

In addition Westmoreland V W Audi; Please control your dog; Write Now etc. Prices from £12.

6th February 1992 — HAPPY & GLORIOUS
5 × 24p stamps showing Her Majesty as Head of State; Head of the Church of England; Head of the Royal Family; Head of the Armed Forces; and Head of the Commonwealth.

SPECIAL HANDSTAMPS
(1)	First Day of Issue — Philatelic Bureau	3	—	*Royal Mail*
(2)	First Day of Issue — Buckingham Palace, SW1	3	—	*Royal Mail*
(3)	Happy & Glorious, National Postal Museum, EC	4	—	*Royal Mail*
(4)	Happy & Glorious, Brian Reeve Cover Series, Windsor	4	10	*B. Reeve 2*
(5)	Happy & Glorious, Victorian Prints No. 65, London SW1	4	7	*Brad VP No 65*
(6)	Happy & Glorious, Church Bell Ringers, Westminster SW1	4	7	*LFDC 103*
(7)	Happy & Glorious, Commonwealth Institute, London SW8 .	4	9	*Bradbury*
(8)	Happy & Glorious, Windsor, Berks.	4	15	*Bradbury*
(9)	Happy & Glorious, Queen Elizabeth II, TV Times, SW1	4	5	*Benham*
(10)	40th Anniv. Accession Elizabeth II, Sandringham	4	9	*BLCS 72*
(11)	40th Anniv. Accession Elizabeth II, Windsor Castle	4	9	*BLCS 72*
(12)	40th Anniv. Accession Elizabeth II, Buckingham Palace	4	9	*Benham SG 15*
(13)	40th Anniv. Accession Elizabeth II, Balmoral Castle	4	9	*Benham SG 15*
(14)	40th Anniv. Accession Elizabeth II, Westminster Abbey	4	17	*B'ham (500) 72*

1992

	ordinary covers £	official covers £	
(15) Fortieth Anniv. Accession, MAJESTY, London W1	4	8	*CoverCraft*
(16) Fortieth Anniv. Long Live the Queen, Buckingham Palace, SW1 .	4	8	*CoverCraft*
(17) Sooty World Museum, 40 Years of Sooty	4	12	*Arlington*
(18) Forty Years Royal Flying, Queen's Flight BF 1992 PS	4	12	*RFDC 100*
(19) City of London Celebrates 40 Happy & Glorious Years, EC ..	4	4	*MGN/SG/RMail*
(20) First Day of Issue — Europe '92, City of London EC	4	—	*Royal Mail*

C.D.S. POSTMARKS

(21) Buckingham Palace, London SW1	75	
(22) Canterbury or York — Head of Church ....*each*	6	
(23) Catterick Garrison — Head of Armed Forces.....................	6	
(24) Duke of Yorks School — DoY appears on centre stamp as a baby ..	7	
(25) Any Field Post Office	8	
(26) House of Commons, London SW1	15	
(27) House of Lords, London SW1	20	
(28) Kensington High Street, London W8 — Commonwealth Institute	7	
(29) Sandringham	100	
(30) Scone — the Coronation Chair stone	12	
(31) Terminal 2 or 4, Heathrow — where H.M. first set foot on British soil as Queen	15	
(32) West Newton — nearest PO to Sandringham House	10	
(33) Windsor	7	
(34) Windsor Castle..	80	
(35) Windsor Great Park..	9	

In addition covers are known with the following CDS postmarks: Coronation Parade, Queen Elizabeth Avenue, Queens Parade, Queens Road, Queen Street, Royal Parade, Trafalgar Square. Prices range from £5.

SLOGAN POSTMARKS

Please control your dog; Alder Hey; Royal School for Deaf Children; Post Code Windsor. Prices from £7.

10th March 1992 — TENNYSON

Portraits of Tennyson together with characters from his poems, viz: 24p 'Vivien'; 28p 'The Miller's Daughter'; 33p 'The Lady of Shalott'; 39p 'Mariana'.

SPECIAL HANDSTAMPS

(1) First Day of Issue — Philatelic Bureau	3	—	*Royal Mail*
(2) First Day of Issue — Isle of Wight....................................	3	—	*Royal Mail*
(3) Tennyson Centenary, Grange de Lings, Lincoln	4	10	*B'ham (500) 73*
(4) Lord Tennyson, Charge of the Light Brigade, Winchester....	4	5	*BLCS 73*
(5) Centenary of Tennyson, The Revenge, Bude, Cornwall	4	5	*BLCS 73*
(6) Tennyson Idylls of the King, Tintagel, Cornwall	4	5	*Benham L29*
(7) Tennyson Centenary, Brian Reeve, Isle of Wight	4	10	*B Reeve 3*
(8) Tennyson Centenary, The Poetry Society, London SW1	4	8	*CoverCraft*
(9) Lord Tennyson, Victorian Print, Freshwater, Isle of Wight...	4	7	*Brad VP No 66*
(10) Lord Tennyson, Haslemere, Surrey	4	10	*Bradbury*
(11) Lord Tennyson, Hagworthingham, Spilsby, Lincs.	4	20	*Bradbury*
(12) The Tennyson Society, Somersby, Spilsby, Lincs................	4	6	*LFDC 104*
(13) The Salvation Army, Newport, Isle of Wight	5	7	*S. Army*
(14) First Day of Issue — Europe '92, City of London	5	—	*Royal Mail*
(15) Disbandment of Number 60 Squadron BF 2318 PS.............	5	6	*RAF FDC 1*

C.D.S. POSTMARKS

(16) Freshwater Bay or Freshwater – Tennyson's home (Farringford) ..*each*	10	
(17) Haslemere — Tennyson's home (Aldworth)	7	
(18) House of Lords, London SW1	20	
(19) Louth — where he attended Grammar School.....................	7	
(20) Tetford — near to Somersby, his birthplace......................	9	
(21) Tintagel — inspired 'Idylls of the King'	7	
(22) Trinity Street, Cambridge — he attended Trinity College	8	

In addition covers are known with the following CDS postmarks: King Arthurs Way, Sebastopol, Tennyson Rd., Tennyson Ave., Trumpington and Winchester. Prices range from £6.

SLOGAN POSTMARKS

Glasgow's Alive with Culture; Please control your dog; Write Now! Say it Better in a Letter. Prices from £8.

**PLEASE READ THE GENERAL NOTES
AT THE BEGINNING OF THIS CATALOGUE**
These often provide the answers to enquiries received.

133

7th April 1992 — EUROPA

24p Columbus; 24p Olympics; 24p Paralympics;
39p Operation Raleigh; 39p Expo.

		ordinary covers £	official covers £	
SPECIAL HANDSTAMPS				
(1)	First Day of Issue – Philatelic Bureau	3	—	*Royal Mail*
(2)	First Day of Issue – Liverpool	3	—	*Royal Mail*
(3)	Landfall of the Americas, Columbus 500th Anniv., Bristol...	5	—	*n.o.c.*
(4)	Columbus 500, Brian Reeve, Liverpool	4	10	*B Reeve 4*
(5)	Columbus Quincentenary, Greenwich, London SE10	4	10	*Bradbury*
(6)	America Yours to Discover, New York, Lincoln	4	6	*LFDC 105*
(7)	America Yours to Discover, California, Halifax	4	7	*Brad VP No.67*
(8)	500th Anniv. Columbus Discovery of America, Portsmouth.	4	10	*B'ham (500) 74*
(9)	500th Anniv. Columbus Discovery of America, Greenwich ..	4	5	*BLCS 74*
(10)	Captain Cook's Endeavour, Whitby, N. Yorks.	4	6	*S Muscroft*
(11)	Peterborough, City of Europe	4	12	*N V Rly*
(12)	King George's Fund for Sailors 75th Anniversary, SW1......	4	6	*CoverCraft*
(13)	First Day of Issue — Europe '92, City of London	4	—	*Royal Mail*
(14)	1992 Olympic Games, Manchester	4	5	*BLCS 74*
(15)	76th Anniversary of No. 56 Squadron BF 2319 PS	5	6	*RAF FDC 2*
(16)	The Royal Belfast Hospital for Sick Children, Belfast	5	10	*R.B.H.S.C.*
(17)	Walk Through Space Exhibitions, Jodrell Bank	5	12½	*Bradbury*
C.D.S. POSTMARKS				
(18)	Chelsea — Headquarters of 'Operation Raleigh'	6		
(19)	Croydon — Headquarters of British Paralympics	6		
(20)	Maritime Mail, London I.S.	15		
(21)	Raleigh	10		
(22)	Stoke Mandeville	7		
(23)	Wandsworth — Headquarters of British Olympic Assoc.	6		

In addition covers are known with the following CDS postmarks: Boston, Hagley Road
Birmingham, Lilleshall, Liverpool, Much Wenlock, New York, The Chart,
The Quarterdeck, Washington, Westward Ho!, Whitechapel. Prices range from £5.

SLOGAN POSTMARKS

(24)	Arcadian Festival, Birmingham	15	

In addition: Please control your dog; Post Haste, Inverness; Tenovus Scotland fights disease;
Hearts of Oak; Railway History, Ashford; PO Charter Croydon. Prices range from £7.

16th June 1992 — ENGLISH CIVIL WAR

24p Pikeman, 28p Drummer, 33p Musketeer, 39p Standard Bearer

SPECIAL HANDSTAMPS				
(1)	First Day of Issue — Philatelic Bureau	3	—	*Royal Mail*
(2)	First Day of Issue — Banbury, Oxfordshire	3	—	*Royal Mail*
(3)	350th Anniv. Civil War, The Sealed Knot, Edgehill, Banbury...	4	10	*Bradbury*
(4)	350th Anniv. Civil War, Edgehill Battle Museum, Banbury..	4	9	*Bradbury*
(5)	350th Anniv. Civil War, The Commandery, Worcester	4	8	*Bradbury*
(6)	350th Anniv. Civil War, Cromwell Museum, Huntingdon	4	6	*LFDC 106*
(7)	350th Anniv. Civil War, Victorian Print, Naseby	4	7	*Brad VP No.68*
(8)	350th Anniv. Civil War, National Army Museum	4	5	*BLCS 75*
(9)	350th Anniv. Civil War, Robert Devereaux, Newbury	4	8	*Benham L30*
(10)	350th Anniv. Civil War, Oliver Cromwell, Huntingdon	4	5	*BLCS 75*
(11)	350th Anniv. Civil War, Prince Rupert, London EC	4	10	*B'ham (500) 75*
(12)	350th Anniv. Civil War, Raising of the Standard, Nottingham .	4	10	*Benham SG17*
(13)	350th Anniv. Civil War, History Today, Kineton, Warks.	4	6	*BLCS 75*
(14)	Start & Finish Civil War, 1642-51 Bredon Covers, Worcester	4	5	*Bredon Crrs*
(15)	Whitefriars, Coventry, 1642 The Civil War 1651	4	7	*Coventry CC*
(16)	English Civil War Society, Hull	4	5	*CoverCraft*
(17)	The Navy Goes Over to Parliament, Portsmouth	4	8	*Benham L30*
(18)	Edgehill, Banbury, Oxon, Brian Reeve Cover Series	4	10	*B Reeve 5*
(19)	The Lawn Tennis Museum, Wimbledon SW19	4	6	*L.T.Museum*
(20)	First Day of Issue — Europe '92, City of London EC	4	—	*Royal Mail*
(21)	75th Anniversary of 101 Squadron	4	5	*RAF FDC 3*
C.D.S. POSTMARKS				
(22)	Castle Boulevard, Nottingham – Raising of the Standard ...	7		
(23)	House of Commons, SW1	15		
(24)	House of Lords, SW1	20		
(25)	Huntingdon – Birthplace of Oliver Cromwell	8		
(26)	Kineton, Warks – nearest Post Office to Edgehill	7		
(27)	Marston – Battle of Marston Moor	7		

PRICES & CONDITION – PLEASE READ GENERAL NOTES

134

		ordinary covers £	official covers £

(28) Naseby – Battle of Naseby 7

(29) Other sites of battles: Dunbar, Lostwithiel, Newbury, Powick, Ribbleton, Sidbury, Stow-on-the-Wold, Wash Common..*each* 7

(30) Oliver's Battery, Winchester.. 8

(31) Southwell – where Charles I surrendered 8

In addition covers are known with the following CDS postmarks: Castle Donington, Cropredy, Edgehill (Scarborough), Kingsland, Lichfield, Oxford, Preston, Trafalgar Square, Worcester. Prices range from £5.

SLOGAN POSTMARKS

(32) Storming of Preston – Battle and Pageant 10

(33) Hull Festival 1992 13

In addition: Guild Preston; North Yorks Moors Railways. Prices range from £5.

21st July 1992 — GILBERT & SULLIVAN

18p Yeoman of the Guard, 24p The Gondoliers, 28p The Mikado, 33p Pirates of Penzance, 39p Iolanthe

SPECIAL HANDSTAMPS

(1)	First Day of Issue – Philatelic Bureau	3	—	*Royal Mail*
(2)	First Day of Issue – D'Oyly Carte, Birmingham	3	—	*Royal Mail*
(3)	D'Oyly Carte Opera Company Birmingham	4	6	*LFDC 107*
(4)	Birthplace of Sir Arthur Sullivan – Lambeth Walk SE11	4	7	*Brad VP No 69*
(5)	Royal Academy of Music, London NW1	4	8	*Bradbury*
(6)	The Gilbert & Sullivan Society, Strand, London WC2	4	10	*Bradbury*
(7)	Birthplace of Richard D'Oyly Carte, Soho, London W1	4	15	*Bradbury*
(8)	The Mikado, 150th Anniv. Sir Arthur Sullivan, Savoy WC2 .	4	10	*B'ham (500) 76*
(9)	The Yeoman of the Guard, Sir Arthur Sullivan, The Tower EC1...	4	6	*BLCS 76*
(10)	The Pirates of Penzance, Sir Arthur Sullivan, Penzance	4	6	*BLCS 76*
(11)	Iolanthe, The Sullivan Society, S. Kensington SW7	4	8	*Benham L32*
(12)	The Gondoliers, The Sullivan Society, Weybridge, Surrey...	4	8	*Benham L31*
(13)	Sir Arthur Sullivan Sesquicentenary, the Savoy, London WC2.....	4	6	*CoverCraft*
(14)	Ruddigore, The Sorcerer etc., G & S Operas, Halifax	4	6	*Savoyards*
(15)	Damart, Grand Prize Draw, Gilbert & Sullivan, Bingley	4	8	*Arlington*
(16)	Gilbert & Sullivan Society (Torbay) Paignton	4	10	*G&S Torbay*
(17)	Symphony of Stamps, National Postal Museum, EC	4	—	*Royal Mail*
(18)	The Salvation Army, Penzance, Cornwall...........................	4	5	*H.R.*
(19)	Sir Arthur Sullivan, 1842-1992, London SE11	4	10	*B Reeve 6*
(20)	75th Anniversary No.47 Squadron BF 2321 PS	4	6	*RAF FDC 4*
(21)	The Royal Tournament, Earls Court BF 2330 PS................	5	—	*n.o.c.*
(22)	First Day of Issue – Europe '92 City of London	4	—	*Royal Mail*
(23)	Hampton Court Place, Int. Flower Show, Hampton Court....	5	8	*CoverCraft*
(24)	Shoreham-by-Sea Station Upgrade Brighton to Cardiff.......	5	15	*Benham R7*
(25)	Introduction of Pad Cancelling Machine at SHC Cardiff.....	5	—	*Royal Mail*

C.D.S. POSTMARKS

(26) Birmingham, or Tower Hill B'ham – D'Oyly Carte Opera Co. 6

(27) House of Commons – Iolanthe 39p value 15

(28) House of Lords – Iolanthe 39p value............................... 20

(29) Kingsway (Television House) – near to Savoy Theatre........ 8

(30) Lambeth Walk – Birthplace of Sir Arthur Sullivan............. 7

(31) Paignton – first performance of Pirates of Penzance 6

(32) Penzance – Pirates of Penzance...................................... 6

(33) Regent Street – where Gilbert and Sullivan first met 8

(34) Trafalgar Sq. – nearest P.O. to Birthplace of W. S. Gilbert.... 7

In addition covers are known with the following CDS postmarks: Broadwick Street, Castle Green, The Circle, Gilbertstone, Harrow & Weald, Haymarket, Old Windsor, Pindore Street, Seething Lane, Prices range from £5.

SLOGAN POSTMARKS

(35) Smugglers' Adventure, Hastings 8

In addition: Maritime Mail; Belfast Harpers; Brooklands, Weybridge; PO Charter; BBC Radio Llandudno; Edinburgh Tattoo; Royal Mail Preston; Royal Mail Cardiff; Southend Borough Centenary. Prices range from £5.

> **PLEASE READ THE GENERAL NOTES AT THE BEGINNING OF THIS CATALOGUE**
> These often provide the answers to enquiries received.

15th September 1992 — GREEN ISSUE
24p Acid Rain; 28p Ozone Layer; 33p Greenhouse Effect;
39p Bird of Hope

		ordinary covers £	official covers £	
SPECIAL HANDSTAMPS				
(1)	First Day of Issue – Philatelic Bureau	3	—	*Royal Mail*
(2)	First Day of Issue – Torridon	3	—	*Royal Mail*
(3)	Without conservation we die, Red Squirrel, Kendal	4	7	*BLCS 77*
(4)	Without conservation we die, Cardigan, Dyfed	4	7	*BLCS 77*
(5)	Without conservation we die, Bristol Zoo, Bristol	4	7	*BLCS 77*
(6)	Without conservation we die, Marsh Fritillary, Oxford	4	7	*BLCS 77*
(7)	Without conservation we die, London Zoo, NW1	4	7	*BLCS 77*
(8)	Without conservation we die, The Osprey, Aviemore	4	7	*BLCS 77*
(9)	Without conservation we die, Howletts, Canterbury	4	7	*BLCS 77*
(10)	Without conservation we die, The Dormouse, Worcester	4	7	*BLCS 77*
(11)	Damaged Environment Kills Wildlife, Brownsea Island	4	10	*B'ham (500) 77*
(12)	Water Wildlife, Otterhampton, Bridgwater	4	6	*BLCS 77*
(13)	Sutton Ecology Centre & Royal Mail Serving the Community	4	15	*SEC & RM*
(14)	The Barn Owl Trust, Ashburton, Devon	4	6	*CoverCraft*
(15)	Green Charter, City of Plymouth	4	6	*LFDC 108*
(16)	Greenacres, Aylesford, Kent	4	7	*Brad VP No. 70*
(17)	Preserve our Planet, Coventry & East Mercia Co-op, Nuneaton	4	8	*Bradbury*
(18)	Leicester on top of the World	4	10	*Bradbury*
(19)	Carsington Water, Britain's Newest Reservoir, Carsington	4	12	*Bradbury*
(20)	Green Issue, Fair Isle, Shetland, Brian Reeve	4	10	*B Reeve 7*
(21)	Manchester Metrolink, Environmentally Friendly Transport	4	5	*Dawn*
(22)	First Day of Issue – Europe '92, City of London EC	4	—	*Royal Mail*
(23)	75th Anniversary No.74 Squadron BF 2322 PS	4	6	*RAF FDC 5*
(24)	Shell UK Exploration and Production, Cowdenbeath	4	8	*P.P.S.*
(25)	'In the Beginning . . .' Salvation Army, Greenford, Middx.	4	5	*S. Army*
(26)	National Postal Museum, London	4	—	*Royal Mail*
C.D.S. POSTMARKS				
(27)	Balham, SW12 – Green Party Headquarters	10		
(28)	Glasshouses	8		
(29)	Greenacres, Greenfields, Green Island, Greenlands, Green Street, Forest Green, The Green ....*each*	6		
(30)	Islington N1 – Green Peace Headquarters	10		
(31)	Kew Gardens – conservation and seed bank	8		
(32)	Leicester – first Environment City	7		
(33)	Paradise	12		

In addition covers are known with the following CDS postmarks: Boat of Garton, Globe Road, Greeness, Greenlaw, Greenside, Hope, Hopes Green, Nettleham, Park Road, Rainhill, Shepherd's Bush, Slimbridge, Sunnyside, World's End, Wren's Nest. Prices range from £5.

SLOGAN POSTMARKS		
(34)	Leicester – Britain's first Environment City	7
(35)	Skegness is SO Bracing	12
(36)	Enrico Fermi 50 Years Controlled Nuclear Fission	25
(37)	Tropical Places – exotic holiday specialists	7

In addition: Wall's virtually fat free; Stamp Collecting Greatest Hobby; Please Control your Dog. Prices range from £5.

13th October 1992 – SINGLE EUROPEAN MARKET
24p Artist's interpretation of British star on European flag

SPECIAL HANDSTAMPS				
(1)	First Day of Issue – Philatelic Bureau	2	—	*Royal Mail*
(2)	First Day of Issue – Westminster	2	—	*Royal Mail*
(3)	First Day of Issue – Europe '92 City of London	3	—	*Royal Mail*
(4)	Autumn Stampex, London SW1	3	—	*Royal Mail*
(5)	British Presidency The European Community, Downing Street	3	9	*B'ham (500) 78*
(6)	The Single Market, Westminster, London SW1	3	7	*BLCS 78*
(7)	LUX Europae European Arts Festival, Edinburgh	3	6	*BLCS 78*
(8)	CBI Investing for the New Europe, London WC1	3	5	*LFDC 109*
(9)	Single European Market, Dover, Kent	3	7	*Brad VP No. 71*
(10)	Single European Market, Parliament Street, London SW1	3	6	*B Reeve 8*
(11)	European Commemorative 50 Pence Issue, Llantrisant	3	5	*Royal Mint*
(12)	Liverpool FC – FA Cup Winners – In Europe	3	4	*Dawn*
(13)	Manchester United in Europe UEFA Cup	3	4	*Dawn*
(14)	Leeds United – League Champions into Europe	3	4	*Dawn*
(15)	Saltaire, Shipley East Yorks 1853 Gallery Salts	3	4	*1853 Gallery*
(16)	75th Anniversary of No.111 Squadron BF 2336 PS	3	4	*RAF FDC 6*
(17)	HMC International	3	4	*HMC Int.*

Single European Market

	ordinary covers £	official covers £
C.D.S. POSTMARKS		
(18) Birmingham – venue for European Summit	5	
(19) House of Commons, SW1	10	
(20) House of Lords, SW1	15	
(21) Industrial and Trading Estates – various ....*each*	5	
(22) Lombard Street, or Stock Exchange.................*each*	5	
(23) Maritime Mail	7	
(24) Market, Market Place or Newmarket................*each*	5	
(25) Newbridge, Dover or Aycliffe, Dover (Tunnel) ....*each*	5	
(26) Paquebot – various	6	

In addition covers are known with the following CDS postmarks: Mastrick, Northern Parliament Parliament Street, Pounds, Runcorn (Shopping Centre), Saltaire, Starcross, Summit.
Prices range from £5.

SLOGAN POSTMARKS		
(27) Birmingham (surrounded by circle of stars)	7	
(28) Europe for Workers Safety and Health	15	
(29) The Visaservice – Passports Renewed	5	
(30) Maritime Mail	10	

In addition: WHSmiths; Royal Mail Children in Cities; Post Office Charter; Hearts of Oak.
Prices range from £4.

10th November 1992 — CHRISTMAS

Stained glass windows – Arts & Crafts Movement:
18p St. James's Church, Pangbourne; 24p St. Mary's Church, Bibury;
28p & 39p Our Lady & St. Peter's Church, Leatherhead; 33p All Saint's Church, Porthcawl

SPECIAL HANDSTAMPS			
(1) First Day of Issue – Philatelic Bureau	3	—	*Royal Mail*
(2) First Day of Issue – Bethlehem, Llandeilo, Dyfed	3	—	*Royal Mail*
(3) First Day of Issue – Pangbourne	3	—	*Royal Mail*
(4) Stained Glass at Canterbury Cathedral	4	5	*BLCS 79*
(5) Stained Glass Castle Howard, York	4	5	*BLCS 78b*
(6) All Saints, Middleton Cheney, Banbury	4	7	*Benham L33*
(7) St. Peter & St. Paul, Cattistock, Dorset	4	7	*Benham L33*
(8) St. Michaels Church, Forden, Welshpool, Powys	4	7	*Benham L34*
(9) All Hallows Church, Allerton, Liverpool	4	7	*Benham L34*
(10) St. Martin's Church, Brampton, Cumbria	4	7	*Benham L33*
(11) Christchurch, Cambridge	4	10	*B'ham (500) 79*
(12) Bethlehem, Dyfed, Victorian Print No.72	4	7	*Brad VP No.72*
(13) Godshill, The Church of the Lily Cross, Isle of Wight	4	6	*LFDC 110*
(14) Our Lady & St. Peter's Catholic Church, Leatherhead	4	10	*Bradbury*
(15) St. Mary's Bibury, Glos	4	6	*CoverCraft*
(16) Peace on Earth, All Saint's Porthcawl	4	6	*CoverCraft*
(17) The Stained Glass Museum, Ely, Cambs	4	6	*CoverCraft*
(18) Christmas, Canterbury Cathedral	4	10	*B Reeve 9*
(19) Cambridge, Christmas 1992	4	6	*Cam. S.C.*
(20) Christmas Blessings to all Mankind, Salvation Army, Westminster	4	6	*S. Army*
(21) National Postal Museum, City of London EC	4	—	*n.o.c.*
(22) Happy Christmas, Royal Mail City of London EC1	4	—	*n.o.c.*
(23) Seasons Greetings from Liverpool FC in Centenary Year	4	6	*Dawn*
(24) Seasons Greetings from Newcastle United in Centenary Year	4	6	*Dawn*
(25) CEAC 7 COSAC London SW1 (Conf. of European Affairs Cttee)	4	—	*n.o.c.*
(26) 75th Anniversary No.84 Squadron BF 2338 PS	4	6	*RAF FDC 7*

C.D.S. POSTMARKS		
(27) Bibury – relevant to 24p value	5	
(28) Leatherhead – relevant to 28p and 39p values	5	
(29) Pangbourne – relevant to 18p value	5	
(30) Porthcawl – relevant to 33p value	5	

In addition covers are known with the following CDS postmarks: All Saints, Church, Ely, Glasshouses, Holy Island, Jerusalem Street, Nasareth, St. James, St. Marys, St. Nicholas, St. Peters.
Prices range from £4.

SLOGAN POSTMARKS		
(31) Leeds Lights Up – 9 Miles of Illuminations	6	
(32) Happy Christmas, Please Post Early – Inverness	12	
(33) A Happy Christmas, The Post Office, Wick	15	
(34) Jesus is Alive! – Manchester	25	

In addition: Shetland for 93; Please control your Dog; Write now etc; Senders Name and Address.
Prices range from £5.

CHRISTMAS BOOKLET: Covers bearing pair or block of
4 × 18p stamps from booklet with relevant postmark

(these have margin at top and bottom).................*from*	3	
Full pane of ten stamps on cover ....*from*	10	

1992

19th January 1993 — SWANS

600th Anniversary of Abbotsbury Swannery: 18p Mute Swan Cob;
24p Cygnets; 28p Mute Swan Breeding Pair;
33p Mute Swans Eggs; 39p 'First Winter' Mute Swan

		ordinary covers £	official covers £	
SPECIAL HANDSTAMPS				
(1)	First Day of Issue – Philatelic Bureau	3	—	*Royal Mail*
(2)	First Day of Issue – Abbotsbury, Dorset	3	—	*Royal Mail*
(3)	First Day of Issue – London	4	—	*Royal Mail*
(4)	The Wildfowl & Wetlands Trust, Caerlaverock, Dumfriesshire ...	4	7	*BLCS 80*
(5)	The Wildfowl & Wetlands Trust, Castle Espie, Co. Down ...	4	7	*BLCS 80*
(6)	The Wildfowl & Wetlands Trust, Martin Mere, Liverpool ...	4	7	*BLCS 80*
(7)	The Wildfowl & Wetlands Trust, Slimbridge, Glos.	4	5	*BLCS 80*
(8)	The Wildfowl & Wetlands Trust, Llanelli, Dyfed	4	7	*BLCS 80*
(9)	600th Anniversary Abbotsbury Swannery, Weymouth	4	15	*Benham SG18*
(10)	Bird Watching, No.1 Bird Magazine, Peterborough	4	6	*Benham*
(11)	Stratford upon Avon	4	10	*B'ham (500) 80*
(12)	Dyers' Hall, London EC4	4	6	*LFDC 111*
(13)	The Vintners' Company, London EC4	4	7	*Brad VP No.73*
(14)	The Swan Sanctuary, Egham	4	10	*Bradbury*
(15)	Tercentenary of the Independent Chapel, Swanland	4	7	*S'land Priory*
(16)	Old Swan Corps, Old Swan, Liverpool	4	6	*S. Army*
(17)	Swan Lifeline Cuckoo Weir Island, Eton, Windsor	4	6	*CoverCraft*
(18)	Swan Trust, Berwick upon Tweed	4	6	*CoverCraft*
(19)	75th Anniversary No.115 Squadron BF 2347 PS	4	6	*RAF FDC 8*
(20)	People in the Post (Modern) National Postal Museum	4	—	*n.o.c.*
(21)	William Shakespeare, Stratford (swan in design)	4	—	*n.o.c.*
C.D.S. POSTMARKS				
(22)	Abbotsbury – Abbotsbury Swannery	6		
(23)	Egham – Swan Sanctuary	7		
(24)	Sandy – Headquarters of RSPB	8		
(25)	Slimbridge – Wildfowl Trust	7		
(26)	Swanland, Swanpool or Old Swan ....*each*	7		
(27)	Thetford – British Trust for Ornithology	8		

In addition covers are known with the following CDS postmarks: Fleet, Hanley Swan, Henley-on-Thames, House of Lords, Ilchester, Mickley, Old Bewick, Swanmore, Swansea. Prices range from £5.

SLOGAN POSTMARKS
Postcode, Doncaster; Colourful Greetings Stamps. Prices range from £5.

2nd February 1993 — GREETINGS

10 designs of 1st Class stamps on the theme of 'gift giving', viz:
Long John Silver; Tweedledee and Tweedledum; Just William; Toad and Mole;
Bash Street Kids; Peter Rabbit; the Snowman;
Big Friendly Giant; Rupert Bear; Aladdin

SPECIAL HANDSTAMPS				
(1)	First Day of Issue – Philatelic Bureau	5	—	*Royal Mail*
(2)	First Day of Issue – Greetland	5	—	*Royal Mail*
(3)	First Day of Issue – London	5	—	*Royal Mail*
(4)	Badger	6	—	
(5)	Daresbury, Warrington	6	8	*Bradbury*
(6)	The Scottish Literary Museum, Lady Stair's House, Edinburgh ..	6	8	*BLCS 81*
(7)	Centenary of Beatrix Potter, Kensington, London W8	6	8	*BLCS 81*
(8)	Big Friendly Giant, Great Missenden, Bucks	6	8	*BLCS 81*
(9)	Aladdin, The Arabian Nights, Manchester	6	8	*Benham D189*
(10)	Alice in Wonderland, Oxford	6	3(s)	*Benham*
(11)	Rivers Corner, Sturminster Newton, Dorset	6	10	*B'ham (500) 81*
(12)	Peter Rabbit Centenary, Near Sawrey, Ambleside	6	3(s)	*CoverCraft*
(13)	Waterstone's, London	6	8	*Waterstone's*
C.D.S. POSTMARKS				
(14)	Far Sawrey – home of Beatrix Potter	7		
(15)	Fleet Street – where the 'Beano' is published	7		
(16)	Greet, Birmingham	7		
(17)	Oxford – home of Lewis Carroll	7		

In addition covers are known with the following CDS postmarks: Badger's Mount, Bearpark, Blackfriars Road, Braemar, Bromley Common, Bunny, Cross Hands, Earls Court, Exchange, Fulham Palace Road, Great Missenden, Hassocks, Kensington High Street, Molehill Green, Portobello Road, Rupert Street, Stock Exchange, Tweedle, Waterstone, William Street, The Willows. Prices range from £6.

SLOGAN POSTMARKS
(18)	Brighten your Mail – Use Colourful Greetings Stamps	8

In addition: Write Now, etc. Prices range from £5.

16th February 1993 — MARINE TIMEKEEPERS

24p, 28p, 33p, 39p: Four layer's of Harrison's "H4" Clock
Celebrating the 300th anniversary of the birth of John Harrison

SPECIAL HANDSTAMPS	ordinary covers £	official covers £	
(1) First Day of Issue – Philatelic Bureau	3	—	Royal Mail
(2) First Day of Issue – Greenwich	3	—	Royal Mail
(3) First Day of Issue – John Harrison 1693-1776, London	3	—	Royal Mail
(4) Tercentenary of John Harrison – Queen Elizabeth 2, Southampton	4	3(s)	Benham
(5) Tercentenary of John Harrison – RMS Queen Mary, Southampton	4	3(s)	Benham
(6) Tercentenary of John Harrison – The Cutty Sark, Greenwich	4	6	BLCS 82
(7) Tercentenary of John Harrison – SS Great Britain, Bristol	4	6	Benham L35
(8) John Harrison First Accurate Marine Chronometer, Portsmouth	4	3(s)	Benham
(9) John Harrison First Accurate Marine Chronometer, Plymouth	4	10	B'ham (500) 82
(10) HMS Belfast John Harrison, London SE1	4	3(s)	Benham
(11) 300th Anniversary of John Harrison HMS Victory, Portsmouth	4	6	BLCS 82
(12) The Antiquarian Horological Society, Ticehurst	4	7	Bradbury
(13) British Watch & Clockmaker's Guild, Burnham on Crouch	4	6	LFDC 112
(14) British Horological Institute Ltd, Newark, Notts	4	7	Brad VP No.74
(15) John Harrison Tercentenary, Greenwich	4	6	CoverCraft
(16) British Sailors' Society, 175th Anniversary, Southampton	4	6	SP
(17) 80 Years of Service No.1 Squadron BF 2346 PS	4	6	RAF FDC 9
(18) The Salvation Army Medical Fellowship 1943-1993 London EC4	4	6	S. Army
(19) First Day of Sale, Windsor	5	—	n.o.c.

C.D.S. POSTMARKS		
(20) Clockface, St. Helens, or Clock House Parade	6	
(21) Greenwich – from where all measures of time and position are based	6	
(22) Maritime Mail, London I.S.	8	
(23) Meridian Centre, Newhaven	15	
(24) Paquebot – various	7	
(25) New Invention, Willenhall, West Midlands	5	
(26) New Crofton, Wakefield – nearest P.O. to Birthplace of Harrison	5	

In addition covers are known with the following CDS postmarks: The Chart, Hampstead,
The Quarterdeck, Theobalds Road, Watchet, Whitby. Prices range from £4.

SLOGAN POSTMARKS		
(27) Maritime Mail, London I.S.	15	
(28) SWATCH Swatch the World	40	

In addition: Bedford Borough Council – Waste Watchers.
Safeway, Plymouth; Royal Mail can help your Business. Prices range from £5.

16th March 1993 — ORCHIDS

18p Dendrobium hellwigianum; 24p Paphiopedilum Maudiae 'Magnificum';
28p Cymbidium lowianum; 33p Vanda Rothschildiana;
39p Dendrobium vexillarius var. albiviride

SPECIAL HANDSTAMPS			
(1) First Day of Issue – Philatelic Bureau	3	—	Royal Mail
(2) First Day of Issue – Glasgow	3	—	Royal Mail
(3) First Day of Issue – London	3	—	Royal Mail
(4) Royal Botanic Gardens, Kew, Richmond, Surrey	4	5	BLCS 83
(5) The Botanical Gardens & Glasshouses, Birmingham	4	6	BLCS 83
(6) The Botanic Gardens, Glasgow	4	6	BLCS 83
(7) The Botanic Gardens Park, Belfast	4	6	BLCS 83
(8) The Royal Botanic Garden, Edinburgh	4	6	BLCS 83
(9) The Oldest Botanic Gardens in Britain, Oxford	4	6	BLCS 83
(10) Royal Orchid Service, Thai Airways, Heathrow, Hounslow	4	10	Benham SG20
(11) World Orchid Conference, Glasgow	4	10	B'ham (500) 83
(12) The Worshipful Company of Gardeners, London EC	4	6	LFDC 113
(13) Royal Botanic Garden, Edinburgh	4	7	Brad VP No.75
(14) The Orchid Society of Great Britain	4	6	CoverCraft
(15) 79 Years of Service, No.30 Squadron BF 2348 PS	4	6	RAF FDC 10
(16) Official Opening Derwentside LDO Consett, Co. Durham	4	—	n.o.c.
(17) Opening of New Post Office, Southend-on-Sea	4	10	Bradbury

C.D.S. POSTMARKS		
(18) Botanic Gardens, Belfast	6	
(19) Glasgow – venue of World Orchid Conference	6	
(20) Kew Gardens, Richmond, Surrey	6	
(21) Royal Hospital Chelsea – Chelsea Flower Show	8	

In addition covers are known with the following CDS postmarks: Flowery Field; Glasshouses;
Montague Terrace, Edinburgh. Prices range from £5.

SLOGAN POSTMARKS
Marie Curie Daffodil Day. Prices from £5.

11th May 1993 — ART IN THE 20th CENTURY

24p Henry Moore – Family Group; 28p Edward Bawden – Kew Gardens;
33p Stanley Spencer – St. Francis and the Birds;
39p Ben Nicholson – Still Life, Odyssey 1

		ordinary covers £	official covers £	
SPECIAL HANDSTAMPS				
(1)	First Day of Issue – Philatelic Bureau	3	—	*Royal Mail*
(2)	First Day of Issue – London SW	3	—	*Royal Mail*
(3)	First Day of Issue – London	3	—	*Royal Mail*
(4)	Courtauld Institute Galleries 20th Century Art, London WC2	4	6	*BLCS 84*
(5)	20th Century Art, Paul Nash, Dymchurch, Kent..................	4	9	*B'ham (500) 84*
(6)	Henry Moore OM CH, 20th Century Art, Leeds.................	4	10	*Benham SG21*
(7)	Ben Nicholson, St. Ives, Cornwall..................................	4	3(s)	*Benham*
(8)	Stanley Spencer, Cookham, Herts..................................	4	3(s)	*Benham*
(9)	Edward Bawden, Saffron Walden, Essex	4	3(s)	*Benham*
(10)	National Portrait Gallery, London WC2	4	6	*Westminster Coll'n*
(11)	Royal College of Art, Kensington Gore, London SW7........	4	6	*LFDC 114*
(12)	Sir Joshua Reynolds 1723-1792, London W1.....................	4	7	*Brad VP No.76*
(13)	Swiss National Tourist Office London Centenary 1893-1993	4	6	*CoverCraft*
(14)	The British Council Promoting Britain Abroad	4	6	*CoverCraft*
(15)	75th Anniv. RAF Frank Wootton Aviation Artist Lympne, Kent ..	4	6	*BLCS 84*
(16)	75th Anniversary No.216 Squadron BF 2349 PS	4	6	*RAF FDC 11*
(17)	We Remember Cyprus, Malaya and Suez BF 2368 PS	4	—	*n.o.c.*
(18)	The Salvation Army, Sunbury Court, Sunbury on Thames ..	4	6	*S.Army*
C.D.S. POSTMARKS				
(19)	Albemarle Street, London – near to Royal Academy	6		
(20)	Braintree – birthplace of Edward Bawden......................	5		
(21)	Carbis Bay – home of Ben Nicholson	6		
(22)	Castleford – birthplace of Henry Moore........................	5		
(23)	Cookham – birthplace of Stanley Spencer	6		
(24)	Denham Green – birthplace of Ben Nicholson	5		
(25)	Great Bardfield – home of Edward Bawden......................	6		
(26)	Kew Gardens – depicted on 28p stamp	5		
(27)	Much Hadham – Henry Moore Foundation	6		

In addition covers are known with the following CDS postmarks: Pembroke Street, Bedford;
Trafalgar Square, WC2; Tufton Street, SW1; Vauxhall Bridge Road, SW1.
Prices range from £4.

SLOGAN POSTMARKS			
(28)	Barnes Cray School Arts Week, Dartford	15	
(29)	Royal Mail Supports the Arts is Magic Festival, Glasgow	5	
(30)	Milton Keynes International Festival Folk Art	20	

In addition: Royal Mail Can Help Your Business. Prices from £5.

15th June 1993 — ROMAN BRITAIN

24p Claudius (Gold Coin, British Museum) found at Bredgar, Kent;
28p Hadrian (Bronze Sculpture, British Museum) found in the River Thames;
33p Roma (Gemstone, Legionary Museum, Caerleon) found at Caerleon;
39p Christ (Mosaic, British Museum) from a villa at Hinton St. Mary

SPECIAL HANDSTAMPS				
(1)	First Day of Issue – Philatelic Bureau	3	—	*Royal Mail*
(2)	First Day of Issue – Caerleon	3	—	*Royal Mail*
(3)	First Day of Issue – London	3	—	*Royal Mail*
(4)	The Ermine Street Guard, Eboracum, York	4	6	*LFDC 115*
(5)	Camulodunum, Roman Britain, Colchester, Essex	4	7	*Brad VP No.77*
(6)	Roman Britain, Caerleon, Gwent	4	5	*Benham L37*
(7)	Roman Britain, Chester, Cheshire	4	5	*Benham L37*
(8)	Roman Britain, Newcastle upon Tyne	4	9	*Benham SG21*
(9)	Roman Britain, Bath, Avon	4	9	*Benham SG21*
(10)	Roman Britain, Colchester, Essex	4	5	*Benham L37*
(11)	Roman Britain, Invasion A.D. 43 Canterbury, Kent	4	5	*Benham L37*
(12)	The White Cliffs Experience, Dover, Kent	4	5	*Benham L36*
(13)	The Largest Roman Palace in Britain, Fishbourne, Chichester	4	5	*BLCS85*
(14)	The Roman Villa Chedworth, The National Trust, Cirencester	4	5	*BLCS85*
(15)	Roman Britain, Cirencester, Gloucestershire	4	5	*Benham L37*
(16)	Roman Britain, Walbrook, London EC4	4	5	*Benham L37*
(17)	Roman Britain, St. Albans	4	9	*B'ham (500) 85*
(18)	Museum of Antiquities, Newcastle-upon-Tyne	4	6	*CoverCraft*
(19)	Museum of London, London Wall EC2Y 5HN	4	6	*CoverCraft*
(20)	Lactodorum, Towcester, Northants	4	6	*Sponne School*
(21)	Royal Air Force Locking, Weston-super-Mare...................	4	15	*RAF Locking*
(22)	Naming of New Relief Lifeboat, Fleetwood, Lancs..............	4	6	*Pilgrim*
(23)	The Salvation Army, International Headquarters	4	6	*S.Army*

(Please note this list is incomplete. C.D.S. and Slogan postmarks will be added in the next edition.)

20th July 1993 — INLAND WATERWAYS

24p Grand Junction Canal; 28p Stainforth & Keadby Canal;
33p Brecknock & Abergavenny Canal; 39p Crinan Canal

SPECIAL HANDSTAMPS

		ordinary covers £	official covers £	
(1)	First Day of Issue – Philatelic Bureau	3	—	*Royal Mail*
(2)	First Day of Issue – Gloucester.....................................	3	—	*Royal Mail*
(3)	First Day of Issue – London	3	—	*Royal Mail*
(4)	The Inland Waterways Association, Market Harborough....	4	6	*LFDC 116*
(5)	Grand Union Canal 1793-1993, Foxton Locks, Leicestershire	4	7	*Brad VP No.78*
(6)	The Canal Musem, Stoke Bruerne	4	6	*Benham*
(7)	Conserving the Environment, British Waterways, The Wharf, Braunston	4	6	*Benham*
(8)	Conserving the Environment, British Waterways, Lochgilphead, Argyll	4	6	*Benham*
(9)	Conserving the Environment, British Waterways, Sheffield, Yorks.	4	6	*Benham*
(10)	Conserving the Environment, British Waterways, Newport, Gwent	4	6	*Benham*
(11)	Canals 200, Grand Junction Canal, British Waterways, Northampton ...	4	6	*Benham*
(12)	Canals 200, Crinan Canal, British Waterways, Ardrishaigh, Argyll	4	6	*Benham*
(13)	Canals 200, Stainforth & Keadby, British Waterways, Sheffield, Yorks. .	4	6	*Benham*
(14)	Canals 200, Brecknock & Abergavenny, Brecon, Powys	4	6	*Benham*
(15)	The Mary-Anne Worsley Marina, Manchester, The Salvation Army	4	6	*S.Army*
(16)	77 Years of Service by No. 51 Squadron BF2383PS..............	4	6	*RAF*

(Please note this list is incomplete. More postmarks, including the CDS and Slogans, will be added next year).

1993

FUTURE ISSUES

1993

10th Aug :	Beatrix Potter £6 Prestige Booklet
14th Sept :	Autumntime (Fruit)
12th Oct :	Sherlock Holmes
9th Nov :	'A Christmas Carol'

1994

Dates to be announced
Order may change

Railway Mania
25th Anniversary of Investiture
Centenary of Picture Postcard
European Discoveries
'D' Day Landings
Golf
Summertime
Channel Tunnel
Christmas

PLUS

Greeting Stamps
Prestige Booklet (N. Ireland)

DEFINITIVE ISSUES
Including Booklet Panes, Coils, Postage Dues, Framas and Regionals

GENERAL NOTES

Please also read the General Notes at the beginning of this catalogue.

Prices and Condition

1839-1951 Prices vary considerably, according to condition, for all early definitives on first day cover. **The prices quoted are for good covers with clear postmarks.** Superb examples will probably realise a better price whilst covers in poor condition will fetch less.

1952 to date Prices are for good clean covers with clear postmarks. With the exception of the earlier issues (1950s) covers are usually available unaddressed (or with small printed labels etc.) and the prices reflect this.

Format

This section falls into three broad categories covering the following dates:

1839-1936 Unless otherwise stated prices are for any postmark on plain (i.e. un-illustrated) envelopes.

1936-1970 Prices are given for both plain and illustrated covers, once again with any postmark. Where known relevant postmarks exist, these have been listed.

1971 – to date All prices are for illustrated covers. The two column price structure now reflects covers with the more sought after Windsor postmarks or covers with any other type of postmark.

Scope

All new varieties and formats of definitive stamps where known on first day cover are included, e.g. changes in phosphor, perforations and papers. Different se-tenant formats from booklets and coil strips are also to be found in this section, as are regionals, postage dues and frama labels.

Booklets In the main these are included if their content (whether different se-tenant format or changes in perfs etc.) has been altered to those previously available.

First Days of New Services Whilst not strictly FDCs, covers marking the first day of new Post Office services, e.g. Recorded Delivery, Speedpost etc. are also included.

All prices from 1839-1936 are for plain (un-illustrated) covers except where stated.

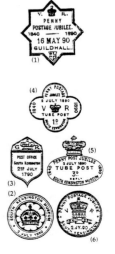

Date of Issue		QUEEN VICTORIA (1837-1901)	£
5 Dec	1839	Uniform 4d Post	300
10 Jan	1840	First Day of Universal Penny Post	375
6 May	1840	The Mulready 1d Stationery	2,500
6 May	1840	1d Black (imperf.) THE FIRST POSTAGE STAMP....	28,000
8 May	1840	2d Blue (imperf.)	25,000
22 Feb	1855	2d Blue (perforated, Plate 4)	2,500
7 Mar	1865	6d Deep Lilac	1,800
1 Oct	1870	½d Rose red (small format) on Asylum cover	1,000
		½d Rose red (small format) printed on postcard	600
12 Apr	1872	6d Deep Chestnut	1,200
1 Sept	1873	1s Green	3,250
1 Jan	1880	1d Venetian red	900
1 Aug	1883	6d First Day of Inland Parcel Service	400
1 Jan	1887	5d Dull Purple & Blue (Jubilee issue)	900

	Uniform Penny Postage Jubilee – official envelopes	
16 May	1890	Guildhall handstamp (No. 1)	50
2 Jul	1890	South Kensington handstamp (No. 6)	30
		South Kensington handstamps (Nos. 4 or 5)..........*each*	70
		South Kensington handstamps (Nos. 2 or 3)..........*each*	50
		All 5 S. Kensington handstamps on one cover	125

| 15 Sept | 1892 | 4½d Green & Carmine (Jubilee issue) | 3,000 |
| 17 Apr | 1900 | ½d Blue-green (Jubilee issue) | 900 |

KING EDWARD VII (1901-1910)

Date	Year	Description	£
1 Jan	1902	½d Blue-green	75
		1d Red	75
		2½d Blue	250
		6d Purple	350
		The above four values on one cover	800
		-do- with Parliament Street C.D.S.	1,000
1 Nov	1909	4d Brown-orange (on postcard)	400
13 Jul	1911	4d Orange	1,200

KING GEORGE V (1910-1936)

Imperial Crown Watermark

Date	Year	Description	£
22 Jun	1911	½d Green	75
		ditto on Junior Philatelic Society cover	275
		1d Red	50
		The above two values on one cover	150
		Pair of covers with Westminster Abbey C.D.S.	2,500
1 Jan	1912	Redrawn ½d and 1d	1,200
25 Jan	1912	**Wilkinson Meter Mail**	
		First day of new experimental machine	275

Royal Cypher Watermark

Date	Year	Description	£
17 Jan	1913	½d Green	600
8 Oct	1912	1d Red	450
15 Oct	1912	1½d Red-brown ....(Int. Stamp Exhib. h/s £650)	450
20 Aug	1912	2d Orange	450
18 Oct	1912	2½d Blue ....(Int. Stamp Exhib. h/s £700)	500
9 Oct	1912	3d Violet	600
15 Jan	1913	4d Grey-green	1,100
30 Jun	1913	5d Brown; 9d Agate – on one cover	2,000
1 Aug	1913	6d Purple	1,600
		7d Olive	1,600
		8d Black-yellow	1,800
		10d Turquoise	2,200
		1s Bistre	2,200

High values — 'Sea Horses'

Date	Year	Description	£
13 Jun	1913	2s 6d Brown	2,000

Postage Dues

Date	Year	Description	£
20 Apr	1914	½d Green (on cover or postcard)	350
		1d Red (on cover or postcard)	400
		2d Black	450
		5d Brown	750

Photogravure (Block Cypher Watermark)

Date	Year	Description	£
19 Nov	1934	½d Green	10
24 Sep	1934	1d Scarlet	10
20 Aug	1934	1½d Red-brown	10
21 Jan	1935	2d Orange	30
18 Mar	1935	2½d Blue	20
		3d Violet	30
		2½d and 3d values on one cover	65
2 Dec	1935	4d Grey-green	60
		9d Olive-green	90
		4d and 9d values on one cover	250
17 Feb	1936	5d Yellow-brown	550
24 Feb	1936	10d Turquoise-blue	600
26 Feb	1936	1s Bistre-brown	600
		Set of eleven (or nine) plain covers	1,800
		All eleven values on one cover with dates as above	2,500

All prices from King Edward VIII reign are for plain and illustrated covers (where known). The abbreviation n.k. indicates not known to exist.

Date of Issue		KING EDWARD VIII (1936)	Plain £	Illus. £
1 Sep	1936	½d, 1½d, 2½d	4	100
		ditto King Edward, Banff C.D.S.	100	n.k.
		ditto Windsor C.D.S.	150	n.k.
		ditto Kingstanding, Birmingham C.D.S.	n.k.	150
14 Sep	1936	1d	8	100
		ditto King Edward, Banff C.D.S.	120	n.k.

KING GEORGE VI (1936-1952)

Low values — original issue

Date of Issue			Plain	Illus.
10 May	1937	½d Green, 1d Scarlet, 2½d Ultramarine	1	20
		ditto Windsor machine postmark	n.k.	100
30 Jul	1937	1½d Red-brown	1	15
31 Jan	1938	2d Orange	5	35
		3d Violet	5	35
		2d and 3d values on one cover	12	80
21 Nov	1938	4d Grey-green	8	n.k.
		5d Brown	8	n.k.
		4d and 5d values on one cover	25	n.k.
30 Jan	1939	6d Purple	20	n.k.
27 Feb	1939	7d Emerald-green	10	n.k.
		8d Carmine	10	n.k.
		7d and 8d values on one cover	30	n.k.
1 May	1939	9d Olive-green	50	n.k.
		10d Turquoise-blue	70	n.k.
		1s Bistre-brown	70	n.k.
		9d, 10d, and 1s values on one cover	275	n.k.
29 Dec	1947	11d Plum	35	100
		Set of fifteen values on eight or more covers	500	n.k.

High values — 'Arms' Design

Date of Issue			Plain	Illus.
4 Sep	1939	2s 6d Brown	750	n.k.
9 Mar	1942	2s 6d Yellow-green	950	n.k.
21 Aug	1939	5s Red	350	n.k.
30 Oct	1939	10s Dark blue	1,500	n.k.
30 Nov	1942	10s Ultramarine	1,800	n.k.
1 Oct	1948	£1 Brown	110	n.k.

Low values — change to pale colours

Date of Issue			Plain	Illus.
1 Sep	1941	½d Pale green	10	n.k.
11 Aug	1941	1d Pale scarlet	10	n.k.
28 Sep	1942	1½d Pale red-brown	30	n.k.
6 Oct	1941	2d Pale orange	20	n.k.
21 Jul	1941	2½d Pale ultramarine	20	25
3 Nov	1941	3d Pale violet	60	n.k.
		Set of six covers	150	n.k.
2 Oct	1950	4d Change of colour — light ultramarine	15	75
3 May	1951	Low values — colour changes: ½d, 1d, 1½d, 2d, 2½d	5	30
		ditto Battersea C.D.S. postmark (Festival of Britain)	10	60
		1s Booklet	—	200
		'Festival' High values: 2s 6d, 5s, 10s, £1*	125	650
		ditto Battersea C.D.S. postmark or slogan*	n.k.	900

(on one cover or set of four covers)

QUEEN ELIZABETH II £.s.d. ISSUES (1952-1970)

LOW VALUE DEFINITIVES

Date of Issue			Plain	Illus.
5 Dec	1952	1½d, 2½d	1	5
6 Jul	1953	5d, 8d, 1s	5	30
31 Aug	1953	½d, 1d, 2d	6	30
2 Nov	1953	4d, 1s 3d, 1s 6d	25	125
18 Jan	1954	3d, 6d, 7d	25	75
8 Feb	1954	9d, 10d, 11d	40	150
		Set of all 17 values on matching covers	150	550

'CASTLES' HIGH VALUES

		Plain £	Illus. £
23 Sep	1955 2s 6d, 5s — on one or two covers	50	400
	2s 6d Value only: Carrickfergus C.D.S. on illustrated cover ..	—	250
1 Sep	1955 10s, £1 — on one or two covers	150	450
	10s, £1 — Edinburgh C.D.S.	—	625
	10s only — Edinburgh C.D.S.	150	—
	£1 only — Windsor Castle C.D.S.	250	—
	Set of 4 values on two or more matching covers............	225	1,250
17 Jul	1956 **DEFINITIVE:** 3d St. Edward Crown wmk	100	—

GRAPHITE-LINED ISSUES

		Plain £	Illus. £
19 Nov	1957 ½d, 1d, 1½d, 2d, 2½d, 3d — Southampton postmark ...	40	80

Graphite lines were printed under the gum on the back of the stamps as an experiment in automatic letter sorting. They were used in connection with machinery at Southampton.

FIRST REGIONAL STAMPS

		Plain £	Illus. £
18 Aug	1958 **3d** with appropriate regional postmarks:		
	Wales or Scotland..each	2½	10
	Northern Ireland or Isle of Man ....each	3	25
	Guernsey or Jersey..each	3	15
	Set of six covers	20	90
29 Sep	1958 **6d and 1s 3d** with appropriate regional postmarks:		
	Wales or Scotland..each	2½	20
	Northern Ireland	4	30
	Set of three covers	15	70
9 Feb	1959 **DEFINITIVE: 4½d** New value	20	175

PHOSPHOR-GRAPHITE ISSUES

		Plain £	Illus. £
18 Nov	1959 ½d, 1d, 1½d, 2d, 2½d, 3d, 4d, 4½d — Southampton postmark	40	100

Similar to the Nov 1957 issue, but with the addition of phosphor bands on the front.

		Plain £	Illus. £
27 Jun	1960 **DEFINITIVE:** 6d Phosphor issue...........................	—	200

PHOSPHOR BANDS ISSUE

		Plain £	Illus. £
6 Jul	1960 ½d, 1d, 1½d, 2d, 2½d, 3d, 4d, 6d, 1s — Southampton pmk	—	100

Inauguration of Phosphor Line Sorting Machine.

		Plain £	Illus. £
1 Feb	1961 **RECORDED DELIVERY:** First Day of new service	60	—
29 Jan	1963 **REGIONALS:** Scotland, 3d, 6d, 1s 3d (with phosphor bands)		
	Scottish postmark	40	100
15 Jul	1963 **REGIONALS:** Isle of Man 3d on chalky paper — I.O.M. pmk	60	250
15 Jul	1963 **BOOKLET:** 2s (2 panes of 4×2½d; 1 pane 3×½d + 1×2½d)		
	Se-tenant pane on cover	30	90
	4×2½d pane on cover............................	40	75
	This booklet was issued primarily for holiday resorts.		
6 Sep	1963 **BOOKLET:** 2s Reprint of above — both panes	50	85
8 Jun	1964 **REGIONALS:** 2½d with appropriate regional postmarks		
	Isle of Man..	4	25
	Guernsey or Jersey......................................each	3	20
1 Jul	1964 **BOOKLET:** 2s (4 se-tenant panes of 2×2½d + 2×½d)		
	Se-tenant pane on cover with either Bournemouth,		
	Ryde, Salisbury, Stratford or Winchester postmark	n.k.	3
	Brighton & Hove slogan pmk	6	—
1 Jul	1964 **DEFINITIVE:** 2½d (wmk sideways) from 2s booklet	10	30
17 May	1965 **DEFINITIVES:** 4d Deep ultramarine — New shade .	30	75
	3d Deep lilac — One phosphor side band ...	30	75

The issue dates of these stamps were originally planned for 28th April (4d) and 29th April (3d). These were deliberately postponed until 17th May being the official date of issue and the date of the change in the letter rate. Covers are known to exist with earlier dates.

Date of Issue			Plain £	Illus. £
21 Jun	1965	**BOOKLET:** 6s (3 panes of 6×4d) — one pane on cover	50	150
16 Aug	1965	**BOOKLET:** 2s (2 panes: 2×1d + 2×3d; 4×4d) — both panes .	50	150
		Se-tenant pane only	15	70
6 Dec	1965	**BOOKLET:** Christmas 3d Booklet pane	—	200
7 Feb	1966	**REGIONALS:** 4d (Wales, Scotland, N.I., I.O.M. Guernsey & Jersey)		
		Set of six covers with regional postmarks.............	6	40
		4d Scotland — Phosphor issue	1	8
15 Feb	1967	**DEFINITIVE:** 7d — Phosphor issue	200	—
1 Mar	1967	**REGIONALS:** 9d, 1s 6d (Wales, Scot., N.I.) Phosphor issue		
		Set of three covers with regional F.D.I. postmarks	—	7
		Wales — special 'New Stamp Issue . . .' slogan postmark	—	15
		N.I. — special 'New Stamp Issue . . .' slogan postmark	—	15
9 Jun	1967	**DEFINITIVE:** 5d — Phosphor issue	100	—
28 Jun	1967	**DEFINITIVES:** 8d, 1s — Phosphor issue	150	—
		DEFINITIVES: New style (Machin Head)		
5 Jun	1967	4d, 1s, 1s 9d ....(Illus. cover with Windsor F.D.I. £1½)	—	½
8 Aug	1967	3d, 9d, 1s 6d ......(Illus. cover with Windsor F.D.I. £1½)	—	½
5 Feb	1968	½d, 1d, 2d, 6d ....(Illus. cover with Windsor F.D.I. £1)	—	½
1 Jul	1968	5d, 7d, 8d, 10d ......(Illus. cover with Windsor F.D.I. £1)	—	½
21 Sep	1967	**BOOKLET:** 6s Machin (3 panes of 6×4d) — one pane	5	100
25 Mar	1968	**BOOKLET:** 10s Machin 'Livingston' cover		
		3 panes (6×4d; 6×3d; 6×1d) Stampex pmk	10	100
		DEFINITIVES: 'Castles': Unwatermarked paper		
6 Dec	1967	£1 (London Underground special cover and special handstamp)...	—	500
16 Apr	1968	5s and 10s...	400	n.k.
3 Jul	1968	2s 6d	n.k.	300
6 Apr	1968	**BOOKLET:** 2s Machin (2 panes: 2×1d + 2×3d; 4×4d) ...	20	70
4 Jun	1968	**DEFINITIVE:** 2s 6d Chalky paper	150	250
10 Jul	1968	**BOOKLET:** 4s 6d (2 panes of 6×4d; 1 pane 6×1d)		
		— pair of different panes on cover..........	20	90
28 Aug	1968	**DEFINITIVE:** 1s 6d PVA Gum	—	150
4 Sep	1968	**REGIONALS:** 4d Brown, 5d Blue (Wales, Scotland, N.I., I.O.M., Guernsey, Jersey) Set of 6 — regional pmks	2	10
		Wales: 'New Stamps' slogan pmk	3	25

16 SEP 1968: THE BEGINNING OF TWO-TIER POST 1st Class 5d, 2nd Class 4d				

Date of Issue			Plain £	Illus. £
16 Sep	1968	**BOOKLETS:** 2s (2 panes: 4×4d; 2×4d + 2 labels).....	5	12
		-do- Windsor postmark	8	30
		4s 6d (2 panes of 6×4d; 1 pane 6×1d) — 2 different panes	10	50
		10s (2 panes 6×4d; 2 panes 6×5d; 1 pane 4×1d + 2×4d)		
		— set of three different panes on cover	15	75
16 Sep	1968	**COIL STRIP:** 4d Pair on cover	20	150
16 Sep	1968	**DEFINITIVE:** 4d (one phosphor band)	10	25
16 Oct	1968	**BOOKLET:** 6s (3 panes 6×4d) — one pane on cover ..	15	75
27 Nov	1968	**BOOKLET:** 5s (2 panes 6×5d) — one pane on cover ..	15	75
29 Nov	1968	**DEFINITIVE:** 9d PVA Gum	—	50
6 Jan	1969	**DEFINITIVES:** 4d Red, 8d Turquoise — Colour changes	—	½
		Windsor postmark	—	2½

Date of Issue			Plain £	Illus. £
8 Jan	1969	**BOOKLET:** 10s (Same composition as 16 Sep 1968 but 4d colour change) — 3 panes............	20	75
26 Feb	1969	**REGIONALS:** 4d Colour change — set with 6 regional pmks.	2	5
3 Mar	1969	**BOOKLET:** 2s (Same composition as 16 Sep 1968 but 4d colour change) — 2 panes............	5	50
5 Mar	1969	**DEFINITIVES: Machin High Values** — 2s 6d, 5s, 10s, £1	2	10
		Windsor F.D.I. postmark	3	15
		Stampex special handstamp	4	25
		ditto Stampex official cover	—	25
27 Aug	1969	**MULTI-VALUE COIL STRIP:** 1s (2×2d, 3d, 1d, 4d)	½	1
		Windsor postmark	1	4
1 Dec	1969	**STAMPS FOR COOKS £1 BOOKLET** 4 panes (15×5d; 2 panes of 15×4d; 6×4d, 6×1d, 3×5d)		
		Set of 4 panes — MMBoard, Thames Ditton handstamp	7	40
		Se-tenant strip from multi-value pane — MMB handstamp .	2	15
10 Dec	1969	**DEFINITIVE:** 1s 6d Phosphor coated paper —		
		Southampton postmark	1	5
3 Mar	1970	**BOOKLET:** 5s 'PHILYMPIA' (2 panes 6×5d) — one pane	5	40
		Stampex special handstamp		
28 Sep	1970	**REGIONAL:** Scotland 9d, unwatermarked	3	20
16 Nov	1970	**DEFINITIVE:** 1s 9d PVA Gum	n.k.	150

QUEEN ELIZABETH II DECIMAL ISSUES (1970 to date)

All prices for illustrated covers.			Windsor Postmark £	Other pmks £
17 Jun	1970	**TO PAY LABELS:** 10p, 20p, 50p, £1 New values	—	450
17 Jun	1970	**DEFINITIVES:** 10p, 20p, 50p, New values	4	1
		First Issue of British Decimal Stamps, Windsor special handstamp...	9	—

15 FEB 1971: 1st Class 3p, 2nd Class 2½p

15 Feb	1971	**DEFINITIVES:** ½p, 1p, 1½p, 2p, 2½p, 3p, 3½p, 4p, 5p, 6p, 7½p, 9p New values		
		F.D.I. postmarks with 'Delayed by GPO Strike' cachets......	2½	1
		Authentic C.D.S. postmarks — a few sub offices were open during strike....................................	—	12
		F.P.O. (Field Post Offices) pmks — open during strike ..	—	7
15 Feb	1971	**BOOKLETS:** 10p (2×2p + 2×½p; 2×1p + 2×1½p) Vertical format		
		25p (5×2½p + label; 4×2½p + 2 labels; 5×½p + label)		
		30p (2 identical panes of 5×3p + label)		
		50p (6×3p; 4×3p + 2×2½p side band; 5×2½p (centre band) + label; 5×½p + label)		
		Set of ten panes (with GPO strike cachets)	90	40
		Set of three se-tenant panes only (with GPO strike cachets).	40	15
15 Feb	1971	**MULTI-VALUE COIL STRIP:** 5p (2×½p; 2×1p; 1×2p) with GPO strike cachet	4	2
		Note: these were not officially available until 11 March 1971 — covers sometimes occur with this issue date		
15 Feb	1971	**COIL STRIPS:** 2½p Vertical or Horizontal..............	—	500
		3p Vertical or Horizontal................	—	500
15 Feb	1971	**TO PAY LABELS:** ½p, 1p, 2p, 3p, 4p, 5p, New values		
		Authentic C.D.S. postmarks — 15 February 1971 .	—	350
		Official date of release — 11 March 1971 with C.D.S. postmarks................................	—	75

Date of Issue		Windsor Postmark £	Other pmks £
7 Jul 1971	**REGIONALS:** 2½p, 3p, 5p, 7½p (Wales, Scot., N.I., I.O.M.) Regional special F.D.I. handstamps — set of four covers......	—	8
14 Jul 1971	**BOOKLET:** 10p (2×2p + 2×½p; 2×1p + 2×1½p) Horizontal format	300	250
23 Jul 1971	**BOOKLET:** 30p (2 identical panes 5×3p + label imperf in margin*) One pane on cover	150	100
11 Aug 1971	**DEFINITIVE:** 10p Small design — change of format	2	½
17 Sep 1971	**BOOKLETS:** 25p (5×2½p + label; 4×2½p + 2 labels; 5×½p + label) Labels imperf in margin* — 3 panes on cover .. 50p — Contains 4 panes, only two of which differ from 17th February issue: labels imperf in margin* (5×2½p (centre band) + label and 5×½p + label) 2 panes on cover	150 150	100 100
	Changes introduced as an aid to the blind — so that they could distinguish the stamps from the labels.		
24 Dec 1971	**CHRISTMAS BOOKLETS** 25p (3 panes 5×½p + label; 5×2½p + label; 4×2½p + 2 labels) 50p (1 pane only: 5×2½p + label – different to 25p booklet) Four panes on set of covers .... ditto more commonly found with Southampton postmark ... *The remaining 50p panes were as previously issued in February (6×3p; 4×3p + 2×2½p) or duplicated the above (5×½p + label)*	120 —	75 75
24 May 1972	**WEDGWOOD £1 BOOKLET:** 4 panes (12×3p; 6×2½p + 6×3p; 9×2½p; 2×2½p + 4×½p) Complete panes on set of 4 covers — Barlaston special h/s ... Complete panes on set of 4 covers – Bureau special h/s Se-tenant pane + 2 se-tenant strips — Barlaston h/s .... Se-tenant pane + 2 se-tenant strips — Bureau h/s .... *N.B. General Note re 'Prestige Booklets' – Prices are for covers bearing the complete pane of stamps + descriptive text. Covers with stamps only are worth considerably less.*	— — — —	90 60 20 10
23 Aug 1972	**DEFINITIVE:** 3p Gum Arabic	—	40
13 Sep 1972	**DEFINITIVE:** 2½p Gum Arabic	—	40
22 Sep 1972	**DEFINITIVE:** ½p Gum Arabic	—	40
22 Sep 1972	**REGIONALS:** 2½p (Scottish) Gum Arabic .... 2½p (Welsh) Gum Arabic .... All three stamps on one cover — any postmark	— —	40 40 100
31 Oct 1972	**DEFINITIVE:** 4p Gum Arabic	—	60
6 Dec 1972	**DEFINITIVE:** £1 — Redrawn '£' sign F.D.I. postmarks.................... Larger style Windsor F.D.I. postmark..................	7 20	2 —
14 Dec 1972	**REGIONAL:** 3p (Scottish) Gum Arabic	—	40
1 Feb 1973	**DEFINITIVE:** 50p Phosphor coated paper Southampton C.D.S. postmark.......................... Other C.D.S. postmarks .... National Postal Museum special handstamp	— — —	110 90 130
2 Apr 1973	**TO PAY LABEL:** £5 New value..............................	—	450
6 Jun 1973	**DEFINITIVE:** 6p Gum Arabic	—	100
6 Jun 1973	**REGIONAL:** 3p (Welsh) Gum Arabic .... Both stamps on one cover — any postmark	— —	40 90
22 Aug 1973	**DEFINITIVE:** 3½p PVA/Dextrin Gum..................	—	40

Date of Issue			Windsor Postmark £	Other pmks £
		10 SEP 1973: 1st Class 3½p, 2nd Class 3p		
10 Sep	1973	**DEFINITIVE:** 3p One phosphor band (centre)..........	20	10
10 Sep	1973	**DEFINITIVES:** 3p GA + 3p PVA/Dextrin Gum ⎫ 1p, 2p PVA/Dextrin Gum ⎭	50	—
27 Sep	1973	**DEFINITIVE:** £1 'Contractors' paper......................	—	500
9 Oct	1973	**DEFINITIVE:** ½p PVA/Dextrin Gum......................	—	40
24 Oct	1973	**DEFINITIVES:** 4½p, 5½p, 8p New values...............	2	½
30 Oct	1973	**DEFINITIVE:** 6p PVA/Dextrin Gum........................	—	125
12 Nov	1973	**DEFINITIVES:** 4p, 10p PVA/Dextrin Gum..............	—	125
14 Nov	1973	**BOOKLET:** 50p (2 identical panes: 5×3½p + blank label, with 1 pane 5×3p (centre band) + blank label) Two different panes on cover...............................	130	75
30 Nov	1973	**DEFINITIVE:** 20p 'Contractors' paper....................	—	400
12 Dec	1973	**BOOKLET:** 35p (2 identical panes: 5×3½p + blank label) One pane on cover......................................	130	70
23 Jan	1974	**REGIONALS:** 3p One phos band + 3½p, 5½p, 8p New values (Wales, Scotland, N.I.) Regional special F.D.I. handstamps — set of three covers	—	4
10 Feb	1974	**SELF ADHESIVE LABELS:** ½p, 1p, 1½p, (3p+5p),(½p+5p)	—	250
20 Feb	1974	**DEFINITIVE:** 50p 'Contractors' paper....................	—	400
22 Mar	1974	**DEFINITIVE:** 9p PVA/Dextrin Gum.......................	—	125
19 Jun	1974	**SELF ADHESIVE LABELS:** 3p, 3½p..................	—	50
		24 JUN 1974: 1st Class 4½p, 2nd Class 3½p		
24 Jun	1974	**DEFINITIVE:** 3½p One phosphor band (centre).......	25	4
21 Aug	1974	**TO PAY LABEL:** 7p New value..............................	—	40
4 Sep	1974	**DEFINITIVE:** 6½p (2 phosphor bands) New value ...	2½	1
9 Oct	1974	**BOOKLET:** 45p (2 identical panes: 5×4½p + blank label) One pane on cover..	100	60
23 Oct	1974	**BOOKLET:** 35p (2 identical panes: 5×3½p centre phosphor band + blank label) One pane on cover..	100	60
6 Nov	1974	**REGIONALS:** 3½p (One phosphor band) + 4½p New value (Wales, Scotland, N.I.) Regional special F.D.I. handstamps — set of three covers	—	3
13 Nov	1974	**DEFINITIVE:** 4½p Experimental phosphor coated paper with two phosphor bands added Windsor postmark.. *Stamps were distributed to Cambridge, Aberdeen and Norwich — hence these postmarks have particular relevance* ....each	12 —	3 20
15 Jan	1975	**DEFINITIVE:** 7p New value (two phosphor bands)... 7p New value (phosphor omitted)	1 20	½ 7½

149

Date of Issue			Windsor Postmark £	Other pmks £

17 MAR 1975: 1st Class 7p, 2nd Class 5½p

17 Mar	1975	**DEFINITIVE:** 5½p One phosphor band (centre).......	4	1
21 May	1975	**DEFINITIVE:** 2½p Two phosphor bands.................	10	4
21 May	1975	**REGIONALS:** 5½p One centre band (Wales, Scot., N.I.)		
		Set of three regional postmarks — no special		
		handstamps were available	—	10
		N.I. only — Ulster Crusade slogan......................	—	10
		The above four stamps (2½p + 3×5½p)		
		Regionals) on one cover	10	3
18 Jun	1975	**TO PAY LABEL:** 11p New value............................	—	40
24 Sep	1975	**DEFINITIVES:** 6½p One centre phosphor band; 8½p Two phosphor bands – new value ⎫	1	½

29 SEP 1975: 1st Class 8½p, 2nd Class 6½p

24 Nov	1975	**SPEEDPOST:** First Day of new service	—	25
3 Dec	1975	**MULTI-VALUE COIL STRIP:** 10p (2×½p, 1p, 2p, and 6p)	4	1
14 Jan	1976	**REGIONALS:** 6½p, 8½p New values (Wales, Scot., N.I.) Regional special F.D.I. handstamps — set of three covers	—	2½
28 Jan	1976	**COIL STRIPS:** 6½p and 8½p vertical.....................	n.k.	150
25 Feb	1976	**DEFINITIVES:** 9½p, 10½p, 11p, New values ⎫ 9p, 10p, Colour changes ⎬ 20p Small format ⎭	5	2
		Stampex special handstamp	—	7
10 Mar	1976	**BOOKLET:** 10p (2×½p; 3×1p and 1×6p) One pane on cover..	3	1
24 Mar	1976	**DEFINITIVE:** 8½p Experimental phosphor coated paper ...	1½	½
14 Jul	1976	**BOOKLETS:** 65p (10×6½p); 85p (10×8½p) Two panes on pair of covers...............................	80	30
13 Oct	1976	**COIL STRIPS:** 6½p and 8½p horizontal..................	100	80
20 Oct	1976	**REGIONALS:** 10p, 11p New values (Wales, Scotland, N.I.) Regional special F.D.I. handstamps — set of three covers	—	3
24 Jan	1977	**SPEEDPOST:** Extension of service........................	—	125
26 Jan	1977	**BOOKLETS:** 2 @ 50p (2×½p; 2×1p; 2×6½p; 4×8½p) both panes, right and left format (mirror image) on cover	12	4
26 Jan	1977	**DEFINITIVES:** 6½p One left phosphor band ⎫ from above 6½p One right phosphor band ⎬ booklet	12	2
2 Feb	1977	**DEFINITIVES:** 50p Small design — change of format	2	1
		£1 Design change; £2, £5 New values	16	8
		All four values on one cover	20	9

13 JUN 1977: 1st Class 9p, 2nd Class 7p

13 Jun	1977	**BOOKLETS:** 2 @ 50p (2×1p; 3×7p; 3×9p) both panes, right and left format (mirror image) 70p (10×7p); 90p (10×9p) pair on cover	8 20	4 9
13 Jun	1977	**DEFINITIVES:** 7p One left phos. band ⎫ from above 7p One right phos. band ⎬ 50p bkt.	5	1½

1977

Date of Issue		Windsor Postmark £	Other pmks £
13 Jun 1977	**COIL STRIPS:** 7p, 9p Vertical — pair on cover..........	100	45
13 Jun 1977	**SACHET BOOKLETS:** 30p, 60p — pair	150	—
31 Oct 1977	**DEFINITIVES:** 6p, 7p, 9p, 10p Halley Press	225	175
16 Nov 1977	**COIL STRIPS:** 7p, 9p Horizontal — pair on cover	100	45
14 Dec 1977	**MULTI-VALUE COIL STRIP:** 10p (2×½p; 2×1p; and 7p)	1½	½
14 Dec 1977	**DEFINITIVES:** ½p Centre phosphor band } from above 1p Centre phosphor band } coil	1	½
18 Jan 1978	**REGIONALS:** 7p, 9p, 10½p New Values (Wales, Scot., N.I.) Regional special F.D.I. handstamps — set of three covers	—	5
8 Feb 1978	**BOOKLET:** 10p (2×½p; 2×1p; 1×7p + label) One pane on cover...	1	½
26 Apr 1978	**DEFINITIVE:** 10½p Colour change	1	½
15 Nov 1978	**CHRISTMAS BOOKLET:** £1.60 (10×9p; 10×7p) ..	5	2
5 Feb 1979	**BOOKLETS:** 70p (10×7p) Kedleston Hall; 90p (10×9p) Tramway Museum, Crich. Pair of covers with Derby pmk.	—	90
	Pair of covers with appropriate pmks.	—	100
	Issued in conjunction with the opening of Derby Mechanised Letter Office, and to promote the use of postcodes in Derby area.		
15 Aug 1979	**DEFINITIVES:** 11½p, 13p, 15p New values	1	½
	20 AUG 1979: 1st Class 10p, 2nd Class 8p		
20 Aug 1979	**DEFINITIVE:** 8p Centre phosphor band	½	¼
20 Aug 1979	**DEFINITIVE:** 10p Phosphor coated paper + two phos. bands	1	½
	Gutter pair on cover	2	¾
28 Aug 1979	**BOOKLETS:** 2 @ 50p (2×2p; 2×8p; 3×10p + label) Both panes, right and left format (mirror image) on cover....	5	2
28 Aug 1979	**DEFINITIVES:** 8p One left phosphor band } from above 8p One right phosphor band } booklet	1	½
3 Oct 1979	**BOOKLETS:** 80p (10×8p); £1 (10×10p) pair on cover	5	2½
3 Oct 1979	**DEFINITIVE:** 10p Preprinted phos. paper from £1 bkt. above	1	½
10 Oct 1979	**DEFINITIVES:** 1p, 2p Preprinted phosphor paper } 5p, 20p Phosphor coated paper }	1	½
17 Oct 1979	**BOOKLET:** 10p (2×1p; 1×8p + label) 'London 1980'......	1	½
14 Nov 1979	**CHRISTMAS BOOKLET:** £1.80 (10×10p; 10×8p) ..	3½	2
14 Nov 1979	**COIL STRIPS:** 8p, 10p Vertical — pair on cover	40	10
12 Dec 1979	**DEFINITIVES:** 1p, 2p Phosphor coated paper } 8p Enschedé printing }	1	½
16 Jan 1980	**MULTI-VALUE COIL STRIP:** 10p (2×1p, 8p + two labels)	1	½
30 Jan 1980	**DEFINITIVES:** 4p Colour change } 12p, 13½p, 17p, 17½p, 75p New values }	3	1½
	4 FEB 1980: 1st Class 12p, 2nd Class 10p		
4 Feb 1980	**DEFINITIVE:** 10p Centre phosphor band..............	1	½
	10p ditto on Phosphor Coated Paper..	75	25
4 Feb 1980	**BOOKLETS:** 2 @ 50p (3×2p; 2×10p; 2×12p + label) both panes, right and left format (mirror image)	8	3
	£1 (10×10p); £1.20 (10×12p) pair on cover	10	4

Date of Issue			Windsor Postmark £	Other pmks £

Date of Issue		Windsor Postmark £	Other pmks £
4 Feb 1980	**DEFINITIVES:** 10p One left phos. band ⎫ from 50p 10p One right phos. band ⎰ bkt. above	2	1
	12p Two phos. bands — from 50p bkt. above	2½	1
16 Apr 1980	**WEDGWOOD £3 BOOKLET:** 4 panes (9×12p; 9×10p; 6×2p; 4×12p + 4×10p + 1×2p)		
	Complete panes on set of 4 covers — Barlaston special h/s ...	—	7
	Complete panes on set of 4 covers — Bureau special h/s	—	6
	Se-tenant pane only — Barlaston special handstamp..........	—	2
	Se-tenant pane only — Bureau special handstamp.............	—	1
	N.B. prices for complete pane (stamps and illustrations)		
21 May 1980	**DEFINITIVES:** 2p, 5p, House of Questa printing ⎫ 20p Waddington printing ⎬ 50p Non-phosphor ⎭	2	1
11 Jun 1980	**COIL STRIPS:** 10p and 12p from coils — pair on cover	50	40
25 Jun 1980	**BOOKLETS:** 2 @ 50p Chambon Press printing (3×2p; 2×10p; 2×12p + label) Both panes, right and left format (mirror image) on cover....	60	40
23 Jul 1980	**REGIONALS:** 10p Centre band; 12p, 13½p, 15p (Wales, Scotland, N.I.) Regional F.D.I. special handstamps — set of three covers	—	6
27 Aug 1980	**BOOKLET:** 10p (2×1p; 1×8p + label) 'London 1980' Chambon Press Printing — one pane on cover ...	2	1
27 Aug 1980	**DEFINITIVE:** 11p Phosphor coated paper..............	3	2
22 Oct 1980	**DEFINITIVES:** 3p Colour change, 22p New value....	1	½
22 Oct 1980	**DEFINITIVES:** -do- on both PCP1 and PCP2 (4 vals)........	10	5
12 Nov 1980	**CHRISTMAS BOOKLET:** £2.20 (10×12p; 10×10p)	4½	3
10 Dec 1980	**DEFINITIVE:** ½p Phosphor coated paper	1	½
14 Jan 1981	**DEFINITIVES:** 2½p, 11½p Colour changes; ⎫ 14p, 15½p, 18p, 25p New values ⎭	1½	1
	26 JAN 1981: 1st Class 14p, 2nd Class 11½p		
26 Jan 1981	**BOOKLETS:** 2 @ 50p (1×½p; 1×1p; 3×11½p; 1×14p) Both panes, right and left format (mirror image) £1.15 (10×11½p); £1.40 (10×14p) pair on cover	3½ 6	1½ 3
26 Jan 1981	**DEFINITIVES:** 11½p One left phos. band ⎫ from 50p 11½p One right phos. band ⎰ bkt. above	2	1
	14p Two phos. bands — from 50p bkt. above	2	1
11 Mar 1981	**COIL STRIPS:** 11½p and 14p stamps from coil — pair on cover.................................	50	35
8 Apr 1981	**REGIONALS:** 11½p, 14p, 18p, 22p New values (Wales, Scotland, N.I.) Regional F.D.I. special handstamps — set of three covers	—	6
6 May 1981	**BOOKLET:** £1.30 (4×11½p; 6×14p) — pane on cover	3	1½
	National Stamp Day — Birmingham special handstamp	—	3
	National Stamp Day — British Library special handstamp ..	—	3
	National Stamp Day — Cameo Stamp Centre special handstamp .	—	3
	National Stamp Day — London EC special handstamp	—	3
26 Aug 1981	**BOOKLETS:** 2 @ 50p (3×2½p; 2×4p; 3×11½p) Both panes, right and left format (mirror image) on cover....	7	2
26 Aug 1981	**DEFINITIVES:** 2½p, 4p both with two phosphor bands — from 50p booklet above	2	1

152

2 Sep 1981 MULTI-VALUE COIL: 11½p (1×2½p + 3×3p) 'Readers Digest'   2   1

Note: Although issued in June for a Readers Digest promotion, these were not placed on sale by the P.O. until 2nd September. Covers with June, July and August dates do exist and will command a premium. (June dates from £50)

11 Nov 1981 CHRISTMAS BOOKLET: £2.55 (10×11½p; 10×14p)   7   3

7 Dec 1981 DEFINITIVES: 4p, 20p, Phosphor coated paper Waddington printing   15   5

30 Dec 1981 MULTI-VALUE COIL: 12½p (1×½p + 3×4p) 'Readers Digest'   2   1

27 Jan 1982 DEFINITIVES: 5p Colour change,
12½p, 16½p, 19½p, 26p, 29p New values }   4   2

---

1 FEB 1982: 1st Class 15½p, 2nd Class 12½p

---

1 Feb 1982 BOOKLETS: 2 @ 50p (1×½p; 4×3p; 3×12½p)   4   1½
     Both panes, right and left format (mirror image)   4   1½
     £1.25 (10×12½p); £1.55 (10×15½p) pair...   6   3
     £1.43 (4×12½p + 6×15½p)...............   4   1½

1 Feb 1982 DEFINITIVES: 12½p One left phos. band
     12½p One right phos. band   } from 50p
     3p Two phos. bands   } bkt. above   3   1
     ½p Two phos. bands (short) }
     15½p Two phos. bands — from £1.43 bkt. }

1 Feb 1982 COIL STRIPS: 12½p and 15½p stamps from coil — pair on cover   40   25

24 Feb 1982 REGIONALS: 12½p, 15½p, 19½p, 26p New values (Wales, Scotland, N.I.)
     Regional F.D.I. special handstamps — set of three covers ....   —   6

19 May 1982 STANLEY GIBBONS £4 BOOKLET: 4 panes
     (6×12½p; 7×12½p + 1×2p + 1×3p; 6×15½p; 9×15½p)
     Complete panes on set of 4 covers — London WC special h/s   —   10
     Complete panes on set of 4 covers — Plymouth special h/s...   —   10
     Complete panes on set of 4 covers — Bureau special h/s ......   —   8
     Se-tenant pane only — London WC special handstamp.......   —   3
     Se-tenant pane only — Plymouth special handstamp ....   —   3
     Se-tenant pane only — Philatelic Bureau special h/s ....   —   2½
     N.B. Prices for complete panes (stamps and text).

9 Jun 1982 TO PAY LABELS: 1p, 2p, 3p, 4p, 5p, 10p, 20p, 25p, 50p, £1, £2, £5, New style
     Stratford-upon-Avon permanent pictorial handstamp..   —   300

10 Nov 1982 CHRISTMAS BOOKLET: £2.50, (10×12½p; 10×15½p)   6   3
     These were sold at a discount of 30p (value of stamps £2.80) and the stamps were printed on the reverse with a star.

30 Mar 1983 DEFINITIVES: 3½p, 17p Colour changes
16p, 20½p, 23p, 28p, 31p New values }   5   3

---

5 APR 1983: 1st Class 16p, 2nd Class 12½p

---

5 Apr 1983 BOOKLETS: 50p (2×1p; 3×3½p; 3×12½p).............   2   1
     Gloucester special handstamp ....   —   5
     ditto on Benham 'silk' official cover .....   —   6
     booklet cover depicts Gloucester Old Spot Pig
     £1.25 no change from 1 Feb 1982 ....   —   —
     £1.60 (10×16p).............................   5   3
     £1.46 (4×12½p; 6×16p)   5   3

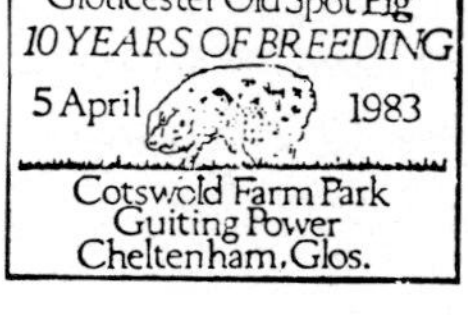

Date of Issue			Windsor Postmark £	Other pmks £

5 Apr 1983 **DEFINITIVES:** 1p Centre band ⎫ from 50p 3½p Centre band ⎬ bkt. above 16p Two phos. bands — from £1.46 bkt. ⎭ — **2** — **1**

20 Apr 1983 **COIL STRIP:** 16p stamp from coil **10** **3**

27 Apr 1983 **REGIONALS:** 16p, 20½p, 28p New values (Wales, Scotland, N.I.)
Regional F.D.I. special handstamps — set of three covers .... — **5**

3 Aug 1983 **PARCEL POST DEFINITIVE:** £1.30 .... **6** **3½**
Philatelic Bureau special handstamp .... — **4**
London E16 special handstamp .... — **6**
Parcel, First Day of Sale, Centenary Postcard Sailsbury special h/s .... — **10**
Hampstead C.D.S. .... — **17**
Hampstead C.D.S. (Pre-released 1st Aug: date of centenary)... — **40**

10 Aug 1983 **BOOKLET:** £1.45 (10×16p)................................... **7½** **3**
Sold at 15p discount and printed with letter 'D' on reverse.

10 Aug 1983 **DEFINITIVE:** 16p 'D' Underprint from above booklet .. **3** **1½**

14 Sep 1983 **ROYAL MINT £4 BOOKLET:** 4 panes
(2 @ 6×12½p; 9×16p; 6×16p + 2×3½p + 1×3p)
Complete panes on set of 4 covers — Llantrisant special h/s . — **10**
Complete panes on set of 4 covers — Bureau special h/s — **8**
Se-tenant pane only — Llantrisant special handstamp . — **4**
Se-tenant pane only — Bureau special handstamp .... — **2**
N.B. Prices for complete panes (stamps and illustrations).

2 Nov 1983 **REGIONAL:** 16p (Scotland) Advanced coated paper
Edinburgh Philatelic Counter handstamp .... — **1**

9 Nov 1983 **CHRISTMAS BOOKLET:** £2.20 (20×12½p) **5** **2**
Sold at a 30p discount with star printed on reverse.

9 Nov 1983 **DEFINITIVE:** 12½p 'Star' Underprint from above bkt. .. **2** **1**

14 Dec 1983 **DEFINITIVE:** 10p Phosphor coated paper............... **2** **1**

10 Jan 1984 **REGIONALS:** 12½p, 16p, (Wales) Perforation change Cardiff Philatelic Counter handstamp ...... — **2**

21 Feb 1984 **DEFINITIVES:** 5p, 75p Perforation change............ **2** **1**

28 Feb 1984 **REGIONALS;** 12½p, 16p (N.I.) Perforation change Belfast Philatelic Counter handstamp .... — **4**

1 May 1984 **'FRAMA' LABELS:** ½p-16p (32 values) on six covers **—** **25**
Cambridge special handstamp .... — **25**
Philatelic Bureau, Edinburgh, special handstamp. — **20**
London EC special handstamp........................... — **25**
Southampton special handstamp .... — **25**
Windsor special handstamp................................ **20** —
Set of six covers with related C.D.S. postmarks..... — **100**

19 Jun 1984 **DEFINITIVES:** 17p Advanced coated paper............ **2** **1**
26p Advanced coated paper............ **75** **n.k.**

10 Jul 1984 **DEFINITIVE:** 2p Perforation change **2½** **1**

14 Aug 1984 **MULTI-VALUE COIL:** 13p (1×1p; 3×4p).............. **1½** **½**

Date of Issue		Windsor Postmark £	Other pmks £
28 Aug 1984	**DEFINITIVES:** 13p, 18p, 22p, Colour changes } 24p, 34p New values	3	2
28 Aug 1984	**PARCEL POST DEFINITIVE:** £1.33 new value	6	3
	Hampstead C.D.S. postmark..............................	—	10
28 Aug 1984	**'FRAMA' LABELS:** 16½p, 17p New values............	2	1

> 3 SEP 1984: 1st Class 17p, 2nd Class 13p

Date of Issue		Windsor Postmark £	Other pmks £
3 Sep 1984	**BOOKLETS:** 2 @ £1.54 (4×13p; 6×17p)		
	Both panes, right and left format (mirror image)	5	3½
	50p (3×1p; 2×4p; 3×13p)	3	1
	£1.30 (10×13p); £1.70 (10×17p) pair on cover ..	15	6
3 Sep 1984	**DEFINITIVES:** 13p One left phos. band 13p One right phos. band } from £1.54 booklet 17p Two phosphor bands	2	1
3 Sep 1984	**COIL STRIPS:** 13p, 17p stamps from coils — pair on cover ..	15	3
4 Sep 1984	**CHRISTIAN HERITAGE £4 BOOKLET:** 4 panes (2 @ 6×13p; 6×17p; 7×17p + 1×13p + 1×10p)		
	Complete panes on set of 4 covers — St. Mary le Strand spec. h/s .	—	10
	Complete panes on set of 4 covers — Canterbury special h/s	—	8
	Complete panes on set of 4 covers — Bureau special handstamp...	—	7
	Complete panes on set of 4 covers — Christian Heritage slogan pmk.	—	35
	Se-tenant pane only — St. Mary Le Strand special h/s........	—	4
	Se-tenant pane only — Canterbury special handstamp	—	3
	Se-tenant pane only — Bureau special handstamp	—	2½
	Se-tenant pane only — Christian Heritage slogan postmark	—	15
	N.B. Prices for complete panes (stamps and illustrations).		
23 Oct 1984	**REGIONALS:** 13p, 17p, 31p New Values } (Wales, 22p Colour change } Scot., N.I.)		
	Regional F.D.I. special handstamps – set of three covers	—	6
8 Jan 1985	**THE TIMES £5 BOOKLET:** 4 panes (9×13p; 6×17p; 9×17p; 2×4p + 4×13p + 2×17p + 1×34p)		
	Complete panes on set of 4 covers — London WC special h/s	—	13
	Complete panes on set of 4 covers — Bureau special h/s	—	10
	Se-tenant pane only — London WC special handstamp.......	—	5
	Se-tenant pane only — Bureau special handstamp.............	—	4
	N.B. Prices are for complete panes (stamps and illustrations).		
8 Jan 1985	**DEFINITIVES:** 4p Left phosphor band 4p Right phosphor band } from above booklet 34p Two bands	3½	2
19 Feb 1985	**DEFINITIVE:** 75p Change of paper	75	n.k.
5 Mar 1985	**BOOKLET:** £1.55 (10×17p)...................................	7½	3
	Sold at 15p discount with letter 'D' printed on reverse.		
5 Mar 1985	**DEFINITIVE:** 17p 'D' Underprint from above booklet ..	2	1
25 Jun 1985	**REGIONAL:** 17p (Scotland) Phosphor coated paper/PVA Gum Edinburgh Philatelic Counter handstamp..........	—	2
16 Jul 1985	**DEFINITIVE:** 10p Advanced coated paper	2	1
17 Sep 1985	**PARCEL POST DEFINITIVE:** £1.41 New value ...	4	2
	With Parcel Post cancellation..............................	—	10
17 Sep 1985	**DEFINITIVE:** 31p Advanced coated paper	2	1

Date of Issue			Windsor Postmark £	Other pmks £
29 Oct	1985	**DEFINITIVES:** 7p, 12p, Colour change	2	1
		These stamps were issued during 'ITALIA' and covers exist with Philatelic Bureau handstamp and special cachet	—	4
29 Oct	1985	**DEFINITIVE:** 12p as above with Star underprint	1½	½
		4 NOV 1985: 1st Class 17p, 2nd Class 12p		
4 Nov	1985	**BOOKLET:** 50p (3×17p + label) .... *Sold at 1p discount with Star printed on reverse.*	2½	1
12 Nov	1985	**COIL STRIP:** 12p Centre Band, Vertical	8	2
4 Dec	1985	**REGIONAL:** 31p (Scotland) Re-drawn lion Edinburgh Philatelic Counter handstamp	—	150
7 Jan	1986	**DEFINITIVE:** 1p Advanced coated paper	2½	1
7 Jan	1986	**REGIONALS:** 12p (Wales, Scotland, N.I.) Colour change Regional F.D.I. special handstamps — set of three covers	—	4
14 Jan	1986	**BOOKLETS:** £1.20 (10×12p Centre Phosphor band) £1.50 (4×12p; 6×17p)	6 6	2½ 2½
14 Jan	1986	**DEFINITIVES:** 12p One left phos. band } from £1.50 12p One right phos. band } booklet	2	1
25 Feb	1986	**DEFINITIVES:** 2p, 5p Advanced Coated Paper	2	1
25 Feb	1986	**REGIONAL:** 17p (Wales and N.I.) Advanced Coated Paper Cardiff and Belfast Philatelic Counter handstamps – pair...	—	2½
18 Mar	1986	**BRITISH RAIL £5 BOOKLET:** 4 panes (9×12p; 6×17p; 9×17p; 2×17p + 6×12p + 1×31p)		
		Complete panes on set of 4 covers — Crewe special handstamp	—	15
		Complete panes on set of 4 covers — Bureau special handstamp...	—	12
		Complete panes on set of 4 covers — T.P.O. postmarks...	—	25
		Complete panes on set of 4 covers — Stratford Railway slogan pmk.	—	30
		Se-tenant pane only — Crewe special handstamp	—	5
		Se-tenant pane only — Bureau special handstamp	—	4
		Se-tenant pane only — T.P.O. postmark	—	7½
		N.B. Prices for complete panes (stamps and illustrations).		
18 Mar	1986	**DEFINITIVE:** 31p Two phos. bands from above booklet.	4	2
29 Apr	1986	**REGIONALS:** 17p, 31p Advanced Coated Paper (Scotland) 12p Perforation change (Scotland) 3 values on cover with Edinburgh Philatelic Counter h/s	—	2½
13 May	1986	**DEFINITIVES:** 4p, 20p Advanced Coated Paper (Questa) ..	2	1
24 Jun	1986	**DEFINITIVES:** 26p, 34p Advanced Coated Paper....	2	1
11 Jul	1986	**DEFINITIVE:** 12p New phosphor ink	40	25
29 Jul	1986	**BOOKLETS;** 50p (2×1p; 4×12p) .... £1 (6×17p) *Sold at 2p discount*	2 7	1 3
12 Aug	1986	**BOOKLET:** 50p (3×17p + label) *Sold at 1p discount..* *Different to 4 Nov 1985 issue — no Star underprint*	2½	1½
2 Sep	1986	**PARCEL POST DEFINITIVE:** £1.50 New value ...	4	2
23 Sep	1986	**COIL STRIP:** 12p (Horizontal format) stamp from coil...	3	1
7 Oct	1986	**DEFINITIVE:** 75p New paper (Coated Papers Ltd.) } 28p Advanced Coated Paper }	5	2

Date of Issue		Windsor Postmark £	Other pmks £

---

20 OCT 1986: 1st Class 18p, 2nd Class 13p

---

20 Oct 1986 **BOOKLETS:** 50p (1×1p; 1×13p; 2×18p) 'Roman Britain' ..... — 2½ / 1
Roman Britain St. Albans, Herts. special h/s.... — / 3½
50p (1×1p; 2×5p; 3×13p) 'Pond Life' .... — 2½ / 1
£1 (1×13p; 5×18p) *Sold at 3p discount* ... — 3 / 2
£1.30 (10×13p); £1.80 (10×18p) pair on cover ... — 12 / 5

20 Oct 1986 **DEFINITIVES:** 5p Centre phos. band } from above
18p Two phos. bands } booklet — 2½ / 1

21 Oct 1986 **COIL STRIPS:** 13p, 18p stamps from coil — pair on cover ... — 20 / 7

4 Nov 1986 **REGIONAL:** 13p (Scotland) 'Questa' printing
Edinburgh Philatelic Counter handstamp .... — / 1½

2 Dec 1986 **CHRISTMAS BOOKLET:** £1.20 (10×13p) .... — 5 / 3
Sold at 10p discount with Star printed on reverse
Glastonbury special handstamps (3 different) ....*each* — / 6

2 Dec 1986 **DEFINITIVE:** 13p 'Star' underprint from above booklet — 2½ / 1½

6 Jan 1987 **REGIONALS:** 18p (Scotland, Wales, N.I.)
Regional F.D.I. special handstamps — set of three covers .... — / 4

27 Jan 1987 **DEFINITIVE:** 13p New phosphor ink .... — 2½ / 1
Introduced to overcome problem of discolouration.

27 Jan 1987 **BOOKLETS:** 2×50p, £1, £1.30 — set of 4 .... — 35 / n.k.
Same format as 20 Oct 1986 but with new phosphor ink.

27 Jan 1987 **REGIONALS:** Advanced Coated Paper (Questa)
Scotland: 22p, 26p, 28p; Wales 26p, 28p, 31p; N.I. 26p, 28p
Regional Philatelic Counter handstamps — set of three ...... — / 6

3 Mar 1987 **P & O £5 BOOKLET:** 4 panes
(6×13p; 9×13p; 9×18p; 1×1p + 2×13p + 5×18p + 1×26p)
Complete panes on set of 4 covers — Falmouth special h/s ... — / 16
Complete panes on set of 4 covers — Bureau special h/s — / 12
Se-tenant pane only — Falmouth special handstamp.... — / 5
Se-tenant pane only — Bureau special handstamp .... — / 4

3 Mar 1987 **DEFINITIVES:** 1p (side phos.); 26p (2 phos. bands)
included in P&O Booklet .... — 3 / 2

14 Apr 1987 **REGIONALS:** 13p (Scotland, Wales, N.I.) Coated Papers Ltd.
31p (N.I.) Advanced Coated Paper
Regional Philatelic Counter handstamps — set of three ...... — / 5
13p (Wales) Dextrim gum — Wales pmk .... — / 12

14 Apr 1987 **BOOKLET:** £1.80 (10×18p) Advanced Coated Paper — 5 / 2½

5 May 1987 **DEFINITIVE:** 3p Advanced Coated Paper .... — 2 / 1

23 Jun 1987 **COIL STRIP:** 1p stamp from strip (1,000×1p) .... — 2 / 1
Specifically issued for large users of post (Readers Digest).
used on 'Readers' Digest' envelope...................... — 10 / n.k.

4 Aug 1987 **'WINDOW' BOOKLETS:** 52p (4×13p); 72p (4×18p);
£1.04 (4×26p); £1.30 (10×13p); £1.80 (10×18p)
Set of five panes on cover .... — 25 / 15
*Each pane is printed with a selvedge around all four sides
giving the appearance of small 'sheetlets'. An operational test
market to assess customer reaction took place at Bristol,
Nottingham, Preston and York.*
Any of these postmarks — set of five covers.......... — / 25

Date of Issue			Windsor Postmark £	Other pmks £
4 Aug	1987	**DEFINITIVE:** 26p Redrawn numeral (from £1.04 Window booklet)............................	20	6
15 Sep	1987	**PARCEL POST DEFINITIVE:** £1.60 New value ...	4	3
29 Sep	1987	**BOOKLETS:** 50p (1×1p, 2×5p, 3×13p)	2½	1
		Belfast pmk. (bkt. fea. Mount Stewart Gdns., N.I.).	—	3
		£1 (1×13p; 5×18p) *Sold at 3p discount* ..	3½	2
		Baker St. C.D.S. (bkt. fea. Sherlock Holmes)...	—	25
		These two booklets were produced with straight edges (i.e. outer long edges had no perforations) – in an attempt to satisfy philatelists requirements.		
29 Sep	1987	**DEFINITIVES:** 1p, 5p, 13p, 2 @ 18p Values with single straight edge from the above booklets	3	2
9 Feb	1988	**FINANCIAL TIMES £5 BOOKLET:** 4 panes (6×13p; 6×18p; 9×18p; 6×13p + 1×18p + 1×22p + 1×34p)		
		Complete panes on set of 4 covers — London EC4 special h/s	—	15
		Complete panes on set of 4 covers — Bureau special h/s	—	12
		Complete panes on set of 4 covers — Relevant C.D.S.	—	30
		Se-tenant pane only — London EC4 special handstamp	—	5
		Se-tenant pane only — Bureau special handstamp	—	4
		Se-tenant pane only — Relevant C.D.S.	—	12
9 Feb	1988	**DEFINITIVES:** 13p One phos. right 13p One phos. left 13p Centre phos. band 18p, 22p, 34p } New Questa printing from above booklet	5	4
23 Feb	1988	**DEFINITIVES:** 2p, 75p Redrawn numerals	2	1
		2p printed on paper supplied by Henry and Leigh Slater.		
18 Mar	1988	**MULTI-VALUE COIL STRIP:** 13p (1×1p; 3×4p) ACP	20	10
29 Mar	1988	**REGIONALS:** 18p (Scot., Wales) Henry and Leigh Slater paper		
		Philatelic Counter handstamps — pair of covers	—	2½
3 May	1988	**COIL STRIP:** 18p stamp from coil...........................	2	1
26 Jul	1988	**DEFINITIVES:** 2p, 4p, 5p, 75p Harrison's printing...	2½	1½
26 Jul	1988	**COIL STRIP:** 1p stamp from coil............................	5	2
23 Aug	1988	**DEFINITIVES:** 14p, 19p, 23p, 27p, 32p, 35p New values 20p, 28p Colour changes }	5	3
23 Aug	1988	**'WINDOW' BOOKLETS:** 56p (4×14p); 76p (4×19p); £1.08 (4×27p); £1.40 (10×14p); £1.90 (10×19p)		
		Set of five panes on cover..................................	25	15
		Issued on trial at Bristol, Nottingham, Preston and York.		
		Set of five panes with any of these postmarks	—	30

5 SEP 1988: 1st Class 19p, 2nd Class 14p

5 Sep	1988	**BOOKLETS:** 50p (1×14p; 2×19p + label) *Sold at 2p discount* .	2½	1½
		£1 (2×14p; 4×19p) *Sold at 4p discount* ...	3½	2
		£1.40 (10×14p); £1.90 (10×19p) pair on cover ...	10	7
5 Sep	1988	**COIL STRIPS:** 14p sideways and longways delivery, 19p		
		The three stamps on cover	8	3
5 Sep	1988	**MULTI-VALUE COIL STRIP:** 14p (1×2p; 3×4p)...	3	1

Date of Issue			Windsor Postmark £	Other pmks £
11 Oct	1988	**'WINDOW' BOOKLETS:** 56p, 76p, £1.08, £1.40, £1.90 Set	30	10
		Stamp contents as for 23 Aug issue, but selvedge replaced by stright edges at top and bottom of stamp panes. Printed by Harrisons.		
		£1.40, £1.90 Pair	15	8
		Printed by Questa — no selvedge, stamps fully perforated. These are the first 14p and 19p litho printings.		
11 Oct	1988	**DEFINITIVES:** 14p, 19p Litho printing (Questa)	2	1
		14p, 19p, 27p Straight edges, top and bottom (Harrison)	5	3
18 Oct	1988	**DEFINITIVES:** £1 (Carrickfergus Castle); £1.50 (Caernarfon Castle); £2 (Edinburgh Castle); £5 (Windsor Castle)		
		First Day of Issue, Philatelic Bureau special h/s....	—	20
		First Day of Issue, Windsor special handstamp.....	25	—
		*Castle High Values, Carrickfergus special handstamp ..	—	30
		*Castle High Values, Caernarfon special handstamp	—	30
		*Castle High Values, Edinburgh special handstamp	—	30
		*Castle High Values, Windsor special handstamp	30	—
		*Special handstamp on Benham official cover ....*each*	35	35
		Set of 4 single stamp covers with appropriate postmarks	—	25
		Windsor C.D.S. pmk.	125	—
		Windsor Castle C.D.S.	175	—
		Edinburgh C.D.S. pmk.	—	125
		Caernarfon C.D.S. pmk	—	150
		Carrickfergus C.D.S. pmk..................................	—	250
		Set of 4 single stamp covers with appropriate C.D.S. postmarks	—	200
8 Nov	1988	**REGIONALS:** 14p Colour change; 19p, 23p, 32p New values (Scotland, Wales, N.I.) Regional F.D.I. special handstamps — set of three.	—	6
24 Jan	1989	**'WINDOW' BOOKLETS:** 56p, 76p	4	2
		Stamp contents as for 23 Aug 1988 but panes have three straight edges.		
21 Mar	1989	**SCOTS CONNECTION £5 BOOKLET:** 4 panes (6×14p; 6×19p; 9×19p; 5×14p + 2×19p + 1×23p + label)		
		Complete panes on set of 4 covers — Inverness special h/s ...	—	15
		Complete panes on set of 4 covers — Bureau special h/s	—	12
		Se-tenant pane only — Inverness special handstamp....	—	5
		Se-tenant pane only — Bureau special handstamp	—	4
21 Mar	1989	**DEFINITIVES:** 14p (side phos. band); 19p, 23p (2 phos. bands) From above booklet	5	3
25 Apr	1989	**BOOKLET:** £1 (2×14p; 4×19p) *Sold at 4p discount*	4	2
		ditto Walsall Security Printers special handstamp	—	6
		ditto Wallsal C.D.S. pmk.	—	30
		printed by Walsall Security Printers with straight edges		
25 Apr	1989	**DEFINITIVES:** 14p, 19p Straight edged (Walsall printers)	2	1
25 Apr	1989	**REGIONAL:** 19p (Scotland) Coated Papers Ltd. Edinburgh Philatelic Counter handstamp	—	2
20 Jun	1989	**REGIONAL:** 19p (Wales) Coated Papers Ltd. Cardiff Philatelic Counter handstamp	—	2
26 Jun	1989	**'WINDOW' BOOKLET:** £1.90 (10×19p) Jumelle press .	5	2
10 Jul	1989	**'WINDOW' BOOKLET:** £1.40 (10×14p) Jumelle press .	4	2
8 Aug	1989	**BOOKLET:** 50p Chambon press	2	1
		Contents the same as 5 Sep 1988 issue		

Date of Issue		Windsor Postmark £	Other pmks £

22 Aug 1989 'WINDOW' BOOKLETS: Non-Value Indicators
56p (4×2nd Class stamps) ⎫
76p (4×1st Class stamps) ⎬ Walsall Security printers
£1.40 (10×2nd Class stamps) ⎫
£1.90 (10×1st Class stamps) ⎬ Harrison Printers

Set of four panes on cover — Windsor special h/s		20	—
Set of four panes on cover — Philatelic Bureau special h/s ...		—	15

22 Aug 1989 NON-VALUE INDICATORS:

1st, 2nd (Walsall) — 2 values on cover		3	1
1st, 2nd (Harrison) — 2 values on cover		3	1

19 Sep 1989 'WINDOW' BOOKLETS: Non-Value Indicators
£1.40 (10×2nd Class) ⎫
£1.90 (10×1st Class) ⎬ Questa Printers: pair of covers

		10	7

19 Sep 1989 NON-VALUE INDICATORS:

1st, 2nd (Questa) — 2 values on cover		3	1

26 Sep 1989 DEFINITIVES: 15p, 20p, 24p, 29p, 34p Colour changes ⎫
30p, 37p New values ⎬

		5	3

2 OCT 1989: 1st Class 20p, 2nd Class 15p

2 Oct 1989 BOOKLETS: 50p (2×15p; 1×20p; + label) ....

		2	1½
£1 (5×20p + label)		3	2

2 Oct 1989 'WINDOW' BOOKLET:

£1.16 (4×29p) for overseas postcards		3	2

10 Oct 1989 MULTI-VALUE COIL STRIP: 15p (1×3p; 3×4p)...

		2	1

Produced for special mailings by large users.

16 Oct 1989 COIL STRIPS: 15p, 20p horizontal ⎫
15p, 20p vertical ⎬ pair of covers

		6	4

28 Nov 1989 REGIONALS: 15p Colour change; 20p, 24p, 34p
New values (Scotland), Wales, N.I.)

Regional F.D.I. special handstamps — set of three		—	7

28 Nov 1989 WINDOW BOOKLET: Non-Value Indicators

60p (4×2nd Class) — Harrisons		15	—

The pane has three straight edges (top, right and bottom).

5 Dec 1989 WINDOW BOOKLET: Non-Value Indicators

80p (4×1st Class) — Harrison		15	—

The pane has three straight edges (top, right and bottom).

10 Jan 1990 PENNY BLACK ANNIVERSARY:
*For the purposes of this catalogue these stamps have been
treated as a commemorative issue. The stamps issued in
booklet form are listed below.*

30 Jan 1990 'WINDOW' BOOKLETS:
Containing Penny Black Anniversary stamps
60p (4×15p) ⎫
80p (4×20p) ⎬ four panes on cover
£1.50 (10×15p) ⎪
£2 (10×20p) ⎭

		20	8

30 Jan 1990 BOOKLETS: Containing Penny Black Anniversary stamps
50p (2×15p; 1×20p + label) — Harrison printing
£1 (5×20p + 1 label) — Harrison printing
£1 (5×20p + 1 label) — Walsall Security Printers

Set of three panes on cover		12	7

13 Mar 1990 DEFINITIVE: 50p Colour variation ....

		2	1

1990

20 Mar 1990 **LONDON LIFE £5 BOOKLET:** 4 panes as follows:
4×20p Alexandra Palace 'Europa' commemoratives
2 panes of 6×20p Penny Black Anniversary stamps
1 pane: 1st, 2nd N.V.I., 15p + 20p; 15p + 20p + 29p
Penny Black Anniversary; 50p + label

	Windsor	Other
Complete set of 4 panes — Tower Hill special h/s	—	15
Complete set of 4 panes — Philatelic Bureau special h/s	—	12
Complete set of 4 panes — Stamp World special h/s	—	16
Complete set of 4 panes — Stamp World on Benham official cover	—	20
Complete set of 4 panes — Victorian Heritage special h/s....	—	16
Complete set of 4 panes — Victorian Heritage on CoverCraft official cover	—	25
Complete set of 4 panes — mixed handstamps as above	—	15
Complete set of 4 panes — relevant C.D.S. or slogan postmarks ...	—	20
Se-tenant pane only — Tower Hill special handstamp...	—	5
Se-tenant pane only — Bureau special handstamp	—	4
Se-tenant pane only — Stamp World special handstamp	—	6
Se-tenant pane only — Stamp World on Benham official cover.....	—	8
Se-tenant pane only — Victorian Heritage special h/s ..	—	6
Se-tenant pane only — Victorian Heritage on CoverCraft official cover	—	8
Se-tenant pane only — Pobjoy Mint Penny Black slogan pmk......	—	8

17 Apr 1990 **'WINDOW' BOOKLETS:**
Penny Black Anniversary stamps:
80p (4×20p) Harrison (previously Walsall) 3 straight edges
£1.50 (10×15p) Questa (previously Harrison) full perfs
£2 (10×20p) Questa (previously Harrison) full perfs
Standard definitives:
£1.16 (4×29p) 3 straight edges

	Windsor	Other
Set of four panes on cover	20	12

17 Apr 1990 **DEFINITIVES:** The above booklets give 8 new varieties

	Windsor	Other
— on one or two covers	7	4

12 Jun 1990 **'WINDOW' BOOKLETS:**
Penny Black Anniversary stamps:
£1.50 (10×15p) Walsall — 3 straight edges
£2 (10×20p) Walsall — 3 straight edges

	Windsor	Other
Set of two panes on cover	10	4

7 Aug 1990 **'WINDOW' BOOKLETS:** Non-Value Indicators
60p (4×2nd Class stamps)
80p (4×1st Class stamps) — Walsall Security printers
£1.50 (10×2nd Class stamps)
£2 (10×1st Class stamps)
£1.50 & £2 (make-up as above) Harrison printers
£1.50 & £2 (make-up as above) Questa printers

	Windsor	Other
— eight panes on cover	40	25

7 Aug 1990 **DEFINITIVES:** The above booklets give 10 new varieties

	Windsor	Other
— on one or more covers	7	4

4 Sep 1990 **DEFINITIVES:** 10p, 17p, 22p, 26p, 27p, 31p Colour changes
33p New value

	Windsor	Other
	4	2½

4 Sep 1990 **BOOKLETS:**

	Windsor	Other
50p (3×17p) *Sold at 1p discount*	2	1
£1 (2×17p; 3×22p)	3	1½

4 Sep 1990 **DEFINITIVES:** 17p (left band); 17p (right band) + 22p
(2 bands) — from above booklets .....

	Windsor	Other
	2	1

17 SEP 1990: 1st Class 22p, 2nd Class 17p

17 Sep 1990 **COIL STRIPS:** 17p, 22p, vertical format ....

	Windsor	Other
	5	4

17 Sep 1990 **'WINDOW' BOOKLET:** £1.24 (4×31p) Walsall printers

	Windsor	Other
	3	2

Date of Issue		Windsor Postmark £	Other pmks £
27 Nov	1990 **MULTI-VALUE COIL STRIP:** 17p (1×5p; 3×4p)...	1	½
4 Dec	1990 **REGIONALS:** 17p, 22p, 26p Colour changes; 37p New value (Scotland, Wales, N.I.)		
	Regional F.D.I. special handstamps — set of three	—	8
19 Mar	1991 **AGATHA CHRISTIE £6 BOOKLET:** 4 panes as follows: (6×22p + 2×33p + label; 9×22p; 2 panes @ 6×17p)		
	Complete set of 4 panes — Philatelic Bureau h/s..........	—	12
	Complete set of 4 panes — Marple, Cheshire h/s..........	—	12
	Complete set of 4 panes — Orient Express h/s.............	—	13
	Complete set of 4 panes — Sunningdale h/s.................	—	13
	-do- various C.D.S. pmks: Sunningdale; Victoria Street; Harrogate; Torquay or Trafalgar Square .*each*	—	20
	4 panes: Take a Bite out of Crime slogan postmark	—	25
	Se-tenant pane only — Philatelic Bureau h/s	—	4
	-do- Marple, Orient Express or Sunningdale h/s..........	—	6
	-do- appropriate CDS pmks as listed above	—	10
	-do- Take a Bite out of Crime slogan postmark	—	12½
14 May	1991 **REGIONALS:** 22p (Wales); 22p, 26p, 37p (Scotland) Coated Papers Ltd — pair of covers with relevant Philatelic Counter handstamps	—	5
6 Aug	1991 **'WINDOW' BOOKLETS:** Non-Value Indicators 68p (4×2nd); 88p (4×1st) ⎫ Walsall £1.70 (10×2nd); £2.20 (10×1st) ⎭ £1.70 (10×2nd); £2.20 (10×1st) ⎫ Questa £2.20 (10×1st) Harrison ⎭		
	set of 7 panes on cover	25	12
10 Sep	1991 **DEFINITIVES:** 6p, 18p, 24p, 28p, 34p, 35p. Colour Changes ⎫ 39p New value ⎭	4½	3
	-do- with 'New Postage Rates' slogan pmk	—	6
10 Sep	1991 **BOOKLETS:** 50p (2×24p; 2×1p) ⎫ pair of covers £1 (4×24p; 2×2p) ⎭	4½	3
	-do- with 'New Postage Rates' slogan pmk	—	6
	16 SEP 1991: 1st Class 24p, 2nd Class 18p		
16 Sep	1991 **'WINDOW' BOOKLETS:** £1.32 (4×33p) ⎫ Walsall £1.56 (4×39p) ⎭ printers	7	3
	-do- with 'New Postage Rates' slogan pmk	—	10
16 Sep	1991 **COIL STRIPS:** 18p, 24p, vertical format	5	4
	-do- with 'New Postage Rates' slogan pmk	—	9
1 Oct	1991 **MULTI-VALUE COIL STRIP:** 18p (2×5p; 2×4p)...	1	½
19 Nov	1991 **DEFINITIVE:** 18p Enschedé printing	1	½
3 Dec	1991 **REGIONALS:** 18p, 24p, 28p Colour changes 39p New value (Scot., Wales, N.I.)		
	Regional F.D.I. special handstamps — set of three	—	8
21 Jan	1992 **DEFINITIVES:** 3p Redrawn value; 50p A.C.P.	2	1
11 Feb	1992 **COIL STRIPS:** 33p, 39p vertical format...................	5	3
25 Feb	1992 **WALES PRESTIGE £6 BOOKLET:** 4 panes as follows: (2×24p + 2×18p + 2×33p + 1×1st Class + 1×2nd Class + label; 4×39p 'Wintertime' stamps; 6×18p; 6×24p)		
	Complete set of 4 panes — Philatelic Bureau h/s..........	—	12
	Complete set of 4 panes — Cardiff handstamp.............	—	12
	Complete set of 4 panes — Stampex, London SW1 h/s .	—	14
	Complete set of 4 panes — Snowdon Mountain Rly h/s.	—	14
	-do- various C.D.S. pmks: Llanberis, The Hayes, Cardiff; St. Fagans, Cardiff; Cardiff etc. ....*each*	—	20
	Se-tenant pane only — Philatelic Bureau h/s	—	4
	Se-tenant pane only — Cardiff handstamp..................	—	5
	Se-tenant pane only — Snowdon Rly, or Stampex h/s ...	—	6
	Se-tenant pane only — relevant C.D.S. pmk.........*from*	—	8

Date of Issue

Date of Issue	Description	Windsor Postmark £	Other pmks £
24 Mar 1992	**DEFINITIVES: SECURITY PRINTING**		
	'CASTLES': £1, £1.50, £2, £5		
	First Day of Issue — Philatelic Bureau h/s	—	14
	First Day of Issue — Windsor handstamp	16	—
	*Castle High Values — Carrickfergus special h/s	—	17
	*Castle High Values — Caernarfon special h/s	—	17
	*Castle High Values — Edinburgh special h/s	—	17
	*Castle High Values — Windsor special h/s	17	—
	*Special handstamps on Benham 'official' covers ..*each*	25	25
	Castle High Values 'Security Printing' Windsor h/s	18	—
	-do- on A. G. Bradbury 'official' cover	27	—
	Windsor C.D.S. or Windsor Great Park C.D.S........*each*	30	—
	Windsor Castle C.D.S.	100	—
	Edinburgh C.D.S. or Caernarfon C.D.S. ....*each*	—	25
	Carrickfergus C.D.S.	—	30
	Set of 4 single stamp covers + relevant C.D.S. pmks	—	35
28 Jul 1992	**BOOKLET:** 78p (Kelloggs) 2×39p	6	3
8 Sep 1992	**'WINDOW' BOOKLET:** £1.32 (4×33p) Dextrin Gum	4	2½
27 Oct 1992	**TOLKEIN PRESTIGE £6 BOOKLET:**		
	4 panes as follows:		
	(2×18p, + 2×24p, + 2×39p, + 1 × 1st Class,		
	+ 1×2nd Class; 6×18p; 2 panes 6×24p)		
	Complete set of 4 panes — Bureau h/s or Oxford h/s	—	13
	Complete set of 4 panes — Rings End, March h/s	—	15
	Complete set of 4 panes — Bagendon, Cirencester h/s..	—	15
	Complete set of 4 panes — Meriden, Middle England h/s....	—	16
	-do- with relevant C.D.S. postmarks	—	20
	Se-tenant pane only ....*from*	—	5
9 Feb 1993	**'WINDOW' BOOKLET:** Non-Value Indicators		
	£2.40 (10×1st Class) — Walsall ACP + PVA	6	3
	The pane has straight edges at the top and bottom.		
9 Feb 1993	**BOOKLET:** £1 (4×24p; 2×2p) – Walsall ACP	4	2
	The pane has straight edges at left and right.		
9 Feb 1993	**DEFINITIVES:** The above booklets give 6 new varieties		
	— on one or more covers	5	2
2 Mar 1993	**DEFINITIVE: £10 BRITANNIA**		
	First Day of Issue — Philatelic Bureau handstamp	—	15
	First Day of Issue — Windsor	16	—
	First Day of Issue — London	—	18
	Windsor handstamp (depicting Britannia)	20	—
	-do- on A. G. Bradbury 'official' cover	25	—
	*£10 High Value — Britannia, Porth handstamp	—	20
	*£10 High Value Definitive — Dover, Kent handstamp	—	20
	*Britannia Way, London SW6 handstamp	—	20
	*Any of the above on Benham 'official' covers	—	25
	Spring Stampex special handstamp	—	20
	Eur-Apex BPT special handstamp	—	20
	Britannia C.D.S. (Bacup or Porth) ....*each*	—	25
	Windsor C.D.S.	25	—
	Windsor Castle C.D.S.	100	—
	Maritime Mail or Paquebot C.D.S. ....*each*	—	22
	Other relevant C.D.S. ....*each*	—	22
6 Apr 1993	**'WINDOW' BOOKLETS:** Non-Value Indicators		
	96p (4×1st Class) ⎫ Harrison		
	£2.40 (10×1st Class) ⎭		
	72p (4×2nd Class) ⎫ Walsall		
	£2.40 (10×1st Class)* ⎭		
	£1.80 (10×2nd Class) Questa		
	— five panes on cover	18	10
	Printed on OBA free paper — perfs all round with		
	elliptical perforations.		
	*Walsall £2.40 — these stamps have two phosphor bands		
	(instead of phosphor coated paper).		
27 Apr 1993	**DEFINITIVE:** 6p Enschedé printing	1	½
8 Jun 1993	**DEFINITIVES:** 1p, 5p, 10p Enschedé printings	1	½

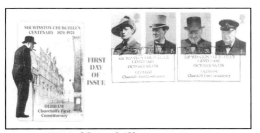

PLEASE MENTION THIS CATALOGUE WHEN REPLYING TO ADVERTISEMENTS

COVER ALBUMS

Safety First!
All Stanley Gibbons cover albums are now supplied with 'Polyprotec' leaves as standard; this offers considerable advantages over traditional materials in that it does not crease or tear easily, does not degrade and gives considerable protection against ultra-violet light.

THE NEW PIONEER COVER ALBUM
A fully padded binder in a choice of black, green or red. Holds up to 40 covers in a high capacity, low priced album, ideal for the beginner.

THE MALVERN COVER ALBUM
Another great value album suitable for collectors at all levels. The 4-ring arch fitting binder contains 19 double-pocket leaves, 1 single pocket leaf and holds up to 78 covers in all. Available in blue, green, black or red. The Malvern binder is now fully padded for extra luxury.

THE NEW CLASSIC COVER ALBUM
A compact de-luxe album with 20 'Polyprotec' leaves offering full protection for up to 40 covers and two clear fly leaves to hold an index of notes. Available in black, red or blue and supplied in a protective slip box.

THE UNIVERSAL COVER ALBUM
The cover album which allows stamps, booklets and presentation packs to be housed all together.

and COLLECTA COVER ALBUMS TOO!
The very popular range of Collecta Albums are also available direct from us. Please write for full details of the Stanley Gibbons cover album range to:

Hugh Jefferies,
Stanley Gibbons Publications Ltd.,
Parkside, Christchurch Road,
Ringwood, Hampshire BH24 3SH
Telephone: 0425 472363

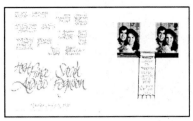

I have been fortunate to have access to a limited stock of absolutely superb covers produced by FINE ART COVERS. *The illustrations for each issue were specially commissioned with each artist being carefully selected for a style sympathetic to the subject. Each cover was limited to a maximum of 850 - each one numbered and signed by the artist.* The following covers are available:

1984 Christmas ......£13.00 ❏	1986 Halley................£9.50 ❏
1985 Trains ....£25.50 ❏	1986 Queen's Birthday£4.00 ❏
1985 Insects............£10.00 ❏	1986 Species at Risk£12.50 ❏
1985 Composers.....£13.00 ❏	1986 Medieval Life ...£9.50 ❏
1985 Royal Mail .....£18.00 ❏	1986 Games ....£5.50 ❏
1985 Safety at Sea...£10.00 ❏	1986 Royal Wedding£17.50 ❏
1985 King Arthur...£10.00 ❏	1986 Parliament ....£3.50 ❏
1985 Film Year........£13.00 ❏	1986 RAF ....£19.50 ❏
1985 Christmas ......£12.50 ❏	

The collection (save£42) ....£164.50 ❏

OTHER COVERS FROM STOCK

Official covers all with full set :

1986 Christmas - Thames Barrier £10.00
1988 Armada - Kellogs £10.00
1988 Armada - Thames Barrier....................£35.00
1989 Lord Mayor - Middlesborough £4.00
1989 Christmas - Whitby Abbey....................£4.00
1990 RSPCA - Cat Protection League £4.00
1990 Penny Black M/S - Bath (Muscroft) £4.00
1990 Queen Mother - Bowes Museum...........£4.00
1991 Science - Loughborough University £4.00
1991 Space - Crop Circle Study Group £5.00
1991 Christmas - Lindisfarne Gospels...........£4.00
1992 Europa - Tall Ships £5.00

£10 Britannia Definitive

Windsor (Britannia) handstamp..................£19.50
Paquebot, London CDS...............................£19.50
Both postmarks are on Philart 'Luxury Covers'

Please Write or Phone for Details of our
NEW ISSUE SERVICE
and
FIRST DAY COVER AUCTIONS

Sajal Philatelics

4, AMEN CORNER, MITCHAM ROAD, TOOTING, LONDON SW17 9JE
Telephone : 081-672 6702 Fax : 081-682 2752

PLEASE MENTION THIS CATALOGUE WHEN REPLYING TO ADVERTISEMENTS

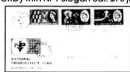
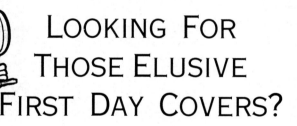

Famous Regiments

(41) £4.75

The Blues & Royals

(42) £4.75

The Life Guards

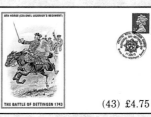

(43) £4.75

The Battle of Dettingen

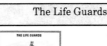

(44) £4.75

Bath Tattoo

(45) £6.75

The Royal Tournament

(46) £4.75

The Welsh Regiment

(47) £4.75

Devonshire & Dorset Regiment

(48) £4.75

The Scots Guards

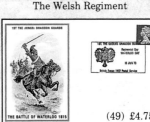

(49) £4.75

The Battle of Waterloo

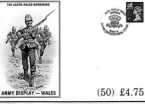

(50) £4.75

The South Wales Borderers

(51) £4.75

The Green Howards

(52) £4.75

Kings Royal Hussars

(53) £4.75

The Royal Scots

(54) £4.75

Scottish Borderers

PAIR OF COVERS

(55) £9.75

Rorkes Drift Centenary

To order: List your requirements and send with a cheque/PO made payable to A. G. BRADBURY.
Sorry no credit cards.   Overseas please remit in £ Sterling and add £1
A. G. BRADBURY, 3 LINK ROAD, STONEYGATE, LEICESTER LE2 3RA

The Abbey Collection 1

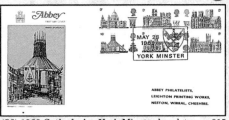

(56) 1969 Cathedrals - York Minster handstamp £15

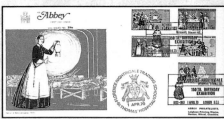

(57) 1970 Anniversaries - Florence Nightingale h/s £20

(58) 1970 Christmas - Bethlehem handstamp £3

(59) 1971 Christmas - Bethlehem handstamp £5

(60) 1971 Literary - London EC handstamp £7

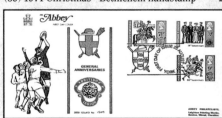

(61) 1971 Anniversaries - York handstamp £12

(62) 1971 Universities - Colchester handstamp £12

(63) 1972 Polar Explorers £9

(64) 1972 Anniversaries - London EC handstamp £7

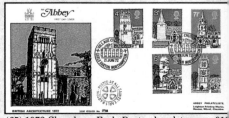

(65) 1972 Churches - Earls Barton handstamp £13

To order: List your requirements and send with a cheque/PO made payable to A. G. BRADBURY.
Sorry no credit cards. Overseas please remit in £ Sterling and add £1
A. G. BRADBURY, 3 LINK ROAD, STONEYGATE, LEICESTER LE2 3RA

The Abbey Collection 2

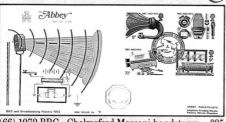

(66) 1972 BBC - Chelmsford Marconi handstamp   £25

(67) 1972 Silver Wedding - Windsor handstamp   £6

(68) 1972 Christmas - Bethlehem handstamp   £4

(69) 1973 Explorers - Denbigh FDI   £18

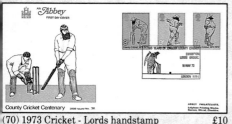

(70) 1973 Cricket - Lords handstamp   £10

(71) 1973 Parliament - SW1 handstamp   £5

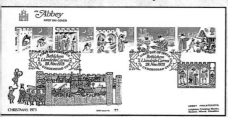

(72) 1973 Christmas - Bethlehem handstamp   £5

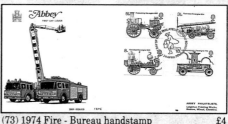

(73) 1974 Fire - Bureau handstamp   £4

(74) 1975 Architecture - Chester handstamp   £15

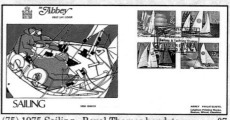

(75) 1975 Sailing - Royal Thames handstamp   £7

To order: List your requirements and send with a cheque/PO made payable to A. G. BRADBURY.
Sorry no credit cards.   Overseas please remit in £ Sterling and add £1
A. G. BRADBURY, 3 LINK ROAD, STONEYGATE, LEICESTER LE2 3RA

The Abbey collection 3

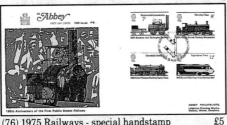

(76) 1975 Railways - special handstamp £5

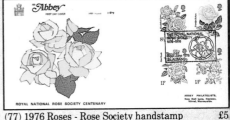

(77) 1976 Roses - Rose Society handstamp £5

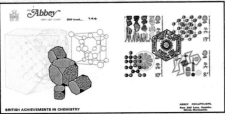

(78) 1977 Chemistry - Royal Institute handstamp £6

(79) 1977 Silver Jubilee - Windsor handstamp £4

(80) 1977 Wildlife - Bureau handstamp £5

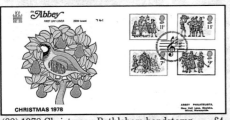

(81) 1978 Horses - Peterborough handstamp £4

(82) 1978 Christmas - Bethlehem handstamp £4

(83) 1979 Dogs - Crufts handstamp £5

(84) 1979 Flowers - Kew handstamp £5

(85) 1979 Year of Child - Winnie the Pooh h/s £

To order: List your requirements and send with a cheque/PO made payable to A. G. BRADBURY.
Sorry no credit cards.   Overseas please remit in £ Sterling and add £1
A. G. BRADBURY, 3 LINK ROAD, STONEYGATE, LEICESTER LE2 3RA

G.B. FIRST DAY COVER
New Issue Service

1993 Greetings —
Waterstone's special handstamp
and Rupert Bear meter mark

1991 Dogs—
Spillers Foods with Birmingham
Dogs Home Special Handstamp

1992 Christmas —
Post Office cover with
"Jesus is Alive Slogan" postmark

1988 Sport —
Official cover with Villa Road
CDS postmark

COMPLETE NEW ISSUE SERVICE FOR

G.B. FIRST DAY COVERS   **SPECIAL, CDS AND SLOGAN POSTMARKS**
PHQ POSTCARDS   **AIRLETTERS**   **BENHAM 'SILKS'**

We have a comprehensive stock of past issues, a selection of which
is shown above of more special items produced.

WANTS LISTS ARE WELCOME FOR PRICING.

We also supply **new issues** for G.B. stamp booklets, stamps and cylinder blocks.
In addition **new issues** for Europe and the rest of the world, plus thematics.
For details and current lists, write to —

JOHN G. RICE STAMP CO.

'Kalahari', I Streetly Drive, FOUR OAKS, SUTTON COLDFIELD B74 4PY

British Postmark Bulletin
The Magazine for Postmark and First Day Cover Collectors

The British Postmark Bulletin is the Royal Mail's magazine for Postmark collectors, providing full information on all forthcoming special handstamps and postmark slogans.

To receive your Bulletin on a regular basis place your order now with:

British Philatelic Bureau
FREEPOST
20 Brandon Street
EDINBURGH EH3 0HN

Annual subscriptions (post free)	
UK and Europe	£10.00
Rest of World (Air)	£21.75

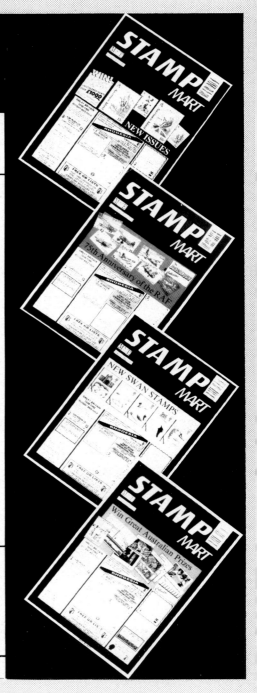

Beautiful covers - yours to treasure

ART ON STAMPS Ref (86)

The latest Art in the 20th Century stamps together with the superb Royal College of Art special first day of issue postmark. Each cover also bears the arts stamps from the past years including the very best of British artists (Constable, Stubbs Turner, etc.) **£9.75**

CORONATION ANNIVERSARY Ref (87)

Superb 40th Anniversary cover with the now scarce 25th anniversary stamps and a genuine 1953 stamp issued for Her Majesty's Coronation **£9.75**

SAVE THE OZONE Ref (88)

Each cover is signed by the whole 'Global Concern' team from their base camp at Eureka in the Canadian North-West Territories. The covers depict their balloon taking off for its trip across the North Pole. Printed in full colour with silver and blue foiling. **£5**

1993 DICKENS FESTIVAL Ref (89)

A commemorative cover and handstamp marks the 1993 Dickens Festival at Rochester. These covers not only feature the 1970 Dickens set of stamps, but also a special Greetings stamp depicting a PENNY RED and antique pen from the time of Charles Dickens **£7.50**

CORONATION DOUBLE Ref (90)

A very unusual item bearing the 1978 Coronation (25th Anniversary) stamp and postmarked DOUBLE WITH the 40th Anniversary stamp and postmark - a genuine double postmark on cover together with the original 1953 Coronation stamp plus cachet **£7.50**

ELVIS Ref (91)

USA produced Elvis first day cover - the stamps which 'ROCKED' the US postal service ! You saw it on the news - now you can own one of these original USA covers **£4.75**

To order: List your requirements and send with a cheque/PO made payable to A. G. BRADBURY. Sorry no credit cards. Overseas please remit in £ Sterling and add £1

A. G. BRADBURY, 3 LINK ROAD, STONEYGATE, LEICESTER LE2 3RA
Telephone (0533) 705367 (office hours)

PLEASE MENTION THIS CATALOGUE WHEN REPLYING TO ADVERTISEMENTS